The Oral and
the Written Gospel

The Oral and
the Written Gospel

*The Hermeneutics of Speaking and Writing
in the Synoptic Tradition, Mark, Paul, and Q*

WERNER H. KELBER

FORTRESS PRESS   Philadelphia

Library of Congress Cataloging in Publication Data

Kelber, Werner H.
  The oral and the written Gospel.

  Bibliography: p.
  Includes index.
  1. Bible. N.T. Gospels—Criticism, interpretation,
etc. 2. Bible. N.T. Mark—Criticism, interpretation,
etc. 3. Bible. N.T. Epistles of Paul—Criticism,
interpretation, etc. 4. Oral tradition. I. Title.
BS2555.2.K44   225.6′63   82-7450
ISBN 0–8006–0689–2   AACR2

9604E82   Printed in the United States of America   1–689

To Mary Ann

Contents

Contents

Abbreviations

AAWB.PH	Abhandlungen der k. Akademie der Wissenschaften zu Berlin—Philologisch—historische Klasse
AGAJU	Arbeiten zur Geschichte des antiken Judentums und des Urchristentums
AJT	*American Journal of Theology*
AnBib	Analecta Biblica
ARW	*Archiv für Religionswissenschaft*
ASNU	Acta seminarii neotestamentici upsaliensis
ATR	*Anglican Theological Review*
BETL	Bibliotheca ephemeridum theologicarum lovaniensium
BEvT	Beiträge zur Evangelischen Theologie
BFCT	Beiträge zur Förderung christlicher Theologie
BHT	Beiträge zur Historischen Theologie
Bijdr	*Bijdragen*
BJRL	*Bulletin of the John Rylands Library*
BMMLA	*Bulletin of the Midwest Modern Language Association*
BSOAS	*Bulletin of the School of Oriental and African Studies*
BWANT	Beiträge zur Wissenschaft vom Alten und Neuen Testament
BZ	*Biblische Zeitschrift*
BZNW	Beihefte zur Zeitschrift für die neutestamentliche Wissenschaft
CBQ	*Catholic Biblical Quarterly*
CBQMS	Catholic Biblical Quarterly Monograph Series
CJ	*Classical Journal*
ConBNT	Coniectanea biblica, New Testament
ConNT	*Coniectanea neotestamentica*
ContRev	*Contemporary Review*
CP	*Classical Philology*
EvTh	*Evangelische Theologie*
ExpT	*Expository Times*
FRLANT	Forschungen zur Religion und Literatur des Alten und Neuen Testaments
GBS	Guides to Biblical Scholarship Series
GRBS	*Greek, Roman, and Byzantine Studies*
HSCP	*Harvard Studies in Classical Philology*
HSCL	*Harvard Studies in Comparative Literature*

HTR	*Harvard Theological Review*
HZ	*Historische Zeitschrift*
Int	*Interpretation*
JAAR	*Journal of the American Academy of Religion*
JAF	*Journal of American Folklore*
JBL	*Journal of Biblical Literature*
JBLMS	Journal of Biblical Literature Monograph Series
JBR	*Journal of Bible and Religion*
JR	*Journal of Religion*
JSNTSup	Journal for the Study of the New Testament—Supplement Series
JTS	*Journal of Theological Studies*
LingBib	*Linguistica Biblica*
LonQHR	*London Quarterly and Holborn Review*
MoRev	*The Missouri Review*
NLH	*New Literary History*
NovT	*Novum Testamentum*
NovTSup	Novum Testamentum—Supplements
NTAbh	Neutestamentliche Abhandlungen
NRT	*La nouvelle revue théologique*
NTS	*New Testament Studies*
ÖkTNT	Ökumenischer Taschenbuchkommentar zum Neuen Testament
PAPS	*Proceedings of the American Philosophical Society*
PhT	*Philosophy Today*
PTMS	Pittsburgh Theological Monograph Series
RP	Religious Perspectives
RR	*Radical Religion*
SANT	Studien zum Alten und Neuen Testament
SBL	Society of Biblical Literature
SBLDS	Society of Biblical Literature Dissertation Series
SBM	Stuttgarter biblische Monographien
SBT	Studies in Biblical Theology
SCHNT	Studia ad corpus hellenisticum novi testamenti
SE	*Studia Evangelica*
SJT	*Scottish Journal of Theology*
SNT	Studien zum Neuen Testament
SNTSMS	Society for New Testament Studies Monograph Series
SO	Symbolae osloenses
StudOr	Studia orientalia
SUNT	Studien zur Umwelt des Neuen Testaments
TAPA	*Transactions of the American Philological Association*
TCLP	*Traveaux du Cercle Linguistique de Prague*
TDNT	G. Kittel and G. Friedrich (eds.), *Theological Dictionary of the New Testament*

TorSTh	Toronto Studies in Theology
TS	*Theological Studies*
TU	Texte und Untersuchungen
TUMSR	Trinity University Monograph Series in Religion
TZ	*Theologische Zeitschrift*
UNDCSJCA	University of Notre Dame Center for the Study of Judaism and Christianity in Antiquity
USQR	*Union Seminary Quarterly Review*
WMANT	Wissenschaftliche Monographien zum Alten und Neuen Testament
ZDA	*Zeitschrift für deutsches Altertum und deutsche Literatur*
ZTK	*Zeitschrift für Theologie und Kirche*
ZNW	*Zeitschrift für die neutestamentliche Wissenschaft*

Foreword

Oral tradition is no new concept in biblical studies, though development of the concept has progressed unevenly. In the late seventeenth century, at the inception of modern biblical scholarship, Richard Simon (1638–1712) had already noted that unwritten tradition lay back of written texts. The textual bias of high-literacy culture for some time prevented Simon's suggestion from having much effect, even when the Romantic concern with folk origins awakened a new interest in oral tradition. But with the form criticism of Hermann Gunkel (1862–1932) the oral background of biblical texts became a major question which scholarship has never since been willing or able to dismiss. The present book makes the question of oral tradition far more urgent than it had been even for Gunkel. It reshapes the concept of oral tradition in the biblical world so radically that it may well appear a new concept from now on.

Today it is possible to know in greater depth than Gunkel's generation, or even Rudolf Bultmann's, could know what oral tradition in itself really is. Even great scholars tend to assimilate the unknown to the known, the unfamiliar to the familiar. Earlier scholars, biblical and other, in ways of which they could not have been aware, modeled their ideas of oral narrative on their experience of narrative composed in writing, or their ideas of oral thought processes on the thought processes familiar to them in their own chirographic world. They made some adjustments, of course, but it was at the time impossible to make adjustments that were more than perfunctory.

A growing mass of scholarship, which Werner Kelber knows in depth, has now made detailed knowledge of oral thought forms accessible as never before. This scholarship ranges from Milman Parry's pioneering studies of the patterns of thought and expression in ancient Greek epic through Parry's and Albert Lord's and others' field work with present-day oral bards in Yugoslavia. The scholarship includes Eric Havelock's assessment of the ways in which the Greek alphabet radically reorganized the ancient oral Greek psyche, and further work by anthropologists such as Jack Goody, by psychologists, and by linguists on oral cultures around the globe, as well as studies of residually oral texts spreading from medieval and Renaissance Europe to eastern Asia. We can now appreciate in depth the psychodynamics of what I have styled primary oral cultures, cultures with no knowledge whatsoever of writing, and of residually oral cultures, where the thought forms of primary orality variously assert themselves with ever-diminishing force as the technology of writing, later reinforced and transformed by print, is interiorized in the psyche.

For all its deep sensitivity to oral backgrounds of texts, biblical scholarship up to the present has hardly attended at all to the new work, initiated chiefly by Americans, that has revealed the distinctive psychodynamics of the orally constituted mind. Because of lack of understanding of oral psychodynamics, as Werner Kelber states in his Preface, neither form criticism nor redaction criticism nor other biblical scholarship has succeeded in producing a truly oral hermeneutic. Indeed, one might say that biblical scholarship generally has not even tried to produce such a hermeneutic, differentiated from a textual hermeneutic, for one has to be acquainted with the mass of extrabiblical scholarship just mentioned to become aware that such a differentiated hermeneutic is even called for or possible.

A sophisticated oral hermeneutic opens the way to deeper understanding not merely of orality but of texts themselves. Textuality shows clearly its own distinctive, rich, and complex psychodynamics, when it is set against orality, with which writing always maintains some sort of reciprocal relationship. By attending to orality as such as well as to textuality, by explaining the forms and functions peculiar to oral speech and thereby throwing into high relief the patterns of thought and expression peculiar to texts, by calling attention to the predisposition of Q and of Paul to favor oral speech over writing in significant ways (not in every way), Werner Kelber's study of the synoptic tradition, and particularly of Mark, casts brilliant new light on the place of the written gospel in the totality of tradition, a light which promises to revitalize our sense of what the biblical tradition is and to make possible a new range of developments in biblical scholarship.

WALTER J. ONG, S.J.
University Professor of Humanities
Professor of Humanities in Psychiatry
Saint Louis University
Past President (1978), Modern Language
Association of America

Preface

All cultural activity is transmitted through available forms of communication. The artist, for example, finds both opportunities and limitations in the particular material used for inventive expression. Artistic creativity is tied to terms dictated by the chosen medium. What has been recognized in the arts at least since G. E. Lessing is equally valid in the realm of language. Human consciousness is structured into thought by available forms of communication. Thinking is indebted to the medium through which knowledge is acquired. The oral medium, in which words are managed from mouth to ear, handles information differently from the written medium, which links the eye to visible but silent letters on the page. This axiom forms the premise of my work. When rigorously applied to biblical studies it yields new and somewhat startling insights into hermeneutics. This book discusses orality and textuality, and the interaction between the two at various points in the early Christian tradition.

The contemporary transformation of oral and literate words through electronic devices has made us sensitive to the power of the medium itself. Now most of us know that a new medium stores and refracts information in ways that will deeply influence the state of human consciousness. Living on the threshold of the third medium stage may provide us with the necessary distance to accord orality and textuality in our biblical heritage a more adequately differentiated treatment.

I have written this book out of a concern for what seemed to me a disproportionately print-oriented hermeneutic in our study of the Bible. Walter J. Ong, who has amply documented the problem outside the field of biblical studies, has termed it the "chirographic bias" of Western intellectuals, and Lou H. Silberman has, in the words of Marshall McLuhan, drawn critical attention to the "Gutenberg galaxy" in which much of biblical scholarship is conducted. In New Testament studies the problem manifests itself in the inability of form criticism to produce an oral hermeneutic, our misconceived search for *the original* form of oral materials, the collaboration of form with redaction criticism in reconstructing tradition according to the paradigm of linearity, and a prevalent tendency to perceive the written gospel in continuity with oral tradition. The current revival of the Griesbach hypothesis, which seeks to explain the Markan text as a conflation of Matthean and Lukan texts, is further testimony to the triumph of visualism and our growing inability to come to terms with spoken words in the synoptic tradition. A steady output of Gospel Synopses, which highlight similar words and word constructions by underlinings and the use of color, place the highest premium on visualist qualities. Printed arrangements of this kind favor closed-system thinking and maximize the impression that the synoptic problem is entirely soluble in literary, source-critical terms. These and other scholarly developments suggested to me that we may have lost touch with the ground of speech in the tradition. We treat words primarily as records in need of interpretation, neglecting all too often a rather different hermeneutic, deeply rooted in biblical language that proclaims words as an act inviting participation. We like to think of textuality as the principal norm of tradition, whereas I wish to show that speaking was a norm as well, and writing often a critical reflection on speech, and also a transformation of it.

It was my intention to avoid being prejudiced in favor of either orality or textuality. When, for example, I refer to the spoken word as being innocent of the linguistic fall into written exteriority, I do not wish to romanticize orality at the expense of writing, but I describe writing as it appears to an oral mentality. Likewise, when I picture the written gospel as creating a novel world out of the debris of deconstructed speech, I do not mean to glorify the powers of textuality, but I describe textuality's treatment of spoken words. This book aims to broaden biblical hermeneutics by developing a sympathetic understanding of both the oral and the written word, and by studying ways in which one acts upon the other.

I have refrained from discussing positions recently taken by James M. Robinson and Helmut Koester, who view the gospel of Mark as a corrective to gnostic Christianity. In part I did so because their relevant works were not accessible to me at the time of this writing, and in part because my linguistically oriented work by and large shies away from history of religion categories such as gnosticism or apocalypticism. But my own independently conducted work has led me to confirm and further develop the insight first achieved by M. Eugene Boring that Mark is more in discontinuity than in continuity with oral, prophetic speech. Different scholarly approaches appear to be on the verge of breaking the predominant tradition-historical model of the gospel as a natural product of antecedent trends in the synoptic tradition. Perhaps the gospel is related more by contradiction than by evolution to what has gone before.

Indeed, the very genre of the written gospel may be linked with the intent to provide a radical alternative to a preceding tradition.

Now I wish to add a word about this book and its relation to my previous publications. In *The Kingdom in Mark* I developed a thesis concerning the purpose and genesis of the gospel based on a redaction-critical reading of Mark 1–13. *The Passion in Mark,* a multiauthored collection of essays published under my editorship, interpreted Mark 14–16 in light of the gospel's internal narrative logic, and not, as was still customary at the time, in relation to the political and legal history of the first century c.e. A clear consensus emerging from the essays was the conviction that the entire gospel comprises a narrative unity—a thesis now virtually taken for granted. My first attempt at reading the gospel in its entirety as a coherent, integral story was undertaken in *Mark's Story of Jesus.* Subsequently my interest turned from literature to language itself, both in its oral and written modality. What may appear to be a narrowing of interests ironically served the purpose of deepening my perspective. In "Mark and Oral Tradition" I studied the gospel's place in the wider world of speaking and writing, exploring specifically its links with the synoptic transmission of traditions. These explorations are to a considerable extent expanded in the present volume. Within the context of my work, *The Oral and the Written Gospel* attempts to transpose my literary thesis of Mark to the level of linguistic reflection, and to consider Mark's linguisticality in relation to speaking and writing in the synoptic tradition, Paul, and Q.

The first debt I wish to acknowledge is to Walter J. Ong, S.J. This book is inconceivable without Ong's lifelong probings into the intricacies of the transformation of the word. From him I have received the intellectual incentive and relevant heuristic tools for the writing of this study. The application of many of Father Ong's insights to the early Christian tradition, however, is entirely my own work. I alone carry responsibility for this book. Herbert N. Schneidau subjected the bulk of the manuscript to a painstaking reading, improving language and style, demanding clarity, questioning concepts, and relentlessly exposing positivism, linguistic or otherwise. I have benefited immeasurably from his criticism, which was of a kind all scholars hope to receive from a distinguished colleague, but only few of us ever do obtain. Both Schneidau and Ong impressed upon me an appreciation for *alienation* as a potentially constructive force in human life and linguistic transactions, liberating me from an entirely negative assessment of the concept in existentialist philosophy. M. Eugene Boring's work on early Christian prophecy and

Preface

my own more theoretically conceived hermeneutic have been converging for some time. I greatly appreciate his generosity in allowing me to read his massive manuscript *Sayings of the Risen Jesus* prior to its publication by Cambridge University Press. My indebtedness to him is substantial and duly recorded in chapter 5. Etienne Trocmé, valued friend and colleague, has my sincere thanks for providing me with his manuscript "The Passion as Liturgy." In addition, I thank John Dominic Crossan for matters of parable and paradox, absence and aniconicity, Robert W. Funk for leading the way in *Language, Hermeneutic, and Word of God,* Erhardt Güttgemanns for radically questioning the hermeneutics of form and redaction criticism in *Candid Questions,* and last but not least Paul Ricoeur for teaching me to think language.

The criticism given me by the readers of preliminary stages of the manuscript, William R. Baird, John Dominic Crossan, Robert Jewett, Howard C. Kee, and James Sellers has been of significant help to me. Professor Niels C. Nielsen, chairman of the Department of Religious Studies, Rice University, has provided me with the lavish gift of time when it was most needed. I owe a special word of gratitude to Mrs. Sylvia Louie whose diligent and impeccable typing of the manuscript has helped me through a long and hot Houston summer.

I have dedicated this book to my wife, Mary Ann.

Rice University
September 1981

WERNER H. KELBER

1. The Pre-Canonical Synoptic Transmission

The most difficult initial problem in the history of literacy is appreciating what preceded it.

M. T. Clanchy, *From Memory to Written Record*

For apart from a consideration of its social setting, no statement about the origin and function of oral tradition may be accepted as valid.

John G. Gager, *Kingdom and Community*

We still march along the straight black line of the Gutenberg galaxy.

Lou H. Silberman, "Habent Sua Fata Libelli"

"Beginnings are apt to be shadowy,"[1] and so it is with the beginnings of the synoptic tradition. If speaking is recognized as the primary means of early Christian communication, the difficulty in coming to terms with speech must likewise be acknowledged. Spoken words vanish at the moment of their utterance. For this reason alone, speaking and the principles governing oral transmission are difficult to document. Among the contributions to our perception of early Christian forms of speech and processes of communication, Rudolf Bultmann's *History of the Synoptic Tradition* ranks as a major achievement of twentieth-century New Testament scholarship.[2] More than any other single work it provided the norms and set the course for the form-critical investigation of the synoptic transmission of traditions. Major systematic alternatives to Bultmann's model were suggested on the one hand by the Scandinavian school under the leadership of Birger Gerhardsson,[3] and from a very different angle by Erhardt Güttgemanns who operated out of a post-Bultmannian German context.[4] In the broadest terms, this chapter reviews and carries forward the debate over this shadowy world of early Christian oral transmission.

Apart from the works of Bultmann, Gerhardsson, and Güttgemanns, perhaps the single most important advance in knowledge relevant to early

Christian processes of transmission has come from American and British specialists in oral culture. The American studies of Milman Parry,[5] Albert B. Lord,[6] Eric A. Havelock,[7] Walter J. Ong, S.J.,[8] Berkley Peabody,[9] and the British contributions by Ruth Finnegan[10] and Jack Goody,[11] as well as a growing body of folklore studies,[12] have vastly enhanced our understanding of the oral medium and its lifeworld. Interestingly, neither European nor American biblical scholarship has profited in depth from the Anglo-American oralist school. Only Güttgemanns has reflected on the Parry-Lord theory of creative oral composition and grasped its implications for form and redaction criticism.[13] The main reason for this neglect, one suspects, is the tendency among biblical scholars to think predominantly, or even exclusively, in literary, linear, and visual terms. Despite, and in part because of form-critical assumptions, it is difficult, if not impossible, to find in biblical scholarship a genuine appreciation of orality as a linguistic phenomenon in its own right.

It is the specific purpose of this chapter to revise the theses of the synoptic transmission put forward by Bultmann and Gerhardsson and to initiate a reconsideration of the synoptic model with the help of categories developed by the Anglo-American school and along the lines suggested by Güttgemanns. We shall first revisit Bultmann's *History of the Synoptic Tradition,* and next reexamine Gerhardsson's challenge to the classic Bultmannian model. A third part will then develop a new model of the pre-Markan processes of oral transmission based on current Anglo-American studies in orality. In light of our new thesis we shall in a fourth part return to Bultmann and Gerhardsson and critically appraise fundamental assumptions shared by both of them.

RUDOLF BULTMANN'S MODEL OF EVOLUTIONARY PROGRESSION

Steady consultation of Bultmann's *History of the Synoptic Tradition* by biblical scholars has tended to enhance its fame as an encyclopedic source of information at the cost of obscuring its larger conceptual scheme. The isolation and identification of tradition units and the determination of their social settings and motivations comprises but one aspect of the work. The other aspect concerns an observation of the alterations undergone by the speech forms and a study of the so-called tendencies of the synoptic tradition. Bultmann's intention clearly was to recapture the initial phase of Jesus materials, both in terms of composition forms and tradition processes. In contemporary linguistic terminology, he aimed at a synchronic and a diachronic comprehension. Although the diachronic perspective is frequently buried under a myriad of analytical data, it was Bultmann's stated goal to write a comprehensive history of the synoptic tradition, from its inception in the form of oral speech units, to changes in the process of their transmission, all the way to their written fixation in the gospels.[14]

While not ruling out the possible existence of pre-Markan texts and Markan access to them,[15] Bultmann was essentially concerned with what he termed *Kleinliteratur*.[16] In his view, the synoptic tradition owed its ascertainable existence to the anonymous matrix of the community, "the folk." Social settings, rather generally defined as preaching, teaching, apologetics, polemics, and parenesis, produced stylized linguistic forms, the hallmarks of collective composition. What guided Bultmann and the form critics in these observations was a general principle of the interplay between social and linguistic forces: communal settings leave a distinct imprint on language, and language behaves predictably in response to social requirements. Accordingly, the synoptic material is not composed by individuals, but arises out of typical situations in the life of the community. Anonymity, collectivity, and nonliteracy were thus considered the formal attributes of the synoptic tradition, and together they epitomize the concept of *Kleinliteratur*. In sum, Bultmann intended to come to terms not with consciously and artistically reflective literature, but with communally shaped and shared folk traditions.

As Bultmann saw it, early Christian communities of faith became operative in the aftermath of Jesus' life and death. This understanding was predicated on the notion of a sharp discontinuity between the historical Jesus and the kerygmatic Christ. Bultmann was not oblivious to the fact that to some extent the synoptic tradition "resumed the message of Jesus and through its preaching passed it on."[17] But in his view, this process of continuation did not illuminate the essential problem of the relationship between Jesus and tradition. The essential thing was the disciples' Easter faith that perceived and for the most part articulated Jesus, his words and deeds, in a new perspective. "All that went before appears in a new light—new since the *Easter faith in Jesus' resurrection* and founded upon his faith."[18] Henceforth, Jesus the messenger of the kingdom has been displaced by Christ who is present in the kerygma.[19] "The proclaimer became the proclaimed."[20] The bulk of the kerygma has either been formulated in the light of Easter faith or passed through its prism.

Bultmann illustrated a considerable number and variety of regularities and tendencies operative in the synoptic tradition: dogmatic motifs,[21] novelistic embellishments,[22] the law of single perspective,[23] the rule of scenic duality,[24] an inclination toward differentiation and individualization,[25] the transposition of narrative material into direct speech,[26] the law of repetition,[27] and many more proclivities. Among them Bultmann stressed what appeared to him to be a dominant trend—the inclination toward growth and expansion. This trend provided the chief impulse for the movement from single saying to gospel composition. Sayings grew together,[28] multiplied by analogous formation,[29] and underwent expansion by secondary additions.[30] New sayings joined the stream of tradition,[31] developed into groups of sayings,[32] and formed catechisms and speech complexes.[33] Apophthegmatic controversy stories showed a tendency to grow around dominical sayings[34] or, vice versa, sayings exhibited generative powers to produce apophthegmatic narratives.[35] Miracle stories developed out of sayings[36] or grew as a result of the tendency to elaborate the miraculous.[37] One similitude was juxtaposed with another so as to produce a double similitude.[38] The passion narrative underwent successive stages of growth before Mark connected it with traditions pertaining to the life of Jesus.[39] There were, to be sure, countertendencies. Sayings did not necessarily require framing by concrete scenes, or evolve into chains of sayings. They could well remain unattached.[40] Sayings might be abridged,[41] and direct speech turned into indirect speech.[42] But those were exceptions to the rule. The bulk of the observed tendencies registered some form of growth, and it was growth that constituted the dominant trend of the synoptic tradition. Single units showed a tendency to grow, to accumulate material, and cluster together. Materials in isolated and clustered form joined the stream of traditions, were sustained by it, and in turn accelerated the momentum toward still larger and more complex formations. One can readily form a mental picture of Bultmann's general model of the synoptic tradition as a process of aggregate growth.[43]

If one presses the question as to the motivating causes for the growth of tradition and the genesis of gospel composition, Bultmann gives a twofold answer. On the one hand, the gospel resulted from forces inherent in the pre-canonical, synoptic stream of traditions. According to what can justly be called the principle of *intrinsic causation,* the tradition itself exerted pressure toward ever more comprehensive manifestations, so that Mark's "project can only be explained in terms of the gravity inherent in the tradition."[44] The material evolved as if decreed by natural law, so that "it is permissible to say that a coherent presentation of the life of Jesus based on the existent tradition of separate and small collections was bound to come."[45] Propelled by their own gravity, the pre-Markan springs and streamlets had little choice but to flow into the gospel reservoir. Sayings, miracles, similitudes, and apophthegms developed step by step along a generally predictable route. Single units evolved into larger and ever more elaborate entities that were sooner or later destined to fall into the conventional pattern of the gospel narrative. It was a process as natural as that of biological evolution: simplicity grew into complexity.

The concept of intrinsic causation was closely allied with that of pure form. It was a distinct aim of Bultmann's form-critical work to determine the *original form* of folk traditions.[46] The original form served as basis for observing secondary developments and tendencies; and the dominant trend, generally, was from purity and simplicity toward complexification. Together these two concepts of original form and intrinsic causation determine the evolutionary ascent of the synoptic tradition.

On the other hand, the gospel was shaped by a theological motivation that arose in a type of Hellenistic Christianity to which both Mark and Paul belonged.[47] Specifically, it was the Christ myth of Pauline persuasion (1 Cor. 11:23–26; 15:3–7; Phil. 2:6–11; Rom. 1:3–4; 3:24; 6:3–4; 10:9) that exerted its influence upon the Palestinian Jesus traditions.[48] This myth imposed theological unity upon the heterogeneous Jesus traditions and brought the gospel composition to completion.[49] To be sure, the Palestinian traditions were bound to grow sooner or later into a narrative of Jesus' life and death, but it was Hellenistic Christianity that hastened the process toward gospel composition.

Mark, representative of Hellenistic Christianity, received credit for the making of the written gospel. None of the sources prior to Mark had connected the traditions into a continuous story of the life and death of Jesus.[50] Not unexpectedly, however, Mark's role in the process of gospel composition was confined to that of chief negotiator. His principal achievement consisted in facilitating the merger of Palestinian traditions with the Hellenistic kerygma.[51] Since both were already full-grown religious entities prior to Mark, the evangelist's literary activity manifested itself in the fusion of two tradition complexes—neither one of which he had made any significant contribution to. As for the synoptic tradition, Mark merely brought to fruition what had already been well on the way toward gospel formation. By the time the tradition had reached him, it required only minor redactional touches to bring it to natural completion: linking devices of time and place, the insertion of one story into another, introductions, postscripts, summaries, and the like.[52] In general, Mark "refrained from exercising major redactional influences on the transmitted material."[53] His performance was of an editorial more than authorial nature. As for the Hellenistic Christ myth, it was not, of course, of Markan making either. Its appropriation by Mark, an exponent of Hellenistic Christianity himself, was natural and did not seem to require inordinate theological, linguistic efforts.

Irrespective of its validity, Bultmann's thesis of the fusion of two tradition complexes might itself have suggested to him considerable complications in the process of gospel formation. How could two admittedly heterogeneous tradition complexes[54] have come together in the gospel without strain and struggle? One feels bound to raise this question since Bultmann regarded the relation of Palestinian to Hellenistic Christianity as "the one principal problem of early Christianity,"[55] and was inclined to view this cultural shift from one to the other as far more significant than the linguistic change from oral to written.[56] From this perspective, would not the merger of Palestinian traditions with the Hellenistic Christ myth have signaled a novel stage in the course of early Christian theological history? Bultmann did make reference to the intermediary role of Jewish-Hellenistic Christianity. As far as he could tell, this stage was responsible for the translation of the Palestinian traditions into Greek.[57] Beyond that, he did not pursue this matter in the *Synoptic Tradition*. Thus, while reference to Jewish-Hellenistic Christianity tends to enhance the impression of a smooth cultural transmission and to promote the notion of an unproblematic genesis of the gospel, it sheds no light on the alleged merger of the Palestinian traditions with the Hellenistic Christ myth.

What strengthened Bultmann's model of an effortlessly evolutionary transition from the pre-gospel stream of tradition to the written gospel was his insistence on the irrelevance of a distinction between orality and literacy. In most cases it was considered "immaterial (*nebensächlich*) whether the oral or the written tradition has been responsible; there exists no difference in principle."[58] By dispensing with the necessity of discriminating between oral and written, Bultmann was thus able to apply laws derived from texts and textual transactions to the reconstruction of a predominantly oral history. Observations made on Matthew's and Luke's handling of Mark and Q were now extendible into the pre-gospel history of tradition.[59] All synoptic materials, whether in oral or in written form, were by virtue of their nature as *Kleinliteratur* subject to the same rules and regulations. Although acknowledging the primacy of pre-Markan orality, Bultmann could therefore claim that the traditions passed into literary fixation imperceptibly and without measurable complications. Since the final gospel product "offers nothing in principle new, but merely completes what was already begun in the earliest oral tradition, it [the gospel composition] must be considered in organic connection with the history of the pre-gospel material."[60] The stream of tradition flowed naturally into the gospel, and Mark remained beholden to oral tradition, exercising little freedom vis-à-vis inherited materials. Indeed, so closely was the gospel allied to oral tradition that it eludes a literary classification.[61]

At rare instances Bultmann intimated a somewhat more complicated relationship between oral and written. In discussing the redaction of speech material, that is, the complexification of *logoi* into speech units, he noted that "in the oral tradition there exists a natural, albeit not exactly definable, limit to such cluster formations; this limit can only be superseded in the written tradition."[62] But he headed off possible implications by denying the written speech complexes any systematic unity and thematic force: "Luckily, that did not happen in the synoptic gospels."[63] The expression "luckily" gives away his profound aversion to ascribing any compositional, integrative powers to the evangelists. At another point he appeared to assume a connection between oral atrophy and the need for gospel-type compositions.[64] But these and other observations were never seriously pursued. In principle, Bultmann held that the gospel extended and preserved a fundamentally oral profile. Mark grew out of orality, but he never outgrew it.

In what to this date constitutes one of the more perceptive critiques of Bultmann's *Synoptic Tradition,* E. P. Sanders stated that Bultmann did not derive the tendencies of the synoptic tradition from an analysis of folk literature, as is widely assumed.[65] Bultmann did not demonstrate, for example, that expansion of pure forms was an established tendency in folklore. "For the most part, students of folklore do not emphasize the kind of laws of transmission about which Bultmann spoke and which concern us here."[66] For his own part, however, Sanders was reluctant to undertake what seemed a logical step toward correction. Dissatisfied with Bultmann's principle of discerning laws of transmission on the basis of Matthean and Lukan alterations of Mark and Q, and deploring his failure to consult folklore in earnest, Sanders himself refrained from exploring current studies on orality. Instead, he turned to the gospel manuscript tradition, the early church Fathers, and the apocryphal gospels for clues to the synoptic tendencies and those of the pre-canonical tradition.[67] In taking this course he acted out of the conviction he shared with Bultmann—and a majority of New Testament scholars, one suspects—concerning the irrelevance of a distinction between oral and written tradition: ". . . the tendencies of the one are presumably the tendencies of the other."[68]

There emerges from Bultmann's *History of the Synoptic Tradition* a perception of pre-Markan synoptic processes as a virtually irresistible movement toward the gospel composition. The gospel itself "has grown out of the immanent developmental drive which resides in the tradition, itself fashioned from diverse motives, and out of the Christ myth of Hellenistic Christianity."[69]

Today it is no exaggeration to claim that a whole spectrum of major assumptions underlying Bultmann's *Synoptic Tradition* must be considered suspect: Easter faith as watershed and point of departure for the tradition, the notion of the original form and its compulsory development into progressively more complex and hybrid formations, collective consciousness as the shaping force both of oral materials and gospel textuality, the concept of "setting in life" as the sociological determinant of oral forms, the heuristic value of the categories of Palestinian versus Hellenistic, and the thesis of an intrinsic gravitational or teleological pull toward the gospel composition. More than anything else, however, one must question Bultmann's failure to appreciate the actuality of living speech as distinct from written texts. Fundamentally what is being put in question here is the model of the virtual inevitability of synoptic evolution from oral simplicity to gospel complexity, and a tendency to minimize the effect of the transition from oral motion to textual still life. The question is whether the form-critical thesis that the gospels "are only the last link in the chain of a linear development over a longer period of time"[70] has not misconstrued the transmission of the synoptic traditions and trivialized the genesis of Mark.

BIRGER GERHARDSSON'S MODEL OF PASSIVE TRANSMISSION

Birger Gerhardsson deserves credit for having launched a major systematic challenge to form criticism. He correctly discerned the inability of the form critics to draw a *concrete* picture of the *technical* aspects of oral transmission. The settings in life, diversely affirmed as preaching, teaching, apologetics, polemics, and parenesis, remain distressingly vague, and reflections on a plausible mechanism of the actual transmission processes are almost nonexistent in form-critical literature.[71] But the core of Gerhardsson's critique was directed at such form-critical theses as the communal participation in the shaping and creating of tradition, anonymous gospel origins, and above all the postulated historical unreliability of the gospels. Indeed, the underlying, nagging question in all his explorations is that of the "historical credibility of the Gospels."[72] Gerhardsson's model of the synoptic transmission warrants scrutiny, partly because it offers valid corrections to form criticism, and mostly because its assumptions have lingered on and impeded a fresh approach to the synoptic tradition.

In developing a model of the transmission of religious traditions Gerhardsson turned to Rabbinic Judaism of the Tannaitic and Amoraic periods.[73] The Tannaitic scholars were responsible for the codification of the oral lore into the Mishna, and are commonly dated from the fall of Jerusalem (70 C.E.) to the beginning of the third century. Gerhardsson, interestingly, projected Tannaitic origins as far back as 10 C.E.[74] Amoraic scholarship stretched from the completion of the Mishna to the end of the fifth century. On the analogy of the Rabbinic transmission of traditions Gerhardsson subsequently drew up a model of its Christian counterpart, relying primarily on the early church Fathers, Luke-Acts, and Paul. The net result was the affirmation of an essential similarity between Rabbinic and Christian transmission processes.

It is not inconsequential that Gerhardsson commenced his investigation of Rabbinic techniques of transmission with *written* materials.[75] Three settings were recognized for scriptural transmission. A *professional* context[76] was provided by "Scripture specialists,"[77] scholars trained in the art of fixing and reproducing textual traditions. Their chief concern was the faithful and flawless preservation of texts. They worked in connection with colleges of scriptural learning, whose center was located in Jerusalem. The second context for the written Torah was *educational*.[78] Teachers, skilled in the Scriptures, taught their pupils to read the sacred texts in elementary schools which existed in most towns and villages of Israel. The nature of instruction was conservative and tradition-bound. The children had to read the texts until they knew them "by heart."[79] This "mechanical learning,"[80] the memorization of texts without necessarily understanding their content, played a vital part in Rabbinic elementary education. Worship was yet another setting that contributed to the preservation and continuation of tradition. The reading of texts had long been a standard feature in synagogue services. This third context was thus *liturgical*.[81] In sum, the transmission of traditions was a deliberate, methodical process, operating exclusively in contexts that favored the verbatim retention of sacred materials. It is again worth noting that these observations which laid the ground for Gerhardsson's model of the Christian transmission were consciously made on *written* traditions.

The oral Torah was transmitted alongside written documents.[82] Responsibility for retaining oral materials once again lay in the hands of specialists and their disciples. "An élite" of "skilled professional traditionists"[83] functioned as teachers and reciters in an elaborate educational program, of which the aforementioned elementary Scripture schools were but one aspect.[84] As was the case with the written Torah, Jerusalem also furnished leadership in the cultivation of the oral Torah.[85] The "fundamental role" in oral transmission was thus played by specialists,[86] and the primary setting was the classroom.[87] While it is true that "the people as a whole are to some extent the bearers of tradition,"[88] they carried the material primarily in the form in which it had been legitimized by the authorities. One notes a virtual exemption of the oral Torah from active social engagement. Authorities steered the course of oral transmission safely through the messiness of ordinary life.

Memorization was the technique by which oral transmission was carried on. The material was mechanically committed to memory before efforts were made toward interpretation.[89] Time and again words were recited by teachers, repeated by students, individually and in chorus, in turn corrected by the teachers, until the students knew them by heart. "A Rabbi's life is one continual repetition."[90] It was this principle of literal repetition and memorization of recited words that assured the process of oral transmission.

Where there is memory in Gerhardsson's scheme, manuscripts are never far away. Orally memorized traditions were either dependent on texts, or evolved from midrashic Scripture exegesis, or, when unconnected with texts, still served in the capacity of textual interpretation.[91] In addition, students enlisted the aid of private notebooks and scrolls to facilitate memorization.[92] The oral Torah, "when compared with the written, had an interpretative, particularizing, complementary and sometimes modifying function."[93] It was not really an entity in its own right. When one remembers that Gerhardsson had initially derived the norms of transmission from textuality, one is inclined to read his subordination of the oral to the written Torah as a consequence of his methodological and linguistic priorities. How firmly Gerhardsson saw the oral Torah underwritten by textual authority is manifested by his consistent application of literary terminology to oral speech in such expressions as "oral text,"[94] "collections of oral textual material,"[95] "oral passages of text,"[96] "oral literature,"[97] "memory-texts,"[98] "repetition-texts,"[99] and the like. Both teachers of oral tradition and oral materials themselves are regarded as "living books" that served to complement collections of scrolls.[100] In the end, there exists no substantial difference between the processes of oral versus written transmission: both are empowered by the same mechanism of mechanical memorization.

Gerhardsson seemed to defend his blurring of oral and written dynamics by arguing that sharp distinctions between the two media were alien to Rabbinic hermeneutics.[101] Yet some of his most incisive observations stressed the very opposite point. He noted the transcultural phenomenon of antagonism toward the written word at times when writing began to assert itself over the oral lifeworld. Transitions from orality to literacy were liable to feed doubts as to whether the new medium was able "to reproduce the full life, power and meaning of the spoken word,"[102] and aroused various states of confusion, anxiety, and hostility. To prove this point, Gerhardsson cited the example of the controversy between Pharisees and Sadducees over the status of the oral Torah. The Pharisaic cultivation of the oral Torah, whose normative standing the Sadducees rejected, created the condition for a "conscious and definite formulation of the distinction between written and oral Torah."[103] Objections to converting spoken into written words have left their mark on Tannaitic and Amoraic hermeneutics as well.[104] One searches in vain, for example, for rules that would permit note-taking in the process of learning oral materials. Private notes were "illegitimate in principle and therefore formally suppressed."[105] So deeply entrenched was the issue of oral versus written in Rabbinic Judaism that Gerhardsson could refer to it as "this classical Talmud problem."[106] His own chirographically slanted interpretation of Rabbinic hermeneutics is thus at odds with his observation of a pervasive Rabbinic consciousness of media differences.

Papias, Justin, Irenaeus, and the anti-Marcionite gospel prologue furnished Gerhardsson with general information about the transmission of Jesus traditions.[107] He acknowledged the inclination of these early authorities to view the gospels as emergency measures, their skepticism toward the written word, their testimony to a predominantly oral matrix of the gospels, and their awareness of the gospels' oral functioning. Moreover, he recognized the difficulty they had in assigning a formal literary category to the written gospels.[108] In this connection he linked the beginnings of the Jesus movement with Pharisaic Judaism and the distinction it had made between the oral and the written Torah: "It is against such a background that we must see the fact that for several decades the tradition concerning Christ appears to have been carried orally."[109] And yet, while postulating a chiefly oral transmission of the synoptic tradition, he refrained from an actual exploration of the synoptic material. As a matter of actual practice he envisioned Christian disciples, on the analogy of Rabbinic students, taking notes and using notebooks for the purpose of writing down "parts of the tradition concerning Christ."[110] Such written materials, together with oral traditions, furnished the sources out of which the gospels were fashioned.[111] When the early church Fathers Justin, Irenaeus, and Eusebius referred to the gospels as *hypomnēmata* and *apomnēmoneumata,* they chose a terminology which "might be said to stand closest to the private notes of the school tradition."[112] Finally, it appears that Gerhardsson agreed with, or at least did not seem to challenge, the post-apostolic concept of the evangelists as reliable traditionists—Matthew and John as disciples of Jesus, Mark and Luke as followers of prominent apostles.[113]

Gerhardsson's chief witness for the origins of the synoptic tradition was Luke, the author of Acts.[114] Although he conceded the apologetic and tendentious nature of the Lukan composition,[115] he still accepted the evangelist's views as normative for the history of the early Christian tradition. Jerusalem served as the "doctrinal centre of early Christianity":[116] here the *logos tou kyriou* was taught by "the college of the twelve."[117] As Jesus himself had practiced midrashic exegesis,[118] so did his apostolic followers likewise engage in "Scripture research."[119] In part their proclamation proceeded from texts, and in part it was presented freely, "but still in connection with the text."[120] The apostolic doctrine encompassed not merely material in *loci* formation, but already the cardinal points of Jesus' life and death, as programmatically outlined in the speeches of Acts.[121] The core of the written gospels, therefore, existed already in the *logos tou kyriou* of the Jerusalem doctrinal authorities.

The role of Paul in this scheme is seen in essential continuity with the doctrinal *logos*, the authorities, and the centrality of Jerusalem.[122] The apostle had conceived of the church as a unity, "having its centre in Jerusalem."[123] Apart from his reliance on Old Testament Scripture, he had received the authoritative doctrinal substance from the Jerusalem apostles.[124] 1 Cor. 15:3ff., "undoubtedly from Jerusalem,"[125] was representative of the preaching of Paul and the apostles in general. The eucharistic tradition of 1 Corinthians 11, moreover, was derived "from Jesus via the college of Apostles."[126] Jesus himself was "the Apostle's doctrinal authority,"[127] and "Paul was extremely interested in receiving tradition from the Lord."[128] Whether based on apostolic authority or that of Jesus, the tradition available to Paul existed in the form of "some oral or written equivalent of one of our Gospels."[129]

Gerhardsson's model of the synoptic tradition may be summarized in the following points. The *origins* of the tradition were neither rooted in the preaching of the church nor even in Jesus himself.[130] He looked back to something that already existed, the Torah in written and oral form. Jesus was a teacher of the Torah,[131] who linked his words and deeds closely with the Torah, and "required his disciples to memorize" his sayings.[132] The *conditions* for transmission were inaugurated with his ministry, solidified by the midrashic exegesis of the Jerusalem church, and given "a new point of departure" by the Easter experiences.[133] The *carriers* of tradition were primarily authority figures, with Jesus himself as the principal authority, and the twelve as "the first link in the chain of tradition."[134] The *technique* of transmission was that of methodical learning by way of continual repetition.[135] The *medium* of transmission was partly oral in the form of memorized texts and partly written in the form of "notebooks and private scrolls."[136] The *process* of transmission developed in "a rather straight line"[137] and "unbroken path"[138] from Jesus via a methodical passing on of "Jesus texts"[139] to the gospels. Changes that undoubtedly did take place in the course of transmission were confined to "interpretative adaptations."[140] Communal needs colored the tradition, but did not create it.[141] The transmission clarified and completed, but never radically altered the portrait of Jesus.[142] On the whole, the *nature* of the tradition is characterized by fixity, stability, and continuity. The *reason* for transmitting material was not merely the inspiration or correction of faith, but transmission itself. Indeed, the primary purpose for transmission was the deliberate act of communicating information "for its own sake."[143] The gospel, finally, is the written edition of Jesus' teachings and eyewitness reports, and exists in organic unity with tradition.

A number of Gerhardsson's contributions, not normally acknowledged by his critics, deserve recognition. He showed an awareness that "the greater part of the ancient literature is intended for the ears as much as, if not more than, the eyes."[144] The appreciation of language as sound existed side by side in antiquity with a skepticism toward the written word.[145] The Rabbis were generally opposed to silent reading and practiced recitation in rhythmic, cantillated fashion.[146] Rhythm, catchwords, and succinct phrasing exercised mnemonic functions in the process of memorization. In this context, Gerhardsson even mentioned the studies on rhythm and gestures in Rabbinic Judaism and in the language of Jesus by Marcel Jousse, S.J., studies which differ sharply, however, from his own thesis of mechanical memorization.[147] Moreover, Gerhardsson acknowledged the oral principle of arranging materials by association.[148] Oral techniques of composition are thus not necessarily in accord with concerns for precise historical preservation.[149] Furthermore, he was conscious of the important concept of imitation in oral culture: speaker and spoken words are closely connected, and the pupil learns by imitating the teacher's words as well as his life style.[150] At points Gerhardsson even alluded to the disappearance of traditions, the silence and the dead seasons, when words lie dormant or fade away.[151] Unfortunately, these insights which could have inspired a model of oral transmission more in accord with contemporary studies in orality remained incidental to his central thesis of a passive and authoritative transmission of traditions.

Among the numerous critical points brought up by Gerhardsson's reviewers, the following six warrant consideration. First, we have indicated his pervasive chirographical bias. While he admits that orality was the predominant medium of the synoptic tradition, he does not reflect upon it in relation to the synoptic materials. It must be emphasized that Gerhardsson's critique of form criticism does not rest on a study of synoptic traditions and their relation to the gospel. This "would require an independent monograph."[152] Second, the issue—raised by Morton Smith[153] and Jacob Neusner[154]—of a precarious backdating of Rabbinic pedagogics to the period of the second temple remains a valid one. The watershed significance of 70 C.E. for Jewish (and Christian) history is difficult to overrate.[155] Third, the synoptic gospels fail to attest to Jesus' teaching according to the rules of mechanical memorization. This is noteworthy if one claims that the gospels "essentially provide us with an historically reliable picture of Jesus of Nazareth."[156] Fourth, the concept of centrality of place (Jerusalem) and unity of message (*logos tou kyriou*) is no longer tenable.[157] The bulk of the synoptic material is not likely to have been legitimized by the Jerusalem authorities and passed on from them to Mark. Fifth, Luke's treatment of early Christian hermeneutics cannot be considered normative for a historical reconstruction of the synoptic transmission of traditions. The notion of Jesus as expounder of Scripture (Luke 4:16–22; cf. 24:27) reflects this evangelist's literary, visualist proclivities more than the linguistic realities of the life of Jesus. "That the Jesus-tradition as a whole does not represent scriptural exposition—nor haggadic scriptural exegesis—hardly needs to be demonstrated."[158] Sixth, Gerhardsson's concept of authoritative teaching and learning by verbatim repetition confuses oral remembering with mechanical memorization, as will be shown below.

ORAL TRANSMISSION AS PROCESS OF SOCIAL IDENTIFICATION AND PREVENTIVE CENSORSHIP

Contemporary theorists of orality appear virtually unanimous in emphasizing the linguistic integrity of the difference between spoken versus written words. The manner and degree of difference is controversial, ranging from A. B. Lord's proposition that the two media are "contradictory and mutually exclusive,"[159] to R. Finnegan's suggestion of overlaps and interactions,[160] to W. J. Ong's thesis that successive stages both reinforce and transform preceding ones.[161] But there is agreement to the effect that the circumstances of performance, the composition, and the transmission of oral versus written materials are sufficiently distinct so as to postulate separate hermeneutics.

In the broadest terms, oral and written compositions come into existence under different circumstances. A speaker addresses an audience in front of him, and its presence in turn affects the delivery of his speech.

There is a sense in which performer and audience share in the making of the message. An author, by contrast, writes for readers who are normally absent at the time and from the place of writing. This relative detachment from social context allows the author to exercise controls over his composition in a manner unknown to the performer of live speech. The speaker, in order to assure remembrance and transmission of information, has to employ linguistic devices such as formulaic speech and mnemonic patterning. What is transmitted orally, therefore, is never all the information available, but only the kind of data that are orally pliable and retrievable. What lives on in memory, moreover, is what is necessary for present life. Neither oral composition nor oral transmission can ever escape the influence of audience and social circumstances. Textual composition and transmission, on the other hand, enjoy a measure of freedom from mnemonic imperatives and social pressure. Everything written is potentially transmissible, and transmissible with verbatim accuracy unheard of in the oral lifeworld. The psychodynamics, furthermore, of oral transmission, the carrying of words from mouth to ear, are fundamentally different from operations that handle the interactions of "frozen" words with the discerning eye.

Recognition of the distinct linguistic differences of orality versus textuality raises questions about Bultmann's and Gerhardsson's models of synoptic transmission. While both concede a predominantly oral process, they tend to think of words more in terms of record than of what they really are in speech: events in sound. One may assume, therefore, that the synoptic transmission may not be as straight and linear and the transition toward the gospel as casual and unobtrusive as Bultmann and Gerhardsson suggested.

"The world into which Christianity was born was, if not literary, literate to a remarkable degree."[162] It is a truism that the early Christian movement does not typify a cultural stage predating the growth of literacy. While the beginnings of mostly pictographical scripts reach as far back as the fourth millennium, prealphabetic forms of Semitic writing developed in the Near East during the second millennium. The recently discovered state archives of the Syrian city of Ebla date back to the third quarter of the third millennium B.C.E., the royal archives at Mari to the first half of the second millennium B.C.E., and the Amarna letters to the latter half of the second millennium B.C.E. The existence of still more archives, a Sumerian at Nippur, a Hittite at Bogazköy, and of Assyrian libraries at Ashur (1100 B.C.E.), Nineveh (800–650 B.C.E.), and Nimrod (705–614 B.C.E.), reveal the human passion for writing and systematically collecting written documents in the ancient Near Eastern world.[163]

The historical roots of the Hebraic consonantal alphabetic script date back to the twelfth century B.C.E., and a complete alphabetic script was introduced in Greece not long before 800 B.C.E. The kind of veneration accorded in Jewish culture to the scrolls, both as physical objects and as carriers of revelation, is without parallel in classical antiquity.[164] The discovery of several hundred manuscripts and thousands of fragments at Kirbet Qumran and related regions in the Judean desert has done much to enrich our knowledge of literate Judaism. Life in this desert community was centered on the cultivation of the written word, and revelation was intrinsically bound to textuality. Paleographical and text-critical studies of the Dead Sea Scrolls have made it virtually certain that no text of the Old Testament postdates the Maccabean age.[165] Moreover, countless fragments of unknown literature found at Qumran have expanded the already existing vast body of pseudepigraphical material. The Hellenization of the Near East further accelerated the general use and spread of the written word. Books were plentiful in the Hellenistic period, and already toward the end of the third century B.C.E. the author of Ecclesiastes stated wearily: "Of making many books there is no end" (12:12). The most famous of all libraries in classical antiquity was at Alexandria; it was founded by the Macedonian rulers of Egypt, the Ptolemies, in the third century B.C.E. The Septuagint project stands out as a spectacular monument to linguistic competence in handling and translating texts. Little wonder that Hellenistic Jews regarded it as a work of inspiration, as the story of its miraculous origin in the so-called *Letter of Aristeas* suggests. Three major and a number of minor Jewish recensions of the Septuagint reinforce the impression of a developed manuscript culture in the centuries preceding the rise of Christianity. Clearly, the Christian movement sprang up in a milieu that both in its Jewish and in its Hellenistic loyalties had long set a high premium on the written word.

While the Dead Sea Scrolls have advanced our knowledge of literate Judaism beyond all expectations, direct historical, sociological, and linguistic parallels drawn between the covenanters and Christian beginnings are nevertheless for the most part misleading. Qumran originated in an internal priestly struggle and by separation from the center of power. The Christian movement, however, came into existence in response to an itinerant, charismatic prophet. Qumran's Teacher of Righteousness was presumably of Zadokite lineage and an accomplished student of Scripture, as was the core group of his original followers. By contrast, neither the founding figure of the Christian movement nor the nucleus of his early followers enjoyed the educational privileges that came with priestly descent. Qumran formed a tightly controlled community, whereas the Jesus movement began with a scattering of individuals and groups of people. The dissenting priests were heirs to a sophisticated urban culture of scriptural learning and professional handling of texts. But there is nothing in the formative stage of the Jesus movement to suggest the scriptorium as the cradle or locus of transmission of traditions.[166] These conspicuous differences must alert us against projecting the literary proficiency of the Qumran scribal experts upon early synoptic processes of transmission.

Granted that the early Christians lived in a world that was no stranger to literacy, the scope and impact of the written word must be assessed in relation to the total situation. A sense of domination by texts and the primacy of the written word is an experience of the world after Johannes Gutenberg. Throughout antiquity writing was in the hands of an élite of trained specialists, and reading required an advanced education available only to few.[167] "In general there was a low level of literacy."[168] Indeed, the ability to read and write remained confined to a minority of people until the nineteenth century.[169] Father Ong, who has spent a lifetime in studying oral hermeneutics and its impact on cultures past and present, emphatically states the case for the pervasiveness of orality: "In antiquity the most literate cultures remained committed to the spoken word to a degree which appears to our more visually organized sensibilities somewhat incredible or even perverse."[170] Because the vast majority of people were habituated to the spoken word, much of what was written was meant to be recited and listened to. The practice of writing did thus not immediately make literacy the new model of linguistic behavior, nor were oral speech forms and habits summarily extinguished by literature. The oral medium was tenacious, and literacy by itself slow in undermining the world of oral values.[171] Orality, therefore, which had been humankind's sole or predominant medium for millennia, dominated long after the introduction of writing.

While the craft of writing has deep roots in ancient Near Eastern culture, and was a veritable preoccupation for parts of Judaism, the precanonical, synoptic tradition must still be viewed as being firmly indebted to the oral medium. The oral matrix of the material corresponds with the sociological identity of the early Jesus movement. In antiquity, writing was essentially a product of urbanization and compact settlements; in rural areas language was almost entirely confined to face-to-face communication.[172] The movement of the historical Jesus was largely a rural phenomenon. "The synoptic tradition is located in small and often anonymous Galilean places."[173] Rural location and an ambivalence toward largely Hellenistic city culture is what the Jesus movement had in common with contemporary renewal and resistance movements. Under those conditions, speaking was the norm of communications rather than trafficking in texts, and word of mouth was the principal medium of transmission.

It remains the abiding achievement of form criticism to have focused attention on the predominantly oral nature of the bulk of the pre-canonical, synoptic tradition. Undoubtedly, form criticism, especially as it applies to gospel studies, is beleaguered from many sides and in dire need of a drastic reformulation. But this need must not blind us to the fact that all too often the critique of form criticism is permeated with a positivistic concern and a fear that it undermines the *historical* basis of Christian faith. Our own concern, and that of form criticism, is primarily language, not history, and our question is whether form criticism succeeded in thinking through orality in strictly oral terms.[174]

It is imperative to trace the very phenomenon of early synoptic orality to Jesus himself. Like Socrates, he moved and discoursed in the oral medium, without—as far as is known—ever committing a word to writing. The only time tradition catches him in the act of writing, it depicts him moving his finger on the ground (John 8:1–11). In this (textually precarious) story of the adulterous woman, Jesus' "writing" is a parody of formal, literary writing and the permanence that comes with texts and words etched on stone. Wind and weather will soon sweep away what was written on the ground; hence it is fitting that we are never told what he wrote.[175] In the only canonical passage reflecting on Jesus' educational, linguistic background (John 7:15), he is characterized as a man of literacy and probably scriptural knowledge (*grammata oiden*), but without formal rabbinic schooling (*mē memathēkōs*). The specifically scribal, Rabbinic model of Jesus the authoritative interpreter of the Torah was clearly shaped by the theological interests of Matthew. All four canonical gospels, however, supply us with the general picture of Jesus as speaker of authoritative and often disturbing words, and not as reader, writer, or head of a school tradition. Insofar as he is featured as a prophetic speaker and eschatological teacher, moving from one place to another, surrounded by listeners and engaged in debate, the gospels will have retained a genuine aspect of the oral performer. His message and his person are inextricably tied to the spoken word, not to texts.

It could be said that the impact Jesus made on friends and foes alike was to no small degree due to his choice and implementation of the oral medium. Spoken words breathe life, drawing their strength from sound. They carry a sense of presence, intensity, and instantaneousness that writing fails to convey. "One cannot have voice without presence, at least suggested presence."[176] Moreover, sounded words emanate from one person and resonate in another, moving along the flow and ebb of human life. They address hearers directly and engage them personally in a manner unattainable by the written medium. One can well imagine Jesus' words interacting with people and their lives, and enacting presence amidst hearers.

As is well known by most ancient cultures, living words, especially those uttered by charismatic speakers, are the carriers of power and being.[177] Precisely what this means can best be demonstrated by an initial comparison with written words. Writing is the technique of making words visible. This exteriorization of language tends to foster the impression of visible signs in separation from the actuality they refer to. In linguistic terms, writing forces the distinction between signs on surfaces, the signifiers, and the content with which they are being charged, the signified. It lies in the nature of written language that it can be abstracted from its signification. Spoken words are not visible apart from their signifiers. In the absence of exterior manifestations, oral discourse appears to be more intimately allied with the actuality to which it refers. When sounded words are thus known to be effective in the act of speaking, it takes but one small step to regard them "as being of the same order of reality as the matters and events to which they refer."[178] In addition, oral language is always personalized. Speaker and hearers together create situations wherein words come into being. Spoken words, therefore, can produce the actuality of what they refer to in the midst of people. Language and being, speaker, message, and words are joined together into a kind of unity. This powerful and binding quality of oral speech we shall henceforth refer to as *oral synthesis*.[179] It is not a universal rule governing orality, but it is more nearly true of spoken words than of written ones.

If Jesus was a charismatic speaker, he risked his message on the oral medium and did not speak with a conscious regard for literary retention. As oral performer he had neither need nor use for textual aids, nor did he speak with an eye toward textual preservation. The thesis that he taught with a concern for posthumous *literary* longevity is very unlikely and smacks of modern projection. As speaker of words and teller of stories, he shared the fate of all oral performers prior to the electronic age that his words would not only be misunderstood, but vanish the very instant they came into being. The power and being of his living words incurred the steep price of oblivion and even loss—unless a mechanism existed that facilitated survival.

The beginnings of what came to be the Christian tradition undoubtedly go back to Jesus' own speaking. He sought out people because he had something to say, and part of what he said and did will already have been passed on during his lifetime. For this reason alone, one must disagree with Bultmann's thesis of the post-Easter commencement of the tradition. There is the additional problem that the postulated rupture between proclaimer and proclaimed, under the impact of Easter faith, goes beyond synoptic evidence. Heinz Schürmann has sampled sayings dealing with kingdom, repentance, judgment, love of enemy, eschatological preparedness, and other topics that show no trace of post-Easter formulation.[180] They could have been spoken after Easter, but not necessarily. One might also ask whether the bulk of the synoptic miracle stories and parables gives concrete evidence for having been conceptualized in the light of Easter faith. If, moreover, one pays attention to oral hermeneutics, the Bultmannian concept of post-Easter as the christological watershed loses still more of its persuasive force. In oral culture, we observed, words are endowed with the special quality of presentness and personal authority. In early Christian culture, speakers who speak in Jesus' name could function as carriers of his authority. The name itself was endowed with wonder-working power.[181] Through the agency of the oral medium their voice carried the voice of Jesus, and Jesus continued speaking in their words (Luke 10:16). Irrespective of Easter faith, Jesus could thus continue his role as proclaimer and assume presence in prophetic words. Because the oral medium is exceptionally equipped to appropriate authoritative presence, Easter will hardly have caused the irrevocable christological rupture Bultmann envisioned. Lastly, it bears remembering that Easter is transmitted to us in the words of the tradition. To extrapolate it from its linguisticality and make it the fountainhead of tradition is to give it an unwarranted positivistic status. As we have it, Easter is part of tradition, and not its prime mover.

Bultmann's thesis of the post-Easter beginnings of the tradition has still deeper implications. Earlier we noted its connection with a radical distinction between kerygma and history. For Bultmann, the Jesus of history became the proclaimed Christ in the light of Easter faith. To James Robinson goes the honor of having pointed out the inadequacy of this terminology: "The current modern categories 'kerygma' and 'history' have foisted upon us a distinction which is neither in the language of the sources nor in our relation to the sources."[182] But if the categories of kerygma and history misapprehend the history of the transmission of traditions, then post-Easter has likewise ceased to be of value. Bultmann's concept of the post-Easter beginnings of tradition is a case in point of the current crisis in categories in New Testament scholarship.[183]

Unlike Socrates, Jesus did not have a single literary heir to collect and interpret his message. He preached and recruited more among the rural population of Galilee than among the urban middle class. Not a writer himself, he apparently never instructed his followers to record his words and the story of his life and death for the benefit of educated readers. There is no hard evidence that any of his personal followers committed his living words to the confining space of parchment or papyrus. Acts 4:13 refers to Peter and John as nonliterate and common men (*anthrōpoi aggramatoi . . . kai idiōtai*). There is no need to revive the romantic notion of the simple, or even boorish, Galilean fishermen, but what must be recognized is that the cultural, linguistic disposition of most of Jesus' earliest followers was formed by oral habits, displaying only tenuous connections with literate culture.

There is little justification for limiting the transmission of traditions to the twelve apostles. While they were important traditionists, they were by no means the only ones. Teachers and prophets have long been suspected of having had a hand in the process of synoptic transmission,[184] but it is only with the recent study by Gerd Theissen[185] and the forthcoming work by M. Eugene Boring[186] that their role has been placed on a firmer footing. In addition to disciples, apostles, teachers, and prophets, the "common folk" cannot be ruled out from the telling of stories. Those who were healed or exorcised, impressed or offended by Jesus became the potential carriers of tradition. Of all the modalities of language—oral, chirographic, typographic, and electronic—orality is by far the most democratic. Speaking is the prerogative of "Everyman." It is in fact the sole medium of most people in antiquity, and authorities can influence but not entirely control speech to the extent imagined by Gerhardsson.

By the same token, Jesus' words were not destined to be memorized by authorities, but rather to be remembered by both ordinary people and close followers. "The emphasis on memorization forms one strand of the extreme romantic view."[187] One searches the synoptic gospels in vain for so much as a glimpse of authoritative memorization by means of continual repetition. None of the canonical gospels depicts Jesus as being insistent on verbatim learning of his words. Nor is there any indication that apostles, teachers, prophets, or ordinary people were trained in what Gerhardsson considered to be a Rabbinic tradition of memorization. His thesis of a virtually passive transmission, that is, the passing on of words intact and in virtual isolation from social involvement, conjures up the image of a single, one-directional pattern of the synoptic tradition. But this notion of an unbroken process of transmission is unrealistic, and it explains neither oral transmission nor the making of Mark.

Note-taking as a preliminary step toward the composition of a gospel, a concept embraced by Gerhardsson, has recently been endorsed by the classical scholar George Kennedy.[188] He rested his case on the celebrated report of the mysterious presbyter, preserved by Papias, and documented for us by Eusebius (*Hist. Eccl.* 3.39.15). On Kennedy's interpretation, Papias described Mark's note-taking of Peter's teachings, and not the evangelist's composition of our extant gospel. We shall here reflect on the issue whether Papias reports the writing of notes, or that of the gospel.[189] In favor of Kennedy's thesis are the following four points: (1) Papias does not expressly describe the composition of what looks like Mark's gospel. (2) Justin (*Apol.* 66.3), *Irenaeus* (*Adv. haer.* 3.1.1–5), and Eusebius himself may have been responsible for a misreading of the Papias report. Following Papias's description of Mark's recollections (. . . *emnēmoneusen . . . apemnēmoneusen . . .*) of Peter's teachings, they may have erroneously equated these apostolic *apomnēmoneumata* with written gospels.[190] (3) The unmistakably apologetic tone of Papias could be in defense of note-taking: Mark's writing, while lacking systematic, sequential order, is nevertheless in accord with Petrine preaching. (4) The fragmentary *Letter to Theodore,* attributed to Clement, and discovered and published by Morton Smith, depicts Mark as a circumspect literary agent of his written notes (*hypomnēmata*).[191]

Kennedy's proposal is not without problems. The following four points could be argued: (1) According to Papias, Mark wrote down "what has either been said or done by the Lord" (*ta hypo tou kyriou ē lechthenta ē prachthenta*). By itself, this formulation does not militate against the form of gospel. (2) Justin, Irenaeus, and Eusebius, in equating the apostolic *apomnēmoneumata* with written gospels, may thus not have misunderstood Papias. (3) Papias's apologetic tone could equally well be in defense of the episodic form of the written gospel.[192] Admittedly, the gospel was lacking in compositional elegance, but it remained faithful to the voice of Peter. This could be the argument of a man who preferred "the living and abiding voice" over information derived from books (*Hist. Eccl.* 3.39.4). (4) According to Eusebius, Clement in his *Hypotyposeis* depicted the Markan composition as a direct transcription of unwritten teachings (*Hist. Eccl.* 2.15.1–2; 6.14.6). At least in Eusebius's mind, there does not seem to have been an intermediary stage of note-taking.

On balance, Papias's report remains as controversial as ever. Almost every word of this text is susceptible to multiple readings. It may portray the writing of notes, but it does not require us to think of Mark's gospel as having grown out of texts by degrees.

Whatever the intention of Papias's report, it is hardly possible to underrate the linguistic complexities of the pre-canonical, synoptic transmission. The concept of a predominantly oral phase is not meant to dispense with the existence of notes and textual aids altogether. The Q tradition, other sayings collections, anthologies of short stories, parables, miracles, and the like could well have existed in written form. But many of these texts served as simple recording devices and will not have transcended an essentially oral state of mind. Writing, in these cases, was not sufficiently interiorized to make accessible to readers and hearers the inner connectedness of Jesus' life and death. It might further be suggested that texts were not always used verbatim in the form of *Vorlagen*. Texts to be used for the composition of other texts were often assimilated through hearing and "interior dictation" more than strict copying. Those textual aids could well be present to writers in an oral mode of apperception.[193] The lines of orality and textuality were indeed blurred in those instances. The medium situation of the synoptic transmission was thus a complex one, and we shall never know its full actuality, let alone the precise shadings and degrees of interplay between the two media.

As has been known since Aristotle, the three constituents of the speech-act are speaker, audience, and speech.[194] In current linguistic terminology, these are called the encoder, the decoder, and the message.[195] To the speaker—encoder—belongs the input of information, to the audience —decoder—the output of information, and the message constitutes the information to be passed along. As words are carried from persons to persons, an interaction develops between speakers, hearers, and message. The process of communication is contingent on the nature of this interaction.

This model suggests that oral speech is invariably socialized. Spoken words have no life apart from speakers and hearers; they always transpire in social contexts. If we are to honor oral speech, we must honor the lifeworld of people as well. This means that a theory of oral transmission is deficient unless it embraces the social dimension.

To say, with Gerhardsson, that oral transmission operates more or less mechanically and apart from any real social engagement is to misapprehend the very nature of oral discourse. If, for example, sayings of Jesus struck a responsive chord in the hearts of hearers, these hearers might not only remember them, but pass them on to family and friends. Thus was set into motion the process of oral transmission. If, furthermore, these former hearers of Jesus' sayings, who had turned into speakers of the sayings, managed to engage a new audience, then the survival—at least for the time being—of the words was assured. Survival and continuity of spoken words was thus not simply a matter of passive transmission, but rather was intimately connected with their social relevancy and acceptability. Remembrance and transmission depended on the ability to articulate a message in such a way that it found an echo in people's hearts and minds. Primarily those sayings, miracle stories, parables, and apophthegmatic stories will have had a chance of survival that could become a focus of identification for speakers and hearers alike. This is not to dismiss the possibility that a group retained words precisely because they were alien or even offensive to its experience. The very oddness of the message could render it unforgettable. But a genuine incentive for transmission will have arisen from identification with words, not from a lack of it. In short, oral transmission is controlled by the law of *social identification* rather than by the technique of verbatim memorization.

The scope of our reflections will permit only two examples, representative of the sayings and narrative tradition, that illustrate the rule of social identification in oral transmission. The first example resumes and carries further the insights developed by Theissen in his classic article on itinerant radicalism.[196]Theissen's study focused on sayings—mostly from Q, or Q and Mark—which offend one's deeply rooted feelings of belonging to place and home (Matt. 8:20//Luke 9:58), the spirit of conventional family piety (Matt. 10:37//Luke 14:26; Matt. 8:22//Luke 9:60), and a natural attitude of respect for and pride in property and wealth (Matt. 19:24//Luke 18:25//Mark 10:25; Matt. 10:10//Luke 10:4). As Theissen properly perceived, sayings that counsel hatred toward father, mother, wife, and children, and the abandonment of home, place, fields, and possessions, raise questions as to their continued believability and social survival. Why were they passed on until their reception into the gospels? Who could take seriously an ethic in praise of homelessness and in favor of the disruption of family life? What were the social conditions for the transmission of this antisocial message?

According to the rule of social identification, these antisocial sayings must have been remembered and preserved by people for whom they rang true. Those who accepted this ethical radicalism, Theissen argued, could do so because it verified their own disestablished, migratory existence. "Only on the periphery of society does this ethos have a chance."[197] This forces the conclusion that one has to do with early Christian itinerant prophetic personalities, charismatics of homelessness, who considered themselves the loyal followers of Jesus. They had adopted Jesus' vagrant mode of living together with the very words that gave support to such a life. Consequently, they could identify with Jesus in a manner such that their voice was that of Jesus, and Jesus was present in their words: "He who hears you hears me, and he who rejects you rejects me" (Luke 10:16). As Jesus, so did they suffer the consequences of a rootless life. They were suspect in the eyes of settled society, taken for beggars and vagabonds, exposed to hunger and thirst, enduring loneliness and persecution. Plainly, the taking of notes and the cultivation of writing was a world apart from the life style of these prophetic transmitters of Jesus' sayings. They needed no aids in writing because they practiced the message they preached.

The antisocial gospel will have found its most enthusiastic sympathizers among people who were themselves living on the periphery of society, that is, those economically and socially disenfranchised representatives of the largely rebellious country population. "The synoptic transmission of anti-social sayings belongs undoubtedly to the few ancient traditions in which those groups found a voice which normally remain silent."[198] These were the people predisposed by their very experience as outsiders to perceive and accept the ethical radicalism of poverty, homelessness, rejection, and break with family ties. The social milieu for transmitting these antisocial sayings will therefore have been to a large degree the unsettled and—for established society—unsettling fringe, the margin of society. There the people lived who spoke and listened to the antisocial gospel, not because they studied and memorized it, but because it was true to their lives.

Theissen's study is impressive because it combines characteristic sayings of the synoptic tradition, a model of oral transmission, and a plausible social milieu into a grand thesis which accounts for oral transmission according to the rule of social identification.

Its merits notwithstanding, the thesis raises a question that goes to the core of form-critical philosophy. It may not be realistic to confine the transmission of the antisocial sayings to one social group, the charismatic itinerants. These prophets will have been the principal, but not necessarily the exclusive, carriers of the antisocial message. Experience teaches us that one can well remember and reproduce information without living out its content in one's personal life. By the same token, members of the more settled classes could identify with these sayings as a matter of principle, and still not apply them in actuality. The concept of *social identification* allows characteristic speech forms to serve as focus of identification for more than one social group. The question is thereby raised about the form-critical thesis of *setting in life*, the notion that forms of speech are tied to specific social settings. Janice Capel Anderson, in a study of eighteenth and nineteenth century German folklore scholarship, observed that *setting in life* was not as dominant a methodological issue for the forerunners of form criticism as it came to be for biblical form criticism itself.[199] On the other end of the spectrum, the contemporary Anglo-American oralist school does not seem to operate with this concept either.[200] As is well known, Bultmann's results, and those of other form critics, were notoriously unsatisfactory in this regard. Indeed, he himself expressed a sense of resignation in the conclusion of the *Synoptic Tradition*: "In this [the transmission of traditions] it is certainly difficult to say in detail which precise pieces of tradition played a role in concrete situations of the life of the community."[201] *Setting in life,* while helpful in many cases and productive in Theissen's case, tends to be unnecessarily restrictive with regard to the real life of oral discourse. Distinct forms of speech can and do function in more than one social setting.

If the movement is to grow, its followers must seek to win more broadly based audiences. Because oral tradition thrives on group expectations, a more durable success hinges on oral ability to appeal to and solidify broad interests. A shift from social marginality toward mainstream society will therefore entail toleration of more widely acceptable viewpoints.

Our second example illustrates the role of social identification with respect to miracle stories. The impact miracles have upon audiences differs from that of the antisocial sayings. As a rule, the healed person in the stories is either released to his or her family or encouraged to spread the good news. If as a result of the healing the person follows Jesus, he or she does so voluntarily, and not in compliance with the extreme injunction to abandon one's previous mode of living. Generally, miracle stories function so as to integrate the physically abnormal into mainstream society. While the antisocial sayings reinforce social marginality, the miracles tend to remove the label of social deviancy. In consequence, miracle stories embrace a social world broad enough for both physical deviants and physically normal people to find social identification. It is precisely because they are acceptable to a wider spectrum of society that they cannot be pinpointed to a single social setting. Contrary to the modern perception of the supernatural eccentricity of miracles, these stories are characteristic of high social mobility in antiquity. The sheer quantity of miracle stories in the synoptic tradition (and also in John) may well serve as an index of their popularity.

Orality and social world cooperate through the vehicle of a formulaic mode of communication. Both the effectiveness and the memorability of spoken words is enhanced in direct proportion to their conformity with rhythmical, acoustic demands. If a saying is to enjoy social survival, it is to be articulated in accordance with mnemonic formalities. Charles Fox Burney,[202] Harris Birkeland,[203] Matthew Black,[204] Robert Tannehill,[205] and above all Marcel Jousse[206] have shown us the extraordinary degree to which sayings of Jesus have kept faith with heavily patterned speech forms, abounding in alliteration, paranomasia, appositional equivalence, proverbial and aphoristic diction, contrasts and antitheses, synonymous, antithetical, synthetic, and tautologic parallelism, and the like. Bultmann,[207] Martin Dibelius,[208] Theissen,[209] and others have documented the predictable traits of the synoptic miracle stories. As a result, these stories have come to serve the dictates of oral utility, and Jesus the miracle worker has been typecast in a fashion that lends itself to habitual, not verbatim, memorization. Compositions in patterned and predictable form are therefore a well-known feature in oral life. What is more, oral life is not merely embellished by rhetorical conventionalities, but it lives from them. Thoughts in orality are not merely clothed in patterned forms, and formalized language is not merely a matter of added skill, but oral thinking consists in formal patterns from the start.[210] So much does information depend on form, and spirit on style, that in orality one could almost say that the form is the soul of the message.

The formulaic quality of oral speech must not suggest mechanized learning processes, and oral clichés are not to be confused with literal consistency. Verbatim memorization as a key factor in oral transmission has been abandoned by the majority of experts, who now admit the inevitability of change, flexibility, and degrees of improvisation.[211] Finnegan, who rejects a single and universal set of laws governing oral behavior, has nevertheless arrived at the conclusion that "it is the variability rather than the verbal identity of orally transmitted pieces that is most commonly noted."[212] Literalness, "which has almost become a fetish with literary scholars,"[213] is foreign to oral transmission. The inability of spoken words to evade social life inescapably involves them in the whirling wheel of social change. Oral formulas, clichés, and commonplaces assure remembering and transmission. At the same time, oral formulas, clichés, and commonplaces are changeable, adaptable, and interchangeable. There are virtually limitless possibilities for the oral performer to improvise basic patterns of oral compositions. He may maximize the use of stock features, "slot in" new ornamental or substantive material into formulaic lines, add introductions and conclusions. "New information and new experiences are continually grafted on inherited models."[214] It would be wrong, therefore, to conceive of orally patterned speech as the retarded language of robot minds. Who would dare make such a judgment on the language of Homer or Jesus? In the hands of the oral performer, oral forms become flexible instruments. Depending on rhetorical powers and skills, one's speech "may be highly concentrated, full of ambiguity and resonance, poetry in fact."[215] Thus when one documents formulaic stability, one should keep in mind compositional variability, and when one refers to oral patterns, one must not forget creative implementation. "This mid-state between fixed and free . . . is the traditional cultural condition."[216]

While Gerhardsson's concept of passive transmission is untenable, his skepticism in regard to the communal, nonindividualistic origin of the tradition is not without justification. The form-critical thesis of the communal genesis of sayings and stories is burdened with an eighteenth and nineteenth century mystique of "the folk," a nostalgic belief in the creative spontaneity of the community. This idea of communal composition, nurtured, among others, by a romantic and nationalistic strand of folklorists, "is seldom accurate or helpful."[217] Individual spokesmen and spokeswomen have emerged as recognizable transmitters and creators of oral compositions. Many of the individual disciples, apostles, prophets, teachers, and ordinary followers of Jesus will forever remain anonymous, but this is not the same as saying that the Jesus traditions are rooted in the anonymous matrix of the community. Community, we stressed, does form a crucial aspect of oral communication, but not in the sense of obliterating individual performers. Spoken words enter into a social contract, thrive on communal response, and, if they are to be successful, share in and play on collective interests. But this functional and essential need of orality to lean on social life in no way dispenses with the individual performer of oral compositions.

If one postulates a process of oral transmission controlled by professionals trained in the art of verbal memorization, the line of oral succession remains intact, irrespective of social implications. If, however, one acknowledges the peculiar dialectics of oral behavior and social realities, the forgetting or rejection of a message is as much to be expected as its remembrance and transmission. There is no rule that decrees growth and development as the dominant and inevitable fate of oral life. Granted orality's involvement in the caprices of social life, discontinuity will no less be a fact than continuity. Not all the words of Jesus will have met with understanding, let alone full enthusiasm. There must have been a multitude of words, sayings, and stories that never appeared in our gospels. If a message is alien to an audience, or a matter of indifference, or socially unacceptable, it will not be continued in the form in which it was spoken. It will either have to be altered, that is, adjusted to prevailing social expectations, or eliminated altogether. This fundamental fact of *preventive censorship*[218] has not adequately been taken into account by a scholarship whose prime focus was (and is) on linear growth patterns. But auditory amnesia and resultant discontinuity constitute an epistemological issue for oral transmission no less important than the indeterminacy principle for classical physics. Forgetting is a form of death ever present in oral life. No model of oral transmission may be said to be valid that does not seriously reflect on and integrate amnesia, broken paths, and rejection of tradition. The rule of preventive censorship, in the extreme, states that a tradition that cannot overcome the social threshold to communal reception is doomed to extinction. Loss and discontinuity no less than growth and continuity dictate the realities of oral life.

The alterations caused by preventive censorship can take multiple forms. The shrinking and condensation of an oral tradition, for example, is a known fact in oral communication. In that case, the speaker minimizes the use of stock features, shuns all frills and flourishes, and prunes the story of anything that exceeds its elementary character. This "selective retention of information" is known from psychological studies of rumor transmission.[219] A story may be told with a flair for detail, frequent repetitions, and digressions. The hearers in turn may wish to protect themselves from forgetting by holding on to the core of the story. It will then be remembered in its essential features, unencumbered by whatever is seen as superfluous. Vincent Taylor's experiment in oral transmission went so far as to conclude that selective retention was the regular feature: ". . . the tendency of oral transmission is definitely in the direction of *abbreviation* . . ."[220] One can well imagine a prophetic figure maximizing his oral performance in relatively ornate style, and his audience reducing the message to its structural skeleton. Precisely for the purpose of assuring a tradition's continuity, "the general form or outline of a story remains intact, but fewer words and fewer original details are preserved."[221]

In addition to growth and loss, or expansion and compression, a multiplicity of tendencies determines the course of oral transmission. Stock features are combined and reshuffled in endless variations, one theme is substituted for another, the order of sequence is changed, features are adopted from related or unrelated materials, and variant compositions are forever in the making. Taken as a whole, oral transmission shows many faces and inclinations. It exhibits "an insistent, conservative urge for preservation"[222] of essential information, while it borders on carelessness in its predisposition to abandon features that are not met with social approval. On the other hand, it can show infinite flexibility in molding a message so as to make it compatible with social needs. It can also exercise powers of innovation by attracting and creating fresh materials. When grasped in their total impact, these tendencies would appear to question the wisdom of imputing a single, directional dimension to oral transmission.

Together with the model of synoptic evolution we must forgo the one closely connected with it, that of *original form*. The form-critical search for the archetypal composition, and the compulsion to honor it as a first rung in the evolutionary ladder betray the bias of textuality and ignorance of oral behavior. The works of Milman Parry and Albert B. Lord have made it incontrovertibly plain that each oral performance is an irreducibly unique creation. If, for example, Jesus spoke a saying more than once, the first utterance did not produce "the original," nor was the second one a "variant" thereof, because each moment of speech is wondrously fresh and new. The concepts of *original form* and variants have no validity in oral life, nor does the one of *ipsissima vox*, if by that one means the authentic version over against secondary ones. "In a sense each performance is 'an' original, if not 'the' original."[223] Moreover, if each utterance constitutes an authentic speech act, then the question of transmission can never be kept wholly separate from composition.[224] In speaking, transmission involves an act of composition, or at least re-creation. All too often when we think of transmission of traditions, we think of it primarily as the passing on of fixed forms. In other words, we think of it in literary terms. In orality, *tradition is almost always composition in transmission*. From this perspective, too, oral transmission enacts a multiplicity of discrete instances of speech rather than a continuous process of solidification of speech into written forms.

A word must still be added about Gerhardsson's sociolinguistic model that gave reason and support to passive transmission. His was a vision of a central place of authority and a fundamental unity of message. This essentially monolithic model does not survive critical inquiry. We have discussed the social engagement of only two forms of oral speech, the antisocial sayings and the miracle stories. If one casts the net more widely across the synoptic tradition, a profusion of speech forms emerges that is nothing short of bewildering. Apart from diversity in forms, this synoptic polymorphism has been found to carry a wide range of religious and ethical convictions. The key to this virtual explosion of voiced opinions and remembered stories lies in the oral medium itself. Unattached to material surfaces, words flow freely, are repeated and adjusted, spoken one next to another, and yes, even set against each other. Speech in the early period thrived in a social world in which apostles and common followers speeded up the process of verbal and geographical proliferation, and prophets, unbound by place or commissioned by a local community, and authorized by the Spirit, prompted a rapid if irregular dissemination of words. It is, we shall see, a function of the written gospel to "implode" this oral heterogeneity and to linearize oral randomness. The notion of synoptic plurality of forms and views, of carriers and social contexts, has long since filtered from the avant-garde to the rank and file of New Testament scholarship, and has now entered the consciousness of systematic theologians, as witnessed in the pointed statement by Edward Schillebeeckx: "We can no longer in fact start, as people used to do at one time, from the single *kerygma* of a Jerusalem mother church, as it was called, which only later on branched out in various directions. The facts contradict that."[225] One must declare unworkable the model of a tightly knit community of early Christians committed to the preservation and transmission of a single gospel.

From the start, Jesus' own words and those of his followers were subject to the rules governing all oral commerce with social life. Some words will have come to an abrupt halt at one place only to be revived at another, while others may have gently coasted into oblivion never to be recollected again. Some traditions will have arrived in relatively unbroken fashion in the gospels, while many made it only after undergoing more or less drastic metamorphoses. The oral history prior to Mark is a pulsating phenomenon, expanding and contracting, waxing and waning, progressing and regressing. Its general behavior is not unlike that of the stock market, rising and subsiding at more or less unpredictable intervals, and curiously interwoven with social and political realities. Or, to use a different metaphor, the oral synoptic traditions represent proliferating tracks going in various directions, some intersecting with one another, others bound for a head-on collision, some running together and apart again, some fading and resurging. But all together they do not mount up to a preordained march controlled by the law of intrinsic causality. Interestingly, this multilateral model of pre-canonical orality was perceived by the very scholar who pioneered the redaction-critical approach to the gospel of Mark, Willi Marxsen. His perception of the theological integrity of the text caused him to reconsider the conventional linear model of the synoptic tradition, and to insist that "the traditional material scatters into every direction."[226] To him it was plain that the nature of the synoptic transmission was more diffuse than strictly evolutionary, and that the gospel, therefore, could not have very comfortably arisen out of oral drives and habits.

THE DOMINANT PARADIGM OF LINEARITY

Glaring differences notwithstanding, Bultmann's model of intrinsic causation and aggregate growth and Gerhardsson's model of inert tradition and passive transmission hold deeply shared assumptions in common. In the first place, both dismiss the relevance of a differentiated treatment of orality versus textuality. Media differences are blurred or belittled in regard to synoptic processes. Second, each postulates a single directional course of transmission. Although both scholars acknowledge a predominantly oral phase of the synoptic tradition, each chooses to reduce the dynamics of living words to the straight path of linearity. Third, both assume a smooth transit from oral transmission to gospel composition, and likewise regard the gospel as being in unbroken continuity with its oral precursors. For Bultmann, the gospel is the expected result of pre-gospel processes, and for Gerhardsson the gospel's genetic code has been inscribed into tradition at its very inception. In their entirety, these three assumptions have given scholarly impetus to the paradigm of synoptic linearity that has gained wide currency and undeserved acceptance.

It has been the objective of this chapter to expose these three assumptions and to challenge the resultant paradigm. The failure to treat orality as a medium in its own right and apart from textuality has been identified as the root cause for the imposition of linearity upon oral life and the trivialization of the genesis of Mark.

Literacy is so deeply implanted in every twentieth-century biblical scholar that it is difficult to avoid thinking of it as the normal means of communication and the sole measure of language. Fierce loyalty to literary values and procedures may account for the startling fact that form and redaction criticism, although originally committed to the exploration of two different media, collaborated in perpetuating the paradigm of synoptic linearity. Form criticism had difficulty in treating oral units truly as spoken words that conformed to the laws of acoustics and oral remembering. The tendency was to identify *original forms* and to assume their compliance with the rule of growth. Redaction criticism, on the other hand, was inclined to perceive pre-gospel materials as textually tangible tradition. Hence, the redactional feasibility of regression from the gospel's text to prior textual stages appears to be as much taken for granted as the form-critical model of an evolution of oral units by successive stages of accretion. Instinctively united by common interests, form criticism joined ranks with redaction criticism in projecting and reinforcing the model of synoptic transmission as a geometrically progressive and progessively textual development toward the gospel. Unobservantly a dominant visual perspective has taken control of the synoptic tradition, and an astoundingly simple diagrammatic vision has imposed itself upon the processes of transmission. This disquieting hermeneutical development has occurred in the absence of actual evidence of pre-gospel textuality, let alone oral/textual evolution, and in the presence of a considerable deposit of orally patterned synoptic materials.

If orality is perceived as a speaking of living words in social contexts, a concept of the pre-canonical, synoptic transmission emerges that is at variance with the paradigm of linearity. In its entirety, the pre-Markan oral tradition diverges into a plurality of forms and directions. Variability and stability, conservatism and creativity, evanescence and unpredictability all mark the pattern of oral transmission. To organize the oral mainstream into a linear scheme, and to declare it an unbroken trajectory toward textuality is to eye it through the distorting lens of hindsight.

Perhaps the greatest difficulty one faces in breaking the paradigm of linearity is to apprehend that "speech as output does not imply direction."[227] Written words run along a single visiospatial direction that the eye can follow in the process of reading. Voiced words well up in a person, and in a moment of sounded presence fill the interior of another person. In this speaking actuality, language is distinguished by the absence of visual characteristics. Spoken words are invisible, and they are given permanent representational embodiment only at the price of negating their very nature, which is sound. Ong has stated the case most persuasively:

> Strange though it seems to us, sound in its own actuality cannot be measured. Its reality eludes diagrammatic representation. This is a hard truth for technological man to accept: to him the measurements in space appear to be what is real in sound, though quite the opposite is true— the diagrams are unreal by comparison with sound as a psychological actuality.[228]

One principal device used for the purpose of visually representing language is the line. Spoken language consists in speech acts, countless instances of utterance and dialogue, separated by intervals of nonspeaking. But speech unconnected by tracts of time and space is hard to bear for our literate minds. It is the intervals, the vacuums, that we seize upon and set about filling in. In connecting one speech act to another by a line, perhaps even a rising line, one has technically accommodated orality to the model of textuality where letters and words are put down next to one another. On a deeper level, the line humanizes oral randomness by creating the illusion of orderly succession. It is a fiction that due to its visual powers of persuasion impresses itself all the more vividly upon us. Now we can "see" speaking and relish and measure its progress in time and space. The visual artifact of the line helps us to achieve the spatialization and, if we follow an ascending line, the temporalization of sounded words. Exceedingly graphic and deeply comforting as the paradigm of linearity is, it is nonetheless one of those fictions that we tend to forget are fictitious.

NOTES

1. Rachel L. Carson, *The Sea Around Us* (New York: New American Library, 1960), p. 9.

2. Rudolf Bultmann, *The History of the Synoptic Tradition,* Eng. trans. John Marsh (New York: Harper & Row, 1963). In view of the noted difficulties pertaining to the translation, all citations are offered in our own translation of the German original: *Die Geschichte der synoptischen Tradition,* FRLANT 29, NF 12, 8th ed. (Göttingen: Vandenhoeck & Ruprecht, 1970). The references refer the reader to the German edition, and in parenthesis to the American edition by Harper & Row.

3. Birger Gerhardsson, *Memory and Manuscript: Oral Tradition and Written Transmission in Rabbinic Judaism and Early Christianity,* ASNU 22 (Lund: C. W. K. Gleerup; and Copenhagen: Ejnar Munksgaard, 1961); idem, *Tradition and Transmission in Early Christianity,* ConNT 20 (Lund: C. W. K. Gleerup, 1964); idem, *The Origins of the Gospel Traditions* (Philadelphia: Fortress Press, 1979). Cf. also Harald Riesenfeld, *The Gospel Tradition* (Philadelphia: Fortress Press, 1970), pp. 1–29, 51–74.

4. Erhardt Güttgemanns, *Candid Questions Concerning Gospel Form Criticism: A Methodological Sketch of the Fundamental Problematics of Form and Redaction Criticism,* Eng. trans. William G. Doty, PTMS 26 (Pittsburgh: Pickwick Press, 1979).

5. Milman Parry, "Studies in the Epic Technique of Oral Verse-Making, I: Homer and Homeric Style," *HSCP* 41 (1930): 73–147; idem, "Studies in the Epic Technique of Oral Verse-Making, II: The Homeric Language as the Language of an Oral Poetry," *HSCP* 43 (1932): 1–50; idem, "Whole Formulaic Verses in Greek and Southslavic Heroic Songs," *TAPA* 64 (1933): 179–97.

6. Albert B. Lord, *The Singer of Tales,* HSCL 24 (Cambridge, Mass.: Harvard University Press, 1960).

7. Eric A. Havelock, *Preface to Plato* (Cambridge, Mass.: Harvard University Press, Belknap Press, 1963); idem, *The Greek Concept of Justice: From Its Shadow in Homer to Its Substance in Plato* (Cambridge, Mass.: Harvard University Press, 1978).

8. Walter J. Ong, S. J., *Ramus, Method, and the Decay of Dialogue* (Cam-

bridge, Mass.: Harvard University Press, 1958); idem, *Ramus and Talon Inventory* (Cambridge, Mass.: Harvard University Press, 1958); idem, *The Presence of the Word: Some Prolegomena for Cultural and Religious History* (New Haven, Conn., and London: Yale University Press, 1967; paperback edition: Minneapolis: University of Minnesota Press, 1981); idem, *Why Talk?* (Corte Madera, Calif.: Chandler & Sharp, 1973); idem, "Agonistic Structures in Academia: Past to Present," *Interchange* 5 (1974): 1–12; idem, "Mass in Ewondo," *America* 131 (1974): 148–51; idem, "Milton's Logical Epic and Evolving Consciousness," *PAPS* 120 (1976): 295–305; idem, "From Mimesis to Irony: The Distancing of Voice," *BMMLA* 9 (1976): 1–24; idem, *Interfaces of the Word: Studies in the Evolution of Consciousness and Culture* (Ithaca, N.Y., and London: Cornell University Press, 1977); idem, *Fighting for Life: Contest, Sexuality, and Consciousness* (Ithaca, N.Y., and London: Cornell University Press, 1981), pp. 118–48, passim.

9. Berkley Peabody, *The Winged Word: A Study in the Technique of Ancient Greek Oral Composition as Seen Principally through Hesiod's Works and Days* (Albany: State University of New York Press, 1975).

10. Ruth Finnegan, *Oral Literature in Africa* (Oxford: At the Clarendon Press, 1970); idem, "How Oral is Oral Literature?" *BSOAS* 37 (1974): 52–64; idem, *Oral Poetry: Its Nature, Significance and Social Context* (New York and Cambridge: Cambridge University Press, 1977).

11. Jack Goody, *The Domestication of the Savage Mind* (New York and Cambridge: Cambridge University Press, 1977); Jack Goody, ed., *Literacy in Traditional Societies* (New York and Cambridge: Cambridge University Press, 1968); Jack Goody and Ian Watt, "The Consequences of Literacy," in *Literacy in Traditional Societies*, pp. 27–68.

12. Cf. the following journals: *Journal of American Folklore, Folk-Lore Journal, Journal of Folklore Institute, Publications of the Texas Folklore Society, Abstracts of Folklore Studies,* and *New Literary History.* Among reference works the following three will be found to be most useful: Alan Dundes, *Folklore Theses and Dissertations in the United States,* Publications of the American Folklore Society, Bibliographical & Special Series 27 (Austin: University of Texas Press, 1976); Stith Thompson, *Motif-Index of Folk-Literature,* 6 vols. (Bloomington: Indiana University Press, 1966); Dan Ben-Amos, *Folklore Genres,* Publications of the American Folklore Society, Bibliographical and Special Series 26 (Austin: University of Texas Press, 1976).

13. Güttgemanns, *Candid Questions*, pp. 204–11.

14. Bultmann, *Synoptische Tradition*, pp. 1–8 (1–7).

15. Ibid., p. 347 (321).

16. Ibid., p. 5 (4).

17. Rudolf Bultmann, *Theology of the New Testament,* Eng. trans. Kendrick Grobel (New York: Charles Scribner's Sons, 1951), I, p. 33.

18. Ibid., 42–43; *Synoptische Tradition*, p. 373 (348).

19. Rudolf Bultmann, "Das Verhältnis der urchristlichen Christusbotschaft zum historischen Jesus," in *Exegetica,* ed. Erich Dinkler (Tübingen: J. C. B. Mohr [Paul Siebeck], 1967), pp. 445–69.

20. Bultmann, *Theology*, p. 33.

21. Bultmann, *Synoptische Tradition*, p. 307 (283–84).

22. Ibid., pp. 305–7 (282–83), 340 (311–12).
23. Ibid., p. 204 (188–89).
24. Ibid., pp. 335–37 (307–9).
25. Ibid., pp. 337–38 (309–10).
26. Ibid., pp. 340–41 (312–13).
27. Ibid., pp. 342–46 (313–17).
28. Ibid., pp. 86–88 (82–84).
29. Ibid., pp. 88–91 (85–87).
30. Ibid., pp. 91–95 (87–91).
31. Ibid., pp. 105–13 (101–8).
32. Ibid., pp. 348–51 (322–25).
33. Ibid., pp. 160–61 (149–50).
34. Ibid., pp. 53–54 (51).
35. Ibid., pp. 48–49 (47–48).
36. Ibid., p. 246 (230–31).
37. Ibid., p. 243 (228).
38. Ibid., pp. 210–11 (194–95).
39. Ibid., pp. 297–303 (275–80).
40. Ibid., pp. 73–82 (69–79).
41. Ibid., p. 88 (84).
42. Ibid., p. 342 (313).
43. In tracing the generative force of controversy dialogues, Bultmann defined this tendency in words difficult to translate as "die lockere Gesetzmässigkeit der Fortpflanzung der Überlieferung" (ibid., p. 53, n. 6 [51, n. 4]). In detailing the growth of sayings, he stated: "The more or less [of a proclivity toward expansion] is debatable, but *the general tendency of the tradition* is in my judgment beyond question" (ibid., p. 97 [93]).
44. Ibid., p. 373 (347).
45. Ibid., p. 395 (370).
46. Ibid., pp. 7 (6), 83 (79), 93 (89).
47. Ibid., p. 372, n. 2 (347, n. 2).
48. Ibid., pp. 370–73 (345–48); 396 (370). Bultmann finds the Christ myth also in the speeches of Luke-Acts: 2:22–24; 3:13–15; 10:37–41; 13:26–31 (p. 396 [370]).
49. Ibid., pp. 394–97 (369–71).
50. Ibid., pp. 363 (338), 394 (369).
51. Ibid., pp. 372–73 (347–48).
52. Ibid., pp. 362–66 (338–41).
53. Ibid., p. 358 (332).
54. Ibid., p. 330 (303).
55. Ibid., p. 6 (5).
56. Ibid., pp. 253–54 (239).
57. Ibid., p. 330 (303).
58. Ibid., p. 91 (87); cf. pp. 7 (6), 50 (48), 92 (88), 347 (321).
59. Ibid., pp. 7 (6), 97 (92–93).
60. Ibid., p. 347 (321).
61. Ibid., pp. 399–400 (373–74).
62. Ibid., p. 348 (322).

63. Ibid.

64. Ibid., p. 395 (370).

65. E. P. Sanders, *The Tendencies of the Synoptic Tradition*, SNTSMS 9 (New York and Cambridge: Cambridge University Press, 1969).

66. Ibid., p. 18, n. 4.

67. Ibid., pp. 229–71.

68. Ibid., p. 8.

69. Bultmann, *Synoptische Tradition*, p. 399 (373). The translation of this sentence is erroneous. Bultmann wrote: "Es [the gospel] ist erwachsen aus dem immanenten Entwicklungstriebe." The translation reads: ". . . it has grown out of the imminent [sic] urge to development."

70. This is Güttgemanns's correct assessment of the form-critical concept of the genesis of Mark. See *Candid Questions*, p. 100.

71. Gerhardsson, *Memory*, p. 14.

72. Gerhardsson, *Origins*, p. 90; idem, *Memory*, p. 194.

73. Gerhardsson, *Memory*, pp. 17–189.

74. Ibid., p. 30.

75. Ibid., pp. 33–70.

76. Ibid., pp. 43–55.

77. Ibid., p. 48.

78. Ibid., pp. 56–66.

79. Ibid., pp. 63–64.

80. Ibid., pp. 62, 65, passim.

81. Ibid., pp. 67–70.

82. Ibid., pp. 71–189.

83. Ibid., p. 99.

84. Ibid., pp. 85–87.

85. Ibid.

86. Ibid., p. 71.

87. Ibid., pp. 85–92, 159–60.

88. Ibid., p. 71; (cf. idem, *Origins*, p. 63).

89. Ibid., pp. 81, 115, 124–36, passim.

90. Ibid., p. 168.

91. Ibid., p. 90.

92. Ibid., pp. 160–61.

93. Ibid., p. 83.

94. Ibid., p. 79.

95. Ibid.

96. Ibid.

97. Ibid., p. 123.

98. Ibid., p. 141.

99. Ibid., p. 179.

100. Ibid., pp. 99, 94.

101. Ibid., p. 149, n. 2.

102. Ibid., p. 157.

103. Ibid., p. 23.

104. Ibid., pp. 158–63.

105. Ibid., p. 161.

106. Ibid., p. 158.
107. Ibid., pp. 194–207.
108. Ibid.
109. Ibid., p. 202; idem, *Tradition,* p. 23.
110. Gerhardsson, *Memory,* p. 202.
111. Ibid.
112. Ibid., p. 195.
113. Ibid., p. 194. Following Papias, Gerhardsson considers Mark to be the disciple of Peter (pp. 315–16).
114. Ibid., pp. 208–61.
115. Ibid., p. 211; (cf. idem, *Origins,* p. 81).
116. Gerhardsson, *Memory,* p. 276.
117. Ibid., p. 221, n. 2.
118. Ibid., p. 232.
119. Ibid., p. 233.
120. Ibid., p. 234.
121. Ibid., p. 225, n. 1; 243.
122. Ibid., pp. 262–335.
123. Ibid., p. 273.
124. Ibid., pp. 274–88.
125. Ibid., p. 280; cf. 300.
126. Ibid., p. 321.
127. Ibid., p. 311.
128. Ibid., p. 320.
129. Ibid., p. 301. This statement is curiously based on Col. 2:6ff.
130. Ibid., p. 324.
131. Ibid., 326–28. There is a tendency in Gerhardsson's later thinking to modify his model of authoritative memorization and passive transmission. In *Origins* (p. 70) Jesus' identity as teacher of the Law is expressly revoked. Now he is called a "parabolist" who taught "in a prophetic spirit, and with messianic authority." Concession is also made to creative acts in the course of transmission (p. 88), and to the theological nature of the gospels (p. 49).
132. Gerhardsson, *Memory,* p. 328.
133. Ibid., p. 331.
134. Gerhardsson, *Origins,* p. 60.
135. Gerhardsson, *Memory,* pp. 328–29, passim; idem, *Origins,* p. 21.
136. Gerhardsson, *Memory,* p. 335; idem, *Origins,* p. 68.
137. Gerhardsson, *Origins,* p. 53.
138. Ibid., p. 77.
139. Ibid.
140. Ibid., p. 85; cf. p. 58.
141. Ibid., p. 46.
142. Ibid., p. 75.
143. Ibid., p. 77.
144. Gerhardsson, *Memory,* p. 163; cf. p. 47.
145. Ibid., pp. 163, 197, 199.
146. Ibid., pp. 163–68.
147. Marcel Jousse, S. J., *Études de Psychologie Linguistique: Le Style Oral*

Rythmique et Mnémotechnique chez les Verbo-Moteurs (Paris: Gabriel Beauchesne, 1925); idem, *L'Anthropologie du Geste* (Paris: Gallimard, 1974); idem, *La Manducation de la Parole* (Paris: Gallimard, 1975); idem, *Le Parlant, la Parole et le Souffle* (Paris: Gallimard, 1978).

148. Gerhardsson, *Memory*, p. 149; cf. p. 333.

149. Ibid., pp. 182–83.

150. Ibid., pp. 184–89.

151. Ibid., p. 189. In *Tradition* (p. 38, n. 88), Gerhardsson speaks of "the enormous losses of teachers, scrolls and oral texts in connection with the destruction of Jerusalem in A.D. 70."

152. Gerhardsson, *Memory*, p. 324.

153. Morton Smith, "A Comparison of Early Christian and Early Rabbinic Tradition," *JBL* 82 (1963): 169–76.

154. Jacob Neusner, "The Rabbinic Traditions About the Pharisees Before 70 A.D.: The Problem of Oral Tradition," *Kairos* 14 (1972): 57–70.

155. Hans Joachim Schoeps, "Die Tempelzerstörung des Jahres 70 in der jüdischen Religionsgeschichte," in *Aus Frühchristlicher Zeit: Religionsgeschichtliche Untersuchungen* (Tübingen: J. C. B. Mohr [Paul Siebeck], 1950), pp. 144–83.

156. Gerhardsson, *Origins*, p. 79.

157. E. Earle Ellis, "New Directions in Form Criticism," in *Jesus Christus in Historie und Geschichte: Neutestamentliche Festschrift für Hans Conzelmann zum 60. Geburtstag*, ed. Georg Strecker (Tübingen: J. C. B. Mohr [Paul Siebeck], 1975), pp. 299–315. The author postulates the existence of "a closely knit religious movement," over a period of three decades (p. 306), as well as "an extensive complex of written Gospel material" prior to Mark, and even rejects the "entire theory of an 'oral period'" (p. 302). See, by contrast, the sober judgment of C. K. Barrett, *Jesus and the Gospel Tradition* (Philadelphia: Fortress Press, 1968; London: SPCK, 1967), pp. 8–12.

158. Güttgemanns, *Candid Questions*, p. 213.

159. Lord, *Singer of Tales*, p. 129.

160. Finnegan, *Oral Poetry*, pp. 24, 160, 169, passim.

161. Ong, *Presence of Word*, pp. 104, 239, 282; idem, *Interfaces of Word*, pp. 82–83, 215.

162. C. H. Roberts, "Books in the Graeco-Roman World and in the New Testament," in *The Cambridge History of the Bible*, ed. P. R. Ackroyd and S. F. Evans (New York and Cambridge: Cambridge University Press, 1970), I, p. 48.

163. D. J. Wiseman, "Books in the Ancient Near East and in the Old Testament," in *The Cambridge History of the Bible*, ed. P. R. Ackroyd and S. F. Evans (New York and Cambridge: Cambridge University Press, 1970), I, p. 40.

164. Roberts, "Books in Graeco-Roman World," p. 49.

165. Frank Moore Cross, Jr., *The Ancient Library of Qumran and Modern Biblical Studies* (New York: Doubleday & Co., 1958), p. 165.

166. The poet, philosopher, and theologian Johann Gottfried Herder (*Vom Erlöser der Menschen: Nach unsern drei ersten Evangelien*, in *Herders Sämmtliche Werke*, ed. Bernhard Suphan [Berlin: Weidmannsche Buchhand-

lung, 1880], XIX, p. 209) ridiculed the popular Christian assumption of an "apostolic chancellery" in Jerusalem that produced pamphlets and disseminated written gospels.

167. Gerhardsson, *Memory*, p. 233.

168. Wiseman, "Books in Ancient Near East," p. 37.

169. Goody, *Domestication of Savage Mind*, pp. 152–53.

170. Ong, *Presence of Word*, p. 55.

171. Ibid., pp. 53–76.

172. Ong, *Interfaces of Word*, p. 86.

173. Gerd Theissen, *Sociology of Early Palestinian Christianity*, Eng. trans. John Bowden (Philadelphia: Fortress Press, 1977), p. 47; cf. pp. 47–58.

174. For an excellent survey of form-critical scholarship, complete with bibliography, see William G. Doty, "The Discipline and Literature of New Testament Form Criticism," *ATR* 51 (1969): 257–321.

175. I owe this insight to John Dominic Crossan, *Finding is the First Act: Trove Folktales and Jesus' Treasure Parable*, Semeia Studies 9 (Philadelphia: Fortress Press; Missoula, Mont.: Scholars Press, 1979), p. 100.

176. Ong, *Presence of Word*, p. 114.

177. James Alexander Kerr Thomson, *The Art of the Logos* (London: George Allen & Unwin, 1935); Solomon Gandz, "The Dawn of Literature: Prolegomena to a History of Unwritten Literature," *Osiris* 7 (1939): 261–522; Pedro La'in Entralgo, *The Therapy of the Word in Classical Antiquity*, ed. and Eng. trans. L. J. Rather and John M. Sharp (New Haven, Conn., and London: Yale University Press, 1970).

178. John Colin Carothers, "Culture, Psychiatry, and the Written Word," *Psychiatry* 22 (1959): 312.

179. The term *oral* or *auditory synthesis* was introduced by Carothers, "Cultures, Psychiatry, and Written Word," p. 310. Its hermeneutical implications are developed by Ong, *Presence of Word*, pp. 111–38.

180. Heinz Schürmann, "Die vorösterlichen Anfänge der Logientradition: Versuch eines formgeschichtlichen Zugangs zum Leben Jesu," in *Der historische Jesus und der kerygmatische Christus*, ed. Helmut Ristow and Karl Matthiae (Berlin: Evangelische Verlagsanstalt, 1962), pp. 342–70; reprinted in *Traditionsgeschichtliche Untersuchungen zu den synoptischen Evangelien* (Düsseldorf: Patmos-Verlag, 1968), pp. 39–65.

181. Wilhelm Heitmüller, *"Im Namen Jesu": Eine sprach-u. religionsgeschichtliche Untersuchung zum Neuen Testament, speziell zur altchristlichen Taufe*, FRLANT I, 2 (Göttingen: Vandenhoeck & Ruprecht, 1903), p. 242.

182. James M. Robinson, "Kerygma and History in the New Testament," in *Trajectories through Early Christianity* (Philadelphia: Fortress Press, 1971), p. 24.

183. The thesis of the post-Easter beginnings of christology has been further undermined by Willi Marxsen (*The Beginnings of Christology*, Eng. trans. Paul J. Achtemeier and Lorenz Nieting [Philadelphia: Fortress Press, 1979], pp. 20–37) and Eberhard Jüngel (*Paulus und Jesus: Eine Untersuchung zur Präzisierung der Frage nach dem Ursprung der Christologie*, 3d ed. [Tübingen: J. C. B. Mohr (Paul Siebeck), 1967] pp. 290–300).

184. "Wanderlehrer" as agents in the process of synoptic transmission were

already assumed by Carl Friedrich Georg Heinrici, *Der litterarische Charakter der neutestamentlichen Schriften* (Leipzig: Dürr'sche Buchhandlung, 1908), pp. 35–36. See also Amos Wilder, "Form-History and the Oldest Tradition," in *Neotestamentica et Patristica,* NovTSup 6 (Leiden: E. J. Brill, 1962), pp. 3–13. For a compilation of synoptic sayings which have been suspected of having been influenced/composed and transmitted by early Christian prophets, see David E. Aune, "Christian Prophecy and the Sayings of Jesus: An Index to Synoptic Pericopae Ostensibly Influenced by Early Christian Prophets," *SBL Seminar Papers* (Missoula, Mont.: Scholars Press, 1975), II, pp. 131–42.

185. Gerd Theissen, "Itinerant Radicalism: The Tradition of Jesus Sayings from the Perspective of the Sociology of Literature," *RR* 2 (1975): 84–93. Citations are offered in our own translation of the German original: "Wanderradikalismus: Literatursoziologische Aspekte der Überlieferung von Worten Jesu im Urchristentum," *ZTK* 70 (1973): 245–71.

186. M. Eugene Boring, *Sayings of the Risen Jesus: Christian Prophecy in the Synoptic Tradition* (New York and Cambridge: Cambridge University Press, 1982); idem, "How May We Identify Oracles of Christian Prophets in the Synoptic Tradition? Mark 3:28–29 as a Test Case," *JBL* 91 (1972): 501–21; idem, " 'What Are We Looking For?' Toward a Definition of the Term 'Christian Prophet'," *SBL Seminar Papers* (Missoula, Mont.: Scholars Press, 1973), I, pp. 142–51; idem, "Christian Prophecy and Matthew 10:23: A Test Exegesis," *SBL Seminar Papers* (Missoula, Mont.: Scholars Press, 1976), pp. 127–33; idem, "The Paucity of Sayings in Mark: A Hypothesis," *SBL Seminar Papers* (Missoula, Mont.: Scholars Press, 1977), pp. 371–77; idem, "Christian Prophecy and Matthew 23:34–36: A Test Exegesis," *SBL Seminar Papers* (Missoula, Mont.: Scholars Press, 1977), pp. 117–26.

187. Finnegan, *Oral Poetry,* p. 141.

188. George Kennedy, "Classical and Christian Source Criticism," in *The Relationships Among the Gospels,* ed. William O. Walker, Jr. (San Antonio: Trinity University Press, 1978), pp. 125–55.

189. In chapter 5, p. 212, we shall reflect on the linguistic implications of note-taking in relation both to oral speech and to the written gospel.

190. Richard Heard, "The ΑΠΟΜΝΗΜΟΝΕΥΜΑΤΑ in Papias, Justin, and Irenaeus," *NTS* 1 (1954): 122–34.

191. Morton Smith, *Clement of Alexandria and the Secret Gospel of Mark* (Cambridge, Mass.: Harvard University Press, 1973), p. 446. This evidence in favor of Kennedy's thesis was cited by Wayne Meeks, "Hypomnēmata from an Untamed Sceptic: A Response to George Kennedy," in *Relationships Among Gospels,* p. 167.

192. For a defense of Papias in terms of a gospel composition, cf. J. Kürzinger, "Das Papiaszeugnis und die Erstgestalt des Matthäusevangeliums," *BZ,* NF 4 (1960): 19–38; idem, "Irenäus und sein Zeugnis zur Sprache des Matthäusevangeliums," *NTS* 10 (1963): 108–15.

193. The most important reference is Josef Balogh, "Voces Paginarum," *Philologus* 82 (1926): 84–109, 202–40; cf. also S. Sudhaus, "Lautes und leises Beten," *ARW* 9 (1906): 185–200; G. L. Hendrickson, "Ancient Reading," *CJ* 25 (1929): 182–96; W. B. Sedgwick, "Reading and Writing in Classical Antiquity," *ContRev* 135 (1929): 90–94; Henry John Chaytor, "The Medieval

Reader and Textual Criticism," *BJRL* 26 (1941–42): 49–56; Eugene S. McCartney, "Notes on Reading and Praying Audibly," *CP* 43 (1948): 184–87; A. Dain, *Les Manuscrits* (Paris: Société D'Édition "Les Belles-Lettres," 1964), pp. 44–46; Bruce M. Metzger, *The Text of the New Testament: Its Transmission, Corruption, and Restoration* (New York and London: Oxford University Press, 1964), pp. 13, 26–27; H. I. Marrou, *A History of Education in Antiquity,* Eng. trans. George Lamb (New York: Sheed & Ward, 1956), pp. 81, 154, 195.

194. Aristotle, *Rhetoric,* 1.3.1358a39.

195. Peabody, *Winged Word,* p. 169.

196. Theissen, "Wanderradikalismus."

197. Ibid., p. 252.

198. Ibid., p. 264.

199. Janice Capel Anderson, "Grimm's Bible: The Influence of *Deutsche Volkskunde* on the Development of Narrative *Formgeschichte,*" unpublished paper, 1977.

200. Finnegan, *Oral Poetry,* pp. 246–62.

201. Bultmann, *Synoptische Tradition,* p. 395 (370).

202. Charles Fox Burney, *The Poetry of Our Lord: An Examination of the Formal Elements of Hebrew Poetry in the Discourses of Jesus Christ* (Oxford: At the Clarendon Press, 1925).

203. Harris Birkeland, *The Language of Jesus* (Oslo: I kommisjon hos J. Dybwad, 1954).

204. Matthew Black, *An Aramaic Approach to the Gospels and Acts* (Oxford: At the Clarendon Press, 1946).

205. Robert C. Tannehill, *The Sword of His Mouth,* Semeia Studies 1 (Philadelphia: Fortress Press; Missoula, Mont.: Scholars Press, 1975).

206. On the work of Jousse, cf. n. 147 above.

207. Bultmann, *Synoptische Tradition,* pp. 233–60 (218–44).

208. Martin Dibelius, *From Tradition to Gospel,* Eng. trans. Bertram Lee Woolf (New York: Charles Scribner's Sons, 1934), pp. 70–103.

209. Gerd Theissen, *Urchristliche Wundergeschichten: Ein Beitrag zur formgeschichtlichen Erforschung der synoptischen Evangelien* (Gütersloh: Gerd Mohn, 1974), pp. 57–81.

210. Ong, *Interfaces of Word,* pp. 102–16, 191.

211. Ong, *Presence of Word,* pp. 22–35; Finnegan, *Oral Poetry,* pp. 52–69; Lord, *Singer of Tales,* pp. 5, 22, passim; Peabody, *Winged Word,* pp. 110–13, 152, passim.

212. Finnegan, *Oral Poetry,* p. 140.

213. Lord, *Singer of Tales,* p. 4.

214. Havelock, *Preface to Plato,* p. 122.

215. Goody, *Domestication of Savage Mind,* p. 113.

216. Peabody, *Winged Word,* p. 96.

217. Finnegan, *Oral Poetry,* p. 140.

218. The technical term *preventive censorship* was coined by Petr Grigo'evich Bogatyrev and Roman Jakobson, "Die Folklore als eine besondere Form des Schaffens," in *Donum Natalicium Schrijnen* (Nijmegen and Utrecht: N. V. Dekker & Van de Vegt, 1929), p. 903: "Bei der Untersuchung der Folk-

lore muss man stets als Grundbegriff die Präventivzensur der Gemeinschaft im Auge behalten."

219. Ernest L. Abel, "The Psychology of Memory and Rumor Transmission and Their Bearing on Theories of Oral Transmission in Early Christianity," *JR* 51 (1971): 272.

220. Vincent Taylor, *The Formation of the Gospel Tradition* (London: Macmillan & Co., 1933), p. 124.

221. Abel, "Psychology of Memory," p. 276.

222. Lord, *Singer of Tales,* p. 120.

223. Ibid., p. 101.

224. Erhardt Güttgemanns ("Die Linguistisch-Didaktische Methodik der Gleichnisse Jesu," in *Studia Linguistica Neotestamentica* [Munich: Chr. Kaiser, 1971], p. 134) criticizes a lack of methodological differentiation in form criticism between rules of composition and those of transmission: "Dieses Schwanken der Analyse zwischen Diachronie und Synchronie ist für die mangelnde methodologische Reflexion der Formgeschichte bezeichnend." On this point his critique of form criticism does not seem justifiable. One cannot strictly differentiate in orality between synchronic and diachronic rules. Transmission entails composition.

225. Edward Schillebeeckx, *Jesus: An Experiment in Christology,* Eng. trans. Hubert Hoskins (New York: Seabury Press, 1979), p. 84.

226. Willi Marxsen, *Mark the Evangelist: Studies on the Redaction History of the Gospel,* Eng. trans. Roy A. Harrisville et al. (Nashville: Abingdon Press, 1969), p. 17.

227. Goody, *Domestication of Savage Mind,* p. 123.

228. Ong, *Presence of Word,* pp. 44–45. Cf. also Peabody, *Winged Word,* p. 129: "No schematic illustration can pretend to describe the actual discrete stages in the history of an oral tradition."

2. Mark's Oral Legacy

... the real history of religion ... begins with the very most concrete conceptions, and only slowly and gradually do men learn to comprehend what is abstract.

Hermann Gunkel, *The Legends of Genesis*

All types of information stored in the oral repertoire are thus likely to be cast in narrative form, to be represented as doings.

Eric Havelock, *The Greek Concept of Justice*

Even the writing forms of the Early Church are better understood if we keep in mind the primal role of oral speech in the beginning ... Oral speech is where it all began.

Amos N. Wilder, *The Language of the Gospel*

In this chapter we will focus on Mark's indebtedness to oral life and nonliterate consciousness. If speaking came first and set linguistic standards for the synoptic tradition, an importation of oral features into the gospel can well be assumed. Unless one views the text as an erratic boulder fallen from the sky, it is reasonable to expect connections with what preceded its existence. While the pre-gospel transmission does not in itself account for the extant gospel, oral forms and conventions will nevertheless have gained admittance into the written document. Without the contribution of orality the gospel might not even be conceivable. A case can thus be made for a study of the gospel's oral legacy.

There are definite limits to this kind of study. The most serious problem concerns the transportation of language from one medium into another. What used to be spoken words are accessible to us exclusively in the written medium. Events became records of events. This means that once-living words have been silenced; their actual speaking contexts are irretrievably lost. It may also mean that oral forms have become textualized beyond recognition. The situation would seem hopeless if it were not for the fact that the written medium may reinforce forms of speech over the short span, just as it erases them over the long run. The objectifying, controlling power of the written medium, while taking the life out of spoken language, can freeze oral forms and preserve them in fossilized profiles. The fixation of speech acts by writing may even exaggerate their formal characteristics.[1] It is thus not unreasonable to probe a text closely allied with oral life for distinctive features of spoken language.

A genuine appreciation of oral language must move beyond a formal analysis of speech patterns. The study of forms is not an end in itself, and literary purism cannot penetrate to the soul of oral life. While the specific speaking circumstances will forever remain outside our grasp, one should probe oral forms for the manner in which information is organized and conceptualization transacted. The speech forms of the synoptic tradition reveal a multitude of oral needs, functions, and thought processes. Our inquiry will introduce us into a world of oral likes and dislikes, sensibilities and imaginative powers, storage and recall functions, values and norms, preference for similarities and opposites, standardization of themes and persons, strategies for stabilizing and destabilizing audiences, rudimentary christologies, and the like.

This study of Mark's oral legacy is more illustrative than exhaustive.[2] It does not include the passion narrative, which will be treated separately in chapter 5. Among the sayings, we have selected only one group, the so-called *parabolic sayings*. But what may be the most startling fact about sayings in Mark, their very paucity, will occupy us beyond this chapter and in the end help us determine the gospel's posture toward oral tradition. The feature of storytelling has been chosen as the principal representative of the pre-Markan mode of language. This choice is warranted by the fact that the bulk of Mark's gospel is made up of brief tales. We shall first examine four distinct types of stories: healings that we will call *heroic stories*, exorcisms that are named *polarization stories*, apophthegmata that will be termed *didactic stories*, and *parabolic stories*. This last type will claim our special interest because parabolic logic will be shown—in chapters 3 and 5—to be essential for an understanding of the gospel both as textualization of oral materials and as narrative. Next we shall probe the extension of oral techniques and values into Markan syntax and narrative. A third part will focus on orality's handling of Jesus' historical actuality and undertake a general classification of early Christian speech forms in regard to their impact on audiences. A final section will be devoted to the issue of the oral gospel, the possibility of an orally implemented gospel prior to and in preparation for Mark's written composition.

ORAL VOICES AND VALUES

In coming to terms with the oral property of healing stories, it is helpful to distinguish this study from other linguistic objectives. We are not concerned with questing after the *original form*, for no such thing ever existed in oral speech. We do not intend to trace a trajectory of the healing story across the expanse of ancient Near Eastern, Jewish, and Christian cultures, nor are we interested in abstracting the deep code from the message. In approaching Mark's healing stories we encounter a *plurality* of brief tales that are impressive by their *uniformity* of composition and *variability* of narrative exposition, and we seek an explanation for this triple phenomenon in the oral technique of communication.

Heroic Stories

At first sight Mark's gospel registers ten healing stories:[3] *Peter's Mother-in-Law* (1:29–31), the *Leper* (1:40–45a), the *Paralytic* (2:1–12), the *Man with a Withered Hand* (3:1–6), *Jairus's Daughter* (5:21–24, 35–43), the *Woman with a Hemorrhage* (5:25–34), the *Syrophoenician Woman* (7:24–30), the *Deaf Mute* (7:31–37), the *Blind Man of Bethsaida* (8:22–26), and the *Blind Bartimaeus* (10:46–52).

Although our objective is to treat these stories as a matter of recall more than of record, we shall begin with the texts before us. Some familiar ground must first be covered in order to move beyond contemplation of visible forms toward a perception of their speaking actuality. If one adheres to the surface chronology of these stories, following the sequence in which they were told and heard, a fairly predictable progression unfolds. Exposition, performance, and confirmation of the healing form the stories' three component parts, each of which is subdivided into a series of auxiliary motifs.

I Exposition of Healing
    a) arrival of healer and sick person
    b) staging of public forum (onlookers)
    c) explication of sickness
    d) request for help
    e) public scorn or skepticism
II Performance of Healing
    a) utterance of healing formula
    b) healing gestures
    c) statement of cure
III Confirmation of Healing
    a) admiration/confirmation formula
    b) dismissal of healed person
    c) injunction of secrecy
    d) propagation of healer's fame

The healing of *Peter's Mother-in-Law* is told with an incomparable economy of words. Martin Dibelius was so impressed with the story's brevity that he declined to express himself on its narrative form.[4] And yet, Mark 1:29–32 is a healing story reduced to the constitutive parts of the formulaic ground plan (I–a, b, c, d; II–b, c). Part III is missing only in appearance, because a formal conclusion is provided by the woman's service on behalf of Jesus and his company. Her own service expresses confirmation of the miracle. Technically, this amounts to a variation of III–a.

In the story of the healing of the *Leper* both exposition and performance parts are compressed into a crisp sequence (1:40–42), which rushes events from the arrival of the leper to his cure (I–a, d; II–a, b, c). The confirmation part (1:43–45a), however, has swollen into an elaborate narration (III–b, c, d). The elaboration is achieved by exploitation of the conventional features of dismissal, secrecy, and propagation. The dismissal is turned into a mission to the priest, and the secrecy is designed to protect the miracle until its official confirmation. The propagation, because personally undertaken by the man enjoined with silence, produces tension with the motif of secrecy. In spite of secrecy, the news is being published. In this way, dismissal, secrecy, and propagation are woven into a minor plot, the focal part of the healing story, to which I and II are merely introductory. The net effect is a heightening of the enormous significance of the healing.[5]

The story of the healing of the *Paralytic* is arranged around the conventional miracle structure (I–a, b; II–a, c; III–a). Within this arrangement two developments have taken place. In one instance, the feature of the onlookers (I–b) has been expanded. By sheer numbers the onlooking crowd impedes access to the healer and complicates the sick man's arrival. This latter aspect, therefore, requires narrative elaboration, that is, his transportation through the roof of the house. Once his arrival has been accomplished, neither explication of sickness nor request for help are needed. The fact that he overcame the obstacle sufficiently illustrates his desire to be cured (2:1–4). A second development is the narration of a controversy between healer and hostile scribes over the issue of forgiveness of sins (2:6–10). It is a feature not directly accounted for by the compositional structure or a variation thereof. We shall return to the controversy below.[6]

Not unlike the preceding story, the healing of a *Man with a Withered Hand* illustrates both a conventional core and redactional pressures on it. After the arrival of the *dramatis personae* (I–a, b), healer and hostile onlookers engage in a confrontation over the issue of sabbath healing (3:1–5a). This is not a development of the conventional motif of public scorn, for the latter purports to underscore the greatness of healer and healing, whereas the controversy stresses the tragic enmity between the healer and onlookers. The performance part sees a return to formularity (II–a, c), but the acclamation is inverted into a death plot (3:5b–6). By moving the extraneous feature of controversy onto center stage, and by overturning the acclamation, the conventional healing story has been adjusted to the gospel's narration that culminates in the healer's death.

In the story of *Jairus's Daughter* the exposition part (5:21–24, 35–40) has been vastly complicated, while performance (5:41–42b) and confirmation parts (5:42c–43) proceed along routine lines. The motif of request for help (I–d) is voided by an announcement of the sick person's death, a startlingly unconventional feature. A new narrative impulse is required if the story is to be brought to the expected conclusion. Now the healer must take the initiative and seek out the girl. Upon arrival at her father's home (I–a), he encounters the mourning of bystanders. But as he denies the actuality of the girl's death, the bystanders' mourning turns into ridicule (I–e), at which point the story settles back into the conventional healing structure (II–a, c; III–a, c).

In the case of the healing of a *Woman with a Hemorrhage* the commonplaces are unevenly developed. The exposition part (5:24–28) dwells at length on the woman's condition of suffering (I–c). This sets the stage for her deliberate touching of the healer, an act resulting in her instant cure (II–c). The unusual execution of the cure without the healer's conscious participation, and in the absence of a healing formula, necessitates a heavy narrative investment (5:30–33) in order to bring healer and healed into the expected relationship. The healer's search for the woman and her return to him allows for a fairly conventional closing: the healer himself confirms the healing and utters a formula of dismissal (III–b).

In the story of the *Syrophoenician Woman* (7:24–30) the focus of interest falls entirely on the auxiliary motif of request (I–d). The reported cure (II–c) is merely incidental, and the confirmation part is conspicuous by its absence. In its present form, therefore, 7:24–30 gives evidence of a request more than of a healing story.

The healing of the *Deaf Mute* (7:31–37) is a formulaically contrived story with three evenly developed constituent parts. Arrival of the sick, description of sickness, request for help, healing gestures, healing formula, and cure form the expected sequence of exposition and performance parts (I–a, c, d; II–b, a, c). In the confirmation part the tension between secrecy and propagation has been forced to the point of open contradiction, a probable Markan emphasis (III–c, d). The formal conclusion is provided by the chorus acclamation in the form of a praise line (III–a).

The story of the *Blind Man of Bethsaida* (8:22–26) brings the focus entirely upon the performance part. The duplication of the motif of healing gesture (II–b, b) amounts to a narration of the cure in two stages. The first stage of partial seeing leads into a discussion between healer and blind man, and this in turn precipitates full cure (II–c). A drastic reduction of both exposition (I–a, d) and confirmation parts (III–b, c) renders the exposure of part II all the more conspicuous.

In the healing of *Blind Bartimaeus* (10:46–52) the auxiliary motif of request for help (I–d) is made the center of the story. The motif is narrated three times, and a dramatic scene is built around this threefold request: the initial request (10:47) is met with the bystanders' rejection (10:48a), which is followed by a renewal of request (10:48b, c), which in turn produces encouragement (10:49–50) and opens the way for a final request (10:51). The story concludes with a dismissal (III–b) and, finally, a statement of the accomplished cure (II–c).

An obvious point to emerge from this survey of healing stories is their indebtedness to a recognizable commonplace structure. A stock-in-trade of dependable features assures a more or less predictable narrative sequence. If deviations occur from the conventional pattern, the narrative trend is to return toward formulary stability. When a conventional ending is lacking or disturbed, redactional adjustment to the inclusive gospel narrative is evident. Each story forms a coherent unit, and each is identified as a healing story or a development thereof. Although no single story exhausts all narrative possibilities, one can justly conceive of the telling of healing stories as the actualization of a given narrative repertoire.[7]

Despite an essential uniformity in composition, these stories display a remarkable variability in the use of commonplaces. Compositional restraints do not manifest themselves as iron grids upon the material. There is ample room for narrative maneuvering, and no single story is quite like any other. A story can be reduced to its barest requirements or crowded with narrative detail. Virtually no limits are set to variations and combinations of auxiliary motifs. These can be dropped or developed, reshuffled into new scenes or transferred from one component part to another. Repetition of individual features is a special form of variation that serves the progress of the story. Actualization of a single motif at the expense of all others may effect transition toward a new type of story.[8] Major components can be omitted or compressed, reinterpreted or inflated. The story can peak, it seems, at almost any given point of its prescribed sequence. In sum, our study concurs with Vladimir Propp's observation about the "two-fold quality of a folktale: it is amazingly multiform, picturesque and colorful, and, to no less a degree, remarkably uniform and recurrent."[9]

There is a long-standing convention in New Testament scholarship to regard the synoptic miracle stories as indigenous products of Hellenistic culture. Rudolf Bultmann himself was one of its foremost advocates.[10] A more particular version of the thesis states that the healing stories are exponents of a *theios anēr* christology of Hellenistic persuasion.[11] Howard C. Kee has recently challenged the suitability of the Hellenistic paradigm from the perspective of post-exilic Jewish literature.[12] Miracles as signs of eschatological deliverance became "a central ingredient in Jewish eschatological literature."[13] Kee's proposition has much to recommend it, not the least being a redirection of scholarly attention toward the Jewishness of synoptic beginnings. But the question is to be raised whether the categories of Hellenistic versus Jewish, Bultmann's legacy from the German history of religion school, have not outlived their hermeneutical usefulness.[14] Etienne Trocmé, deliberately eschewing history of religion terminology, wondered whether Mark's healing stories might be "neither very Jewish, nor very Greek, but simply perhaps . . . animistic?"[15] In his view, they are traceable to the popular memory of Galilean storytellers, "to be distinguished . . . from the memory of the organized Christian community" of Jerusalem.[16] Trocmé's student, Kenzo Tagawa, followed up on his teacher's suggestion and presented a developed portrait of the folkloristic nature of the synoptic miracle stories.[17] Trocmé's assessment and Tagawa's study are significant in that they orient us away from outmoded history of religion categories and toward a more authentically oral appreciation of the material.

In the scholarly tradition of Trocmé and Tagawa we prefer to understand Mark's healing stories not primarily as expressions of a particular ethnic culture, but as products of the oral medium and of oral mentality. Healing stories transcend cultural bounds. Language, not ethnology, holds the key. The extraordinarily high proportion of stories in Mark and the synoptic tradition must not immediately lead us to assume literary sources. A logical connection exists between storied redundancy and oral transmission, and also between popularity and orality. "In oral styles, the close repetition of entire compositions is to be expected."[18] In a culture dependent on speaking, the repetition of stories is not only desirable but necessary: "knowledge not repeated enough vanishes."[19] The plurality of healing stories is a mute witness to what must have been a lively art of storytelling. Reiteration is assisted by commonplace structures. The same culture that pluralizes stories is inclined to formalize them. If memory alone allows words to survive, any kind of patterning facilitates retention and transmission. The variability in oral transmission/ composition is a feature masterfully documented by Albert B. Lord.[20] In performance the formulaic story is comparable to a musical instrument that is capable of producing an infinite variety of sounds, depending on the skills of the player and the reception by the audience. The narrator plays the role of musician who achieves effects by variation and phrasing: he renders emphatic one part while deemphasizing others. No single rendition is exactly like any previous or subsequent one. Every performance is "true," but no performance is the original or permanent one. In sum, it is the plurality, uniformity, and variability of the healing stories that attests to their oral production and quality of performance.

Oral pressures extend to the stories' mode of dramatization. In the interest of mnemonics, each story records a single-stranded plot with no more than two principal characters making a joint appearance. This rule of *scenic duality*[21] is carefully observed. The focus is either on Jesus and the sick person, or on Jesus and a supplicant on behalf of the sick. Orality prefers personalized stories; in each story a single person is healed. It is the writer of the inclusive narrative who generalizes by reporting the healing of multitudes (1:32–34, 39; 3:7–12). At the same time, none of the characters are developed into individual personalities. The sick persons or their supplicants are virtually exchangeable figures, for "what is preserved has to be typical."[22] What matters is the functioning of roles, not the delineation of characters.[23]

As character Jesus himself remains undeveloped. He appears as an accomplished performer of powerful deeds, but for the most part his healings lack a motive other than the mere presence of sick persons.[24] He heals in fulfillment of his prescribed role of healer. Those traditions that typecast Jesus into the role of healer we shall henceforth call *heroic stories*.[25] It is first and foremost mnemonic necessities that require Jesus to wear the mantle of healing heroism. The oral medium displays little grasp of the prosaic nature of ordinary life. What it remembers is not the ordinary occurrence, but what in some sense is extraordinary. It is part of the genius of orality to center on a single aspect of Jesus, to magnify and light it up, and to narrate it as his essential quality. Life's complexity, as well as its ordinariness, is thereby neglected and in fact abolished. The human condition is reduced to a single dimension, which is inflated to vast proportions. In short, the evocation of the high and heavy deeds intensifies and simultaneously simplifies Jesus. Moreover, certain qualities must be attached to him to make him a figure worth remembering. While the heroic Jesus is elevated to a presence larger than life, he remains deeply committed to life. He enjoys an enlarged status beyond the reach of ordinary mortals, but stays touchingly close to human frailty and mortality. This simplified and heroized Jesus, who acts outside of the common order but retains earthy touches, conforms to the requirements of oral rhetoric, remembering, and reenactment. In terms of narrative composition, of dramatization, and of conceptualization, this Jesus of the heroic stories is a genuine manifestation of *oral christology*.

Polarization Stories

Despite obvious compositional and conceptual affinities with the heroic stories, the exorcisms deserve a separate consideration. Mark acknowledges their existence apart from the heroic stories (1:32–34; 6:13). In general terms, exorcisms have slanted oral heroism toward the agonistic. Three narrative units qualify as exorcism stories:[26] the exorcism at the *Synagogue of Capernaum* (1:21–28), the exorcism of the *Gerasene Demoniac* (5:1–20), and the exorcism of the *Epileptic Boy* (9:14–29). All three stories progress along a path of more or less predictable happenings. Confrontation, expulsion, and acclamation form the three component parts, each of which is subdivided into a series of auxiliary features.

    I Confrontation
        a) meeting of exorcist and possessed
        b) the demon's warding-off formula
        c) the exorcist's rebuke and silencing
    II Expulsion
        a) command to exit
        b) demon's violent exit
    III Acclamation
        a) choral formula
        b) propagation of cure

Following the redactional reference to Jesus' teaching authority (1:21–22), the story of the exorcism at the *Synagogue of Capernaum* steadfastly adheres to the prescribed pattern. All three parts are evenly developed. Initial attention focuses on the aspect of confrontation. The demon struggles to keep the exorcist at bay by identifying his name and identity (I–a, b). The exorcist in turn rebukes the demon and issues a command to keep silent and to exit (I–c; II–a), which sets off the convulsive departure of the demon (II–b). The acclamation part registers the conventional motifs (III–a, b), both of which are accentuated by redactional references to Jesus' teaching authority and the propagation of the cure to "all the surrounding district of Galilee" (1:28).

The story of the exorcism of the *Gerasene Demoniac* is built around the skeleton of stereotypical traits: 5:1–2 (I–a), 5:6–7 (I–b), 5:8 (II–a), 5:13 (II–b), 5:14, 18–20 (III–b). The commonplace nature of the story is reinforced by verbal formularity:[27] *anthrōpos* (5:2; cf. 1:23); *en pneumati akathartō* (5:2; cf. 1:23; 9:25); *kai kraxas phōnē megalē legei* (5:7; cf. 1:23, 26; 9:24); *ti emoi kai soi, Iēsou* (5:7; cf. 1:24); *exelthe to pneuma to akatharton ek tou anthrōpou* (5:8; cf. 1:25; 9:25); *kai exelthonta ta pneumata ta akatharta* (5:13; cf. 1:26). Considerable narrative care is expended on the seriousness of the man's condition (5:3–6). This is a feature reminiscent of the heroic stories. In the case of the exorcism, it stresses the violence of the possessed man, thus heightening the agonistic flavor of the story.

At a crucial point, however, the story strays from thematic commonplaces, verbal grids, and folkloristic embellishments. The exorcist, instead of rebuking and silencing the demonic spirits, enters into negotiations with them concerning their place of destination (5:9–13). This is an extraneous feature that produces a shift from the conventional part of expulsion to the unconventional feature of demonic entry into the herd of swine. As a result, the story develops a double focus: the destruction of the swine is at least as important as the cure of the man. It has fallen upon the acclamation part to reconcile the unconventional with the conventional aspect, and then to return the story to the expected ending.

The unusual departure from narrative formularity requires explanation. Indications of major redactional involvements in the shifting of the focus are lacking. But the story's unconventional angle offers a rare glimpse into political risks taken by early Christian storytellers.[28] The code word *legiōn* (5:9, 15) stirs the imagination of those who live under Roman occupation. The narration of the drowning of the army of swine vents anti-Roman sentiments and encourages wishful thinking with regard to the occupying troops. An explanation for the departure from narrative clichés and for the use of metaphor may thus be found in the allusion to a highly sensitive political issue. The unconventional part makes demands on hearers, but the code word effects a conspiratorial rapport between narrator and hearer.

The story of the exorcism of the *Epileptic Boy* has been enveloped by the Markan theme of discipleship failure (9:14–19, 28–29). Apart from it, the language employed and the features developed disclose the core of a conventional exorcism. Narrative complications arise from the nature of the boy's ailment. His deaf-mute condition requires replacement of the warding-off formula by a scene of tortured convulsion (9:20: I–a), as well as intervention by the father on his behalf. Not being demon-possessed himself, the father pleads for help instead of shouting out toward the exorcist. But his cry for help, while reminiscent of the heroic stories, still echoes the conventional warding-off language (9:24: *kraxas;* cf. 1:23; 5:7). The father's successful intervention allows the story to reach its peak with the rebuke (I–c), the command to exit (II–a), and the demon's violent departure (II–b). Chorus line and propagation motif are missing. They were probably absorbed by the redactional motif of discipleship.

Mark's exorcisms register uniformity in compositional structure and variability in narrative performance. Again we recognize the art and economy of oral composition of narrating in verbal and thematic commonplaces. These are the defining and stabilizing constituents. Remove the clichés, and the heart of the stories is gone. By the same token, the stable constructs offer seemingly inexhaustible narrative license. What is essentially one and the same story can be told in a multitude of different ways. The variability of the narrative repertoire ranges from the accentuation or modification of auxiliary features to the flexible dramatization of component parts all the way to departure from the compositional structure itself. Social conditions may require expansion toward an entirely novel segment. There is, however, an ingrained narrative compulsion to return to expected endings. The speakers compose with the aid of received structures and by improvisation on them. There are as many variant narrations of the same type of story as there are occasions to narrate. Exorcisms are thus constructed on the same oral principle of "variation within the same"[29] that characterized the heroic stories.

The situations dramatized in exorcisms are themselves products of oral making. All three stories narrate a grim adversary relationship between Jesus and forces of evil. Their world is crude and confrontational, not subtle and discreet. Violence and destruction are massively present in each case. The *agōn*, the contest, is a hallmark of oral culture. To the oral mind, "was is a subject preferred to peace,"[30] and life is grasped by its opposites. Struggle and competition, conflict and adversary relations have decided mnemonic advantages over the daily grind and routine, the ambiguity and complexities of life. "Contest between heavily laden type figures is a central operation in an oral culture's retention of its knowledge and its sense of identity."[31] Undoubtedly there is a moral quality attached to the polemics of these stories: the good wins over the evil. But the needs of the medium dominate over the values it transmits. It is the functional need of oral remembering, more than addiction to moral values, that promotes antithetical structuring of knowledge.[32] In view of the preoccupation of exorcisms with polarizing actuality into good and evil, praise and blame, we shall henceforth refer to them as *polarization stories*.

Only an overliterate mind will be inclined to read these stories for more than the obvious. There may be subtle allusions, as in the case of the *Gerasene Demoniac*. But no complex ideological investment is to be expected. Those habituated to storytelling are disinclined, and perhaps not able to reflect on the nature of Jesus and the essence of redemption. Indeed, *nature* and *essence* as concepts are alien to the oral mind. The challenge for the storyteller is not to contemplate Jesus with theological acumen, nor to restore his historical actuality, but rather to make him live in the imagination of the audience. This is ideally done by narrated actions, because "actions and their agents are in fact always easy to visualize,"[33] and adversary relations are a preferred form of action stories. There is an oral, poetic sense, therefore, in which the figure of Jesus demands opposition, a pathological double, and preferably one in personalized form. Evil is not defined as an *It*, but dramatized as a *Thou*, endowed with speech and intelligence. In this personalized fashion, the demons become the defining opposite for Jesus, shaping and sharpening him into a figure of redemptive quality.

Ideological simplicity is a virtue both in the heroic and the polarization stories. Jesus is a wholly unambiguous figure who cures diseases and conquers evil spirits. The terrifyingly ambiguous notion that the protagonist must first be crushed himself for evil to be conquered lies outside the mental horizon of this oral christology of heroism and polarization.

Didactic Stories

The apophthegmatic tradition covers a variety of controversies, double-controversy dialogues, and biographical tales. Our discussion is strictly confined to those controversy stories that culminate in a memorable saying of Jesus. Defined in this fashion, the following six examples provide clear evidence of pre-Markan formulation:[34] *Table Fellowship with Sinners* (2:15–17), the *Issue of Fasting* (2:18–19), *Plucking Corn on Sabbath* (2:23–28), the *Issue of Divorce* (10:2–9), the *Issue of Posses-*

sions (10:17–22), and *Payment of Taxes* (12:13–17). In developed form these stories stage two rounds of conversation:

a) *mise en scène*
b) raising of (provocative) question
c) protagonist's counter-question
d) response by inquirer(s)
e) protagonist's answer: memorable saying

One encounters this dramatization in three stories (10:2–9; 10:17–22; 12:13–17); the other three register a simplified version of only one sequence of query/answer (2:15–17; 2:18–19; 2:23–28). Minor deviations are provided by the addition of closure (10:22), the substitution of opponent by an eager, soon-to-be disillusioned sympathizer (10:17–22), and the protagonist's request for a piece of evidence upon which the burden of proof will rest (12:15–16).

It was Bultmann's view that the apophthegmatic controversies represented a literary form—with few traces of Hellenistic influence, but fashioned in the mode of Rabbinic disputations; their function in the early church was apologetic and polemical.[35] Yet if apophthegmatic stories are to be taken seriously as forms of oral rhetoric, the classification of Jewish versus Hellenistic will at most be of secondary importance. All six stories use dialogue to dramatic effect. As a rule, the drama opens with a controversial issue or situation, or a reference to the intended entrapment of the protagonist. With the exception of the rich man, the agents enter into an adversary relationship. It is incumbent upon the interrogators to raise the issue directly, often provocatively, and to defend the opposite of what will be the story's didactic goal. This process of challenging and denouncing at first what is to be remembered at last implements a teaching *via negativa* through the mechanism of disputation. The listener is drawn into the controversies through the device of polarization of issues and agents. After the debate has climaxed, the listener is left with the final saying. And that is for good reason. The focal sayings, strategically placed at the culmination of the story, are the carriers of the community's social, cultic, and moral values: social intercourse with outcasts (2:17), prohibition of fasting (2:19), suspension of Sabbath law (2:27), ban on divorce (10:9), renunciation of possessions (10:21), and payment of taxes (12:17). It is because of the educational, encyclopedic function of these controversies that we shall henceforth refer to them as *didactic stories*.

What is remarkable about the transmission of ethical norms is that it is not conducted straightforwardly by way of a list of items to be memorized or a philosophical treatise to be contemplated. The didactic stories are a form of speech that combines story with statement. The information to be remembered is implanted in a context that serves as a memory bridge. The scenes and agents are typical rather than unique, but rich in imaginative quality. This is the ultimate objective of the oral process: to make the information virtually present in the mind.[36] Perhaps none of the six didactic stories has made greater impact on popular and artistic imagination than *Plucking Corn on Sabbath*. The actual story line, however, is limited to the plain and uninventive statement that "He was passing through the grainfields on the Sabbath, and his disciples began to make their way along while picking the heads of corn" (2:23, au. trans.). Prosaic though this sentence is, it is highly suggestive, and sparks visual images in the listener. In this fashion, the stories function as mnemonic triggers that help recall information incidentally, rather than mechanistically. As Havelock observed, for knowledge to make a lasting impact on mind and memory, "the pill has to be sweetened."[37] In the case of the didactic stories, the pill is the ethical information, and the story serves as the sweetener.

The didactic stories are a world created to the measure of orality, mnemonically as well as conceptually. They inculcate propriety through the vehicle of memorizable examples, narrated as doings. Codes and mores have become inextricably aligned with human situations, or more accurately, have been made to emanate out of dramatic scenes of disputation. If asked about social directives apart from social settings and doings, the tellers of these stories would wonder what the question meant. Only a mind removed from oral mentality would probe stories and narrators with a curiosity about the *nature* of justice, piety, morality, social and civic responsibility. What this means is that an ethics managed in the form of story is unable to leave the scope of the concrete, or is at least uncomfortable with such a departure. To the storyteller, abstractions have little validity, and discipleship cannot be articulated by recourse to principles. It is thus of decided advantage for speakers and auditors that these stories personalize and actualize the information to be remembered. Ethical directives can now be apprehended in terms of application, rather than generalization.

Parabolic Stories

Mark's gospel records six identifiable parabolic stories: the parable of the *Sower* (4:3–8), the parable of the *Reaper* (4:26–29), the parable of the *Mustard Seed* (4:30–32), the parable of the *Wicked Tenants* (12:1–11), the parable of the *Fig Tree* (13:28), and the parable of the

Doorkeeper (13:34). This remains, however, a restrictive count. Parabolic discourse is strewn across the gospel (2:21–22; 3:23–27; 4:21, 22, 24–25; 7:15; 9:50).[38] Indeed, Mark has associated Jesus, the oral performer, exclusively with parabolic speech (4:33–34). For the Markan Jesus, it seems, the significance of speaking in parables goes beyond those stories technically called parables. Here we shall treat the mnemonic quality of parables and their special characteristics as compared to the heroic, polarization, and didactic stories. Since Mark 4:14–20 offers an allegorical interpretation of the parable of the *Sower,* and allegory appears to have penetrated the parable of the *Wicked Tenants,* the issue of the parable/allegory dichotomy must be addressed. Does allegory detract from and perhaps violate the spirit of parable? There is finally the question of the purpose of parabolic speech. Why does one speak in parables? Of all synoptic speech forms, parable displays by far the greatest hermeneutical intricacies. We shall, for this reason, need to explore further parabolic hermeneutics in chapters 3 and 5 respectively.[39]

The oral propriety of parabolic stories requires little argument. "A parable is an urgent endeavour on the part of the speaker towards the listener."[40] Speaking is the ordinary mode of parabolic discourse, and writing in parables seems almost out of place. In spite of their incontrovertibly-oral nature, however, parables are not susceptible to a uniform compositional structure. Individual parables, we shall see, are mnemonically shaped, and groups of parables are identifiable by common structures, but there is no single synchronic pattern that accommodates all six Markan stories, still less the bulk of the synoptic parables.[41] There is, of course, in parable scholarship no shortage in classification according to theological, ethical, existentialist, philosophical, and structuralist principles.[42] But the legitimate concern for and the relative success in organization should not blind us to the fact that parables are not reducible to a single story line. "The parables do not constitute a set in the same sense as do the Russian folktales studied by Propp, which are reducible to only one fundamental tale."[43] Parables, one might add, are not recognizable by a formulaic, compositional stability in the manner of the heroic, polarization, and didactic stories. Historically, one may trace this compositional latitude of parabolic stories to their linguistic prototype, the Hebrew *mašal* and the Aramaic *mathla,* which embrace an astounding variety of speech forms.[44] But one may also suspect deeper motivations. Is there a connection between Jesus' proclamation of the kingdom in parables and parabolic resistance to synchronic uniformity, which mocks, so it seems, the very principle of total organization?

One of the popularly cherished qualities of parabolic stories is their power to describe everyday life. In vivid language they replay the largely agricultural world of speakers and listeners. Seeds and growing, growth and harvest, fig tree and vineyards, wealthy landowners and slaving laborers are all experiences drawn from Galilean peasant society. Even the story of a murderous rebellion against an absentee landowner, while clearly inspired by Old Testament language and imagery, suggests a realistic feature of first-century Jewish life. A rebellious country population and peasant revolts came to be common experiences at that time. There is thus a sense in which the parables reconfirm their listeners in the very world in which they live. It is in this evocation of the ordinary that they give the impression of being "true to life."

The problem this notion of parabolic realism raises for the mnemonic process is obvious. Ordinariness may well serve as a focus of identification: speaker and hearers recognize themselves in these stories. But what are the chances for stories being repeated and carried on which narrate everyday experiences? Ordinariness allows for instantaneous identification, but hardly for enduring transmission. For this reason alone, plainness cannot be the last word on parabolic stories.

Mnemonic patterning has left its imprint on two Markan parables, and to a lesser degree on a third one. The parable of the *Sower* narrates a sharp contrast between triple failure and triple success of the seed. The parable of the *Mustard Seed* contrasts the smallest of seeds with the largest of plants. Contrasts render these stories orally impressionable, for the display of opposites appeals to the imagination and holds the attention as few rhetorical devices do. In the *Gospel of Thomas* the parable of the *Wicked Tenants* (65:1–16) reports the threefold mission of the owner of a vineyard to his laborers. The trebling, as well as doubling, of narrative features is a favorite oral strategy. If a feature is repeated more than three times, it loses its impact on the audience.[45] In contrast to *Thomas*, Mark's version of the *Wicked Tenants* upsets the balance of the threefold composition by the additional dispatch of many other messengers (12:5b), and by a novel narrative focus: the punishment of the tenants, the transference of the vineyard to others, and the reinstatement of the heir (12:9–11). If one observes that the *Thomas* version appears closer to oral speech, and Mark's story more fully textualized, one has not thereby arrived at the original form. In parabolic speech, as in all other acts of speaking, the original form is a phantom of the literate imagination.

While parables narrate on the level of ordinary life, this ordinariness is frequently put under strain. For about four-fifths of the way through its story the parable of the *Sower* leads one to believe that failure is inevitable, before fate is turned around in the last part. The narration of a stark fiasco at seedtime and in the early stage of growth leaves hearers unprepared for the excessive and excessively accelerating crops at harvest time. In the case of the *Mustard Seed* sole emphasis on the herb's beginning and ending, without regard for the period of growth, twists the story toward the paradoxical.[46] In the *Thomas* version of the *Wicked Tenants* the mistreatment of the first and even the second servant is credible, but the subsequent mission of the son strains our credulity. How could the father have responded to the abuse suffered by two servants by sending his own son, heir of the vineyard, unprotected into the hands of ruthless tenants? Justice is withheld in the end, and all murders go unpunished. One might call this a particularly realistic story depicting life's cruelty, were it not for the father's unrealistic mission of the son. Mark's version of the *Wicked Tenants* flouts all conventional logic. In view of more than two abortive missions and a series of murders, the father's decision to send his son appears entirely ill-conceived. The tenants' assumption, moreover, that they would acquire the land by killing the heir is unrealistic in the extreme. Yet, the son's mission is justified by a new kind of logic. The unexpected rehabilitation of the heir redeems the father's "ill-conceived" decision. But this very rehabilitation introduces a paradox: the one who was cast out of the vineyard is made the keystone.[47] The impression of realism is thus deceiving in all three parables. In each case elements of logical unlikeliness impinge upon the realism of the story, and credibility is stretched to its limits. Elements of surprise, hyperbole, and paradox are lodged in these stories.

The proposition is now widely entertained that in the world of parables not all is "true to life." Some scholars have judged parabolic stories to be "antitraditional in intention,"[48] as delivering an "imaginative shock,"[49] or containing a "trait of hyperbole."[50] Others have recognized parabolic "shock tactics,"[51] "the fractured realism of the parables,"[52] or an "aesthetic mingling of the realistic and the surprising."[53] A consensus appears to be emerging—especially in North American parable studies—that holds this conjunction of the normal with the abnormal to be symptomatic for many parables. Paul Ricoeur has introduced the term *extravagance* to characterize this specific parabolic trait.[54] Parabolic extravagance promotes intensification and exaggeration, risks paradox and hyperbole, and strains or transgresses the hearers' sense of realism. A parable is thus a story that, while it "pretends to be plain and trivial,"[55] holds powers to embrace the "extraordinary within the ordinary."[56] For Ricoeur it is this extravagance that "transforms the poetics of the parables into a poetics of faith."[57] That is to say that the "oddness"[58] of the narrative serves to disconfirm conventional expectations and encourages experimentation with a new logic in defiance of common sense.

Ricoeur's concept of extravagance further illuminates the mnemonic process of parabolic stories. Over and above mnemonic patterning, it is the element of excess and irregularity that eases remembering. The trivial facilitates identification, but oddness makes these stories memorable. For what one remembers is not the pane in the window, but the crack in the pane.

What is noteworthy about most *Markan* parables is that the element of extravagance is moderately developed or even nonexistent. Paradox is most deeply etched into the story of the *Wicked Tenants*. The parables of the *Sower* and the *Mustard Seed* narrate extreme and paradoxical but not necessarily implausible situations. They strain but do not distort everyday experiences of farming and of processes of nature.[59] They ask for readjustment, but hardly for total reorientation of hearers' viewpoints. In the stories of the *Reaper*, the *Fig Tree*, and the *Doorkeeper* the course of ordinary life remains entirely unchallenged and undisturbed. These tales about sowing, self-acting growth, and harvest, about a tree putting forth its leaves and a watchman placed in charge of the master's house are unambiguously implanted in nature and human life. Why is it that the more extravagant parables, which shatter hearers' conventional expectations, are to be found in Matthew and especially in Luke, but not in Mark? Is there, moreover, a connection between the relative paucity of Markan parables and their comparatively moderate tone? We must return to this issue in chapter 5.[60]

The purpose of parables is not exhausted by making known what is more or less common knowledge about sowing and harvest, the process of growth, the desperate brutality of workers in vineyards, a sprouting fig tree, or an unexceptional guard. What all parables have in common is their *metaphorical quality*.[61] "The parable that has only a literal level of meaning does not exist."[62] Whether marked by extravagance or not, a parable is never self-explanatory. It signifies meaning that lies outside its own narrated world. Or, perhaps more cautiously, it gestures beyond itself. Parables invite hearers into the story and through it to a story behind the story. Or, again more cautiously, parables are stories that bespeak something else. One may say, therefore, that the parabolist tells stories without giving them away. Hence the frequent *Weckformel* at the conclusion of a parable: "He who has ears to hear, let him hear."

Owing to their metaphorical quality parables are hermeneutically unfinished products. They encourage but withhold meaning, suggest but conceal understanding. This status of hermeneutical open-endedness renders parables peculiarly dependent on oral, social contextuality. A parable is not meant to be frozen into textuality, but rather to engage hearers "to complete the process built up within the story."[63] Speaker and hearers are thus wholly indispensable to a successful delivery of parabolic speech. Because parabolic language is not self-explanatory but intent on transcending what it says literally, it needs all the help it can get to carry out this delicate transaction. The sounding of words, the gestures of the speaker, facial contact between speaker and hearers, as well as an environment shared by speaker and hearers alike are all crucial aids in conveying meaning without saying it. Two conclusions must be drawn. First, insofar as parabolic language is open-ended, and negotiable in social contexts and by interaction of speaker with hearers, it is a quintessential *oral form of speech*. Of all synoptic speech forms, the parable is the least capable of functioning as an autonomous linguistic object. Contrary to modern aesthetics of literature, parable is first and foremost a speech act delivered by a speaker to hearers. Second, parabolic speech not only lacks *the original form* but also *the original meaning*. No single telling of a parable is quite like any other, and different social contexts suggest multiple hearings. It is not even possible to specify the kingdom of God as *the* referent of *all* synoptic parables.[64] The case for parabolic polyvalency was most persuasively argued by Mary Ann Tolbert.[65] After demonstrating parabolic indeterminacy on a variety of linguistic levels, she concluded that for "a full elaboration of their meaning the parables are dependent on their context. Hence every different context into which they are placed will result in a different interpretation."[66] In other words, the hearing of parables varies with each performance, because hearers and social contexts, the "cocreators" of parabolic speech, are inevitably variables.[67] To sum up, the parables as metaphors invite polyvalent hearings that are negotiated in oral, social contexts. Metaphoricity, orality, and polyvalency militate against the original form and uniform meanings.[68]

The metaphoricity of parabolic stories sheds still more light on their mnemonic quality. Apart from rhythmic patterning and extravagance, the mnemonic attractiveness of parables lies in their hermeneutical inexhaustibility and susceptibility to multiple hearings. Deceptively ordinary as most parables are, they prompt retelling and rehearsing. Simple as they appear to be, they engage and intrigue the mind on account of their concealing and revealing disposition. They bear repeating and require testing because they are never fully narrated. One must say, therefore, that parables, insofar as they are hermeneutically unfinished stories, stimulate a process of interpretation that is never entirely brought to completion or under control.

The concept of allegory has bedeviled parable scholarship and affected our reading of the Markan interpretation of the parable of the *Sower* (4:11–20). Ever since Adolf Jülicher's postulated dichotomy of parable versus allegory, the interpretation is widely held to be inferior to the parable *due to the former's allegorizing posture*. As Jülicher saw it, the many-pointed allegory obscured the lucidity of the one-pointed parable. To this one must first say that the parable of the *Sower* is not a paragon of transparency, but the carrier of the mystery of the kingdom of God, and its interpretation illuminates the mystery more than it obscures it. Jülicher's dichotomy was based on an essentially rationalistic reading of parables.[69] In the second place, the issue of one or two or many points of reference is irrelevant—given the parables' oral polyvalency. A parabolist may emphasize one or two or many features to suggest meaning, and hearers may likewise comprehend only one, a few, or multiple points of comparison. There exists in the world of speaking no absolute distinction between the point-by-point correspondence versus a holistic perception.[70] Thirdly, parables cry out for interpretation due to their metaphorical quality. By making explicit a hermeneutically implicit potential, interpretation acknowledges parabolic metaphoricity. In one sense, therefore, the interpretation discharges the hermeneutical task fallen on hearers and readers alike. There is another sense, however, in which the interpretation goes beyond parabolic intentionality, but it has nothing to do with allegory. In *articulating* meaning, the interpretation transacts the very operation that the metaphoricity of parables suggests cannot be transacted. The explication, above all *written fixedness*, of the interpretation is the crux of the matter, not allegory. This written explication of the interpretation both carries out and goes beyond the orally transacted intentionality of parables. In chapter 3 we note that Mark's whole parabolic scenario of the mystery of the kingdom of God, parabolic speech, insiders versus outsiders, placement of the disciples into the inside, and interpretation for the insiders shows the developed hermeneutical reflectiveness of the writer of the gospel.

The parable of the *Wicked Tenants* is generally considered an allegorical story and often assumed to be inferior to the more "authentic" parables. Linguistically, allegory is not the most penetrating question this parable poses. It is more interesting to explore the reason for our ability to recognize allegory. The "beloved son" (12:6) is disclosed by the inclusive gospel story as Jesus himself (1:11; 9:7). The second servant who is wounded in the head (12:4) will probably refer to John the Baptist (6:27). The tenants (12:8–9) give themselves away as the temple authorities (11:27; 12:12). The vineyard, finally, in the context of Jesus' temple speeches serves as a metaphor for the temple.[71] One must conclude that the allegorical features are primarily due to the parable's interconnectedness with the larger story of the gospel. It is the reader of the gospel more than the hearer of the parable who is conditioned to reading the exclusive parable allegorically. The more penetrating linguistic question this parable raises is thus not allegorization, but textualization. What happens to parables, which are meant to open out to hearers, when they become enclosed by a text? Can parabolic stories still function as parables when they are carried by the gospel's textuality? We shall return to this question in chapter 3, and again in chapter 5.

With parabolic discourse language is pressed toward its limits.[72] When Nathan the prophet dares criticize King David's sin against Uriah, he does so in the form of a parable (2 Sam. 12:1–4), and when Jotham objects to his brother's Abimelech's royal ambitions, he likewise resorts to parabolic talk (Judg. 9:8–15). The message to be delivered in each case can barely be uttered at all, and never in straightforward language. This is symptomatic for speaking in parables. Something is left unsaid, and it is this unsaid that matters most. Parables are more important for what they do not say than for what they say. There is an understanding, whether conscious or not, shared by parabolists that all does not submit to language. It is through the vehicle of the parabolic story that one seeks to gain a hearing for the as yet unexpressed and to break ground for the unheard-of. Transposition of parabolic meaning into propositional language, a congenital defect of much of parable scholarship in the past, is the last thing parables are capable of tolerating.[73] The parabolic commitment is to emancipation from general principles and conventional wisdom, and to the hearing of a new voice. Parables as metaphors may arouse a sense of mystery over the unfathomable reservoir of language, or despair over the inadequacy of spoken words. But hard definitions and set formulations have long lost their purpose in parabolic talk. To give voice to what has as yet not come to expression—that is the paradoxical task fallen upon the speakers of parables.

Whether parables shock hearers out of conventionality or gesture them toward something else, their secret strategy is in all instances seduction by the ordinary with a view toward the extraordinary.

ORAL SYNTAX AND STORY

A quarter of a century of redaction and literary criticism in Mark has woven an intricate tapestry of thematic and linguistic patterns, and almost blinded us to the agglomerate nature of the text. Not only does the author rely on single tales whose oral profile is far from being erased, but short stories constitute the backbone of his narrative. Take the stories away, and the narrative of Jesus' life is gone. Literary criticism notwithstanding, the first observation on Mark 1–13 pertains to this text's transparency on a storied, oral heritage.

The many stories are linked together by stereotypical connective devices: pleonastic *archesthai* with infinitive verbs, preferably of action (2:23; 6:7; 11:15; etc.) and speaking (1:45; 8:31; 14:69; etc.), the adverbial *euthys* and *kai euthys* (1:29; 3:6; 6:54; etc.), the iterative *palin* and *kai palin*, preferably with verbs of movement (2:1; 7:31; 14:40; etc.) and speaking (4:1; 10:1, 10; etc.), the formulaic *kai ginetai* or *kai egeneto* (1:9; 2:15, 23; etc.), and abundant use of paratactic *kai* (9:2; 11:20; 15:42; etc.). These connectives are for the most part derived from the oral repertoire of the gospel's primary building blocks.[74] For this reason they render constructive service in simulating narrative sequentiality *between* single stories much in the same fashion as narrative develops *within* them. In addition to functioning connectively, these devices insinuate the suddenness, urgency, and near-simultaneity of successive events. They line up episodes paratactically like beads on a string, producing a narrative that, especially in the pre-passion section, is jolting more than smoothly flowing and "a grid rather than a plenum."[75] Mark's paratactic narrative engenders a sense of spontaneity. It leaps nervously from one stark episode to the next, propelling the reader forward and offering little encouragement to pause, reflect, and revisit a story. One wonders whether oral connectives, episodic syntax, and breathlessness of prose could not be an index of this gospel's effectiveness on hearers.

What reinforces the action-packed narrative is the oral principle of the interchangeability of actions and words.[76] Actions manifest a didactic intent, which pulls them into the orbit of words, and words embody the vitality of happenings, which makes them indistinguishable from actions. A demonstration of the verbal quality of an action is provided by Jesus' first deed of power (1:21–28). The redundant reference to his teaching at the outset (1:21–22) and the acclamation in terms of a new teaching with authority (1:27; "A new teaching! With authority . . .") accord this exorcism the property of an actualized message. This notion, programmatically enacted with Jesus' first deed of power, is by implication extended to all subsequent deeds.[77] All heroic and polorization stories are a form of powerful speech. Jesus' words, on the other hand, do not merely announce a new time and a reversal of priorities, but put an end to conventional logic and bring a new world into being. His voice carries the power of action. It calls into discipleship, calms the sea, creates friend and foe, cures the sick, and ruins the fig tree. Dialogues and controversies take on the power of events and blend in with pure action scenes. Words carry the force of action, and actions speak as loud as words. It is this reciprocal relationship of deed and word, the word-character of actions and the action-character of words, that further enhances the gospel's *activist syntax.*[78]

A number of stylistic and rhetorical features contribute to the gospel's oral flavor. Folkloristic triads have deeply penetrated the narrative: three disciples are separated from within the twelve, three times Jesus predicts his passion and resurrection, three times he asks the disciples to wake with him at Gethsemane, three times he enters Jerusalem, and three times Peter denies him. The prolific use of the third person plural instead of the passive (5:14; 8:22; 10:13; etc.) is in keeping with the popular style of storytelling.[79] The excessive employment of the historical present, preferably with *legein* (3:32; 8:12; 14:67; etc.) and *erchesthai* (1:40; 3:20; 16:2; etc.), magnifies the gospel's dramatic intensity. Preference for direct speech (1:14–15; 9:11; 11:17; etc.) or the tendency for indirect discourse to become direct speech (1:40; 10:32–33; 14:57–58; etc.) heightens the narrative immediacy. Parenthetical clauses (3:30; 13:14; 16:8c; etc.) enliven the style and serve as *ad hominem* directives. Even if some of these features are traceable to Aramaisms or Semitisms, this does not preclude their oral propensity. Their cumulative effect in Mark adds vividness to the narrative. As for the quality of Mark's Greek, finally, it is a commonplace that it is removed from Attic elegance and more akin to a colloquial version of Koine Greek.[80]

The phenomenon of duality has justly been called "one of Mark's most characteristic features of style."[81] Frans Neirynck has painstakingly assembled a vast amount of Markan pleonasms, redundancies, and repetitions. A few examples must suffice to illustrate the case: compound verbs followed by the same preposition (1:16; 10:25; 15:32; etc.), multiplication of cognate verbs (2:15; 8:6–7; 14:45; etc.), double imperatives (4:39; 14:38; 15:36; etc.), double negatives (1:44; 13:32; 16:8; etc.), *ouk . . . alla* constructions that restate in positive terms a preceding negation (2:17; 6:52; 16:6–7; etc.), local and temporal redundancies (1:32; 11:15; 15:42; etc.), repetition of motifs (3:21, 22; 10:32; 14:41, 42; etc.), double questions (2:7; 8:17; 14:37; etc.), inclusions (1:15; 4:3, 9; 15:16, 20; etc.), repetition of request by realization (5:12, 13; 6:56; 15:11, 15; etc.), and a host of others. Prior to Neirynck scholars attended to Markan duality with a strong interest in source criticism. Duplicate features were taken as evidence for a combination of sources. Hence Neirynck's observation: "As far as I know, no reconstruction of Proto-Mark or Proto-Markan sources has been proposed from which the phenomenon of duplication is totally ruled out."[82] After Neirynck we must accept pervasive duality as a trait "typical for Mark's way of thinking and writing."[83] But how is one to account for duality in Mark, and what are we to make of it? Neirynck has left us without clues.

Above all else duality is a concession to oral needs, not a "sign of the limitations of Mark's art as a writer,"[84] as Vincent Taylor suggested. In a culture dependent on speaking, repetition is neither a stylistic quirk nor a flaw, but a dire necessity.[85] Without recourse to texts, knowledge must be repeated many times over. How else are words to be retained and transmitted? If a text is to appeal to hearers, it must likewise employ the strategy of repetition. In reading a text, the eye can roam the pages, return to a passage, dwell on it, and compare it with other passages. But the auditor is entitled to only one hearing. He or she cannot revert to spoken words and reflect on them. The reflective procedure is not given much of a chance in orality. The ear has to be attuned to live speech and must grasp it momentarily. In those circumstances, repetition is the oral substitute for the eye's privilege to revisit words. The reiteration of words, clauses, and themes allows the hearer to return to and link up with what was said before.

By way of example, we shall reflect on the story of the healing of the *Paralytic* (Mark 2:1–12). Earlier we observed a narrative deviation from the conventional healing pattern in the form of a controversy over the forgiveness of sins (2:6–10). This controversy part is shot through with verbal duplications: *aphientai sou hai hamartiai* (2:5)//*aphientai sou hai hamartiai* (2:9); *dialogizomenoi en tais kardiais autōn* (2:6)// *dialogizesthe en tais kardiais hymōn* (2:8); *egeire kai aron ton krabatton sou* (2:9)//*egeire aron ton krabatton sou* (2:11). A pair of identical "framing" clauses appear to mark off the controversy as an "interpolation": *legei tō paralytikō* (2:5)//*legei tō paralytikō* (2:10). The notions of "framing" and "interpolation" conjure up intricate textual manipulations. Yet the gospel's proximity to oral life may warrant reflection on Lord's proposition: "I do not believe in interpolators any more than I believe in ghosts, even less."[86] Mark may be treating an oral story in order for it to remain functional for the ear more than for the eye. By duplicating the key phrases, he has in effect told the controversy twice. The impact of reiterating verbal clauses allows the ear to recall and hear its way through the unconventional passage. Despite deviation from the norm of healing story, healing and controversy can now be heard as a narrative whole.[87]

What adds weight to the ascription of repetition to orality is the infrequency of verbatim repetitions. "In fact, it can be maintained that pure redundancy is extremely rare in Mark."[88] Often the first reference "is a general statement and the second adds further precision."[89] This double-step redundancy serves both speaker and hearers, narrative and mnemonic needs. The second statement revisits the first but at the same time carries the story forward. Progressive duplication, therefore, fosters recall, but without retarding, and in fact by enhancing the narrative momentum. Dramatic and mnemonic needs are equally served by Mark's double-step technique.

In view of Mark's stylistic devices, the activist syntax, the nature of his Greek, and the art of storytelling, the judgment seems warranted that his "style is that of the speaker rather than that of the writer."[90]

In turning to the gospel's characters, one is struck by a paradox. Many give the impression of being fleshed out in detail, but close scrutiny shows them to be poorly developed. A sizable number of persons, among them the leper, the paralytic, Jairus and his daughter, the Syrophoenician woman, the deaf mute, the hemorrhaging woman, and blind Bartimaeus fail to rise above their typified status in oral presentation. Opposition forces such as the Pharisees, Sadducees, and scribes lack individual profiles. The many are treated as one. Not even Jesus' own relatives are honored with distinct personality traits. John the Baptist might appear to be an exception: he is subject to descriptive treatment as no other person in the gospel (1:4–8). But apart from his programmatic appearance, his baptism of Jesus, his incarceration and death, he remains a person shrouded in obscurity. Herod Antipas, Herodias, and her daughter are admitted into one of the most visually stimulating dramatizations, the circumstances surrounding the Baptist's death (6:14–29). Beyond this single scene, however, they are given no chance to grow into well-formed characters. The passion narrative is crowded with persons who add much to the gospel's "realism." Figures like the woman anointing Jesus, the high priest, Pilate, Barabbas, the soldiers, Simon of Cyrene, the centurion, Joseph of Arimathea, and the women appear removed from an oral, schematic base. And yet, what measure of individuality they have acquired is due more to their function in the passion drama than to artistic skill in developing characters.

By far the most impressively drawn portraits are those of the disciples, Peter, and Jesus. The disciples are indispensable to the gospel narrative. Still, exploitation of character is not the manner by which they are brought to life. It is in their developing relationship with Jesus that their attitudes are revealed and their motives unfolded. In spite of their importance, many of them remain faceless. Judas, James, and John, who together with Peter are set apart from the twelve, are still not portrayed in full. Erich Auerbach was certainly right in contending that Peter showed a distinct mark of individuality: "A scene like Peter's denial fits into no antique genre."[91] As an individual he ranks above all other disciples. He is "the most fully developed character in the entire story other than Jesus."[92] And yet, his individuality does not come into view by virtue of poetic, descriptive powers, but through the actualization of his failing leadership. As for Jesus himself, some of his feelings and affections are expressly recorded: he is moved by anger (1:41;[93] 3:5; 10:14), pity (6:34; 8:2), wonderment (6:6), and love (10:21). This is not to say, however, that his volitional and intellectual life has been fully explored. "The psychology of human development is a modern invention."[94] He enters upon stage without any hint at background and upbringing, "a hero full grown and ready for action."[95] As heroic figure he is drawn in firm and impressive outline. But this life, caught in a series of wonder-working deeds, betrays its connection with oral heroism and cries out for explication and interpretation. The passion narrative brings him a step closer to "realism," and Gethsemane offers an intimate glimpse into his soul's despair. Determined to suffer but plagued by fear, he has taken on the appearance of a "real person."

What one can gather from these observations is that none of the characters, however brief or extended their appearance, is a fully realized, knowable human being. They are not persons in the sense that the author has grasped them from all sides and in the fullest possible completeness. Character development is not the strength of stories rooted in orality. Narration in the form of actions is where the oral interest lies. "In very many situations where the modern writer would expect a psychological analysis, the primitive storyteller simply presents an action."[96] Mark, therefore, cannot be said to conform to the Aristotelian premise that the story is actualized through the characters: quite the opposite. It is through actions, face-to-face dialogues, controversies, and confrontations that characters come to life.[97] Movement and action convey a sense of animation and "real life," obscuring the fact that one has to do with more or less limited artistic characterizations. The woman who anoints Jesus "is characterized only by what she has and what she does."[98] But her actions give her a sense of "reality" and reveal some personal traits. Action scenes, moreover, can be perceived with the mind's eye, and what can be visualized takes on a keen sense of "reality." This, for example, is the poetic secret of Peter's denial. It is a highly visual scene with a strong appeal to the imagination. True to all orally successful stories, it captivates the mind "in order that vision may lead on to vision."[99] Such is the dramatic power of Mark's action scenes that they almost make us forget that it is not the characters who generate the story, but the stories that shape characters.

Mark shares the oral conviction that truth is not to be known nor redemption to be had by concepts estranged from life. This applies with special force to the disciples' relation with Jesus, as narrated by Mark. The information conveyed to the disciples is not given them in propositional statements subject to memorization by heart. Rather, Jesus' entire life and death constitutes a pedagogical paradigm, inspiring the disciples to learn by imitation and participation. Jesus' doings and sayings, his relations and confrontations, and the pattern of his travels spell out a didactic rationale. Unless the disciples learn this paradigm in the concrete act of following, they cannot grasp the truth pertaining to Jesus. For this reason, they are present at the performance of powerful deeds (4:35; 5:31, 37; 6:1, 5, 45; 9:14), are sent on a "trial run" of preaching, exorcising, and healing (6:7–13, 30), observe Jesus' break with his relatives (6:1–6a), participate in feedings (6:35–44; 8:1–10), accompany Jesus on his trips to the temple (11:1–12:44), and witness the passion events—up to the arrest. In addition, they receive private instructions on such matters as the mystery of the kingdom of God (4:10–32), the new morality (7:17–23), Jesus' impending death and resurrection (8:31; 9:31; 10:32–34), the casting out of evil spirits (9:28–29), communal relations (9:35–50), divorce (10:10–12), the acceptance of children (10:13–15), discipleship (10:23–31), servanthood (10:42–45), the end of the temple and the end of history (13:5–37). All this is imparted in the concreteness of Jesus' life and by communion with him. Markan language reflects the activist notion of the learning process. Discipleship as a noun, prepared to meet the requirements of reflection and abstraction, is nonexistent. Discipleship is explicable only in verbal form, for it does not represent an idea, but entails the activity of participating with Jesus on his way.[100] His way embraces the mystery of the kingdom. The way is the thing that matters.

ORALITY AND ACTUALITY,
MYTHOLOGY AND MYTHOCLASM

Speaking was undoubtedly a primary means of keeping the memory of Jesus alive. But what kind of Jesus was it who was remembered in stories and sayings? The early Christian penchant for storytelling, the passion for the concrete, and the impulse to follow Jesus' way seem well disposed toward recapturing the "real story." Must one not assume high competency in preserving the life and person of Jesus among those committed to active discipleship, ethical pragmatism, and the eschewal of lifeless abstractions? What appears obvious is not that at all. If Jesus is to remain a living option, he must enter language in oral or written form. He cannot, somehow magically, escape his linguistic destiny and retreat beyond the bounds of language. His continued existence is inescapably bound up with the entire life of language. But to submit to language is to submit to its special needs and controls. If the oral medium is entrusted with the preservation of information, it will control the data to be selected, the values to be preserved, and therefore the kind of Jesus to be transmitted. Lest he be forgotten, he must comply with oral requirements.

Once entered into speech, Jesus yields to the call of the oral imperative. His words are retold and his deeds are transposed into stories amenable to auditors. That "brevity and conciseness are important virtues"[101] is a truth plainly borne out by Mark's oral legacy. The spoken word, when unassisted by visible signs, must perforce travel light and avoid being overcrowded with meaning. The Jesus who is gathered into patterned episodes is a simplified, heroized, and visually impressive figure whose teachings emanate from controversies and who acts in a world divided into hostile camps. Oral usability prompts the linguistic conduct that prefers type over character, action over tranquility, extravagance over ordinariness, confrontation over harmony, and formularity over fortuity.

The student of oral language can agree with Mircea Eliade, who from the perspective of the study of myth observed that "popular memory refuses to preserve the personal, historical elements of a hero's biography."[102] The issue of the *historical* Jesus is of no import to the tellers and hearers of stories. The modern stance which separates "authentic" from "inauthentic" words or searches for the "real" Jesus behind texts is alien to oral mentality. Stories and sayings are authenticated not by virtue of their historical reliability, but on the authority of the speaker and by the reception of hearers. This must not suggest that orality has lost all rapport with actuality. But it means from the perspective of language that if Jesus is to be continued in the hearts and minds of people, then he must be filtered through the oral medium. What is summoned for transmission is fashioned for mnemonic purposes and selected for immediate relevancy, not primarily for historical reasons. The studied simplicity of stories is designed to meet the needs of oral expediency and social identification more than historical accuracy. In sum, orality's principal concern is not to preserve historical actuality, but to shape and break it into memorable, applicable speech.

Not all synoptic forms of speech offer the Jesus of history the same chance to be heard and remembered. The heroic and polarization stories constitute speech *about* Jesus. Unless one assumes that Jesus narrated his own deeds of power, one must acknowledge followers who adapted him to oral conventions. Oral form and viewpoint were imposed on him from without, as it were. The case is different with parabolic stories that came to us as stories spoken *by* Jesus. To them we must now add the sayings, including those carried by didactic stories that are qualified as Jesus' utterance. Yet even in the case of sayings, the principle of selection is not determined by historical interest: "It would be hard to maintain that any single saying was preserved out of pure detached historical concern."[103] Nonetheless, parables and sayings represent a form of speech that is consonant with Jesus' own language. The difference suggested is between language imposed upon Jesus and that grasped by himself, or between a Jesus who is brought into conformity with the oral imperative and a Jesus who has entrusted himself to it. It is in parables and sayings that we encounter forms in which he made his peace, or, as the case may be, a compromise with orality's special assignments.

Stories and sayings address and engage audiences. Their precise impact is hard to measure due to the operational fluidity of oral life. The interaction of speaker, message, and hearers fluctuates from one performance to the next. Without ignoring oral composition in transmission and parabolic polyvalency, one can nevertheless discern connections between forms of speech and their impact on audiences. If we keep our terms broad and general, a statement can be made about types of speech and their communicative property.

The Jesus of the heroic and polarization stories operates as an ordering presence, inveighing against instability and restoring the structures of the human lifeworld. He is conjured up as one who wrests order from chaos and enables victims, caught in the throes of anomie, to reenter a wholesome social life. Conflicts are mediated, breaches healed, and fears assuaged. Given this stabilizing function, it is difficult to see how hearers could be unsettled, let alone alienated, by the message of these stories.[104] Far from arousing questions about culture, they extend certainties and promise social stability. The alienations exposed are reconciled, the values engendered are constructive, and the truths put forward positivistic. A world is made whole, and participation in it is encouraged. In short, the heroic and polarization stories function in a culture-supportive manner. They tend to operate in favor of what has aptly been termed "the project of making a whole out of one's life."[105]

The *didactic* stories serve informational needs, but the information they carry tends to defy social expectations. Fellowship with sinners overturns Pharisaic ethics, prohibition of fasting subverts the practice of

Pharisaic disciples and those of the Baptist, suspension of the Sabbath law undermines Pharisaic and Jewish piety generally, and ban on divorce upsets Pharisaic interpretation of the Mosaic law. Renunciation of possessions exceeds the commandments more than it upsets them. All five stories exhibit a disorienting potential. The values transmitted enforce a life in discontinuity with or in excess of established norms and practices: ethics subvert more than support one's place in life. But the disjunctive factor must not be exaggerated. An audience of outcasts will hardly be disoriented by the story of Jesus' fellowship with sinners, and people who believe in the indissolubility of marriage will find themselves only confirmed by the ban on divorce.[106] Much will depend on the audience's prevailing social customs and expectations.

Payment of Taxes constitutes a special case of a didactic story. The story's didactic goal, "Render to Caesar the things that are Caesar's, and to God the things that are God's" (12:17), can be put to various oral uses. By emphasis, tone of voice, and gestures the speaker can signal his preferred interpretation, which may be loyalty to the state, or singular, perhaps even zealotically motivated, commitment to God. Still another possibility is to hear the story as an utterly perplexing double statement that inhibits literal compliance.[107] In this version it fails to convey direct information altogether. The story has exploited the disorienting potential to the fullest, or, one might say, it has become a parody of its own didactic assignment. It teaches by withholding information! The affinity to parabolic stories is evident.

The strategy of many parables, we remember, is to be initially supportive, and subsequently in tension with, or even subversive of, conventional logic. Primarily responsible for this narrative process is the element of extravagance. It operates against taking things for granted and aims at making the familiar strange. Paradox and hyperbole, the favorites of parabolic extravagance, shake hearers out of credible assurances and confront them with more or less incredible options. The impact of those parables, unlike that of heroic and polarization stories, inclines toward the culture-subversive. Parabolic speech, in order words, exercises demoralizing pressures on "the project of making a whole out of one's life."

Surprise, hyperbole, and paradox are not limited to parabolic stories. A number of scholars have alerted us to similar devices in a group of sayings.[108] Given this remarkable correlation, one may justly classify such *logoi* as *parabolic sayings*. Among those embedded in Mark at least the following six deserve our attention. The statement, "It is easier for a camel to go through the eye of a needle than for a rich man to enter the kingdom of God" (10:25), is poorly tolerated by many of our students, and by some scholars as well, who seek rationalistic relief from the pressure of the paradox. The saying, carried by a didactic story, "The Sabbath was made for man, not man for the Sabbath" (2:27), is hardly a prudential rule in support of established practices, but rather a harsh challenge to reorder fundamental priorities. A complete reversal of fortunes is anticipated by the saying, "But many that are first will be last, and the last first" (10:31). The significance of the saying for Mark is evidenced by its existence in three versions (9:35; 10:31; 10:44). Gain and loss are placed in an inverse relationship in the saying: "For whoever would save his life will lose it; and whoever loses his life . . . will save it" (8:35). The following saying makes a mocking paradox out of the human project: "What does it profit a man to gain the whole world and forfeit his life?" (8:36). The sixth saying is designed to awaken hearers to the cruel paradox perpetrated by the human arrangement: "For to him who has will more be given; and from him who has not, even what he has will be taken away" (4:25; *Gospel of Thomas* 41). Parabolic thinking, the inversion of priorities and the amplification of paradox, is thus not confined to parabolic stories. It also exists in the primary unit of synoptic speech forms, the sayings of Jesus.

Subversion of conventional logic, the game played by extravagance, does not exhaust the hermeneutical process of parabolic stories. All parables, we noted, entertain a metaphorical proclivity. Ricoeur has stated the matter succinctly: "Miracles, indeed, are stories given as true stories. Parables are stories given as fiction."[109] As metaphors, parables assume a linguistic posture whereby meaning is estranged from words. The parabolist does not entirely say what he means and mean what he says. It is for hearers to step into the breach and find meaning behind the word. This suspension of meaning erodes linguistic certainties, for language that gestures toward meaning instead of delivering it suffers the loss of oral immediacy and eventfulness. A deconstruction of words and a distanciation of words from meaning gets under way in a sense normally attributed to writing. In chapter 5 we shall resume discussion of the peculiar phenomenon that the parable, although a quintessential form of oral speech, embodies the hermeneutical complexities of textuality.

By virtue of disorientation and metaphoricity, parabolic speech poses a threat to what we have called the *oral synthesis*. A parabolic message that states improbabilities or virtual impossibilities may hinder more than help the oral process of drawing hearers and speaker into the space of spoken words. Hearers tuned in on paradoxical stories may be made strangers by and to those stories. If, moreover, the message ceases to be of the same order of reality as the words spoken, the sense of estrangement is further deepened. Hearers may be turned away and become *out-*

siders to the message. This is why one must say that the paradoxical and metaphorical aspects of parabolic speech may have corrosive effects on the oral unity of speaker, message, and hearers.

A breach of oral synthesis remains an ever-present possibility with parabolic speech. But this is by no means bound to happen. Ironically, the very hermeneutical intricacies that weaken oral unity may serve to strengthen it. This aspect is often neglected or ignored in current parable studies. The result can be a lopsided emphasis on parabolic alienation.

What is crucial for an understanding of the parables' possibility of oral synthesis is the fact that nonlinguistic features enter decisively into oral discourse. The context in which oral communication transpires is not purely linguistic, but physical and social as well. The speaker seeks to reach his or her audience by the instinctive use of physiognomic characteristics, the inflection of tone and pitch of voice, the phrasing of words, and tonal manipulation of narrative variables. The hearers may respond during and/or after the narration. Their questions, interjections, applause, and expressions of doubt reflect back on the speaker and sway his or her formulation of the message. Even if an audience is totally silent, the very expressions on faces are reflex mechanisms that will not fail to make their impact on the speaker. As every teacher knows, one enters into a peculiarly symbiotic relationship with students as one modifies, repeats, elaborates, abandons, and invents speech by simply registering facial expressions, not to mention verbal responses. In short, all oral communication passes through the feedback loop. In a broader sense the context is provided by a framework of social, political, religious, economic, cultural, and aesthetic references. This includes the immediate environment shared by speaker and hearers alike. It is in this context of physical interaction and social commonality that oral speech is embedded and from which it receives powerful ideological and situational support. Without this context, words have no existence and understanding is impossible. It may be said, therefore, that in oral speech, both with regard to the effects it achieves and the meaning it creates, nonlinguistic features have priority over linguistic ones.[110]

The *reader* of parabolic *texts* lacks this very physical, social contextuality without which hearers are not inclined to find meaning. This is all the more noteworthy because parables, of all synoptic speech forms, are most needful of the contextual support. The reader, however, abstracts parabolic speech and is forced to treat it in a purely linguistic context. A possible consequence may therefore be that the reader's own distancing posture effects interpretation and exaggerates the parables' alienating potential.

In the oral context of unwritten and partially unspoken significations, the metaphorical leap can be made in the flash of a moment, and parabolic words and meanings fall into place with a magical click. This case is well illustrated by the words of Mr. Jack Wolfskin, an American Indian, addressed to a white man: "You know our language is not at all like yours. In our language, we talk about something and never even mention it. But everybody knows what is meant. We understand from the context."[111] Mr. Wolfskin described an oral functioning of metaphorical language. Speaker and hearers, bonded together by contextuality, transact the hermeneutical process without apparent complications. With like ease the parabolist can coax his hearers via the metaphorical detour into the message behind the story. Those who understand have become *insiders*, and the newly shared knowledge brings hearers and speaker still closer together. Hearers and speaker now partake in a secret. Here is the reason why Ted Cohen can suggest that one aspect of metaphoricity is "the achievement of intimacy."[112] As he sees it, the speaker issues a concealed invitation, the hearers accept it, and the transaction "constitutes the acknowledgement of a community."[113] In the terms suggested here, an oral synthesis develops that is deeply rooted in the ideational and situational support system common to speaker and audience.

Despite the possible achievement of intimacy, it must be remembered that in the case of many parables the meaning shared still embraces a logic that contradicts conventional wisdom. A parabolic story may well unite speaker and hearers, meaning and words, but it does so against and not with the world. In other words, parabolic discourse may retain its culture-subversive quality when, and especially when, it operates out of oral synthesis.

In the broadest terms, Mark's oral legacy presents itself as ordering and disordering discourse. The heroic and polarization stories improvise on more or less stable structures that are rounded off by formal closure. They invite a retelling of what essentially amounts to the same stories. As to their impact on hearers, they foster continuity with culture and may for this reason be called *mythopoetic* discourse. Parables are said to effect "re-orientation by disorientation."[114] This formula will not adequately cover the Markan parables that are, as we noted, peculiarly moderate by comparison with many Matthean and especially Lukan parables. Yet even in Mark's parables the basic conservatism of oral speech suffers a setback. As regards form, they lack security in a common synchronic structure and are almost always without formal conclusion. It is difficult to imagine a parabolic closure by way of a praise line. Parabolic speech is not applauded! Insofar as Mark's parables twist ordinary experiences, put a strain on the imagination, and challenge the hearers' sense of reality, they may be termed *mythoclastic* discourse.[115] Didactic stories stand midway between mythopoetic and mythoclastic speech. Depending on the nature of the saying they carry and on speaking contexts, they may either support or subvert the human arrangement. In the extreme, they abort their didactic mission altogether.

This categorization suggests that in early Christian speech the art of ordering and that of disordering strain against each other. In mythopoetic discourse abnormality is restored to current expectations, whereas in mythoclastic discourse everydayness is twisted toward the paradox. Accommodation to the world is aspired to in one case, the transformation of the world in the other. Interestingly, the mythopoetic viewpoint finds expression in speech forms imposed on Jesus, while the mythoclastic thrust is carried by discourse attributable to Jesus.

ORAL PLURALISM VERSUS ORAL GOSPEL

The discussion of orally identifiable units leads us to question whether we have misinterpreted Mark's oral legacy by seeing it in fragmentation, failing thereby to acknowledge its integrative powers.[116] Can one not expect the little stories to fall in line with the larger story so as to produce an oral gospel? The issue raised is whether there exists in orality the impulse to collect material into an *oral gospel* of the nature and scope of the written gospel. This is to be differentiated from the issue of orality's gravitation toward the *written gospel*, which was treated in the preceding chapter.

The poet, theologian, and philosopher of language Johann Gottfried Herder was the originator of the thesis of the oral gospel, which bears repeating at this point.[117] Herder was thoroughly convinced of the pervasiveness of oral discourse; speaking and preaching was the norm for early Christian communication. Few of Jesus' apostolic followers possessed writing skills, and those who did refrained from using them.[118] Next to apostles and teachers there existed a class of evangelists who stayed in close touch with the apostles and received instruction from them.[119] This "school of evangelists"[120] cultivated the apostolic information consisting of rudimentary data about Jesus' life and death. That was the oral gospel.[121] Once this oral gospel was disseminated by continual delivery, the production of written gospels was "inevitable."[122] In rapid succession the synoptic gospels came to be written down in the years 61–64 c.e. by those who had been trained to be proclaimers of the oral gospel.[123] For Herder, the whole notion of the literary competence of the evangelists, collecting writings, comparing notes, and redacting texts, was unacceptable. He deemed equally impossible the idea that they corrected and redacted texts for the purpose of outclassing one another. Each evangelist wrote a story drawn from oral delivery and without regard for anyone else's gospel.[124] This thesis, Herder argued, explains both the similarities and the differences among the written gospels. The similarities were due to reliance on the *evangelium commune*.[125] The differences were the expected manifestations of oral transmission. The spoken gospel was narrated freely, and different versions of the same story are the rule in orality.[126] Peter, anticipating his imminent death, commissioned Mark, his favorite follower, to write down the oral gospel.[127] Mark, residing in Jerusalem,[128] produced a transcript of the Petrine oral gospel, schematized for memorization and suitable for oral delivery.[129] This gospel, more than the other synoptics, breathes the spirit of living speech.[130] Whereas in the case of Matthew and Luke the pen has altered oral discourse,[131] Mark's gospel is the unadulterated oral version.

In the twentieth century Herder's thesis of the oral gospel has been embraced by Thorleif Boman,[132] Albert B. Lord,[133] and Thomas E. Boomershine,[134] the former in conscious dependence on Herder, Lord and Boomershine without reference to him.

At first blush Herder's thesis appears eminently plausible. Variation of the same basic story is a proven oral principle. Since Herder, however, scholars have been increasingly impressed with the peculiar intractability of the synoptic problem. The profusion of verbatim correspondences and sequential parallelisms is such as to suggest textual interaction of some kind.[135] Redaction and literary criticism, moreover, have convincingly demonstrated that the differences among the gospels represent distinct theological views worked out by writers, not fluctuations symptomatic of oral transmission. One must further ask why Mark, against Matthew and Luke, is granted immunity from the imposition of writing. Lastly, there is no evidence for a class of evangelists entrusted with the declamation of the oral gospel in the form of an extensive narration of Jesus' life, death, and resurrection. The three passages cited by Herder— Acts 21:8, Eph. 4:11, and 2 Tim. 4:5—cannot bear the burden of proof.

In contemplating the feasibility of an oral gospel, one ought not to appeal to the oral compositions of the *Iliad* and *Odyssey*. Exceedingly helpful as the oral studies of Milman Parry, A. B. Lord and B. Peabody are, they do not permit us to draw direct correspondences between the Homeric epics and the gospels. The *Iliad* and the *Odyssey* are oral poetry in metrical language. The gospels are prose narratives with a heavy oral substratum, but in themselves something other than transcribed orality. Nor is it advisable to invoke the stupendous mnemonic talents of the Yugoslav folksinger Avdo Mededović, popularized by the studies of Parry and Lord: "Avdo could sing songs of about the length of Homer's *Odyssey*. An illiterate butcher in a small town of the central Balkans was equalling Homer's feat, at least in regard to length of song."[136] In the case of both the Homeric and the Yugoslav epics the singers were privileged to draw on centuries of accumulated oral culture. Mark's oral legacy, on the other hand, represents a tradition that had barely gotten under way. This must be stressed despite the obvious fact that the synoptic tradition relies on many ancient forms and models. A pluralism of short stories and sayings can well be appreciated in view of the movement's recent and unliterary beginnings. Textuality came early to the tradition, and it is not intrinsically implausible that Mark imposed his writing authority upon an unorganized oral lore.

The stories we have studied exhibit full narrative self-sufficiency. This repays our attention because recent literary criticism has habituated us to seeing the small units as integral parts of the compositional whole. Eminently important as the literary comprehension of the gospel narratives is, we must not lose sight of the fact that many of their component parts represent modes of oral integrity. Our use of them in worship and instruction amply demonstrates their ability to function as self-contained oral units of communication. That they became building blocks for gospels can never be taken for granted, for they are anything but fragmented pieces in need of integration. A heroic story gathers what is perceived to be the truth about Jesus, a polarization story communicates the myth of combat and progress, a didactic story imparts relevant information, and a parable teaches by disorientation. All are autonomous stories, and none are designed to build up a project of Markan proportions.

Mark's stories, moreover, are impressive by their heterogeneity. We have restricted our study to four types of storytelling. A comprehensive analysis would disclose more diverse forms of story and saying. Given this heterogeneity, there exists no imperative need for the telling of a single, comprehensive story about Jesus. There is as little desire in orality for the ethical data to be added up into a systematic scheme as there is for the little stories to be combined into the "full" story. "Absorption in the particular and unconcern with the logical relations of the parts to the whole"[137] is a natural state of oral affairs. One can subscribe to multiple truths and identities without any apparent concern for an encompassing logical arrangement. "The many predominate over the whole."[138] If, as will be shown in the following chapter, Mark's lining up of single stories and sayings entailed a more or less drastic reconstruction of their oral integrity, an oral composition of a developed gospel seems all the more unlikely. In chapter 5, moreover, we will demonstrate that the gospel's entire compositional structure, the placement of stories and sayings into a pre-Easter framework, operates as a countersign to oral hermeneutics.

A. B. Lord himself made a remarkable concession to his thesis of the oral gospel: "In their normal tellings, oral traditional narratives about individuals, whether in verse or prose, only rarely include a single account that begins with birth and ends with death. Most commonly, the separate elements or incidents in the life of the hero form individual poems or sagas."[139] This principle of orality's narrow *foci* is not very different from Eric Havelock's description of oral cognition centering on " 'happenings' (*gignomena*) which are sharply experienced in separate units and so are pluralised (*polla*) rather than being integrated into systems of cause and effect."[140] Even if one were to assume a storyteller uniting the many into a single one, this story would still not be destined to become normative. No universally binding norm can assert itself in speaking actuality, for oral life escapes ownership by any single authority. In orality, one must allow for pluralism, as well as for a certain randomness.

Oral reluctance to program diverse speech forms into a narrative composite receives additional confirmation from Mark's transparency on collections of like materials. The form critics rightly perceived that the very traditions which are most likely to be oral exist in plural form, some even in cluster-like density: miracles, apophthegmatic controversy stories, parables, and *logoi*.[141] By our own definition, heroic and polarization stories are strewn throughout Mark 1–9, didactic stories are assembled primarily in chapters 2, 10, and 12, parabolic stories are crowded into chapter 4, and sayings in chapters 4 and especially 13. One must add to these more hypothetical collections the sayings genre of Q, whose existence has been established with a measure of certainty. What all these collections have in common is a technique of information gathering that betrays the cognitive processes of oral operations. The oral mind collects and clusters similar materials by virtue of analogical or associative thinking.[142] Once an item has proven orally workable, it becomes a magnet for attracting and a measure for producing equivalent entities. Like draws like in this world, and knowledge is gathered and multiplied more than critically developed. Strung together by formal association, stories and sayings form a succession of single impressions or "pluralised instances."[143] But this oral need for like to attract like is ill-equipped to draw heterogeneity into a single, consecutive plot. None of these cluster collections, including Q, can be regarded as connecting links in the tradition's alleged evolution toward the written gospel.[144] Deep-seated and complex as the gospel's indebtedness is to the oral lifeworld, in the last analysis the gospel takes its cue from an authority other than the oral imperative.

NOTES

1. Walter J. Ong, S. J., *The Presence of the Word: Some Prolegomena for Cultural and Religious History* (New Haven, Conn., and London: Yale University Press, 1967; paperback edition: Minneapolis: University of Minnesota Press, 1981), pp. 104, 239, 282; idem, *Interfaces of the Word: Studies in the Evolution of Consciousness and Culture* (Ithaca, N.Y., and London: Cornell University Press, 1977), pp. 82–83, 198, 215.

2. Ulrich Luz, "Das Jesusbild der vormarkinischen Tradition," in *Jesus Christus in Historie und Geschichte: Neutestamentliche Festschrift für Hans Conzelmann zum 60. Geburtstag,* ed. Georg Strecker (Tübingen: J. C. B. Mohr [Paul Siebeck], 1975), pp. 347–74.

3. Rudolf Bultmann, *Die Geschichte der synoptischen Tradition,* FRLANT 29, NF 12, 8th ed. (Göttingen: Vandenhoeck & Ruprecht, 1970), pp. 226–60 (209–44); Martin Dibelius, *From Tradition to Gospel,* Eng. trans. Bertram Lee Woolf (New York: Charles Scribner's Sons, 1934), pp. 37–103; Gerd Theissen, *Urchristliche Wundergeschichten: Ein Beitrag zur formgeschichtlichen Erforschung der synoptischen Evangelien* (Gütersloh: Gerd Mohn, 1974); Vincent Taylor, *The Formation of the Gospel Tradition* (London: Macmillan & Co., 1933), pp. 119–41; Hans Dieter Betz, "The Early Christian Miracle Story: Some Observations on the Form Critical Problem," *Semeia* 11 (1978): 69–81; Antoinette Clark Wire, "The Structure of the Gospel Miracle Stories and Their Tellers," *Semeia* 11 (1978): 83–113; Robert W. Funk, "The Form of the New Testament Healing Miracle Story," *Semeia* 12 (1978): 57–96. For a critical view of the form-critical study of healing stories, see Laurence J. McGinley, S. J., "Form-Criticism of the Synoptic Healing Narratives," *TS* 3 (1947): 203–30.

4. Dibelius, *From Tradition to Gospel,* p. 44.

5. In 1:45b–c the shift in focus from the healed back to the healer forms the transition to the following story.

6. Cf. p. 67.

7. Theissen, *Urchristliche Wundergeschichten,* p. 82; Hendrikus Boers, "Sisyphus and His Rock: Concerning Gerd Theissen, *Urchristliche Wundergeschichten,*" *Semeia* 11 (1978): 28–30.

8. Vladimir Propp, *Morphology of the Folktale,* Eng. trans. Laurence Scott (Philadelphia: American Folklore Society, 1958; 2d rev. ed.; Austin: University of Texas Press, 1968), p. 70.

9. Ibid., p. 19.

10. Bultmann, *Synoptische Tradition,* p. 256 (240).

11. Leander E. Keck, "Mark 3, 7–12 and Mark's Christology," *JBL* 84 (1965): 341–58; Theodore J. Weeden, *Mark—Traditions in Conflict* (Philadelphia: Fortress Press, 1971); idem, "The Heresy That Necessitated Mark's Gospel," *ZNW* 59 (1968): 145–58; Thomas L. Budesheim, "Jesus and the Disciples in Conflict with Judaism," *ZNW* 62 (1971): 190–209; Hans Dieter Betz, "Jesus as Divine Man," in *Jesus and the Historian: Festschrift for E. C. Colwell,* ed. F. Thomas Trotter (Philadelphia: Westminster Press, 1968), pp. 114–33; Moses Hadas and Morton Smith, *Heroes and Gods: Spiritual Biographies in Antiquity* (New York: Harper & Row, 1965); Morton Smith, *The Aretalogy*

Used by Mark, Protocol of the Colloquy 6 (Berkeley, Calif.: Center for Hermeneutical Studies, 1975); Heinz-Wolfgang Kuhn, *Ältere Sammlungen im Markusevangelium*, SUNT 8 (Göttingen: Vandenhoeck & Ruprecht, 1971), pp. 225, 229–30; the basic reference to the *theios aner* concept is Ludwig Bieler, ΘΕΙΟΣ ANHP: *Das Bild des "Göttlichen Menschen" in Spätantike und Frühchristentum*, 2 vols. (Vienna: Oskar Höfels, 1935–36; reprint: Darmstadt: Wissenschaftliche Buchgesellschaft, 1967); for a critique of the concept, cf. Carl R. Holladay, *Theios Aner in Hellenistic Judaism: A Critique of the Use of this Category in New Testament Christology*, SBLDS 40 (Missoula, Mont.: Scholars Press, 1977).

12. Howard Clark Kee, *Community of the New Age: Studies in Mark's Gospel* (Philadelphia: Westminster Press, 1977), pp. 23–30; idem, "Aretalogy and Gospel," *JBL* 92 (1973): 402–22; idem, *Aretalogies, Hellenistic 'Lives,' and the Sources of Mark*, Protocol of the Colloquy 12 (Berkeley, Calif.: Center for Hermeneutical Studies, 1975).

13. Ibid., p. 27.

14. James M. Robinson, "The Dismantling and Reassembling of the Categories of New Testament Scholarship," in *Trajectories through Early Christianity* (Philadelphia: Fortress Press, 1971), pp. 1–19.

15. Etienne Trocmé, *The Formation of the Gospel According to Mark*, Eng. trans. Pamela Gaugham (Philadelphia: Westminster Press, 1975), p. 49.

16. Ibid., p. 52.

17. Kenzo Tagawa, *Miracles et Evangile* (Paris: Presses Universitaires de France, 1966).

18. Berkley Peabody, *The Winged Word: A Study in the Technique of Ancient Greek Oral Composition as Seen Principally through Hesiod's Works and Days* (Albany: State University of New York Press, 1975), p. 4.

19. Ong, *Interfaces of Word*, p. 104.

20. Albert B. Lord, *The Singer of Tales*, HSCL 24 (Cambridge, Mass.: Harvard University Press, 1960).

21. Axel Olrik, "Epische Gesetze der Volksdichtung," *ZDA* 51 (1909): 1–12, esp. 5; Eng. trans.: "Epic Laws of Folk Narrative," in *The Study of Folklore*, ed. Alan Dundes (Englewood Cliffs, N. J.: Prentice-Hall, 1965), pp. 129–41, esp. 134–35.

22. Eric A. Havelock, *Preface to Plato* (Cambridge, Mass.: Harvard University Press, Belknap Press, 1963), p. 87.

23. Propp, *Morphology of Folktale*, pp. 20, 58, 60, 69–70, 74, passim.

24. In Mark 1:41 a motivation appears to be given: Jesus is moved with pity (*splangchnistheis*). The reading is well attested by the Western text, and accepted even by a scholar who is conscious of the technical language of miracle stories, Campbell Bonner ("Traces of Thaumaturgic Technique in the Miracles," *HTR* 20 [1927]: 178–81). But the *lectio difficilior* is frequently preferred: Jesus is moved with anger (*orgistheis*). The pneumatic excitation is a technical feature of healing stories: Kirsopp Lake, "ΕΜΒΡΙΜΗΣΑΜΕΝΟΣ and ΟΡΓΙΣΘΕΙΣ, Mark 1, 40–43," *HTR* 16 (1923): 197–98; Theissen, *Urchristliche Wundergeschichten*, p. 67.

25. The notion of the *heroic origin of literature* and the designation *heroic*

story date back to H. Munro Chadwick, *The Heroic Age* (Cambridge: At the University Press, 1912); H. Munro and N. Kershaw Chadwick, *The Growth of Literature*, 3 vols. (Cambridge: At the University Press, 1932–40). The Chadwicks did not, however, pay close attention to the oral shaping of heroic literature. Both Havelock and Ong have identified the heroic notion as a hallmark of orality: Havelock, *Preface to Plato*, p. 168: "The reason for the heroic paradigm is in the last resort not romantic but functional and technical"; cf. pp. 94, 106–8, 135, 165–93. Ong. *Interfaces of Word*, p. 191.

26. Bultmann, *Synoptische Tradition*, pp. 223–26 (209–12); Dibelius, *From Tradition to Gospel*, pp. 37–103; Theissen, *Urchristliche Wunderge-schichten*, pp. 94–98, passim; Otto Bauernfeind, *Die Worte der Dämonen im Markusevangelium*, BWANT 8 (Stuttgart: Kohlhammer, 1927); Campbell Bonner, "The Technique of Exorcism," HTR 36 (1943): 39–49; idem, "The Violence of Departing Demons," HTR 37 (1944): 334–36; S. Eitrem, "La Magie comme motif littéraire," SO 21 (1941): 39–83; Howard C. Kee, "The Ter-minology of Mark's Exorcism Stories," NTS 14 (1968): 232–46; for a critique of the form-critical study of exorcisms, see McGinley, "Form-Criticism," pp. 203–30.

27. Karl Kertelge, *Die Wunder Jesu im Markusevangelium: Eine redak-tionsgeschichtliche Untersuchung*, SANT 23 (Munich: Kösel-Verlag, 1970), p. 104.

28. Gerd Theissen, *Sociology of Early Palestinian Christianity*, Eng. trans. John Bowden (Philadelphia: Fortress Press, 1977), pp. 101–2.

29. Havelock, *Preface to Plato*, pp. 92, 147, 184, passim.

30. Eric A. Havelock, *The Greek Concept of Justice: From Its Shadow in Homer to Its Substance in Plato* (Cambridge, Mass.: Harvard University Press, 1978), p. 89.

31. Ong, *Interfaces of Word*, p. 210.

32. Agonistic dramatizations enter into writing and resurge strongly in the electronic medium of television. This does not alter the fact that agonistic structures originated in the oral medium.

33. Havelock, *Preface to Plato*, p. 188.

34. Bultmann, *Synoptische Tradition*, pp. 39–73 (39–69); Dibelius, *From Tradition to Gospel*, pp. 37–69; Wilhelm Gemoll, *Das Apophthegma* (Vienna: Hölder-Pichler-Tempsky, 1924); Martin Albertz, *Die synoptischen Streitge-spräche: Ein Beitrag zur Formgeschichte des Urchristentums* (Berlin: Tro-witzsch, 1921); Robert C. Tannehill, "Attitudinal Shift in Synoptic Pronounce-ment Stories," in *Orientation by Disorientation: Studies in Literary Criticism and Biblical Literary Criticism*. Presented in Honor of William A. Beardslee, ed. Richard A. Spencer, PTMS 35 (Pittsburgh: Pickwick Press, 1980), pp. 183–97; idem, "Synoptic Pronouncement Stories: Form and Function," SBL *Seminar Papers* (Chico, Calif.: Scholars Press, 1980), p. 51–56; idem, "Intro-duction: The Pronouncement Story and Its Types," *Semeia* 20 (1981): 1–13; idem, "Varieties of Synoptic Pronouncement Stories," *Semeia* 20 (1981): 101–19.

35. Bultmann, *Synoptische Tradition*, pp. 39–51 (39–49).

36. Havelock, *Preface to Plato*, pp. 187–89.

37. Ibid., p. 51.

38. Charles E. Carlston, *The Parables of the Triple Tradition* (Philadelphia: Fortress Press, 1975), pp. 97–210.

39. Chapter 3, pp. 111–13, 120–29, 131; chapter 5, pp. 215–20.

40. Eta Linnemann, *Jesus of the Parables,* Eng. trans. John Sturdy (New York: Harper & Row; London: SPCK, 1966), p. 19.

41. John Dominic Crossan, *In Parables: The Challenge of the Historical Jesus* (New York: Harper & Row, 1973), pp. 117–19.

42. Bultmann, *Synoptische Tradition,* pp. 179–222 (166–205); Adolf Jülicher, *Die Gleichnisreden Jesu,* 2 vols. (Tübingen: J. C. B. Mohr [Paul Siebeck], I, 1888 [2d ed. 1899], 11, 1899 [2d ed. 1910]); C. H. Dodd, *The Parables of the Kingdom,* 3d ed. (New York: Charles Scribner's Sons, 1961); Joachim Jeremias, *The Parables of Jesus,* Eng. trans. S. H. Hooke, 6th ed. (New York: Charles Scribner's Sons, 1962); Dan O. Via, *The Parables: Their Literary and Existential Dimension* (Philadelphia: Fortress Press, 1967); Erhardt Güttgemanns, "Die linguistisch-didaktische Methodik der Gleichnisse Jesu," in *Studia Linguistica Neotestamentica* (Munich: Chr. Kaiser, 1971), pp. 99–183; Crossan, *In Parables;* idem, *Finding is the First Act: Trove Folktales and Jesus' Treasure Parable,* Semeia Studies 9 (Philadelphia: Fortress Press; Missoula, Mont.: Scholars Press, 1979); idem, *Cliffs of Fall: Paradox and Polyvalence in the Parables of Jesus* (New York: Seabury Press, 1980); Robert W. Funk, *Language, Hermeneutic, and Word of God: The Problem of Language in the New Testament and Contemporary Theology* (New York: Harper & Row, 1966), pp. 123–222; Hans Weder, *Die Gleichnisse Jesu als Metaphern: Traditions- und redaktionsgeschichtliche Analysen und Interpretationen,* 2d ed. (Göttingen: Vandenhoeck & Ruprecht, 1980).

43. Paul Ricoeur, "Biblical Hermeneutics," *Semeia* 4 (1975): 100.

44. Jeremias, *Parables of Jesus,* p. 20.

45. Olrik, "Epische Gesetze," 4–5 (133–34).

46. For a highly suggestive reading of the parable of the *Mustard Seed* against the background of the symbol of the mighty cedar, cf. Robert W. Funk, "The Looking-Glass Tree is for the Birds: Ezekiel 17:22–24; Mark 4:30–32," *Int* 27 (1973): 3–9; reprinted in *Jesus as Precursor,* Semeia Studies 2 (Philadelphia: Fortress Press; Missoula, Mont.: Scholars Press, 1975), pp. 19–26.

47. Cf. chapter 3, p. 127.

48. Crossan, *In Parables,* p. 118.

49. Funk, *Language, Hermeneutic, and Word,* pp. 193, 213, 234.

50. Amos N. Wilder, *The Language of the Gospel: Early Christian Rhetoric* (New York: Harper & Row, 1964), p. 85.

51. Jeremias, *Parables of Jesus,* p. 30, quoting J. J. Vincent, "The Parables of Jesus as Self-Revelation," in *SE* I [TU 73]: 80.

52. Mary Ann Tolbert, *Perspectives on the Parables: An Approach to Multiple Interpretations* (Philadelphia: Fortress Press, 1979), p. 91.

53. Via, *Parables,* p. 106.

54. Ricoeur, "Biblical Hermeneutics," 32, 99, 115, passim.

55. Ibid., p. 98.

56. Ibid., p. 118.

57. Ibid.

58. Ibid., p. 99.

59. Theodore J. Weeden, "Recovering the Parabolic Intent in the Parable of the Sower," *JAAR* 47 (1979): 97–120.

60. Cf. chapter 5, pp. 218–19.

61. Cf. *Critical Inquiry* 5 (1978), special issue on metaphor; Paul Ricoeur, *The Rule of Metaphor*, Eng. trans. R. Czerny with K. McLaughlin and J. Costello, University of Toronto Romance Series 37 (Toronto and Buffalo: University of Toronto Press, 1977); Sheldon Sacks, ed., *On Metaphor* (Chicago and London: University of Chicago Press, 1979); Max Black, *Models and Metaphors* (Ithaca, N. Y., Cornell University Press, 1962); Philip Wheelwright, *Metaphor and Reality* (Bloomington: Indiana University Press, 1962); Sallie McFague, *Speaking in Parables: A Study in Metaphor and Theology* (Philadelphia: Fortress Press, 1975).

62. Madeleine Boucher, *The Mysterious Parable: A Literary Study*, CBQMS 6 (Washington, D. C.: The Catholic Biblical Association of America, 1977), p. 33.

63. Tolbert, *Perspectives on Parables*, p. 45.

64. Earl Breech, "Kingdom of God and the Parables of Jesus," *Semeia* 12 (1978): 15–40.

65. Tolbert, *Perspectives on Parables*, p. 45.

66. Ibid., p. 48.

67. Cf. Tolbert, ibid., p. 70: "For the parables the interpreter is in fact the cocreator."

68. It is to be noted that the imposition of titles forecloses parabolic polyvalency. For example, in oral performance the parable of the *Sower* may be heard as the parable of the *Seed*, or the parable of the *Reaper* as the parable of the *Seed Growing Secretly*. Titles, including those used by the author of this book, are the invention of the parables' literate students, not words spoken or meanings necessarily suggested by speakers in parables.

69. For a reassessment of Jülicher's concept of allegory among biblical scholars, see especially Raymond E. Brown, S. S., "Parable and Allegory Reconsidered," in *New Testament Essays* (Garden City, N. Y.: Doubleday & Co., 1968), pp. 321–33; Boucher, *Mysterious Parable*, pp. 1–25. Of general interest are Angus Fletcher, *Allegory: The Theory of a Symbolic Mode* (Ithaca, N. Y.: Cornell University Press, 1964); Michael Murrin, *The Veil of Allegory* (Chicago: University of Chicago Press, 1969).

70. Boucher, *Mysterious Parable*, p. 23; Charles E. Carlston, "Parable and Allegory Revisited: An Interpretive Review," *CBQ* 43 (1981): 235.

71. Ernst Lohmeyer, "Das Gleichnis von den Bösen Weingärtnern (Mark. 12, 1–12)," in *Urchristliche Mystik: Neutestamentliche Studien*, 2d ed. (Darmstadt: Wissenschaftliche Buchgesellschaft, 1958), pp. 165–70.

72. Funk, *Language, Hermeneutic, and Word*, p. 235: "The parable stands on the frontier of language and mirrors without conceptualizing the kingdom of God."

73. Ibid., pp. 133–52; Norman Perrin, *The New Testament: An Introduction*

(New York: Harcourt Brace Jovanovich, 1974), p. 291; idem, *Jesus and the Language of the Kingdom: Symbol and Metaphor in New Testament Interpretation* (Philadelphia: Fortress Press, 1976), pp. 56, 194, passim.

74. Rudolf Pesch, *Das Markusevangelium*, I (Freiburg—Basel—Vienna: Herder, 1976), pp. 15–20, 90, passim; E. J. Pryke, *Redactional Style in the Marcan Gospel: A Study of Syntax and Vocabulary as Guides to Redaction in Mark*, SNTSMS 33 (New York and Cambridge: Cambridge University Press, 1978), pp. 1–9, 79–99; Theissen, *Urchristliche Wundergeschichten*, pp. 198–99; Gunnar Rudberg, "ΕΥΘΥΣ," ConNT 9 (1944): 42–46.

75. Frank Kermode, *The Genesis of Secrecy: On the Interpretation of Narrative* (Cambridge, Mass., and London: Harvard University Press, 1979), p. 93.

76. Leander E. Keck, "The Introduction to Mark's Gospel," NTS 12 (1966): 360–62; cf. also James M. Robinson, *The Problem of History in Mark: And Other Marcan Studies* (Philadelphia: Fortress Press, 1982), pp. 49–51.

77. Pesch, *Das Markusevangelium*, I, p. 124.

78. The designation *activist syntax* is used by Havelock in reference to orally shaped narrative (Havelock, *Greek Concept of Justice*, pp. 41–45, passim).

79. John Charles Doudna, *The Greek of the Gospel of Mark*, JBLMS 12 (Philadelphia: Society of Biblical Literature and Exegesis, 1961), p. 70; Pryke, *Redactional Style*, pp. 107–8.

80. Vincent Taylor, *The Gospel According to St. Mark*, 2d ed. (London: Macmillan & Co., 1966), pp. 44–54; Doudna, *Greek of Gospel*, pp. 128–36; Trocmé, *Formation of Mark*, pp. 68–72.

81. Frans Neirynck, *Duality in Mark: Contributions to the Study of the Markan Redaction*, BETL 31 (Louvain: Louvain University Press, 1972), p. 49.

82. Ibid., p. 50.

83. Ibid., p. 49.

84. Taylor, *Gospel According to St. Mark*, p. 53.

85. For repetition and duality as a mark of oral style, see Bennison Gray, "Repetition in Oral Literature," JAF 84 (1971): 289–303; Dennis Tedlock, "Toward an Oral Poetics," NLH 8 (1977): 507–19, esp. 513; Harold Scheub, "Oral Narrative Process and the Use of Models," NLH 6 (1975): 353–77; Olrik, "Epische Gesetze," pp. 3–4 (132–33); Peabody, *Winged Word*, p. 3, passim.

86. Lord, *Singer of Tales*, p. 177.

87. Perhaps the time will come when in addition to seeing the text in terms of geometrical patterns, we will learn to hear it in terms of "echo systems" (Havelock, *Greek Concept of Justice*, p. 155), "phonic echoes" (Peabody, *Winged Word*, p. 223), and "clumps of phonic cores" (ibid., p. 207). The first, and to my knowledge only, attempt in this direction was undertaken by Thomas Eugene Boomershine, "Mark, the Storyteller: A Rhetorical-Critical Investigation of Mark's Passion and Resurrection Narrative" Ph.D. diss., Union Theological Seminary, New York, 1974).

88. Neirynck, *Duality in Mark*, p. 46.

89. Ibid., p. 71.

90. Pryke, *Redactional Style*, p. 29; Pesch, *Das Markusevangelium*, I, p. 25.

91. Erich Auerbach, *Mimesis: The Representation of Reality in Western*

Literature, Eng. trans. Willard R. Trask (Princeton, N.J.: Princeton University Press, 1953), p. 45.

92. Boomershine, "Mark, the Storyteller," p. 138.

93. Cf. note 24.

94. Martin Hengel, *Acts and the History of Earliest Christianity,* Eng. trans. John Bowden (Philadelphia: Fortress Press; London: SCM Press, 1979), p. 18.

95. Kermode, *Genesis of Secrecy,* p. 69.

96. Hermann Gunkel, *The Legends of Genesis: The Biblical Saga and History,* Eng. trans. W. H. Carruth (New York: Schocken Books, 1964), p. 60.

97. Robert C. Tannehill, "The Gospel of Mark as Narrative Christology," *Semeia* 16 (1979): 58.

98. Boomershine, "Mark, the Storyteller," pp. 91–92.

99. Havelock, *Preface to Plato,* p. 188.

100. Gerhard Kittel, *"akoloutheō," TDNT* I: 213–15.

101. Birger Gerhardsson, *Memory and Manuscript: Oral Tradition and Written Transmission in Rabbinic Judaism and Early Christianity,* ASNU 22 (Lund: C. W. K. Gleerup; Copenhagen: Ejnar Munksgaard, 1961), p. 136.

102. Mircea Eliade, *Cosmos and History: The Myth of the Eternal Return,* Eng. trans. Willard R. Trask (New York: Harper & Brothers, 1959), p. 46.

103. Frank W. Beare, "Sayings of the Risen Jesus in the Synoptic Tradition: An Inquiry Into Their Origin and Significance," in *Christian History and Interpretation: Studies Presented to John Knox,* ed. W. R. Farmer, C. F. D. Moule, and R. R. Niebuhr (New York and Cambridge: Cambridge University Press, 1967), p. 178.

104. The disorienting factor in the heroic and polarization stories must not be exaggerated. Antoinette Clark Wire ("The Structure of the Gospel Miracle Stories and their Tellers," *Semeia* 11 [1978]: 109) describes the structure of miracle stories "in terms of a circle burst wide open or a mold broken." Paul Ricoeur ("Biblical Hermeneutics," *Semeia* 4 [1975]: 103), while keenly aware of the linguistic difference between miracle stories and parables, nevertheless suggests that in both stories "the course of ordinary life is broken, the surprise bursts out. The unexpected happens; the audience is questioned and brought to think about the unthinkable." This seems an overly disjunctive view with regard to heroic and polarization stories. Due to the popularity of miracle stories in antiquity, ancient hearers will not be as startled by them as modern interpreters are inclined to think. Also, one must carefully differentiate between the miracles' functioning in oral integrity and in gospel textuality. It is in the latter case, we shall see, that they take on an alienating, almost parabolic function.

105. William A. Beardslee, "Parable, Proverb, and Koan," *Semeia* 12 (1978): 157.

106. Joseph A. Fitzmyer, S. J., "The Matthean Divorce Texts and Some New Palestinian Evidence," *TS* 37 (1976): 197–226.

107. Funk, *Jesus as Precursor,* pp. 75–92.

108. William A. Beardslee, "The Wisdom Tradition and the Synoptic Gospels," *JAAR* 35 (1967): 231–40; idem, "Uses of the Proverb in the Synoptic Gospels," *Int* 24 (1970): 61–73; John Dominic Crossan, *Raid on the*

Articulate: Comic Eschatology in Jesus and Borges (New York: Harper & Row, 1976), pp. 69–73; Perrin, *The New Testament,* pp. 291–99; Ricoeur, "Biblical Hermeneutics," pp. 101–2, passim.

109. Ricoeur, "Biblical Hermeneutics," pp. 102–3.

110. Paul Ricoeur, *Interpretation Theory: Discourse and the Surplus of Meaning* (Fort Worth: Texas Christian University Press, 1976), pp. 14–18.

111. Fred McTaggart, *Wolf That I Am: In Search of the Red Earth People* (Boston: Houghton Mifflin Co., 1976), p. 157.

112. Ted Cohen, "Metaphor and the Cultivation of Intimacy," in *On Metaphor,* p. 6. The so-called *Messianic Secret* may well have its origin in parabolic speech and a particular emphasis on its esoteric quality.

113. Ibid.

114. Ricoeur, "Biblical Hermeneutics," p. 114.

115. The designations *mythopoetic* versus *mythoclastic* are taken from Wilder, *Language of Gospel,* p. 129.

116. Theodore J. Weeden, "Metaphysical Implications of Kelber's Approach to Orality and Textuality," *SBL Seminar Papers* (Missoula, Mont.: Scholars Press, 1979), II, pp. 153–66.

117. Johann Gottfried Herder, "Vom Erlöser der Menschen: Nach unsern drei ersten Evangelien," in *Herders Sämmtliche Werke,* ed. Bernhard Suphan (Berlin: Weidmannsche Buchhandlung, 1880), XIX: 135–252; idem, "Von Gottes Sohn, der Welt Heiland," in *Herders Sämmtliche Werke,* pp. 253–424.

118. Herder, "Erlöser," p. 142.

119. Ibid., pp. 213–15.

120. Herder, "Gottes Sohn," p. 384.

121. Ibid., pp. 385–88.

122. Herder, "Erlöser," p. 207.

123. Ibid., p. 147; idem, "Gottes Sohn," p. 422.

124. Herder, "Erlöser," pp. 209–11.

125. Herder, "Gottes Sohn," p. 417.

126. Herder, "Erlöser," pp. 213–15.

127. Herder, "Gottes Sohn," pp. 395–96.

128. Ibid., pp. 262–63.

129. Ibid., pp. 394–95; idem, "Erlöser," pp. 216–17.

130. Herder, "Erlöser," p. 216: "Kein Evangelium hat so wenig Schriftstellerisches und so viel lebendigen Laut eines Erzählenden wie dieses."

131. Ibid.; "Matthäus und Lukas . . . sprechen nicht, sondern sie schreiben. Der Griffel verändert den Ton der Rede."

132. Thorleif Boman, *Die Jesus-Überlieferung im Lichte der neueren Volkskunde* (Göttingen: Vandenhoeck & Ruprecht, 1967), pp. 31, 35, 40, 47, 55, 91, 96.

133. Albert B. Lord, "The Gospels as Oral Traditional Literature," in *The Relationships Among the Gospels: An Interdisciplinary Dialogue,* ed. William O. Walker (San Antonio: Trinity University Press, 1978), pp. 33–91.

134. Thomas E. Boomershine, "Oral Tradition and Mark" (unpublished manuscript, 1979).

135. Joseph B. Tyson, "Sequential Parallelism in the Synoptic Gospels," *NTS* 22 (1976): 276–308.

136. Albert B. Lord, "Avdo Mededović, Guslar," in *Slavic Folklore: A Symposium,* ed. Albert B. Lord (Philadelphia: American Folklore Society, 1956), p. 125.

137. James A. Notopoulos, "Parataxis in Homer: A New Approach to Homeric Literary Criticism," *TAPA* 80 (1949): 21.

138. Havelock, *Preface to Plato,* p. 185.

139. Lord, "Oral Traditional Literature," pp. 39–40.

140. Havelock, *Preface to Plato,* p. 180.

141. Kuhn, *Ältere Sammlungen im Markusevangelium;* Albertz, *Synoptische Streitgespräche;* Paul J. Achtemeier, "Toward the Isolation of Pre-Markan Miracle Catenae," *JBL* 89 (1970): 265–91; idem, "The Origin and Function of the Pre-Marcan Miracle Catenae," *JBL* 91 (1972): 198–221.

142. Ong, *Presence of Word,* pp. 79–87; *Interfaces of Word,* pp. 147–51; Havelock, *Preface to Plato,* pp. 183–85; Lord, *Singer of Tales,* p. 159; Peabody, *Winged Word,* pp. 206–7.

143. Havelock, *Preface to Plato,* p. 218.

144. Kuhn, *Ältere Sammlungen im Markusevangelium,* p. 216. For a discussion of the relationship of written gospel and sayings genre Q, see chapter 5, pp. 199–203, 208–10.

3. Mark as Textuality

To transfer to paper a manner of speech which has been developed by oral tradition may seem on the face of it an easy task, but it is in fact supremely difficult.

James A. K. Thomson, *The Art of the Logos*

Writing is the destruction of every voice, of every point of origin.

Roland Barthes, *Image, Music, Text*

. . . the question remains whether the *insertion* of the parable within the larger framework of the Gospel contributes to its *meaning* as a parable.

Paul Ricoeur, *Biblical Hermeneutics*

Our reflections on the transmission of synoptic oral traditions led us to refute a step-by-step progression toward gospel textuality (chapter 1). The written gospel cannot be properly perceived as the logical outcome of oral proclivities and forces inherent in orality. We have further shown that the gospel took shape in a milieu rich in oral materials and values (chapter 2). That Mark owes much to oral tradition is now evident. But although profoundly nourished by spoken words and probably meant to be spoken itself, the gospel nevertheless exists in written words. Since our own explorations prevent us from taking Mark's writing for granted, it is to it that we must now turn our attention. Broadly, this chapter is concerned with Markan textuality and the nature of its relation to the oral legacy.

With respect to orality we have operated on the premise that the nature of the medium helps determine the form and kind of knowledge preserved. By the same principle, we will now demonstrate connections between the gospel's written medium and the message it helps generate. If, moreover, one asserts the predominantly oral nature of pre-Markan transmission, the gospel marks a departure from one medium and a transition toward another. On the premise, again, of a medium's impact on its message, this transposition of oral voices into written signs may have left traces in the gospel's narrative. Specifically, this chapter explores medium transposition as a key to Markan textuality and probes Mark's gospel for indications of its own medium history.

As stated before, the concept of a predominantly oral synoptic transmission does not dispense with the existence of notes and textual aids altogether. It suggests not the complete absence of textuality, but the presence of a tradition predisposed to an oral ontology of language. Nor is it our claim that the hermeneutical processes described in this chapter are necessarily conscious thought processes of the author. What is maintained, however, is that in Mark textuality asserts itself in its own right, decisively shaping the oral legacy according to the imperative of the written medium.

We shall first discuss Mark's disruption of the oral lifeworld, the textually induced eclipse of voices and sound. Next, we will treat the Markan composition insofar as it reassembles short stories and sayings into a novel unity. The new medium absorbs what it inherits into something quite its own. A third part will inquire into the generic identity of Mark's novel composition. Did he give preference to any single form of speech, or did he grasp an entirely novel form? Finally, we will illustrate medium and message as intersecting phenomena and reflect on the Markan gospel as a narration of its own linguistic history.

TEXTUALITY AS DISORIENTATION

Mark's writing project is an act of daring and rife with consequences. To the extent that the gospel draws on oral voices, it has rendered them voiceless. The voiceprints of once-spoken words have been muted. This is an extraordinary undertaking. If it is agreed that Jesus entrusted his message to the oral medium, the existence of a written gospel is nothing short of remarkable. For the moment, language has fallen silent; the ground of Jesus' speech and that of his earliest followers is abandoned. Sayings and stories are rescued, but at the price of their transportation into and, we shall see, transformation by a foreign medium. The text, while asserting itself out of dominant oral traditions and activities, has brought about a freezing of oral life into textual still life. In short, the oral legacy has been deracinated and transplanted into a linguistic construct that has lost touch with the living, oral matrix.

Mark's writing manifests a transmutation more than mere transmission, which results in a veritable upheaval of hermeneutical, cognitive realities. In orality, we saw, words have no existence apart from speaker and hearers. The tendency is for words to actualize their meaning in the performance of oral delivery. Aided by a common social and physiological contextuality, speaker and hearers cooperate in an effort to assure a direct and immediate hermeneutical transaction; "the meaning of each word is ratified in a succession of concrete situations."[1] With the written gospel the cooperation between speaker and hearers is abolished. "It is this grounding of reference in the dialogical situation that is shattered by writing."[2] Performer and audience no longer jointly participate in the making of the message. The writer works in a state of separation from audiences, and hearers or readers are excluded from the process of composition: "the reader is absent from the writing of the book, the writer is absent from its reading."[3]

The threat posed by the gospel's written form to the oral lifeworld can be restated in terms of a subversion of the *homeostatic balance.*[4] What characterizes orality in distinction from textuality is its intimate association with social life. Oral words are ratified, censured, queried, and rejected in interaction with listeners' interests and expectations. There is for the oral medium no escaping from accountability to hearers. This give-and-take between spoken words and audience pressures generates the homeostatic balance, a continuous process of adjustment of language to communal expectations, of social to linguistic realities. It is this oral equilibrium that is threatened by the gospel's textuality. As text, the gospel has ceased to be directly accountable to audiences. A major effect is that of disestablishment of the precarious balance of homeostatic self-regulation essential for all orally functioning communication. From the perspective of synoptic orality, therefore, the gospel's text marks the breakdown of the authentic act of live communication.

The transcription of sounded words into graphic signs, which results from the textualization of Mark's oral legacy, accords language a separate, bodily identity. Once-invisible words are turned into visible marks that function in the altogether objectifiable artifact of the written gospel. But if words have become visible and knowable apart from sound and hearing, meaning may be suspended and hermeneutical ratification delayed. The text as a linguistic artifact, moreover, is separated from its own writer and open to an infinite range of readers and interpretations. In writing the author loses control over the process of interpretation. In light of these complications engendered by the written medium, Mark's writing project may be conceived as a product of linguistically disjunctive operations: the unity of knower and known, speaker and audience, words and meanings is, however subtly, set ajar. In short, the gospel signals a disruption of the oral synthesis.

Lukas Vischer has documented the reluctance and anxiety even expressed by the early church Fathers with regard to their own writing.[5]

Their seemingly awkward apologies arose out of fear that writing might compromise the Christian gospel. Far from taking writing for granted, they did not perceive it as a process of stabilizing oral impermanence, but rather as a more or less questionable means of releasing words from their normative, oral management. As long as words transpired in the oral medium, speakers remained in charge of the seed they had sown. But language divorced from human contexts and transposed into textuality has fallen outside the control of speakers. It is entirely up to readers, devoid of speaking contacts, to determine the meaning of words. Writings could outlive their own author, and readers were uninvolved in the production of texts. This is a wholly impossible situation for those who believed in the oral propensity and efficaciousness of the gospel! In our terms, the Fathers feared the breakdown of the oral synthesis and the collapse of the homeostatic balance as a result of their writing.

Once again the point is brought home to us that, for those committed to speaking and to the oral gospel, the written gospel was neither necessary nor desirable. Rather it raised the prospect of hermeneutical instabilities that could be avoided by staying with the oral medium.

The transposition of oral forms of speech into gospel textuality did not put an end to speaking. Obviously, it is not within the power of a text to stem the flow of spoken words. The ongoing existence of synoptic orality, especially of the sayings tradition, has been researched by Helmut Koester.[6] He found literal citations to be rare in the Apostolic Fathers (95–150 C.E.). As a rule one encounters variants which are explicable as "freie Überlieferung," that is, as oral transmission rather than textual derivatives. Indeed, Koester showed in case after case that the synoptic material in the Apostolic Fathers harks back to the pre-Markan phase of oral tradition. It is not until the middle of the second century, beginning with Justin Martyr, that the synoptic gospels, especially Matthew and Luke, become *scriptural* authorities vying with and gradually replacing oral transmission.[7]

Granted the ongoing force of synoptic orality, one must nonetheless acknowledge that the gospel's textuality asserts a new technology of communication over the synoptic tradition. But a new technology carries within it the power of reformulating, of reinventing even, the old, familiar message. We will show in this chapter, and especially in chapter 5, that the new technology of writing produced a christology that was in tension with, and a replacement of oral christology. It should be obvious at this point that voices had to be silenced and an oral way of life subverted in order for this gospel to come into existence. In this instance the composition of the message suggests that speaking was no longer the dominant, life-giving force in Christianity. This is so despite the fact that the written gospel was probably designed so as to be recycled into the oral medium.

Still another way of illustrating the project of Markan textuality is to assess its impact on oral pluralism. The pre-Markan traditions, we noted, diverge into a multiplicity of forms and directions. No law of oral transmission decrees a process of accretion toward textual stability. Hence, past states of synoptic orality cannot fully account for the present state of gospel textuality. From this viewpoint also, the gospel's written posture appears extraneous and even hostile to the waxing and waning of oral life. The gospel composition demanded that multiple oral wills and aims, objectives and trends, forms and values be overridden so as to be bent into a single linear direction. There is, therefore, something destructive about Mark's commitment to oral tradition: he embraces it only to disown it. To be sure, textuality may accord one form of speech preferential treatment, especially if the gospel is meant to be spoken aloud. But the fact remains that by appropriating oral pluralism and forcing it under the tyranny of a single, textual perspective, Mark has renounced direct loyalty to multiple oral interest groups.

All items of Mark's oral legacy are subject to decontextualization as they are enlisted in the service of the written gospel. None is excluded, all are affected. Utterances made at different times and places are synchronized and subjugated to an alien medium. Those sundry forms of speech that crossed the threshold to textuality were forced out of circulation and frozen into a static condition. This entails their uprooting from the very ideational and situational contexts which, as we noted earlier, are indispensable for the oral generation of meaning.[8] Language does not thereby go context-free, for the transposition into the new medium key carries with it a crucial shift in contextuality, as will be shown below. It will suffice at this point to observe that textuality extricates all oral speech forms from live performance and social, physiological contextuality. None can serve the purpose they were designed for or operate in the way they used to. All are bereft of the context of communality shared by speaker and hearers alike. Words, in short, are not allowed to have their own say.

Whether one perceives Markan textuality as a silencing of sounded words, or the termination of the dialogical situation, or the disruption of the homeostatic balance, or the attenuation of hearers' participation, or the breakdown of the oral synthesis, or a linearization of oral pluralism, or a decontextualization of words from their authentic oral matrix, its impact on the oral legacy is one of elementary disorientation. In a most acute sense, this gospel feeds "upon the de-activation of the strictly dynamistic component in words as signifiers."[9] While it remains valid that the gospel is composed by frequent recourse to orality, it is not until the latter is uprooted and transformed that the textual construct can take shape. Strictly speaking, therefore, the gospel arises not from orality *per se*, but out of the debris of deconstructed orality.

To treat living words as devitalized, stable objects requires a measure of distance from the oral lifeworld. If, in other words, the thesis of predominant synoptic orality is valid, then Mark, the writer of the text, must have had to assume a critical viewpoint over and even against his oral heritage. To repeat, Mark's employment of oral forms and values is incontrovertible. But to assert Mark's use of orality does not give us full insight into the linguistic dynamics of the gospel's composition. Nurtured by oral drives as the gospel is, it is in the last analysis built on its self-distancing from them.[10] It is by standing apart from live speech, confronting it as a nonparticipant, that Mark gains both freedom and leverage to manipulate words into textuality. Insofar as he operates as a writer, he can best discharge his obligations by becoming an outsider to oral tradition.

When thus probing gospel textuality in relation to its oral legacy, one is confronted with the question whether the text gives evidence for the kind of tensions and conflicts we have postulated for its genesis. Does the gospel reflect estrangement from oral life and alienation from its linguistic heritage? Does it, in plain words, register the trauma of its literacy? The question is the more relevant if one subscribes to Markan priority, assuming that the text is itself the primary record of the transition from orality to textuality.

It has long been conventional to explore the gospel for oral deposits, narrative logic, social connections, genre identity, and deep structures. Oral, literary, social, genre, and structural forces are all to be reckoned with in the formation of the gospel. That the written medium itself may have exerted pressures has as yet not been considered. The text as text is consistently taken for granted. But the medium perspective may prove fruitful at points of linguistic transformation, these crucial shifts from sound to silence. By way of preparation for what can be expected at medium transitions, a brief review of a *cause célèbre* in classical studies may be in order.

In a distinguished book, *Preface to Plato,* Eric H. Havelock reflected on an item of considerable embarrassment to the aesthetic sensibilities of classical scholars: Plato's repudiation of the poets and the poetic experience in books 2, 3, 5, and especially 10 of the *Republic.*[11] Havelock's argument can be summarized in three steps. First, poetry was not in the modern sense an art form that engaged the creative, imaginative faculties. Rather, it had fallen to the poets during the long haul of preliteracy to serve as articulators, collectors, and transmitters of knowledge. They functioned as a kind of social encyclopedia, constituting both an educational and political necessity in ancient Greece.[12] Second, operating exclusively in the oral medium, the poets shaped information in rhythmic, memorable fashion. Learning under those circumstances was essentially a process of recapitulation and emotive identification. The speaker "sank his personality in his performance,"[13] making his audience identify both with his message and himself. One learned by imitation what was being recited by the poets. Hence, *mimesis* became a term applicable to the poetic, educational experience. The urgency of mimesis was to repeat rather than to invent and to sustain group identity more than to upset it. Third, Plato's polemic against poetry must therefore be conceived as being directed toward the normative, oral apparatus of Greek education. In his judgment, knowledge acquired through the mimetic process is of little value:

> He is entering the lists against centuries of habituation in rhythmic memorised experience. He asks of men that instead they should examine this experience and rearrange it, that they should think about what they say, instead of just saying it. And they should separate themselves from it instead of identifying with it; they themselves should become the "subject" who stands apart from the "object" and reconsiders it and analyses it and evaluates it, instead of just "imitating" it.[14]

In Havelock's judgment, the Platonic state of mind that is capable of reflecting on the opinions of others as well as on one's own thought is unthinkable apart from the stimulus of writing and reading. It follows that the Platonic drive toward abstraction and the thing *per se* reflects a new type of mental activity prompted by the effects of the alphabetization of the Greek language and the rise of literacy. From a linguistic perspective, therefore, Plato's ban on the poets marks a revolt of the new literate mentality against the oral hegemony of the Homeric culture.

In turning to Mark's gospel we recall the elaborately staged relationship between Jesus and the disciples.[15] The latter are conceived both as followers of Jesus and prospective carriers of his mandate (3:14–15; 6:7–13, 30). They function as listeners, never writers, and are trained to be activists, not readers. Remembering, not memorization, is their obligation (cf. 8:18). Step by step Jesus initiates them into the logic of his mission. In consistence with this design, the disciples are placed into positions that allow them to acquire knowledge by familiarization with the master's words and by imitation of his deeds. In this fashion the chosen twelve, and among them the three, and above all Peter can receive the relevant information that will enable them to operate as apostolic representatives in the absence of Jesus. What is enacted in this dramatization is thus essentially an educational process. Jesus himself is the mentor, but the information he supplies is never objectified apart from his person and career. His whole life, in typical oral fashion, is an example to be followed or a lesson to be learned. His words and actions, travels and suffering constitute the supreme didactic paradigm that guides the disciples into their apostolic responsibilities. This is, however, nothing less than saying that the relationship between Jesus and his disciples is constructed on the oral principle of *imitatio magistri*,[16] or in Platonic terms on *mimesis,* which has as its chief concern the preservation of tradition.

In Mark's gospel the twelve personify the principal, oral representatives of Jesus. They function in a mimetic process whose function it is to assure continuity of tradition. The tradition to be continued is constituted by the paradigm of Jesus' life and death.

As is well known, Jesus' rebuke of the disciples' comprehension, or rather lack of it, is one of the major unifying themes of the gospel.[17] Although the twelve are placed within auditive immediacy of Jesus and privileged to hear and witness the fundamentals of his life and death, theirs is a failing discipleship. *Both the model of a mimetic relationship and the drama of failing discipleship are drawn with equal care by Mark.* This leads us to suggest that the dysfunctional role of the disciples narrates the breakdown of the mimetic process and casts a vote of censure against the guarantors of tradition. Oral representatives and oral mechanism have come under criticism. If the foremost oral authorities are depicted as failing to perceive the message and mission of Jesus, the conclusion is inevitable that, as far as Mark is concerned, mimesis malfunctioned and did so at a crucial juncture.[18]

In probing the gospel's narrative for clues to the defect, one general answer would be that oral transmission did not work because it could not work. What epitomizes the disciples' frame of mind is a preference for ideological simplicity and heroic actuality. It is a mentality that runs afoul of the kind of theological complexities that, according to Mark, characterize the fullness of Jesus. Above all, it is their sense of mythopoetic presence and stability that constitutes a barrier to full consciousness of Jesus' destabilizing presence and paradoxical career. What is remarkable about the disciples' convictions is the persistence with which they cling to them. Theirs is a christology deeply entrenched and resistant to change. The irony of Jesus' life, the contradiction prompted by his death, the instability produced by his message, and above all the mystery of the kingdom that entails the death of the king are all items alien to the Markan disciples, but dear to the author who dramatized the role of the disciples.

There is a deep logic connecting Mark's textual accomplishment with his indictment of oral process and authorities. If the gospel marks the break with synoptic orality and a move toward thoroughgoing textuality, alienation from the oral apparatus is intrinsic to the gospel's linguistic identity. So deeply is the gospel born out of emancipation from oral norms that its narrative and its medium history have become inseparable. The polemic against the disciples, from this perspective, can hardly be considered peripheral to the gospel. If Mark takes to writing not ultimately in order to continue and preserve, but rather to uproot and transcend oral forms and values, this very motive for his writing may be expected to emerge as a central feature in his story. Critique of the principal oral authorities could be the narrative manifestation of the new consciousness raised by the writer's departure from oral norms and habits. By highlighting the failure of the oral representatives, this gospel writes its case on behalf of its technological innovation. In other words, the gospel articulates the *raison d'être* for its own written existence by dramatizing the breakdown of the mimetic process. The emergence of thoroughgoing textuality and the gospel's narration of the failure of oral transmission are rigorously complementary phenomena.

In addition to the disciples, who stand at the outset of oral transmission, Mark also repudiates oral representatives who are much closer to his own situation. In Mark 13 christs and prophets are singled out for condemnation by the Markan Jesus. More than any other section in Mark this chapter touches most directly on the gospel's social matrix. Analyses have shown that the identity of the persons under attack is to be derived from 13:5b–6, 21–22, verses that refer to one and the same group of people. Accordingly, Mark criticizes early Christian prophets who perform signs and wonders (13:22) and make pronouncements in the name and on the authority of Jesus (13:6).[19]

The crisis triggered by the prophets and its connection with Markan textuality can be reviewed from several angles.

Whether one dates the prophets before or after the fall of the temple,[20] they are in any case closely bound up with the turbulence of the Roman-Jewish War. Mark's careful staging (13:1–4) and disposition of chapter 13 leaves little doubt about the matter.[21] Nothing in Mark's depiction of the prophets suggests a life style of writing and reflection on life. Their proclamation of words and performance of deeds is designed for public consumption in a highly charged political arena. It may not be amiss, therefore, to perceive them as politically committed Jewish-Christian prophets who thrive on speech and action. Mark's production of a text, by contrast, is not a good way of participating in life. Perhaps it is not entirely accidental that his text, which is predicated on a decentering from oral activity, fosters an ideology hostile to oral, prophetic activism. There is a connection, though not necessarily conscious to the writer, between the text founded on withdrawal from oral, active life and its expressed critique of prophetic representatives of the *vita activa*.

A more obvious reason for Mark's objection to the prophets lies in their orally effected presence of Jesus. This phenomenon of consummating presence is contingent on oral language and a specific feature of oral, prophetic language. Texts are signs practicing the deferment of the signified, but spoken words discourage reflection on meaning as something apart from utterance. Operating without transposition into objectified, visible form, sound tends to keep language from falling apart into signified and signifier. The resultant effect of sounded words is one of powerful presence. It is only with the electronic medium that oral words take on a form of signified pastness much like written words. But apart from the electronic medium, voice exists only at the moment of speaking, tending to make present the reality it is referring to. This "absolute proximity of voice and being, of voice and the meaning of being"[22] links oral words with a whole metaphysics of presence and parousia. Authoritative, prophetic speakers, including those in the background of Mark 13:5b–6, 21–22, exploit the presenting power of oral speech to the fullest. Utilizing the prophetic *egō eimi* style of speech, these prophets spoke as representatives of Jesus and embodied in this manner his very authority. Since their words were his words, Jesus continued to speak in their prophetic proclamations. It is possible to conclude, therefore, that the prophets maximized the power of the oral medium for the purpose of continuing the present authority of Jesus, the living Lord.

It is this oral metaphysics of presence that is objectionable to Mark, writer of the gospel. His elaborately constructed apocalyptic speech—Mark 13—serves to discredit the prophets and their *egō eimi* proclamation of the presence of Jesus. The reality of Jesus' presence, Mark argues, was brutally disconfirmed by war and persecution (13:7–13), the destruction of the temple (13:2, 14), and the dispersion of the people (13:15–20). In the first part of the speech (13:5b–23) he defuses a prophetically aroused consciousness of parousia hope (13:7b, 8c, 13b), thereby exposing the proclaimed presence of Jesus as false. From his perspective, the prophets misrepresented Jesus and thus imperiled his status as the living

Lord. Having taken the notion of realized presence away from the prophets, Mark in the second part (13:24–27) projects Jesus' presence into the future. In the third part (13:28–37) he protects the reconstructed future against prophetic errors by assuring the unpredictability of future fulfillment.

While Mark 13 articulates the specific refutation of the "plenipotentiaries of Christ,"[23] the gospel as a whole appears to take an evasive posture toward the presence of the living Lord. As is well known, Jesus as risen Lord does not appear in the gospel, let alone proclaim his presence in the word. He is "not only absent, he is silent."[24] That the absence of resurrection appearance stories is not fortuitous, but connected with the purpose of the Markan composition, has recently been pointed out in a number of studies on Mark and early Christian prophetism.[25] In chapter 5 we shall argue that the entire form of the gospel, that is, the construction of a pre-resurrectional, christological framework, constitutes a written alternative to the oral metaphysics of presence.[26] At this point we observe a logic according to which the resurrected Lord cannot appear in a gospel that objects to the prophetically inspired metaphysics of presence. The connection is between the prophets' orally proclaimed presence of Jesus and Mark's repudiation of them in a written gospel that does not feature the risen Lord.

There is yet another way in which Mark's repudiation of the prophets and prophetic mentality may have a bearing on his writing of the gospel. If, in his view, the authority of Jesus is best safeguarded through the written medium, might one not expect him to be wary of oral words and their prophetically presenting power? Did not the prophets perhaps expose to him a problematic potential of *logoi*, the primary unit of oral speech? If again he resorted to the written medium at least partly in reaction against prophetic words, might one not expect him to select and treat the genre of *logoi* with caution, perhaps with reserve? This is what M. Eugene Boring has recently suggested.[27] The author proceeded from the well-known fact regarding the relative paucity of sayings in Mark. By his own count, the Markan sayings material comprises 27.5 percent, the Matthaean sayings 55.2 percent and the Lukan sayings 48.5 percent of the totals of their respective gospels. "Mark has only a little more than half as much sayings material in his gospel as either Matthew or Luke."[28] From the view of source criticism, the paucity of sayings in Mark has long been a problem for the classic two-source hypothesis and its complementary premises regarding Markan priority and an early dating of Q, the sayings genre. Indeed, if Mark emerged from a predominantly oral synoptic tradition, and Q existed prior to Mark, how does one account for this remarkable scarcity of *logoi* in the gospel? According to Boring, it results from Mark's deliberately reserved attitude toward the sayings genre and the religious posture associated with it: "Mark has so few sayings of Jesus because he is suspicious of Christian prophecy as it is present in his community and expressed in the sayings tradition."[29]

It is noteworthy that in the two instances where Mark presents Jesus as speaker par excellence (4:1–34; 13:5b–37), eschatology and the presence of time are the issue. What is even more astounding is that in each case Jesus' words function so as to disallow any oral sense of presence. The Galilean speech is parabolic in the extreme, articulating the minuteness and grandeur, the hiddenness and revelation of the kingdom, as well as the paradoxical responses to it. Far from being an instantaneous presence accessible to the utterance of *logoi*, the kingdom is said to have a history mysterious in its entirety. *Logoi* must be considered too discrete, direct, and episodic to allow full revelation of the kingdom's mysterious history. What is more, the *logos* is itself ambiguously involved in the mysterious process of the kingdom. According to the interpretation of the parable of the *Sower*, a massive malfunctioning of the *logos* forms an essential part of the mystery of the kingdom (4:14–19). For Mark, the *logos* is thus not an unambiguous carrier of presence. The Jerusalem speech, as we observed, extricates kingdom hopes from past and present implications and projects the presence of the Son of man into the future. In the two major speeches delivered by the Markan Jesus, therefore, his *logoi* have the effect of minimizing more than maximizing the fullness of presence, and of stressing the ambiguity of kingdom and *logos* more than oral presence.

We have focused on the linguistic aspects of the crisis, observing tension between the prophetic enactment of living words and Mark's use of the written medium. The prophets' words had attained their highest pitch of oral efficaciousness in the form of their *egō eimi* pronouncements. They came to be a Christ-event at the moment of utterance, happening in the midst of hearers. But as social events contradicted the power of prophetic words, their proclamation of presence was exposed as false and a crisis of confidence inevitable. The experience of disconfirmation undermined the credibility of prophetic authorities and faith in their oral, prophetic effectiveness. At this point, orality was ill-equipped to deal with the dilemma, for the prophetic, oral use of living words was itself a major part of the problem. Linguistically, Mark responded by disestablishing words from oral life and transposing them into a new key. The novel medium enabled him to stand apart from the crisis and to turn events into records of events, to reflect on them within the larger framework of

Jesus' life and death, and in that context to disown the voices of his prophetic precursors.[30] Not unexpectedly for one faced with the dilemma of oral speech, power, and authorities, Mark exploited the alienating potential of the written medium by underplaying the event-character of words and stressing the absence of the living Lord, rather than his presence, and the mysterious history of the kingdom more than the fullness of present time.

Apart from conflict with the disciples and prophets, Mark's gospel registers consistent hostility toward Jesus' own family. The first time the relatives are mentioned, they are, together with the Jerusalem scribes, relegated to an outside position (3:20–35). One initially learns of the ignoble intention of "those about him" (au. trans.) to take Jesus into custody when they judge him to be mentally deranged (3:21). While "those about him" are on the way to Jesus, he is confronted by another group, the scribes, who charge him with demonic possession and spiritual uncleanliness (3:22–30). In the meantime the former group arrives on the scene and is now identified as "his mother and his brothers" (3:31). "Those about him" (*hoi par'autou*) who came to apprehend (*kratēsai*) Jesus must therefore be identified as "his relatives" (*JB*), or "his family" (*NEB*), rather than "his friends" (*RSV*, 1946 edition). Both relatives and scribes are now linked together by their common attitude against Jesus: they accuse him of mental derangement and demonic possession respectively. The relatives have no sooner arrived when Jesus relegates them to an outsider position. A topological scheme dramatizes the outsider-insider dichotomy. Jesus is inside the house (3:20) with a crowd sitting about him (3:32: *ekathēto peri auton ochlos*), while his mother and brothers are "standing outside" (3:31: *exō stēkontes*). In response, Jesus identifies those around him as the true family of God (3:34), thereby symbolically solidifying the outsider role of his blood relatives. Their status as outsiders will neither be reversed nor relinquished in the remainder of the gospel story.

At the occasion of Jesus' visit to Nazareth, his relatives are mentioned again (6:1–6). The episode narrates his disengagement from his home town and emphatically his break with his family. The initial reception is far from unfriendly, but the people's astonishment (6:2: *exeplēssonto*) turns into embarrassing and derisive questioning. The focus of their queries falls on the issue of Jesus' origin, and their roll call of Mary the mother and his brothers and sisters is designed to expose his ordinary, and perhaps less than ordinary, descent (6:3: *ho hyios tēs Marias . . . kai eskandalizonto en autō*).[31] Jesus meets the challenge by citing the proverb of the prophet who is not without honor except in his own place (6:4).

But the particular phrasing suggests Jesus' distanciation not merely from hometown, but also from relatives in the broad sense and house in the special sense (*en tē patridi autou kai en tois syggeneusin autou kai en tē oikia autou*). Since neither Matthew (13:57), nor Luke (4:24), nor John (4:44), nor *Oxyrhynchus Papyrus* 1.6, nor the *Gospel of Thomas* 31 mentions the family in the broader sense (*syggeneusin*), and only Matthew notes family in the narrow sense (*en tē oikia autou*), and that in adaptation of Mark, the double emphasis on family is uniquely Markan. By both personalizing and reduplicating the reference to relatives, the evangelist has emphasized Jesus' alienation from his family, and especially from those members who figured in the preceding roll call—the mother, the brothers James, Joses, Judas, and Simon, as well as the sisters.

One may well submit that Mark does not seem to conceive of the relatives as symbols of oral authority, nor link Jesus' disengagement from them with the breakdown of tradition. And yet is it thinkable that Mark banished the relatives without awareness of their natural roles as spokesmen and spokeswomen on behalf of the tradition? The early Christian tradition, in any case, was moderately conscious of their importance in the formative stage of the movement (Acts 1:14; 12:17; 15:13; 21:18; John 19:25–27; 1 Cor. 15:7; Gal. 1:19; 2:9, 12; James 1:1; Jude 1:1).

In one case, however, an important relative could well be directly associated with oral transmission and its malfunctioning. In the passion narrative reference is made to a Mary "the mother of James the Younger and of Joses" (15:40), who alternately is called "Mary the mother of Joses" (15:47) and "Mary the mother of James" (16:1). Both J. D. Crossan[32] and T. E. Boomershine[33] have identified this Mary as the mother of Jesus. The only other time the two names associated with Mary, James and Joses, appear in the gospel is in the Nazareth story. There they are introduced as brothers of Jesus, the son of Mary (6:3). The verbal threads that connect 6:3 with 15:40, as well as with 15:47 and 16:1, serve to designate Mary as the mother of Jesus.[34] The reiteration of the names of James and Joses in the passion narrative is entirely in line with Markan narrative techniques; for the evangelist has been shown to resume, in the story of Jesus' death, words, motifs, and names from the preceding story of life.[35] The narrative importance of Mary in the last episodes of the gospel can hardly be exaggerated. One remembers that she, together with Mary Magdalene and Salome, witnesses Jesus' death (15:40), and alone with Mary Magdalene his burial (15:47). In the absence of the apostate disciples, she and the other women personify the crucial link in the final act of communication. When the three women enter the tomb for the purpose of anointing the body, they are commissioned to transmit to Peter and the disciples the decisive news: Jesus' resurrection and his journey to Galilee (16:1–7). But the written gospel concludes with the narration of the abortive mission of the oral message (16:8). Mary, the mother, together with Mary Magdalene and Salome, has thus become instrumental in the final and decisive breakdown of oral transmission. Mark, on this reading, has brought the antecedent negativity toward the family to a climax by implicating an important member in the message that failed.

Even if the identification of Mary as Jesus' mother were judged conjectural, Mark can hardly have been ignorant of the implications entailed in an unfavorable depiction of the family. Family and tribe are the natural locus for the process of learning by familiarization. An author capable of staging the relationship between Jesus and the disciples as a mimetic process will also know that mimesis flourishes in familial relations. The family members are the natural heirs to and transmitters of tradition. It is difficult to avoid the conclusion that Mark, by narrating Jesus' rejection of and by his family, has cancelled a valuable oral connection and undercut a priceless source of transmission. The comforting process of familiarization has been voided by the alienating method of defamiliarization.

We began our discussion of Markan textuality on the premise of a linguistic dislocation. The search for clues to the assumed trauma of literacy has yielded ample evidence. There are various degrees of tension with orality reverberating through the gospel's text. Such specifically Markan features as the absence of a resurrection appearance story, reservation toward the genre of *logoi,* the de-eschatologizing function of the two major speech complexes, and a pervasive deconstruction of a prophetically proclaimed metaphysics of presence form a connected pattern that counteracts the operating power of oral speech. More spectacularly, Mark's writing is fueled with a passion to disown the voices of his oral precursors. One is struck by this gospel's repudiation of the disciples, the prophets, and the family of Jesus. In sociological terms, Mark undermines the very structures that facilitate and legitimize oral transmission: the legitimately appointed authorities, the charismatic authorities, and the hereditary authorities. The very representatives of Jesus, those who can and must be expected to function as official, inspired, and traditional transmitters of his words, are dislodged. The guarantors of the tradition have been evicted.

To ask in exasperation how Mark could bite the hands that fed him is as irrelevant as it would be to charge Plato with treason against the poets. As long as we measure this gospel's anti-oral thrust against standards of continuity, we shall misread and trivialize the novelty of its linguistic operation. But once we acknowledge that a language gained entails perforce a language lost, and that an old world must be revoked for the new one to be installed, we can appreciate this gospel's inherent need to abrogate the authorities of an older order of language. Because the Markan narrative bears the brunt of a transition from the oral to the written medium, it is profoundly marked by a rebellion against orality and its authoritative carriers. The transformation of words into the written medium and antagonism toward the representatives of oral words are interconnected phenomena. Standing at a painfully creative juncture of two language worlds, the Markan text feeds on alienation and in part derives its strength from the very act of overriding oral powers. This plotted narrative which climaxes with the nontransmission of *the* vital oral message reflects back on itself and its own textual communication.[36] So deeply is the new writing consciousness predicated on distance from the old medium, that the text can be said to write its own cancellation of the contract with orality.

TEXTUALITY AS REORIENTATION

The linguistic disorientation we have postulated for the Markan composition manifests itself in a dramatic narrative engagement. In narrating the ill-fated lot of the principal authorities of oral transmission, the gospel has produced a story that is deeply connected with its own linguistic genesis. If, therefore, the written medium is intrinsic to the message, Mark's text as text repays examination. Apart from disorienting oral speech forms, this text has reoriented them into a novel textual construct. Our business here is not with literary criticism, but with the textualization of spoken words, their rebuilding into a new and foreign medium.[37]

In the written gospel words acquire a new authority, a pathos even, unobtainable in oral life. Those voices and stories which were incorporated into textuality are destined to survive. Whatever their interpretation, they are guaranteed longevity, if not perpetuity. Oral fragility has been overcome by "the secret of making the word immortal."[38] A particular rendition of Jesus' life and death is made "safe," fortified against oral decay, variability, amnesia, or floating. It is now fixed in place to be studied, interpreted, copied, and disseminated. With writing a beginning has been made in the synoptic tradition for a manuscript mentality that deals with original form, copies, and textual accuracy—all notions foreign to the oral medium.

As text the gospel exhibits a virtually limitless ability to attract and absorb materials. In speaking, as we noted, language makes a covenant with people. Oral words are spoken and responded to, retained and forgotten by people. Texts, by contrast, are mute. They cannot talk back, and if they are talked back to, they will not respond. Textuality is predicated on a technique that generates verbal existence outside and apart from persons. Writing, therefore, assures gain, whereas speaking risks a loss. Given their nonpersonalized, independent, verbal existence, texts become convenient tools, machines almost, for hoarding information. The shift from utterance to textual silence, therefore, implies a vast increase in storage possibilities. Any oral performance of the life and death of Jesus was necessarily limited to themes, clusters of forms and genres, episodes and incidents. A written presentation can absorb virtually unlimited diversity, without specifically endorsing the multiple oral interest groups. It is a matter of significance, therefore, to observe an intrinsic link between Mark's recourse to writing and textuality's tolerance for sundry and assorted items of information.

An example will demonstrate the heterogeneity of materials embedded in the gospel and the ambitiously absorbent power of its textuality. In Mark 4:35–8:21 the text has assimilated the following reservoir of story types: two sea stories (4:35–41; 6:45–52), six heroic stories (5:1–20; 5:21–24, 35–43; 5:25–34; 6:53–56; 7:24–30; 7:31–37), two feeding stories (6:34–44; 8:1–10), two types of didactic stories (6:1–6; 8:11–13), two controversy stories (7:1–23; 8:14–21), an etiological story (6:7–13), and a martyrological story (6:17–29). If one accepts Paul Achtemeier's extrapolation of two cycles of miracle stories, one would find in them a recognizable pattern of pre-Markan organization. But the cycles, if indeed both of them are pre-Markan,[39] are more indicative of oral clustering than of a causally constructed narrative. The difficulty in plotting 4:35–8:21 was thus considerable: how to bring such heterogeneous stories as the death of the Baptist, the rejection at Nazareth, the mission of the twelve, two miracle cycles, a discussion on ritual purity, and a controversy with Pharisees into a single, coherent arrangement. Needless to say, story is a favorite child of orality. But Mark's implosion of orality's storied pluralism into a comprehensive narrative must be viewed as fundamentally an achievement of textuality.

Writing, the inscribing of graphic signs on surfaces, entails the linearization of language. Speech as verbal output, we remember, does not imply spatial direction; spoken words are preeminently sound, and sound does not lend itself to spatializing patterns. By robbing words of sound, language is made subservient to spatial arrangements. As words are transposed into visible signs, they are lined up in rectilinear rows. The line now becomes a dominant factor in the formation of language.[40]

The effects of linearization upon cognitive processes, largely taken for granted by the modern, literate mentality, are not to be underrated. The most obvious result is the introduction of an ordering agent into language. To allocate each letter, word, and verbal unit to a single position, "where it stands in a definite, permanent, and unambiguous relationship to the others,"[41] is equivalent to the construction of a world. Orality, of course, is perfectly adept at creating ordered stories and epics of stories. But the faculty of writing to apportion items along the artificial construct of the straight line forces a systematic ordering upon language unknown to spoken words. From this viewpoint, the written gospel presents itself as the streamlined regimentation of oral ebb and flow. This act of overriding oral forms and proclivities amounts to more than an ordering of words. It is equivalent to a reordering of tradition. The line recasts oral diffusiveness into a new constellation of linguistic relations.

Writing along the line "introduces the directional factor into verbal communication."[42] The placing of letter after letter and word after word advances semantic sequentiality and quickens the forward momentum of the narrative line. Mark exploits the directional potential of writing by threading a journey that draws hitherto unrelated items onto a single path. The construction of a journey as a literary device for the purpose of uniting oral episodes was recognized by Hermann Gunkel in his study of Genesis: "Usually the narrators make the transition by means of very simple devices from one of the stories to the other. The transition par excellence is the journey."[43] A redactional summary (1:39) suggests that Jesus traveled through all of Galilee, with Capernaum serving as a temporary base (1:21; 2:1), and the lake of Galilee as a provisional goal (2:13; 3:7; 4:1). Six voyage notes (4:35; 5:21; 6:32; 6:45; 8:10; 8:13) impose a directional pattern upon the aforementioned stories (4:35–8:21), settling them along a purposeful route. The gospel's midsection (8:22–10:52) is punctuated with gestures of spatial reference (8:27; 9:33; 9:34; 10:17; 10:32; 10:52) and geographical orientations (8:27; 9:30; 10:32) that serve to align sayings and stories along a way from Caesarea Philippi to Jerusalem. To further reinforce a sense of linear causality, Mark inserted circumspectly phrased passion sayings along the route (8:31; 9:31; 10:33–34) that point forward like arrows to death and resurrection. Thus buttressed by spatial directives, the written lineup gives the storied diversity the appearance of "followability."[44] Oral redundancy and heterogeneity is assimilated to the direction of the line, and the plurality of stories and sayings is comprehensible as a single narrative.

Textuality does not merely chart a path toward the future; it also reaches back into the past. The gospel's retrospective posture manifests itself interiorly and exteriorly.[45] As regards interior reflexiveness, it must first be observed that the written narrative is a more consciously constructed product than an oral story. The writer organizes the material and plots it toward a definite narrative goal. This process of composing with a narrative goal in mind implies a plotting backwards from the anticipated goal. Mark's story is structured from its ending.[46] In the most general terms, Jesus' announced resurrection presupposes his death; death finds its rationale in an antecedent life; death and life are inaugurated and foreshadowed by the Baptist. It is this posterior narrative slant that gives the gospel, together with most textually plotted narratives, a sense of *interior retrospectivity*. The ending is where the construction of most plotted narratives commences. Because the ending determines the plot all the way to its beginning, ending and beginning tend to feed into each other. In Mark, as again in many textually constructed narratives, the beginning anticipates the ending because the ending controlled the beginning. With the announcement of Jesus' journey to Galilee (14:28; 16:7) the narrative turns back on itself, revisiting the beginning of Jesus' career (1:9). The women's failure to pass on the message of life, finally, is highly instructive in regard to interior retrospectivity. The written gospel's ending with the nontransmission of the oral gospel offers a retrospective rationale for the beginning of the written gospel.

As regards *exterior retrospectivity*, textuality accords the gospel a once-for-all character, conferring upon it a sense of pastness. Orality, to be sure, tells stories of things past as well. But the tendency of live performance is to contemporize, that is, to interact with the presence of hearers. Even if the gospel is meant to be spoken, it is a textually filtered and fixed story that addresses hearers' presence as a monument from the past. By exploiting textuality's exterior posteriority Mark retrieves the authority of Jesus who lived, spoke, and healed in Galilee, had died and risen in Jerusalem, and was to return to Galilee. In thus assuring Jesus' authority as essentially belonging to the past, the text construes an alternative to his prophetically proclaimed presence. As noted before, we shall elaborate on Mark's textually constructed, pre-resurrectional framework as an alternative to the oral metaphysics of presence in chapter 5.[47] But it is already obvious that textuality's retrospective reach toward Jesus' past authority and the narrated elimination of all intermediary oral authorities are connected and complementary features. The story's dispossession of Jesus' oral successors is linked in depth with textuality's accomplished repossession of Jesus' past authority.[48]

From textuality's retrospective cast it is but a small step toward its potential for self-reflection and self-criticism. The mnemonics of oral culture require repetition and foster redundancy. Knowledge that has to rely on memory is uneasy about innovative departures from orally stored and transmitted tradition. Thinking, for this reason, proceeds less by deviation from, and more in imitation of, oral forms and authorities. The analytic and self-critical stance is generally alien to orality, and self-preservation is its prevailing mood.[49] In textuality, reflection on words takes priority over mere perpetuation of them. Fundamentally this is because the mind is relieved of the burden of retaining knowledge by remembering. Writing enables one to produce language over a prolonged period of time, at one's own pace, with self-chosen interruptions and without a direct commitment to audiences. The ensuing reflective viewpoint produces double and triple distancing effects.[50] Language laid out before one's eyes entails a retreat from or absence of hearers, engenders a loosening or separation of signified from signifier, and in turn invites reflection upon its own signifying self. In sum, writing is "the fitting form of the alienated insight."[51] One cannot well reflect on Mark's gospel without being struck by the distance it has gained on its linguistic and religious heritage. Linguistically, the indictment of the principal carriers of the Christian tradition must be preeminently the work of a writer. Orality can ill afford undermining its own authorities, and in that process transacting a fresh departure from its received world.

The textualization of spoken words entails an intricate process of linguistic transformation, much of which has remained unexplored. Most crucially, what is involved is a *shift in contextuality*. As we observed earlier, oral language is bound up with a physiological, social, and environmental contextuality. Gestures and facial expressions, pitch and tone of voice, economic and political experiences, and the very locale of discoursing are crucial determinants in the shaping of meaning. This very dependency of oral speech on nonlinguistic factors makes it less plainly a linguistic act than writing. Written language assumes a posture of aloofness from and indifference toward oral checks and balances. The whole referential nexus of physiognomic, social, and environmental commonality is now effaced. Words taken out of nonlinguistic contextuality are pressed into unilateral relations with other, written words. There is no escaping from this novel contextuality that has deprived oral words of their nonlinguistic or extralinguistic support system. Conscripted into the service of textuality, the once-spoken words have to alter their semantic behavior and live up to new hermeneutical responsibilities.

Paul Ricoeur has found the fitting terminology for the linguistic interplay of the *inclusive* gospel story with its *exclusive* elements. The multitude of sayings, parables, and stories (heroic, polarization, and didactic stories) commingle so as to create a "space of intersignification."[52] Accordingly, the text not merely houses diverse materials in close proximity, but sets up a network of interconnections and interactions. In the resultant "process of intersignification,"[53] sayings and stories interpret each other and become interwoven with the inclusive gospel narrative in multiple ways. The transformational impact on the exclusive materials takes on varying modes and degrees of intensity, but it is never wholly absent.

The heroic and polarization stories, once accepted into gospel textuality, are called upon to assume specific narrative tasks beyond their oral functioning. In Mark 4:35–8:21, for example, they operate within a redactionally created, spatial framework that draws fresh energies and new meanings from the stories. Strategically placed onto the back-and-forth path of Jesus' voyages across the lake of Galilee, they serve the process of unification of Jewish and Gentile lands into the new identity of the kingdom of God.[54] As participants in the plotted narrative, heroic and polarization stories are deprived of oral redundancy and clustering, and overlaid with meanings other than mythopoetic heroism. The healings of Jairus's daughter (5:21–24, 35–43) and of the hemorrhaging woman (5:25–34) transcend the type of heroic story highlighting the deeds of a strong man. In the textually controlled context of Jesus' journey they signify his embracement of the Jews as part of the previously announced mystery of the kingdom of God. By the same token, the exorcism of the Gerasene Demoniac (5:1–20) is more than a heroic story with possible anti-Roman sentiments. In Mark's contextuality the story points to the acceptance of the Gentiles as part of Jesus' mission of the kingdom. Likewise, the two healings of blind men (8:22–26; 10:46–52) narrate more than a mythopoetic restoration to physical well-being. Situated at the beginning and ending of a major travel section, they become symbolic of the purpose of Jesus' traveling mission: the opening of eyes not merely in a physical sense, but spiritually in regard to the suffering messiahship of the Son of man. In these and other instances, Markan textuality has brought forth significations barely or not at all present in orality. In traditional, exegetical terminology, the heroic and polarization stories perform an eschatological, constitutive function. Linguistically, we must say, they point to a reality beyond themselves, that of the kingdom of God. This is, however, nothing less than saying that they operate metaphorically. This metaphorical proclivity or sign-character of the synoptic miracle stories has frequently been observed, but Madeleine Boucher deserves credit for having boldly linked it with the linguisticality of parables: ". . . the miracles, as they are treated in Mark, are similar to the parables in having more than one level of meaning and are thus subject to the same misunderstanding as the parables."⁵⁵ Indeed, one of the problems of Mark's disciples is their failure to grasp the metaphorical quality of Jesus' heroic deeds. They are inclined to understand them in the mythopoetic sense of self-authentication, rather than in the parabolic sense of self-transcendence. Once again, one observes tension between the textually induced metaphoricity of the heroic and polarization stories, which brings them into the neighborhood of parables, versus the disciples' attachment to their oral, heroic functioning.

Didactic stories, once contextualized in the gospel, relinquish their role as autonomous carriers of information. Banished into the space of inter-signification, they must conform to a project not only larger than but different from their own. Their chief responsibility, one might say, is now less to people outside the text, than to words within it. The story of *Plucking Corn on Sabbath* (2:23–28), for example, has surrendered its primary oral functioning of satisfying specific informational needs about Sabbath observance. Inserted into a sequence of controversies (2:1–3:6), it contributes to the narrative buildup of Jesus' strange and estranging career. Likewise, *Teaching on Divorce* (10:2–9) is not primarily intended to answer a particular people's moral questions. Placed in the wake of Jesus' announcements of his impending death (8:31; 9:31) and following the exposure of Pharisaic hostility (2:24; 3:6; 7:1; 8:11, 15), this debate with the Pharisees, situated as it is at his arrival in the region of Judea (10:1), strengthens the impression of the inevitable demise of the protagonist. The textualization of the didactic stories heightens their controversial and even mythoclastic potential at the price of weakening their topical, didactic functioning. Moreover, didactic stories, not unlike heroic and polarization stories, are instrumental in signifying the kingdom of God. In Mark's linguistic contextuality, they are designed to shape the contours of a new and highly controversial reality, rather than to serve immediate social needs.

If Markan textualization in effect nudges the oral legacy toward the parabolic, the status of exclusive parables in the text deserves our special attention. A text that appears to favor metaphoricity might be expected to be receptive toward parables, but such is not the case, as we noted before.⁵⁶ By comparison with Matthew and Luke, Mark exhibits few and relatively moderate parables. Lest premature conclusions be drawn from this fact, we reemphasize the hermeneutical paradox of parabolic stories. With parables, language and logic are never quite what one expects. In treating the textualization of parables we shall first observe their actual involvement in the text. Deprived of social contextuality and hearers, parables enter into a veritable maze of hermeneutical complications. The parable of the *Mustard Seed,* for example, is defined as a kingdom parable and can readily operate as such in oral contextuality. But within the textual space of intersignification it relates to the mystery of the kingdom (4:11), interacts with other kingdom references, and finally contributes to the gospel's entire dramatization of the kingdom's story. The parable of the *Sower* is accompanied by its own written interpretation. In that case, the single act of oral transaction has fallen into two separate written records. The interpretation determines the meaning of the parable and rationalizes the mystery intrinsic to all parables. But in the inclusive gospel text the parable and its interpretation are not allowed to form a linguistic enclave. Both parable and interpretation open out to the wider narrative, participate in, and indeed help determine the so-called parable theory. The parable of the *Wicked Tenants* (12:1–11) links up with the "beloved son" references (12:6) in the baptismal and transfiguration stories (1:11; 9:7) and suggests identification of the second servant (12:4) with John the Baptist (6:27), of the tenants (12:8–9) with the temple authorities (11:27; 12:12), and of the vineyard (12:1) with the temple (11:11, 15–18, 27). As observed before, it is this parable's close interaction with surrounding textuality that gives it an allegorical quality.[57] In all instances, intertextual relations yield up latent senses *ad libitum,* producing meanings and complications unmanageable by the oral medium. If one remembers that a text survives its author, it could almost be said that for the reader the shift from social to linguistic contextuality opens up a hall of mirrors, as it were, conjuring up connections and reflections virtually without end.

Our second observation pertains to the hermeneutically unfinished condition of parables.[58] Parabolic stories open out to hearers who serve as cocreators in the formation of meaning. In order to function orally, parables are thus deeply contingent on the living interaction of speakers and hearers. It is this acute dependence on oral, social contextuality that makes parables less amenable to linguistic contextualization. The inclusive text obstructs the open-endedness of the exclusive parables, forcing them to relate to other, intrinsically unrelated, written words, rather than to receptive hearers. Undoubtedly, parables have much to lose by their insertion into the text.[59] This is why we must say that of all pre-Markan forms of speech parables are most resistant to linguistic contextualization. One may well ask to what extent linguistic contextuality can carry parables and preserve their hermeneutical integrity at all; and one can answer that, strictly speaking, a text cannot carry parables without doing damage to them. The presence of few parables in Mark's text is thus not necessarily an indication of lack of sympathy toward them. It could mean the very opposite.

Although the exclusive parables enter into complicated intertextual relations, one can nevertheless observe authorical efforts at controlling the situation. This leads us to reflect on the conspicuous accumulation of parables in Mark 4. The parable of the *Sower* and its interpretation, the parables of the *Reaper* and the *Mustard Seed,* as well as assorted parabolic discourse all cooperate in the making of the so-called parable theory. That theory, we shall argue below, serves to extend parabolic logic across the gospel narrative. Moreover, the rather textualized parable of the *Wicked Tenants* will be shown to tie in closely with the gospel's parabolic logic. Though limited in number, Mark's parables appear for the most part directly engaged in an overriding parabolic purpose.

It could be surmised that the parabolizing tendency of Markan textualization and the limited but focused use of exclusive parables may contribute to the composition of an inclusive, parabolic narrative.

The textual absorption and transformation of speech forms and their arrangement along a followable line allow for extension of cognitive powers into areas formerly not, or only partially, occupied by oral discourse. Although Mark remains a storyteller, unpossessed by speculative interests in space and time, he draws up a map of spatial coordinates and enlarges the vision of the history of the kingdom. Spatially, the traveling Jesus stakes off ground, both sanctifying and desanctifying it. Reaching into Galilee and crossing back and forth over the lake, he divinizes land, designating it as Jewish and Gentile territory. Alternating between the temple and the Mount of Olives, he profanes the sacred place and valorizes its opposite mountain peak. Sitting inside a house, we recall, he spatializes audiences into insiders and outsiders (3:20, 31–35). House and synagogue, lakeside and cities, Galilee and Jerusalem, desert and temple, and the triangle of mount of transfiguration, temple mount, and Mount of Olives embrace a large and meaningful world.

Within this spatial world time is created and the kingdom's story mapped out. At his opening address (1:14–15) Jesus offers thematic guidance by intoning the kingdom leitmotif. But if one asks about the nature of the kingdom and its present actuality, no direct answer is forthcoming. Beginning roughly at midpoint of the gospel (9:1), the kingdom is given as a future entity (9:47; 10:15, 23, 24, 25; 12:34; 14:25; 15:43), anticipating Jesus' paradoxical coronation as King (15:2, 12, 16–20, 31–32) and an incalculable eschaton (13:24–37). Throughout, the kingdom is referred to as something to be received (10:15) and entered into (9:47; 10:14–15, 23–25), or something near at hand (12:34), to be expected (15:43) and celebrated (14:25). Precisely what it is that is present, or absent, or coming, or all three things together, the gospel withholds from the inquirer. Inasmuch as the kingdom resists definition, it attracts the discourse of parables. In his Galilean speech (4:1–34) Jesus hides it in parabolic mystery, concealing knowledge from all but the insiders. Markan textuality in general and the textually constructed speech in chapter 4 in particular complicate the revelation of the kingdom and weaken its sense of oral presence. Written out as it is, the kingdom is more paradox than presence, and mystery rather than possession.

Mark's gospel is no mere custodian, preserving and presiding over the collective memories of the past. What is remarkable about his dealing with oral speech forms is not the limits they impose on him, but the license he takes with them. They are treated less as authorities to be followed than as sources to be exploited. This new license is granted by the written medium. In part, textuality facilitates a redistribution of mental energies. "To memorize anything," Havelock reminds us, "is like lifting a weight and carrying it; it requires . . . energy."[60] Delivered from oral handling of words, Mark is free to engage words in a novel arrangement. In depth, textuality emancipates or alienates from oral necessities. In the words of Walter J. Ong, "writing and print isolate the individual or, if you prefer, liberate him from the tribe."[61] Released from direct audience controls and censorship, "detribalized"[62] as it were from oral formularity and redundancy, Mark the writer is at liberty to shape, arrange, and manipulate words in a manner unheard of in synoptic orality. Operating from a literary distance and hiding his personal identity behind the text, he binds oral pluralism into the new medium of textuality and organizes discreteness into narrative sequentiality. This is how a novel, systematic composition has emerged, governed not by the remembered stories, but by a single organizing intellect in control over them. This less mnemonic, more consciously plotted gospel raises a new world into being and implements a new state of awareness.

The point is reached at last where homage must be paid to the fictionalizing power of textuality. The case for it was recently restated by the literary critic Frank Kermode in close reference to the gospel of Mark.[63] Kermode's critique turned on linguistic positivism, "the gratuitous assumption that a direct relation exists between a sign and a corresponding object 'in reality'."[64] Our reflections on Mark's oral legacy and Markan textuality can only serve to underwrite his argument. The best chance orality had to preserve the Jesus of history was to remember his very own words. Whatever he himself had not entrusted to the speaking mode, that is, most items of his biography, someone else had to submit to the demands of spoken and remembered language. Textuality for Mark solves the problem of mental storage by releasing words from their struggle for survival. Loosened from speaking contexts, words are absorbed into linguistic contextuality and made to partake in the construction of the textually mediated world. Now it is the written medium, not a special contract with the Jesus of history, that reorients oral consciousness. "Bold invention is the prerogative of writers."[65] The implosion and linearization of oral pluralism, the construction of a comprehensive journey, the valorized spatial world, the narration of the kingdom's story, all that gives sayings, parables, stories, and episodes a semblance of plot, sequentiality, and followability is the achievement of the new technique of writing. Hence the conclusion that the gospel's constructive unity is built on the fictionalizing power of textuality.

Perhaps this notion of linguistic license contracted by the written medium may seem excessive. Did Mark not merely undertake a shift in allegiance from hearers to readers, and did the latter not make different though no less constricting demands on him? To this one must respond by reiterating a crucial difference between the composition of oral and written words: the absence or presence of the recipients of the message from its production. Even if the gospel was meant to be recited or read aloud, its writing was nonetheless done in the absence of the hearers. Whatever their reactions to the recited text, they did not participate in its written formation, and they were hardly in a position to alter it. This substantial lessening of audience interference permits the writer to effectively control both the text and its readers.

Who is Mark, donor of the text and hiding behind it, and to whom does he write? Undoubtedly he wishes to narrate a story, but must his story be tailor-made for a historically identifiable community so that its social setting would be mirrored in the story? While hearers and their social world belong "to the oral as its hermeneutical context, inseparably with the linguistic 'meaning' of the linguistic work, such an aid to understanding disappears in the case of the written."[66] Because social contextuality has ceased to be an immediate participant in the linguisticality of texts, it can be derived from the gospel only with extreme caution. This is not to deny that texts are culturally conditioned and related to history. But reconstructions of precise communal histories based on gospel texts erroneously assume an unbroken continuity in the function of contextuality from the oral to the written medium. Erhardt

Güttgemanns has alerted us to this persistent flaw in New Testament scholarship,[67] but our attempts at reconstructing gospel communities continue unabated in Markan and especially Johannine studies. What is there to stop Mark from casting his recipients into fictional roles and walking them through his narrative world? If, in short, Mark's written words are capable of plotting a narrative of Jesus' life and death, could they not effect a fictionalizing of audience or readers as well?[68]

Irony plays its crafty game with the new gospel composition. The text, although a written artifact, conveys a sense of "realism" that in its total impact exceeds that of orality. More to the point, this "realism" is the logical outcome of the manufactured text. Written language, exempt from concerns for self-preservation, is allowed full play. It can live and create out of its interior potential. By keeping recipients at arm's length, textuality is in a position to engage in a reflective construction of the life and death of Jesus. The resultant "realism" is thus not built—as far as is known—on a newly secured proximity to Jesus' history, but on a textually enforced distance from audience and oral speech commitments. Linearization on a large narrative scale strengthens oral vividness.[69] The textually produced space of intersignification allows characters not only to act, but to interact. This gives them psychological depth in excess of oral typecasting. The plotted narrative accords meaning, purpose, and goal to Jesus, all of which appeals to our sense of "realism." And yet, what looks "real" and, we think, less contrived, is in truth the brilliant result of textual plotting.

It is difficult to overstate the success of gospel textuality, its "benign deceit"[70] in seducing readers into taking fact-likeness for factuality. Indeed, so persuasive has the gospel's textuality been in drawing attention away from itself and toward what it has written, that it has until recently escaped inquiry into its own techniques and credentials. Hence, Christian theology's unending zeal to ground faith in a Jesus of history, who is, on dubious principles of authenticity and without serious linguistic reflection, blithely derived from written words.[71] Undoubtedly, Mark aimed at recovering the sacred actuality of Jesus. But his is a *textually* recovered actuality. Orality has already shaped the life of Jesus according to the needs and requirements of its medium. Textuality in turn persists in arranging oral forms to fit its own medium preoccupations. Writing always entails a rewriting of worlds.[72] The result of Markan textuality is thus not a copy of the Jesus of history, but rather an artistic recreation. Art, one remembers, does not produce but illuminate nature, not copy but re-create actuality.[73]

THE GOSPEL AS WRITTEN PARABLE

If the gospel is viewed as having arisen out of a process of decontextualization, transformation, and reintegration, we have thereby sketched the history of its textuality but not its new literary identity. The issue here is the gospel's constructive unity. Into what literary form did Mark organize language? What is the formal, artistic principle determining the linguistic gestalt of the gospel? The conventional designation for this concern is genre criticism.[74] Its objective is to probe authorial compliance with the larger, transpersonal imperatives of literary culture. One may in fairness say that genres are hardly ever fully objectified in any given text. The purpose of genre definitions ought not to be the positing of immutable verities and classical certainties, but experimentation with heuristic tools that allow a holistic grasp of the gospel or any other text. If in the following we find fault with four prominent genre models—tragedy, comedy, aretalogy, biography—we do not wish to dismiss their usefulness altogether. Our critique notwithstanding, each model casts the gospel in a different, illuminating perspective.

Resuming earlier studies on tragic aspects in Mark,[75] Gilbert G. Bilezikian has developed a cogent argument for the gospel's affinity with Greek tragedy.[76] For Mark "action represents the substance of the gospel,"[77] and the dynamic progression of action is played out according to the classic pattern of complication-crisis-denouement. In this Mark is said to have followed, by cultural osmosis more than by conscious design, the structural formula recommended by Aristotle for tragic composition in his *Poetics*.[78] The first half of the gospel produces complication, with the disciples' blindness being "the most pathetic aspect."[79] Peter's confession near Caesarea Philippi marks the critical turning point, and the remainder of the story narrates the hero's downfall. There is much to be said for Bilezikian's thesis that the dramatic movement is sustained by the disciples' deteriorating relations with Jesus, but it is not entirely clear how the gospel's revolutionary dynamics can be built on Aristotle's plot structure. Amos Wilder's often quoted caveat that "Greek and traditional humanistic categories are inadequate as measuring rods"[80] for early Christian literature may not be valid in all instances, but it does apply to Mark's gospel. All canonical gospels contain an element that "rebels against order imposed from the past. This element is most visible in Mark."[81] If Mark is the gospel that dramatizes renewal of the world by subverting its foundation, is it amenable to the formal category of Greek tragedy? Are we blunting the shock effects emanating from the gospel by

117

dignifying it with a cultured, classical designation? How does the gospel's open-endedness conform with the formal closure of Greek tragedy? Does Mark intend "to proclaim the universal relevance of a very Jewish story by telling it in the manner of a Greek tragedy,"[82] or does he perhaps narrate his Jewish story in a form more directly compatible with Jesus the Jew?

Dan O. Via has offered the most penetrating genre analysis of the gospel up to date.[83] While Bilezikian followed the narrative sequence, Via deconstructed the text into a series of textemes. Examining a variety of structural relations of actions, functions, and sequels, he finds the paradigm of death and resurrection, the rhythm of upset and recovery, reverberating on all levels. Since death and resurrection stand at the heart of the comic form, comedy is the generic source from which the text is generated. It is out of a special sense of appreciation for Via's work that the following five issues are being raised. First, if one is dedicated to the proposition that "the New Testament kerygma [sic] belongs to the structure of comedy,"[84] which, moreover, is said to be "a deep, generative structure of the human mind,"[85] why go through the motion and recapitulate the case for Mark? Second, Via admits that "Mark does not really exploit the comic side of these patterns."[86] While "the comic genre . . . generated the Gospel of Mark,"[87] the text in fact belongs to the genre of "tragicomedy" in the modern sense. Tragicomedy, apart from maintaining the life-through-death pattern of comedy, emphasizes the global presence of death and confronts us with uncertainties about Jesus, and, one might add, about ourselves.[88] If tragicomedy is what really matters, is there not a more appropriate category that takes account of Markan uncertainties, metaphorical language, and reversal of roles and expectations? Third, in reflecting on Rom. 9:30ff., a Pauline discourse on righteousness through faith versus righteousness by law, Via suggests that "the narrative form is tragic, the last word being Israel's disobedience."[89] Yet what does this say for Mark who dares end his narrative with the aborted transmission of the message of life? That ending cannot be taken lightly as regards the gospel's genre. Fourth, one wonders whether Via has satisfactorily answered the crucial question with which he has challenged other scholars: why did Mark produce a narrative? To say that the gospel "came to be written because . . . the death and resurrection of Jesus reverberated in the mind of Mark and activated the comic genre,"[90] begs the question. If one believes, as Via does, that both Mark and Paul belong to comedy,[91] why then did this same comic genre in one case produce a narrative, but not in the other? Fifth, there is the question of the application of structuralism to biblical texts, an issue that admittedly deserves a more detailed response than is possible here. Herbert Schneidau, resuming Ricoeur's question about structuralist interpretation of biblical texts, has proposed a differentiation between cybernetic and kerygmatic language.[92] Cybernetic, mythic, and frequently oral communication confirms and repeats structure. Kerygmatic and frequently biblical communication disconfirms and subverts structure.[93] Structuralist interpretation is most aptly applied to cybernetic language and least successfully to kerygmatic language. In Mark's case one wonders whether a text born out of linguistic disorientation and reflecting a deep sense of alienation is adequately grasped by fitting it into stable grids and schemata.

In a joint project undertaken by Moses Hadas and Morton Smith the gospel was found to conform to the ancient genre of aretalogy.[94] The latter was broadly defined as a form of religious biography in which the hero is characterized by the gift of miracle working and impressive teaching, and often suffers martyrdom at the hands of a tyrant. For two reasons New Testament scholars have been reluctant to endorse this proposal. First, the very existence of a literary genre of aretalogy is subject to doubt. As Howard C. Kee has noted,[95] the paradigmatic model of aretalogy, that is, Plato's portrait of Socrates, lacks miracles, and the most fully developed aretalogy, Philostratus's *Life of Apollonius of Tyana*, is without martyrdom.[96] Second, the inclination among New Testament scholars was and is to apply the designation of aretalogy strictly to a source of miracle stories, usually understood to have been written for the purpose of religious propaganda. It is in this restricted sense that Gerd Theissen has recently sought to find the generic key to Mark in aretalogy.[97] He proceeded from the thesis that acclamation is the intended goal of all synoptic miracle stories. This element, he observed, is either absent in Mark or overshadowed by misunderstanding and secrecy. The pre-passion narrative, largely made up of a string of exclusive miracle stories, is thus put in a state of suspense from which it is not released until the centurion's Son of God confession (15:39). It is his climactic confession that rounds out the aretalogical overarching structure (*aretalogischer Spannungsbogen*) and generates an inclusive aretalogical composition. One may wonder, however, whether the miracles are allowed to function as an overarching structure, if one observes with Paul Achtemeier,[98] Hans D. Betz,[99] Helmut Koester,[100] and James Robinson[101] that they have been subjected to critical transformations.[102] In the oral-textual perspectives we have been developing, the issue may be formulated from a different angle. If the process of textualization injects a controversial, metaphorical element into the heroic stories, sharpens the mythoclastic function of the didactic stories, and, as we shall see, introduces a parabolic hermeneutic, one must question whether this thrust toward the mythoclastic and parabolic is compatible with the elevation of the most heroic and mythopoetic form to the position of genre determinant.

Johannes Weiss, one of the first scholars to propose the gospel's relation to the genre of ancient biographies,[103] has at the same time articulated two major objections: the authorial absence from the text, and the lack of birth and childhood stories.[104] Similar questions must be raised in regard to Clyde W. Votaw's more elaborate effort to link the gospel with the biographical accounts of philosopher teachers such as Socrates, or miracle workers like Apollonius.[105] For Philip L. Shuler the gospel is an encomium,[106] a laudatory biographical genre, the principal purpose of which was "to present a portrait of a person in such a way as either to call forth praise from an audience or to persuade an audience of his praiseworthiness."[107] While there is what Shuler calls a *bios factor* present in Mark, encomium is too genteel and bland a category. Charles H. Talbert has come closer to Mark's generic identity by defining the gospel as a biography that aims "to dispel a false image of the teacher and to provide a true model to follow."[108] But the manner of dispelling a traditional model of Jesus and the precise mechanism of reverting roles and expectations moves this gospel toward the parabolic.

Recently a number of scholars have detected a parabolic dimension in the gospels, and especially in Mark. In the latest edition of *Traditions in Conflict,* Theodore Weeden noted cryptically that "the evangelist intended a parabolic effect."[109] Frederick H. Borsch in a popular book on gospels and gospel traditions concluded that the narration of Jesus' life and death "became the consummate parable of the new faith."[110] Robert Tannehill brilliantly traced the narrative role of the disciples in Mark, in effect offering a parabolic interpretation.[111] John R. Donahue, S. J., deserves major credit for a creative reading of the gospel as "a narrative parable of the meaning of the life and death of Jesus."[112] He clearly spelled out the connection between the gospel's leading motif of the mystery of the kingdom and its parabolic nature: it is by shaking conventions and shattering expectations that the gospel beckons toward the mystery of the kingdom of God. John Dominic Crossan, reflecting on the transition from Jesus to tradition, suggested that Rudolf Bultmann's thesis of the Proclaimer becoming the Proclaimed ought to be redefined in terms of the parabler becoming parable: "Jesus announced the kingdom of God in parables, but the primitive church announced Jesus as Christ, the Parable of God."[113] In this connection Crossan specified my own reading of Mark 1–13 in *The Kingdom in Mark* as a genuinely parabolic one.[114] Ricoeur, as noted in an epigraph to this chapter, has wondered whether the role of the exclusive parable in the space of intersignification may not contribute to the meaning of gospel as parable.[115] In a comprehensive structuralist analysis of the spatial world of Mark, Elizabeth Struthers Malbon argued that the narrative was a parable-myth, powered by the reversal of expectations.[116] Amos Wilder long ago sensed that "some of the parables present the larger story in microcosm."[117] Today the matter is expressed more forthrightly, as exemplified by Schneidau, who suggested that the gospels, insofar as they emphasize the difficulty of receiving their message, share the kerygmatic function of parabolic speech: "The parable, therefore, is the typifying form of the Gospel."[118]

It is curious that none of the above scholars, the present writer included, have bothered to consult the gospel about *its* thought on parables. As is well known, the evangelist develops what has been called a parable theory in chapter 4.[119] How is Mark's thesis related to contemporary parable hermeneutics, and what, if anything, does it contribute to the gospel's generic identity?

The intriguingly difficult verses 4:10–12 contain the germ of Mark's so-called parabolic theory. In response to a question concerning parables Jesus states that "to those about him with the twelve" (4:10; au. trans.) the mystery has been given that pertains to the kingdom of God, whereas "to those on the outside" (*ekeinois de tois exō*) everything is "in parables" (4:11). One immediately observes an insider-outsider dichotomy. Insiders are admitted into the mystery of the kingdom, while outsiders are barred from it. The latter are depicted as people who, while seeing and hearing, nonetheless are lacking in comprehension (4:12). Theirs is a situation of everything being "in parables." As often observed, the meaning of parables here has been slanted toward riddle. Parabolic speech, on this riddling notion, casts hearers into outsiders by withholding understanding from them.

This, then, is the heart of the so-called theory on parables: parabolic discourse is the carrier of a cryptic message that casts to the outside those who cannot fathom it, while confirming as insiders those to whom it is revealed.

How did Mark arrive at a parabolic hermeneutic that espouses esoteric teaching with deeply alienating effects? The observation that he derived it from Isa. 6:9–10 (= Mark 4:12) merely begs the question. One must rather ask what encouraged him to link Isaiah's pessimistic verdict about those who see but don't perceive, hear but don't understand, with parabolic discourse.

John C. Meagher has recently explained the Markan theme of esoteric teaching in parables as a strategic device aimed at overcoming contradictions that arose between Jesus' own message and its history of tradition.[120] The historical Jesus, he suggested, was generally known to have spoken parables for the purpose of illumination, not obscuration. After the resurrection, when the tradition about him conflicted with his own pre-resurrectional message, parables were turned into riddles. Consequently, Jesus could be said to have preached all that tradition reported about him because he had taught in a form accessible only to a few, and opaque to others. Esoteric teaching is therefore a continuity-affirming device that reconciles Jesus with the post-resurrectional situation. Meagher's thesis is predicated on two major assumptions that are subject to question. There is first the issue of parabolic hermeneutics. The author states flatly: "Parables are normally instruments of clarification, illustration, illumination, not obfuscation."[121] Parable scholarship has learned much since Adolf Jülicher, above all that parables are not "normally" means of clarification. Whence this confidence in a Jesus who was "generally known to have taught openly and clearly"?[122] There is secondly the issue of Mark's distortion of parables, his redactional "clumsiness," and tradition-historical conclusions drawn from it. That the evangelist has misconstrued the linguisticality of parables is a charge running through much of nineteenth and twentieth century Markan scholarship, but it is, we will show below, unacceptable. Meagher issues an important warning against overestimating the evangelist's literary skills and ambitions. Mark is not the sterling literary genius he appears to be in some recent scholarship. Still, "clumsiness" is hardly an acceptable intellectual category for approaching a text. What is more, to proceed from redactional "clumsiness" toward sorting out stages in the tradition is hazardous in the extreme. The proposition that esoteric teaching served to conform Jesus with conflicting traditions about him remains as unconvincing as the remarkably similar theory by William Wrede who suggested that the Messianic Secret was meant to reconcile an unmessianic life of Jesus with a messianizing tradition.[123] The more obvious linguistic consideration is to associate esoteric teaching in parables not with redactional clumsiness, but with the very hermeneutics of parables.

Contemporary parable scholarship is in a position to appreciate the Markan hermeneutic of esoteric teaching and parabolic alienation, and the corresponding casting of audience into insider and outsider roles. We have noted in the preceding chapter that it is the nature of parables to deviate from literal meaning, evade the event character of oral speech, suspend meaning, and disrupt oral synthesis—all features which complicate and impede the hermeneutical process.[124] In emphasizing the riddling, alienating function of parables, Mark has thus seized upon a hermeneutical potential inherent in parabolic discourse. By the same token, the very parabolic speech that delays comprehension and relegates hearers to the outside may strengthen oral synthesis and locate hearers on the inside. As also noted before, parabolist and audience partake in social contextuality that can facilitate an instantaneous transaction of the hermeneutical process.[125] In that case, speaker and hearers have come to share inside knowledge hidden from those who have now become outsiders. The parable functions as carrier of secrecy. In emphasizing the initiation of the twelve into insider roles, Mark has thus again exploited inherent parabolic potentiality.

We have arrived at an important preliminary conclusion. The features that constitute Mark's so-called parable theory—esoteric teaching and corresponding alienation, and the complementary roles of insiders versus outsiders—reflect genuine implications of parabolic discourse. What we find is neither clumsiness nor misunderstanding, but a developed hermeneutical reflection on parabolic language. Madeleine Boucher has expressed the matter most perceptively:

> The charge made in much of the scholarly literature since the nineteenth century that Mark has distorted the parable as a verbal construct is simply unfounded. Mark has not taken clear, straightforward speech, the parable, and transformed it into obscure, esoteric speech, the allegory. He has rather taken what is essential to the parable, the double-meaning effect, and made it the starting point of a theological theme concerning the audience's resistance to hearing the word.[126]

Mark is not, of course, a philosopher of language who lectures on a theory of parables. Rather he narrates a story that displays notable sensitivity toward parabolic hermeneutic. The precise question, then, is that of the narrative implications of the so-called parable theory. Jesus' parabolic discourse, it is made very clear to the disciples, concerns the kingdom of God (4:10–11). The mystery of the kingdom draws parabolic speech. What is noteworthy at this point is that the theme of kingdom is not exclusively tied to, let alone exhausted by, exclusive parabolic speech. Mark's whole gospel is the proclamation of the kingdom of God. Initiation into the mystery of the kingdom requires that the disciples follow Jesus' way to the very end. But if consciousness of the kingdom is inseparable from the way of Jesus, all aspects of his life and death are pointers toward the kingdom's mystery. The Markan space of intersignification, as noted above, slants individual forms of speech toward the metaphorical, and produces, we now conclude, a thoroughgoing metaphorical text. Mark's gospel in its entirety points beyond itself to the mystery of the kingdom of God. The first criterion for parable, that of metaphoricity, is thereby met by the gospel of Mark.

The metaphorical character of the text may induce us to take seriously statements that tend to extend the concept of the parabolic across the gospel's narrative. When in Mark 4:34 it is narrated that Jesus "did not speak to them without a parable, but privately to his own disciples he explained everything (*panta*)," one must not immediately dismiss this as a redactional oversight. It could well mean that everything Jesus says signifies the kingdom's mystery to which the disciples are privileged insiders. There is Markan justification for stretching parabolic dynamics across the gospel. When, moreover, it is argued that to ousiders "everything (*ta panta*) is in parables" (4:11), the concept of the parabolic and the creation of outsiders is applied once again to the whole story.[127] At this point it can no longer be claimed that Mark argues a particular theory on parables. In effect, what is articulated is the parabolic nature of Jesus' story. Jesus' life and death, as narrated by Mark, transpires according to the hermeneutical process of parable. It functions *ad malam partem* as an impenetrable riddle, and *ad bonam partem* as revelation into the mystery of the kingdom of God.

In turning to the second criterion for parable, that of *extravagance*, one suspects a connection with the insider-outsider dichotomy. At least this feature is the principal narrative candidate in Mark 4:10–12. For the most part, Markan scholarship observed the placement of the disciples onto the inside track, and the author's peculiar reluctance, or inability, to carry out their appointed narrative role. Meagher, for example, observed that the gospel "tends to have the crowds see and hear quite well, while the inner circle has difficulties—nearly the opposite of the policy strangely advanced in chapter 4."[128] Not only has Mark mistakenly connected esoteric teaching with parables, but esoteric teaching is itself "curiously inconsistent with the Gospel at large."[129] In the same vein, Heikki Räisänen proposed that Markan redaction deliberately foiled a parabolic interpretation that came to him from tradition.[130] Since crowds, apparently the outsiders, are depicted in a neutral, or even enlightened posture, whereas the insiders' role of the twelve is virtually turned into its opposite, Räisänen concluded that Mark adopted a parable theory (4:10–12) for the purpose of relativizing it via the thoroughgoing motif of discipleship misunderstanding.[131]

It is, however, Räisänen, Meagher, and many other scholars—not Mark —who have prevented the parabolic story from running its due course.

Insensitive to parabolic extravagance and obsessed with the logic of "normality," they could not see the wood for the trees. Indeed the very feature that they considered out of step with parabolic logic, the rapidly increasing blindness of the inner circle, is the key to the parabolic narrative. If Mark is as rigorous a parabolic thinker as we claim, he cannot narrate the insider-outsider syndrome in such a way as to allow easy and direct identification. The insider-outsider dichotomy, we noted, is a constitutive feature of parabolic language. But a genuinely parabolic story aims at defying the structure of expectancy, even the expected structure of parable! That it is the nature of the parable to turn on itself was keenly discerned by Schneidau:

> A parable is always a parable or, more exactly, the existence of parables is itself a parable. Whatever its messages and whatever utilitarian purposes these suggest and incur, the form itself enacts a further parabolic dramatization of the evanescent nature of any "message," or more precisely, of the uncertainties of interpreting it.[132]

Lest parable be converted into myth, its very own logic requires a parabolic dramatization.

If one recognizes in Jesus' announcement of the kingdom (1:14–15) the high point of the introduction, then the call of the first disciples (1:16–20) marks the formal opening of the narrative proper.[133] With Jesus' calling upon the four to follow him, the dominant theme of discipleship gets under way, and a structure of expectancy is initiated. The subsequent story strengthens this expectancy by letting those who follow Jesus be privy to prominent aspects of his mission of the kingdom: exorcism and teaching with authority (1:21–28), healing (1:29–31), the purpose of journeying (1:38), the shattering novelty of the mission and its collision with a world of traditional values (2:13–17, 18–22, 23–28), as well as the ecumenical proportion of the movement (3:7–12). In an act of far-reaching significance Jesus "makes" the twelve, singling out three by special names (3:13–19). The twelve and especially the three have been appointed to official leadership. Since the three were among the first to be called, the structure of expectancy is reinforced. They can be expected to follow Jesus and to absorb the information indispensable for their functioning as apostolic representatives. There is one crack in the structure of expectancy: Judas is marked as traitor (3:19).

With apostolic leadership firmly established, the author brings the parabolic dimension into narrative focus. The first time Jesus speaks "in parables" (3:23), he does so in condemnation of the Jerusalem scribes who accused him of demonic possession. When the relatives, who consider Jesus mentally deranged, arrive (3:20–21), he relegates them to the outside by identifying those inside the house sitting "about him" (3:34: *tous peri auton*) as the true family of God. By interconnecting the two episodes (3:20–22, 23–30, 31–35), the author strengthens the view that inasmuch as scribes and blood relatives are united in their objection to Jesus, both are cast to the outside. Hence, the very first reference to parabolic speech sets into motion the insider-outsider dichotomy.

No sooner is the insider-outsider scheme confirmed than "those about him [4:10: *hoi peri auton*] with the twelve" are declared participants in the mystery of the kingdom of God (4:11a). In addition to delegating the twelve to the inside, Jesus articulates a most carefully drawn up characterization of the outsiders (4:11b–12). With this placement of the twelve into the role of privileged insiders, the structure of expectancy is completed. But at that very point the insider-outsider scheme is also disclosed as being part of a parabolic process. Indeed, no sooner are the twelve confirmed as insiders over against outsiders than Jesus questions their grasp of parables (4:13). How does lack of comprehension conform with their insider position? The answer is that the very moment the structure of expectancy has been completed and shown to be subject to parabolic logic, the parabolic reversal of roles is ever so slightly set into motion.

Subsequently (4:35–8:21) "Mark shows how Jesus unites the community in a sacrificial existence."[134] In a series of boat trips the Markan Jesus opens the frontier toward Gentile land, connecting it with Jewish land. Two pivotal feedings (6:34–44; 8:1–10) are designed to initiate the disciples into the Jewish-Gentile fellowship. But the logic of his voyages finds no congenial response among them. On the first voyage (4:35–41) they become panic-stricken. Both purpose and goal of the trip elude their comprehension. During the second trip to the Gentiles (6:45–52) they once again fail to overcome adversity and to reach the shore on their own strength. Thereafter their condition is described as one of ignorance about the loaves (= the first feeding) and of hardness of heart (6:52). The motif of ignorance replays an outsider characteristic (6:52: *ou gar synhēkan;* 4:12: *mē synhiōsin*), and hardness of heart, applied earlier and later to opponents (3:5; 10:5), reinforces the impression of the disciples' drift toward the outside. On the final voyage (8:13–21) the decisive step is taken of conferring the entire catalogue of outsider characteristics upon the disciples: lack of understanding, hardness of heart, blindness and deafness (8:17–18). At this point, the systematic application of all outsider characteristics to the insiders has resulted in the overthrow of the structure of expectancy.

But is the reversal sustained? Jesus' final question, "Do you not yet understand?" (8:21) leaves the door open for repentance, a distinct possibility for outsiders (4:12c). Is the gospel narrating a genuinely parabolic story, or does it defuse the paradox and reconcile us with the initial narrative expectation?

Jesus' threefold passion predictions (Mark 8:31; 9:31; 10:33–34) emphasize the irrefutability of his impending death. But as the necessity of the Son of man's suffering is accentuated, so is the failure of the disciples to adopt his model of discipleship. Each passion pronouncement is followed by a glaring case of misconception on the part of the disciples. Peter, the leader, stands exposed as Jesus' satanic adversary (8:33); the disciples are convicted of lack of perception and fear (9:32); James and John, among the first to be called, are found asking for positions of power (10:35–46). The disciples' failure to come to terms with Jesus' suffering is compounded by the apparent obtuseness of the triumvirate regarding the resurrection (9:9–10). A false sense of presence makes Peter, together with James and John, misjudge the proleptic nature of the transfiguration (9:2–8). Unable to perform an exorcism, the disciples default on an obligation that they had earlier been able to discharge successfully (9:14–29; cf. 6:7, 13). Contrary to Jesus' wishes, they obstruct the work of an accomplished exorcist (9:38–41) and rebuke children (10:13–16; cf. 9:36–37). The author, it seems, spares little effort to sharpen the conflict between Jesus and the disciples, and to consolidate thereby the outsider position of the latter. Seeing they do not see, and hearing they do not hear. At the same time, the author has them thoroughly prepared for the Jerusalem events, and he sustains their relation with Jesus into the passion. The reader's (or hearer's) expectation for a final turnabout is thus very much kept alive.

The last time Jesus speaks "in parable," he addresses the parable of the *Wicked Tenants* (12:1–11) to the temple authorities (11:27; 12:12). As his first speech "in parables" (3:23) was designed to set into motion the insider-outsider dynamic, so does his last parable speech likewise cast hearers to the outside. The tenants of the vineyard are turned outside, while the beloved Son, who was killed and thrown outside (12:8), becomes the insider. The implication of the parable is grasped by the temple authorities, the perceived insiders. Although the exclusive parable does not implicate the disciples, it is made to function according to the parabolic logic of the gospel's inclusive parabolic narrative.

In the Jerusalem speech (13:5b–37) Jesus initiates the very disciples whom he had called first into the meaning of the final events. Tannehill has recently suggested that the speech "anticipates a continuing role for the disciples beyond the disaster of chapter 14,"[135] and Norman Petersen has gone even further by stating that Peter, James, John, and Andrew "will be representatives of Jesus up to the time of the parousia."[136] This seems a curious argument to come from literary critics. How can one make assumptions about the role of narrativized persons in the world outside the narrative world without letting the story come to its completion? Petersen correctly states that in accord with the Markan story line "we are compelled to assume that they [the disciples] understood it [Jesus' speech] no more than anything else."[137] Unless there is forthcoming evidence to the contrary, Jesus explains everything to the disciples, who hear but fail to perceive. That there is "lack of any mention"[138] of the disciples' response to the speech is, however, not quite correct. Tannehill points to known connections between the eschatological speech and passion motifs.[139] The speech climaxes in the admonition to endurance (13:13) and vigilance (13:33–37). These are virtues required during passion. But when in the Gethsemane story (14:32–42) the motif cluster of waking-coming-finding-sleeping is resumed, the disciples fail to wake, and sleep instead. Despite Jesus' speech, they consolidate their role as outsiders, consistently undermining hope that they could function as future leaders. Nor can it be said that Jesus' words must come to pass or else his authority is invalidated. In the story world, his words fall on the deaf ears of the disciples; they are disobeyed, not disconfirmed. The hardness of heart of the inner circle does not discredit the authority of Jesus. Nor does Jesus ever promise the actualization of a reunion with the disciples. He merely promises to go ahead of them to Galilee (14:28). They have been informed of the return to Galilee, as they were told everything else pertaining to the mystery of the kingdom. It is up to the disciples to follow the leader and his words.

If the hopes of the gospel's recipients have been kept alive into the passion story, it is there that they are decisively crushed. Far from experiencing a change of heart, the disciples, under the leadership of Peter, play out their roles of outsiders to the bitter end. Peter contradicts Jesus' prediction of the discipleship failure (14:26–29), all the disciples promise to suffer with Jesus (14:30–31), the triumvirate falters at Gethsemane (14:32–42), one disciple betrays Jesus (14:10–11, 43–46), all desert him at the moment of arrest (14:50), and Peter, the last hope, denies Jesus while the latter makes his fateful confession before the high priest (14:53–72).

After the disappearance of the disciples the three women act as vital intermediaries between Jesus and the disciples (16:1–8). This one last time hopes are aroused that the women might repair the broken connection, transmit the message of life, and facilitate the disciples' rehabilitation. But inasmuch as the narrative kindles such hopes, it does everything to wreck them. While the women are indeed commissioned to carry the message of the resurrection to the disciples, they fail to deliver it. Overcome by trembling, astonishment, and fear, they flee (16:8: *ephygon*), as earlier all the disciples had fled (14:50: *ephygon pantes*). As a result, the disciples, who had been absent at the crucifixion and have remained ignorant of the resurrection, never learn that the signal has been given for the reunion with the resurrected one. They are thereby effectively eliminated as apostolic representatives of the risen Lord. With their demise the structure of expectancy is finally and irrevocably reversed, and the narrative has found its proper, parabolic ending. If it is assumed that the "projected meeting in Galilee is the only moment of all those in Mark's narrative world when the disciples could come out from under the cloud of ignorance—when the plot of Mark's narrative could be resolved,"[140] one has dulled the gospel's extravagance and trivialized its oddness. One has, in short, remained undisturbed by parabolic disorientation. The obvious conclusion to be drawn from the open ending is that it is meant to be inconclusive. "The parable," Robert W. Funk states flatly, "does not have a conclusion."[141] This is so because the parable, far from inviting us to settle for familiar, classical perspectives, shocks us out of them toward a new and unfamiliar logic.

TEXTUALITY AS AGENT OF ALIENATION AND LIBERATION

At crucial points of linguistic transit the dynamics of the medium enter into the recorded message to an extent that medium and message become intersecting phenomena. The reasons are intricate and far from being fully explored. But in a general sense, this interpenetration of narrative and medium features is intelligible. When a tradition that was contingent on and grew up in oral speech shifts its mode of communication, it may have to argue its linguistic existence and assignment vis-à-vis the conventional medium and its authorities. One may thus find inscribed in the newly mediated story a rationale for its own medium history. In the early synoptic tradition the oral medium had been sanctioned by Jesus himself. His was a message inherently bound up with speaking. Prophetic and apostolic speakers carried his words and words about him to audiences. In this predominantly oral milieu a writer's reflexive and distancing appropriation of Jesus' words and deeds marked a linguistic and theological departure that may have required justification. It is for this reason that Mark's gospel is not merely concerned with the life and death of Jesus, but also with writing about it.

Mark as a writer, we saw, had to maneuver himself into an outside position vis-à-vis oral tradition. He could not have plotted the gospel without exercising reserve toward the oral metaphysics of presence and contemporizing. Distance from orality gave him the new perspective. Characteristically, the story he wrote favored the outsider and narrated the epistemological paradox of proximity versus distance. There is a tendency for the power of perception of at least some characters to increase in proportion to their distance from Jesus. Those within constant earshot of the teacher do not hear well. Crowds, which do not partake in Jesus' traveling, tend to have a better comprehension. Outsiders such as the Greek woman (6:24–30) and a blind man (10:46–52) become models of faith and discipleship. The Roman centurion, distanced to an extreme by his discharge of duty, nonetheless more clearly than anyone else in the narrative perceives Jesus as the Son of God. His, not Peter's, is the true confession of Jesus the Crucified. Jesus himself is an outsider who contradicts his own tradition and the expectations of his followers, and in the end is thrown out of the vineyard. That the outsider is a secret insider is both a medium experience and the narrative truth of the gospel.

Mark, the writer, chose the written medium, not to recapitulate oral messages, but to transform them. By this logic, his literary production is inherently linked with alienation from living words. Notably, the story that came to be written down is dominated by a sense of distancing. But it is an alienation hardly comprehensible as apocalyptic world-weariness or gnostic aloofness. Mark's estrangement is from the standard-bearers of oral transmission. In narrating the exclusion of family, the rejection of the prophets, the growing and incorrigible incomprehension of the disciples, and in making the story culminate in the definitive rupture of oral communication, the author has narrated the justification for his own written narrative.[142] The story self-authenticates its new, redemptive medium over against the prevailing authorities of oral transmission. It is a story in which its own medium history is deeply implicated.

Technically, Mark dissociates heterogeneous units from live contextuality, reconstructing them into a new unity. The textual medium alters oral language and its norms, and thereby reconceptualizes the way one perceives christology, the kingdom, and authority. Mark's story reorients basic assumptions held about Jesus and his message. It disconnects the kingdom from central place and traditional expectations, and projects a vision of its incomparable mystery. It is no longer an orally present actuality, but is now connected with the textual recapitulation of Jesus' life and above all death. The gospel's Jesus does not enter into mimetic relations with any oral model. He speaks with unprecedented authority.

Markan christology even defies the scheme of promise and fulfillment.[143] The redemption Jesus offers is at odds with the anticipations of friend and foe alike. The freedom he gives is inseparable from dislocations. The depth of alienation that dominates this gospel is in direct proportion to the profundity of its revelation. That "new wine is for fresh wineskins" (2:22) is technically Mark's medium experience and dramatically his deep theological conviction.

Mark, the storywriter, suffers and accomplishes the death of living words for the purpose of inaugurating the life of textuality. Linguistic and narrative perspectives concur in acknowledging death as the key to life. The protagonist's arduous and paradoxical journey from life to death to life again may thus be conceived as a narrative manifestation of the medium experience of drifting away from oral life in the exercise of writing for life.

For a language that asserts itself by distanciation from the received mode of communication, parable is the ultimate metaphor. The parabolic strategy of reorientation by disorientation that marks this gospel's linguistic genesis has likewise etched itself into its story line. Medium and message are connected by a compelling parabolic logic. It is this logic that shapes the gospel's narrative, disorienting away from oral authorities and reorienting toward the textually recaptured Jesus, and all along gesturing toward the mystery of God's kingdom. There is a deep sense, therefore, in which the gospel as a novel language project narrates the story of its own story.

NOTES

1. Jack Goody and Ian Watt, "The Consequences of Literacy," in *Literacy in Traditional Societies,* ed. Jack Goody (New York and Cambridge: Cambridge University Press, 1968), p. 29.

2. See Paul Ricoeur's essay, "What is a Text? Explanation and Interpretation," in *Mythic-Symbolic Language and Philosophical Anthropology,* by David M. Rasmussen (The Hague: Martinus Nijhoff, 1971), p. 136.

3. Paul Ricoeur, *Interpretation Theory: Discourse and the Surplus of Meaning* (Fort Worth: Texas Christian University Press, 1976), p. 35.

4. Goody and Watt, "Consequences," pp. 27–34.

5. Lukas Vischer, "Die Rechtfertigung der Schriftstellerei in der Alten Kirche," *TZ* 12 (1956): 320–36; cf. also Plato, *Phaedrus,* 274e–277a.

6. Helmut Koester, *Synoptische Überlieferung bei den Apostolischen Vätern,* TU 65 (Berlin: Akademie-Verlag, 1957).

7. Ibid., pp. 122–23, 257–67.

8. Chapter 2, p. 75.

9. James Nohrnberg, "On Literature and the Bible," *Centrum* 2 (1974): 23.

10. Joachim Gnilka, *Das Evangelium nach Markus* (Zurich—Einsiedeln—

Cologne: Benzinger; Neukirchen and Vluyn: Neukirchener Verlag, 1978), I, p. 24: "Nur in einer gewissen, freilich nicht völligen Distanz war das Werk möglich."

11. Eric A. Havelock, *Preface to Plato* (Cambridge, Mass.: Harvard University Press, Belknap Press, 1963).

12. Ibid., pp. 31, 165, passim.

13. Ibid., p. 160.

14. Ibid., p. 47.

15. Chapter 2, p. 70.

16. Birger Gerhardsson, *Memory and Manuscript: Oral Tradition and Written Transmission in Rabbinic Judaism and Early Christianity*, ASNU 22 (Lund: C. W. K. Gleerup; Copenhagen: Ejnar Munksgaard, 1961), pp. 181–85.

17. Joseph B. Tyson, "The Blindness of the Disciples in Mark," *JBL* 80 (1961): 261–68; Theodore J. Weeden, *Mark—Traditions in Conflict* (Philadelphia: Fortress Press, 1971), pp. 52–69; idem, "The Heresy that Necessitated Mark's Gospel," *ZNW* 59 (1968): 145–58; Thomas L. Budesheim, "Jesus and the Disciples in Conflict with Judaism," *ZNW* 62 (1971): 190–209; Etienne Trocmé, *The Formation of the Gospel According to Mark*, Eng. trans. Pamela Gaughan (Philadelphia: Westminster Press, 1975), pp. 120–37; Werner H. Kelber, *Mark's Story of Jesus* (Philadelphia: Fortress Press, 1979); Robert C. Tannehill, "The Disciples in Mark: The Function of a Narrative Role," *JR* 57 (1977): 386–405; Norman R. Petersen, *Literary Criticism for New Testament Critics*, GBS (Philadelphia: Fortress Press, 1978), pp. 49–80; Ernest Best, *Following Jesus: Discipleship in the Gospel of Mark*, JSNTSup 4 (Sheffield: JSOT Press, 1981); David J. Hawkin, "The Incomprehension of the Disciples in the Marcan Redaction," *JBL* 91 (1972): 491–500; Jürgen Roloff, "Das Markusevangelium als Geschichtsdarstellung," *EvTh* 29 (1969): 84; W. Bracht, "Jüngerschaft und Nachfolge," in *Kirche im Werden*, ed. J. Hainz (Munich—Paderborn—Vienna: Schönigh, 1976), pp. 143–65; Karl-Georg Reploh, *Markus—Lehrer der Gemeinde: Eine redaktionsgeschichtliche Studie zu den Jüngerperikopen des Markus-Evangeliums*, SBM 9 (Stuttgart: Katholisches Bibelwerk, 1969); Klemens Stock, *Boten aus dem Mit-Ihm-Sein: Das Verhältnis zwischen Jesus und den Zwölf nach Markus*, AnBib 70 (Rome: Pontifical Biblical Institute, 1975).

18. We are offering here a linguistic assessment of the theme of failing discipleship. For a literary interpretation of the theme, see pp. 125–29.

19. Rudolf Pesch, *Naherwartungen: Tradition und Redaktion in Mk 13* (Düsseldorf: Patmos-Verlag, 1968); Jan Lambrecht, S. J., *Die Redaktion der Markus-Apokalypse: Literarische Analyse und Strukturuntersuchung*, AnBib 28 (Rome: Pontifical Biblical Institute, 1967); Werner H. Kelber, *The Kingdom in Mark: A New Place and A New Time* (Philadelphia: Fortress Press, 1974), pp. 111–16.

20. For example, Willi Marxsen (*Mark the Evangelist: Studies on the Redaction History of the Gospel*, Eng. trans. Roy A. Harrisville et al. [Nashville: Abingdon Press, 1969], pp. 170–73) dates the prophets prior to the fall of the temple, and Pesch (*Naherwartungen*, pp. 218–23) shortly thereafter.

21. Pesch, *Naherwartungen*, pp. 77–106; Lambrecht, *Markus-Apokalypse*, pp. 67–91; Kelber, *Kingdom in Mark*, pp. 109–28; Nikolaus Walter, "Tempelzerstörung und Synoptische Apokalypse," *ZNW* 57 (1966): 38–49.

22. Jacques Derrida, *Of Grammatology,* Eng. trans. Gayatri Chakravorty Spivak (Baltimore and London: Johns Hopkins University Press, 1976), p. 12.

23. Weeden, *Mark,* p. 80.

24. M. Eugene Boring, "The Paucity of Sayings in Mark: A Hypothesis," *SBL Seminar Papers* (Missoula, Mont.: Scholars Press, 1977), p. 377; idem, *Sayings of the Risen Jesus: Christian Prophecy in the Synoptic Tradition* (New York and Cambridge: Cambridge University Press, 1982), p. 202.

25. Weeden, *Mark,* pp. 83–90; Boring, "Paucity of Sayings," pp. 371–77; idem, *Sayings of Risen Jesus,* pp. 195–203; John Dominic Crossan, "Empty Tomb and Absent Lord," in *The Passion in Mark,* ed. Werner H. Kelber (Philadelphia: Fortress Press, 1976), pp. 135–52; idem, "A Form for Absence: The Markan Creation of Gospel," *Semeia* 12 (1978): 41–55; Vernon K. Robbins, "Last Meal: Preparation, Betrayal, and Absence (Mark 14:12–25)," in *Passion in Mark,* pp. 21–40; Werner H. Kelber, "From Passion Narrative to Gospel," in *Passion in Mark,* pp. 160–65.

26. Chapter 5, pp. 207–11.

27. Boring, "Paucity of Sayings," pp. 371–77; idem, *Sayings of Risen Jesus,* pp. 195–203.

28. Boring, *Sayings of Risen Jesus,* p. 196.

29. Ibid., p. 198; idem, "Paucity of Sayings," p. 374.

30. Concerning a crisis in confidence in conjunction with a change in communication from the oral to the written medium, see Eduard Nielsen, *Oral Tradition: A Modern Problem in Old Testament Introduction,* SBT 11 (London: SCM Press, 1954), pp. 60–61. Our linguistic thesis of the genesis of Mark is akin to the one developed by Joseph Blenkinsopp with regard to the canon of the Old Testament (*Prophecy and Canon: A Contribution to the Study of Jewish Origins,* UNDCSJCA 3 [Notre Dame, Ind., and London: University of Notre Dame Press, 1977]). The author observed a close connection between prophecy and the formation of the Old Testament canon. Concern for writing often arose out of conflicting hermeneutics and conflicting claims to authority. The Pentateuchal source P, for example, undercut the entire history of prophecy by returning to distant, cultic origins, and the final version of the Pentateuch itself contributed to the eclipse of prophecy.

31. Ethelbert Stauffer, "Jeschu Ben Mirjam: Kontroversgeschichtliche Anmerkungen zu Mk 6:3," in *Neotestamentica et Semitica: Studies in Honour of Matthew Black,* ed. E. Earle Ellis and Max Wilcox (Edinburgh: T. & T. Clark, 1969), pp. 119–28.

32. John Dominic Crossan, "Mark and the Relatives of Jesus," *NovT* 15 (1973): 81–113.

33. Thomas Eugene Boomershine, "Mark, the Storyteller: A Rhetorical-Critical Investigation of Mark's Passion and Resurrection Narrative," (Ph.D. diss., Union Theological Seminary, New York, 1974), pp. 238–40.

34. Ibid., pp. 238–39.

35. Ibid., pp. 122–25, 238–39, 264–68; Kelber, "From Passion Narrative to Gospel," pp. 153–59.

36. Louis Marin, "The Women at the Tomb: A Structural Analysis Essay of a Gospel Text," in *The New Testament and Structuralism,* ed. and Eng. trans. Alfred M. Johnson, PTMS 11 (Pittsburgh: Pickwick Press, 1976), pp. 73–96, esp. 89–92.

37. An impressive example demonstrating the extraordinary difficulties entailed in the textualization of oral speech has been given by Harold Scheub, "Translation of African Oral Narrative-Performances to the Written Word," *Yearbook of Comparative and General Literature* 20 (1971): 28–36.

38. Havelock, *Preface to Plato,* p. 140.

39. For a critique of the two *pre-Markan* cycles of miracle stories, see Robert M. Fowler, *Loaves and Fishes: The Function of the Feeding Stories in the Gospel of Mark,* SBLDS 54 (Chico, Calif.: Scholars Press, 1981). The author considers the first feeding story (6:34–44) to be Markan, and the second one (8:1–10) traditional. It is Mark who creates doublets and the impression of two cycles.

40. Derrida, *Of Grammatology,* pp. 85–87.

41. Jack Goody, *The Domestication of the Savage Mind* (New York and Cambridge: Cambridge University Press, 1977), p. 68.

42. Ibid., p. 123.

43. Hermann Gunkel, *The Legends of Genesis: The Biblical Saga and History,* Eng. trans. W. H. Carruth (New York: Schocken Books, 1964), p. 81.

44. On the concept of "followability," see Martin Price, "The Fictional Contract," in *Literary Theory and Structure: Essays in Honor of William K. Wimsatt,* ed. Frank Brady, John Palmer, and Martin Price (New Haven, Conn., and London: Yale University Press, 1973), pp. 151–78, esp. 171–76.

45. I owe the designations *interior* and *exterior retrospectivity,* or *posteriority* to Walter J. Ong, S. J., "Maranatha: Death and Life in the Text of the Book," in *Interfaces of the Word: Studies in the Evolution of Consciousness and Culture* (Ithaca, N.Y., and London: Cornell University Press, 1977), pp. 230–71, esp. 240–53.

46. Marxsen, *Mark,* pp. 30–44.

47. Chapter 5, pp. 207–11.

48. Textuality reflects not only linear patterns, forward and backwards thrusts. Once language is objectified, the eye discovers diverse, geometrical arrangements, such as concentric patterns and ring compositions. See above all Joanna Dewey, *Markan Public Debate: Literary Technique, Concentric Structure and Theology in Mark 2:1–3:6,* SBLDS 48 (Chico, Calif.: Scholars Press, 1980).

49. On the Bible as demythologizing, dissociative, and self-critical literature, see Herbert N. Schneidau, *Sacred Discontent: The Bible and Western Tradition* (Berkeley—Los Angeles—London: University of California Press, 1976).

50. On the concept of "distanciation" in connection with writing, see Paul Ricoeur, "The Hermeneutical Function of Distanciation," *PhT* 17 (1973): 129–41; idem, *Interpretation Theory,* pp. 25–44.

51. Schneidau, *Sacred Discontent,* p. 287.

52. Paul Ricoeur, "Biblical Hermeneutics," *Semeia* 4 (1975): 104–5.

53. Ibid., p. 104.

54. Kelber, *Kingdom in Mark,* pp. 45–65; idem, *Mark's Story of Jesus,* pp. 30–42.

55. Madeleine Boucher, *The Mysterious Parable: A Literary Study,* CBQMS 6 (Washington, D. C.: Catholic Biblical Association of America, 1977), p. 80.

56. Chapter 2, p. 61.

57. Chapter 2, pp. 63–64.

58. Chapter 2, pp. 61–62.

59. Thomas J. J. Altizer, *Total Presence: The Language of Jesus and the Language of Today* (New York: Seabury Press, 1980), pp. 3–18; Ulrich E. Simon, *Story and Faith in the Biblical Narrative* (London: SPCK, 1975), p. 64.

60. Havelock, *Preface to Plato*, p. 147.

61. Walter J. Ong, S. J., *The Presence of the Word: Some Prolegomena for Cultural and Religious History* (New Haven, Conn., and London: Yale University Press, 1967; paperback edition: Minneapolis: University of Minnesota Press, 1981), p. 88.

62. Ibid., p. 135, passim.

63. Frank Kermode, *The Genesis of Secrecy: On the Interpretation of Narrative* (Cambridge, Mass., and London: Harvard University Press, 1979).

64. Ibid., p. 108.

65. Havelock, *Preface to Plato*, p. 46.

66. Erhardt Güttgemanns, *Candid Questions Concerning Gospel Form Criticism: A Methodological Sketch of the Fundamental Problematics of Form and Redaction Criticism*, Eng. trans. William G. Doty, PTMS 26 (Pittsburgh: Pickwick Press, 1979), p. 199.

67. Ibid., pp. 120, 197–200, 261–63, passim.

68. Walter J. Ong, S. J., "The Writer's Audience is Always a Fiction," in *Interfaces of Word*, pp. 53–81.

69. On *vividness* as a mark of the gospel's narrative fictionality, see Güttgemanns, "The 'Vividness' of Mark as an Aesthetic Deception," in *Candid Questions*, pp. 380–84.

70. Kermode, *Genesis of Secrecy*, p. 122.

71. The most perceptive American contribution to the issue of the historical Jesus and Christian faith was, in our judgment, made by Van Austin Harvey, *The Historian and the Believer: The Morality of Historical Knowledge and Christian Belief* (Philadelphia: Westminster Press, 1981).

72. Ricoeur, *Interpretation Theory*, p. 42: "The inscription of discourse is the transcription of the world, and transcription is not reduplication, but metamorphosis."

73. Gotthold Ephraim Lessing, *Laokoon*, ed. Dorothy Reich (New York and London: Oxford University Press, 1965); Ernst Hans Gombrich, "Meditations on a Hobby Horse or the Roots of Artistic Form," in *Classic Essays in English*, ed. Josephine Miles, 2d ed. (Boston and Toronto: Little, Brown & Co., 1965), pp. 408–22.

74. Norman Petersen, "So-called Gnostic Type Gospels and the Question of the Genre 'Gospel'" (unpublished paper for SBL Task Force on the Gospel Genre, 1970); William G. Doty, "The Concept of Genre in Literary Analysis," *SBL Seminar Papers* (Missoula, Mont.: Scholars Press, 1972), II, pp. 413–48; James M. Robinson, "On the Gattung of Mark (and John)," in *Jesus and Man's Hope* (Pittsburgh: Pittsburgh Theological Seminary, 1970), I, pp. 99–129; reissued in *The Problem of History in Mark: And Other Marcan Studies* (Philadelphia: Fortress Press, 1982).

75. Donald W. Riddle, "The Martyr Motif in the Gospel According to

Mark," *JR* 4 (1924): 397–410; Ernest W. Burch, "Tragic Action in the Second Gospel: A Study of the Narrative of Mark," *JR* 11 (1931): 346–58; Curtis Beach, *The Gospel of Mark: Its Making and Meaning* (New York: Harper & Brothers, 1959).

76. Gilbert G. Bilezikian, *The Liberated Gospel: A Comparison of the Gospel of Mark and Greek Tragedy* (Grand Rapids: Baker Book House, 1977).

77. Ibid., p. 53.

78. Ibid., pp. 51–55.

79. Ibid., p. 62.

80. Amos N. Wilder, *The Language of the Gospel: Early Christian Rhetoric* (New York: Harper & Row, 1964), p. 44. Bilezikian is conscious of the issue (*Liberated Gospel*, pp. 19, n. 27; 29).

81. William A. Beardslee, *Literary Criticism of the New Testament*, GBS (Philadelphia: Fortress Press, 1970), p. 28.

82. Bilezikian, *Liberated Gospel*, p. 31.

83. Dan O. Via, *Kerygma and Comedy in the New Testament: A Structuralist Approach to Hermeneutic* (Philadelphia: Fortress Press, 1975).

84. Ibid., p. 49.

85. Ibid., p. 93.

86. Ibid., p. 101.

87. Ibid., p. 93.

88. Ibid., pp. 99–103.

89. Ibid., p. 50.

90. Ibid., p. 93.

91. Ibid., pp. 77–90.

92. Schneidau, *Sacred Discontent*, pp. 286–306; idem, "For Interpretation," *MoRev* 1 (1978): 70–88, esp. 79.

93. The terms kerygmatic versus cybernetic correspond to our use of mythoclastic versus mythopoetic.

94. Moses Hadas and Morton Smith, *Heroes and Gods: Spiritual Biographies in Antiquity* (New York: Harper & Row, 1965).

95. Howard Clark Kee, "Aretalogy and Gospel," *JBL* 92 (1973): 402–22; idem, *Aretalogies, Hellenistic 'Lives,' and the Sources of Mark*, Protocol of the Colloquy 12 (Berkeley, Calif.: Center for Hermeneutical Studies, 1975).

96. Gerd Petzke, *Die Traditionen über Apollonius von Tyana und das Neue Testament*, SCHNT 1 (Leiden: E. J. Brill, 1970). The author designates Philostratus's work as religious propaganda literature, but specifically states: "Auf eine Gesamtcharakterisierung des Werkes mit einem Begriff muss verzichtet werden" (p. 60). As for the narration of Apollonius's death, or rather his apotheosis: "Von einem Martyrium des Apollonius kann man nicht sprechen" (p. 185, n. 4).

97. Gerd Theissen, *Urchristliche Wundergeschichten: Ein Beitrag zur formgeschichtlichen Erforschung der synoptischen Evangelien* (Gütersloh: Gerd Mohn, 1974), pp. 211–21. For incisive critiques, cf. Hendrikus Boers, "Sisyphus and His Rock: Concerning Gerd Theissen, *Urchristliche Wundergeschichten*," *Semeia* 11 (1978): 1–48; Paul J. Achtemeier, "An Imperfect Union: Reflections on Gerd Theissen, *Urchristliche Wundergeschichten*," *Semeia* 11 (1978): 49–68.

98. Achtemeier, "Imperfect Union," p. 63.

99. Hans Dieter Betz, "Jesus as Divine Man," in *Jesus and the Historian: Festschrift for E. C. Colwell,* ed. F. Thomas Trotter (Philadelphia: Westminster Press, 1968), pp. 114–33.

100. Helmut Koester, "One Jesus and Four Primitive Gospels," in *Trajectories through Early Christianity* (Philadelphia: Fortress Press, 1971), pp. 187–93.

101. James M. Robinson, "The Problem of History in Mark, Reconsidered," *USQR* 20 (1965): 131–47; reissued in idem, *Problem of History in Mark.*

102. Achtemeier *(Mark* [Philadelphia: Fortress Press, 1975], p. 78) suggests that "Mark continued the process of adapting and interpreting the miracle stories." Betz ("Jesus as Divine Man," p. 121) argues that the miracle tradition underwent "a total transformation when it came into the hands of Mark." According to Koester ("One Jesus," p. 189, n. 105), the miracles "were subjected to the principle of the cross." On Robinson's view ("Problem of History," p. 137), Mark "blunted the proclivities of collections of miracle stories."

103. Johannes Weiss, *Das älteste Evangelium* (Göttingen: Vandenhoeck & Ruprecht, 1907), pp. 6–29.

104. Ibid., pp. 9, 14.

105. Clyde Weber Votaw, *The Gospels and Contemporary Biographies in the Greco-Roman World* (Philadelphia: Fortress Press, 1970).

106. Philip L. Shuler, *The Synoptic Gospels and the Problem of Genre* (Ph.D. diss., McMaster University, 1975).

107. Ibid., p. 169.

108. Charles H. Talbert, *What is a Gospel? The Genre of the Canonical Gospels* (Philadelphia: Fortress Press, 1977), p. 94.

109. Weeden, *Mark,* p. viii.

110. Frederick Houk Borsch, *God's Parable* (Philadelphia: Westminster Press, 1975), p. 98.

111. Tannehill, "The Disciples in Mark."

112. John R. Donahue, S. J., "Jesus as Parable of God in the Gospel of Mark," *Int* 32 (1978): 369–86.

113. John Dominic Crossan, *The Dark Interval: Towards a Theology of Story* (Niles, Ill.: Argus Communications, 1975), p. 124, cf. also 10; idem, *In Parables: The Challenge of the Historical Jesus* (New York: Harper & Row, 1973), p. xiv; idem, *Finding is the First Act: Trove Folktales and Jesus' Treasure Parable,* Semeia Studies 8 (Philadelphia: Fortress Press; Missoula, Mont.: Scholars Press, 1979), pp. 106–7.

114. Crossan, *Dark Interval,* p. 126.

115. Ricoeur, "Biblical Hermeneutics," p. 103.

116. Elizabeth Struthers Malbon, "Narrative Space and Mythic Meaning: A Structural Exegesis of the Gospel of Mark" (Ph.D. diss., Florida State University, 1980).

117. Wilder, *Language of Gospel,* p. 67.

118. Schneidau, "For Interpretation," p. 84.

119. T. A. Burkill, "The Cryptology of Parables in St. Mark's Gospel," *NovT* 1 (1956): 246–62; J. Coutts, " 'Those Outside' (Mark 4, 10–12)," *SE*

II, TU 87 (Berlin: Akademie-Verlag, 1964): 155–57; Fred D. Gealy, "The Composition of Mark IV," *ExpT* 48 (1936): 40–43; Jan Lambrecht, S. J., "Die fünf Parabeln in Mk 4," *Bijdr* 29 (1968): 25–53; Willi Marxsen, "Redaktionsgeschichtliche Erklärung der sogenannten Parabeltheorie des Markus," *ZTK* 52 (1955): 255–71; Robert P. Meye, "Mark 4, 10: 'Those about Him with the Twelve,'" *SE* II, TU 87 (Berlin: Akademie-Verlag, 1964): 211–18; Donald W. Riddle, "Mark 4:1–34: The Evolution of a Gospel Source," *JBL* 56 (1937): 77–90; Eduard Schweizer, "Zur Frage des Messiasgeheimnisses bei Markus," *ZNW* 56 (1965): 1–8; G. H. Boobyer, "The Redaction of Mk 4, 1–34," *NTS* 8 (1961–62): 59–70; C. F. D. Moule, "Mark 4:1–20 Yet Once More," in *Neotestamentica et Semitica: Studies in Honour of Matthew Black*, ed. E. Earle Ellis and Max Wilcox (Edinburgh: T. & T. Clark, 1969), pp. 95–113; Joachim Gnilka, *Die Verstockung Israels: Isaias 6, 9–10 in der Theologie der Synoptiker*, SANT 3 (Munich: Kösel, 1961), pp. 13–86; J. W. Pryor, "Markan Parable Theology," *ExpT* 83 (1972): 242–45; Hendrikus Boers, *Theology out of the Ghetto: A New Testament Exegetical Study Concerning Religious Exclusiveness* (Leiden: E. J. Brill, 1971), pp. 9–25.

120. John C. Meagher, *Clumsy Construction in Mark's Gospel: A Critique of Form- and Redaktionsgeschichte*, TorSTh 3 (New York and Toronto: Edwin Mellen Press, 1979).

121. Ibid., p. 86.

122. Ibid., p. 93.

123. William Wrede, *The Messianic Secret*, Eng. trans. J. C. G. Greig (London: James Clarke & Co., 1971).

124. Chapter 2, pp. 61–62, 74.

125. Chapter 2, p. 75.

126. Boucher, *Mysterious Parable*, p. 83.

127. Friedrich Hauck, *"parabole,"* *TDNT* V: 758.

128. Meagher, *Clumsy Construction*, p. 87.

129. Ibid.

130. Heikki Räisänen, *Die Parabeltheorie im Markusevangelium*, Schriften der Finnischen Exegetischen Gesellschaft 26 (Helsinki: Länsi-Suomi, 1973).

131. Ibid., pp. 27–47.

132. Schneidau, "For Interpretation," p. 85.

133. Leander E. Keck, "The Introduction to Mark's Gospel," *NTS* 12 (1966): 352–70.

134. Simon, *Story and Faith*, p. 75.

135. Tannehill, "The Disciples in Mark," p. 402.

136. Petersen, *Literary Criticism for New Testament Critics*, p. 70.

137. Ibid.

138. Ibid.

139. Tannehill, "The Disciples in Mark," p. 402; cf. also F. Dewar, "Chapter 13 and the Passion Narrative in Mark," *Theology* 64 (1961): 99–107; R. H. Lightfoot, *The Gospel Message of St. Mark* (New York and London: Oxford University Press, 1950), pp. 41–60; Werner H. Kelber, "The Hour of the Son of Man and the Temptation of the Disciples," in *Passion in Mark*, pp. 41–60.

140. Petersen, *Literary Criticism for New Testament Critics*, p. 77.

141. Robert W. Funk, *Language, Hermeneutic, and Word of God: The*

Problem of Language in the New Testament and Contemporary Theology (New York: Harper & Row, 1966; reprint: Missoula, Mont.: Scholars Press, 1979), p. 196.

142. Long before Havelock had developed his thesis on Plato, Hans-Georg Gadamer ("Plato and the Poets," in *Dialogue and Dialectic: Eight Hermeneutical Studies on Plato,* Eng. trans. P. Christopher Smith [New Haven, Conn., and London: Yale University Press, 1980], p. 58) sensed a connection between Plato's act of writing and his criticism of the poets: "The critique of poetry here is simultaneously an ultimate justification for Plato's writings." This is precisely the conclusion we have reached with regard to Mark's critique of the oral authorities.

143. Alfred Suhl, *Die Funktion der alttestamentlichen Zitate und Anspielungen im Markusevangelium* (Gütersloh: Gerd Mohn, 1965).

4. Orality and Textuality in Paul

[Paul] does indeed manifest a rather different disposition to language, written and oral, than is characteristic of the modern view. Perhaps the best way to indicate this difference is to say that he is oriented, not so much to the content of words, as to what they effect, what they set in motion, what room they create for faith. He does not concentrate on a given assertion as a statement about something, but on the invocation as a call to something, as a communication of a reality in which both speaker and hearer may participate.

Robert W. Funk, "Saying and Seeing"

For the letter kills, but the Spirit gives life.

2 Cor. 3:6

So faith comes from hearing, and hearing through the word of Christ.

Rom. 10:17

Whatever kinship may be said to exist between the Markan and the Pauline gospel, it is imperative to note that the apostle wrote letters, whereas the evangelist, as far as we know, did not. A writer of letters has chosen a form that favors extension of one's personal authority into written verbalization. As far as his authorial identity is concerned, Mark has retreated behind his text. Paul, by contrast, plays up his first person singular authority in the manner of oral speech. The letter form allows him to keep in as close touch with the recipients of his message as is possible for a writer, and to address them almost as if he were present in person. The apostle's preference for writing letters, therefore, may point to a fundamentally oral disposition toward language.

The depth of Paul's inclination toward oral gospel and personal presence was revealed by Robert Funk's discovery of the Pauline travelogue, a standard ingredient of the apostle's letters.[1] According to Funk, Paul attached to his letters travel notes that review past and future contacts with his respective communities.[2] What characterizes his travel reflections is the tendency to transcend their traditional, epistolary function of announcing whereabouts and travel plans. It is in the post-Pauline tradition that the travelogue functions in a purely conventional fashion.[3] In the Pauline letters, however, it partakes in an argument over "the apostolic parousia"[4] and its (the parousia's) mediation by letter, emissaries, and personal presence. Consistently the travelogue adds the promise of an oral to the written word, or recalls and wishes to renew the once orally delivered word. This ardent desire to convey the word in person, or through personal representatives, may indicate that the letters do not "bear the apostolic power to the same degree as Paul's personal presence."[5] As harbinger of oral words and personal presence, the travelogue may even be taken to suggest "that Paul wrote reluctantly,"[6] perhaps regarding the oral word more fully effective than letters.[7] It is this Pauline indebtedness to the spoken word and the dialectic of spoken and written language, first brought to our attention by Funk's exposition of the travelogue, that will be developed in this chapter.

First, we shall observe Paul's partiality toward oral discourse that pervades his treatment of gospel, faith, and obedience. This will be followed by a study of the apostle's noted polemic against the Law in terms of an aversion toward the objectified, written word. Third, we will explore the classic antithesis of Law and Gospel as a conflict between two linguistic modalities, *verbum scriptum* versus *viva vox*, and reconnect the belabored theologoumena of justification by faith and righteousness of God with the oral matrix of the preached gospel. Finally, we will focus on Paul's message as it is available to us in written documents. While letters accommodate the oral gospel exceedingly well, they will themselves not entirely escape the impact of the written medium. Throughout, Pauline theology is conceived as a theology of language. Centrally located in the apostle's theology is the issue of the Word of God in its oral and written dimension.

THE ORAL GOSPEL

The thesis advanced here concerns the close affinity of Paul's understanding of gospel with oral hermeneutics. Predominantly oral analogues are the key to the Pauline gospel. We do not suggest the absence of visual analogues altogether. Visual imagery is present in Pauline language, conspicuously so in 2 Corinthians. The Divine Man apostles who stand in the background of this letter indulged in outward, visible signs of redemption, and Paul's refutation tends to pull his language into the orbit of visual conceptualization.[8] Yet even the most prominent example of visual language in 2 Corinthians is susceptible of explanation in terms of the oral gospel. In 2 Cor. 3:12–18 the apostle describes the experience of a vision (or reflection) of and transformation into the likeness of the Lord. It is in the freedom of the Spirit that one sees (or reflects) the glory of the Lord as in a mirror, and one is changed into what one sees. Similarly, the preached gospel may be compared to a light that shines out of darkness into human hearts, conveying knowledge of God (4:4–6). Incontrovertible as Paul's reference to sight and seeing is, it aims at interiorizing the essentially invisible, not at objectifying God or the language of the gospel. Interiorization of vision and inner transformation is entirely consonant with the oral gospel, which, we shall see below, addresses and affects the human heart.[9] What is impermissible for Paul is the objectification of the invisible and a grounding of faith in the externally visible. The invisible alone has eternal significance (4:18; cf. Rom. 8:24–25): "we walk by faith, not by sight" (2 Cor. 5:7).

Twice the apostle links visualizing language with his entry into apostleship. According to 1 Cor. 15:8, Christ "appeared" to or was "seen" by him, and in the same letter a "seeing" of the Lord Jesus is invoked in apostolic self-defense (9:1). Before one interprets Paul's entry into apostleship as an Easter experience of the living Lord, it is advisable to explore the source of visual language in 1 Corinthians and the extent to which it characterizes Paul's personal reflection on the event outside of Damascus. Willi Marxsen observed that the *ōphthē* in 1 Cor. 15:8 was likely to have been phrased in conformity to the pre-Pauline formula 1 Cor. 15:3b–5.[10] The Lord "appeared" to Paul, as he had formerly "appeared" to Cephas, then to the twelve, to more than 500 brethren, to James and all other apostles. In the case of 1 Cor. 15:8, therefore, and possibly also in 9:1, Pauline terminology may have been shaped by assimilation to tradition. In Gal. 1:15–16, moreover, Paul offers his most extensive personal report on the Damascus event, but without reference to "seeing." Here he writes of the revelation (*apokalypsai*) of the Son in him, while leaving entirely open the mode of revelation. Rather than reading Gal. 1:15–16 in light of 1 Cor. 15:8 and 9:1, it is in accord with the historical sequence of the letters to suggest that the apostle initially perceived his encounter with Christ in revelatory language, before he interpreted the revelation, under the pressure of tradition, in visual terms.[11]

Krister Stendahl, in pursuing earlier observations by Johannes Munck,[12] argued that in Gal. 1:13–16 Paul described his revelatory experience after the model of a prophetic call story.[13] By the grace of God the apostle was set apart and called in the manner of Isaiah (49:1) and Jeremiah (1:5). It follows that "the usual conversion model of Paul the Jew who gives up his former faith to become a Christian is not the model of Paul but ours."[14] Stendahl was rightly concerned to rebut the popular (and sometimes scholarly) misconception of Paul's "conversion" from Judaism to Christianity, as it were, and to protect the Jewish integrity of the apostle. But it should also be kept in mind that the notion of *call* (Gal. 1:15: *kalesas dia tēs charitos autou*) transports us into a particular sensory field, that of sound, speaking and hearing. It is in full accord with his Jewish heritage that the apostle looks and hopes for the unseen and perceives the divinity of God to be invisible, although apprehensible in the works of creation (Rom. 1:20). The God whose divinity is invisible reveals his divine will primarily through calling.[15] God calls people into the presence of Christ (1 Thess. 5:24), calls from Jews and Gentiles (Rom. 9:24), calls into kingdom and glory (1 Thess. 2:12), and calls to peace (1 Cor. 7:15) and freedom (Gal. 5:13). Those who heed divine calling will become "Jews and Gentiles who are called" (1 Cor. 1:24; au. trans. of *autois de tois klētois, Ioudaiois te kai Hellēsin*) and "saints through calling" (Rom. 1:7; 1 Cor. 1:2; au. trans. of *klētois hagiois*). The dominant trait of Paul's apostolic self-consciousness relates to this phenomenology of calling, rather than to seeing. He is primarily an apostle who has been called (Rom. 1:1; 1 Cor. 1:1: *klētos apostolos*), and his calling pertains to the proclamation of the gospel among the Gentiles (Gal. 1:15–16).

It has been suggested that Paul "in setting forth his deepest and most personal experiences in the spirit, or in bodying forth his most vibrant hopes, . . . uses imagery that is auditory."[16] It is fair to say that in Pauline theology the ear triumphs over the eye. When at a rare moment the apostle ponders the "visions and revelations of the Lord" (2 Cor. 12:1), he records his own translation into the third heaven not with respect to what he saw, but in terms of inexpressible words that he heard (2 Cor. 12:2–4). He articulates this translation as an experience communicated to his sense of hearing. Whereas in the synoptic gospels the coming of Jesus, his parousia, is a phenomenon of universal visibility, a blaze of light forcing the attention of every eye amid cosmic darkness (Mark 13:24–27; Matt. 24:26–31; Luke 17:23–24), it is for Paul an event accompanied by momentous sound effects. Its quality is that of "a shout of command," "the voice of an archangel" (au. trans.), and "the trumpet of God" (1 Thess. 4:15–17). One hears the coming of Jesus more than one sees it. Both the resurrection of the dead and the transformation of the living will be effected by the sound of the trumpet (1 Cor. 15:52). The force and pervasiveness of auditory analogues in Pauline literature has rarely received adequate theological appreciation, presumably because they are alien to the modern reader of texts. "The oral state of mind and psychological structures so evident in the Bible are strange to us, as we now know, not because we are 'Western' but because we are typographic folk,"[17] whose philosophical, theological, and scientific tradition is dominated by visual models. In Paul's thinking, life is allied to sound and hearing, while death is disconnected from spoken words, and indeed vulnerable to sound. God "gives life to the dead and calls things that do not exist as existing" (Rom. 4:17; au. trans.). Death, by this logic, is overcome by the very medium of life, the sounding of God's call.

The master metaphor of the apostle's entire program is *gospel*. He employs the term approximately fifty times, more than any other author in the New Testament, and places it into predominantly auditory contexts. The gospel is commonly linked with verbs or nouns denoting the act of speaking. It is preached, spoken, announced, proclaimed (*euaggelizesthai, lalein, kataggelein, kēryssein*), and a matter of confirmation, confession, defense, and participation (*bebaiōsis, homologia, apologia, koinōnia*). In Paul's view, the gospel was promised in advance by the prophets in Scripture (Rom. 1:1–2) but was not in itself a scriptural authority. It is constitutionally and operationally defined in oral terms, not by association with writing and reading. Although Paul does, of course, commit the gospel, or reflections upon it, to letters, his written exposition leaves no doubt that the gospel, when it came alive, was spoken aloud and, if it is to bring life again, must be sounded afresh. Clearly, the writing of a gospel after the manner of Mark is foreign to Paul. The gospel he writes about bears the indelible imprint, or more accurately, echoes the voiceprints of an oral authority.

The oral quality of gospel is corroborated by the fact that *logos* or *logos tou theou* can serve as synonyms for gospel in Pauline language. The Thessalonians have received "the Word" (1 Thess. 1:6), the Corinthians heard the unadulterated "Word of God" (2 Cor. 2:17; 4:2; 1 Cor. 14:36), the Galatians were taught "the Word" (Gal. 6:6), and the Philippians spoke "the Word of God" (Phil. 1:14). Gerhard Kittel has stressed the activist character of *logos* with a seriousness rarely encountered in Pauline scholarship: "In all this the *logos* is always genuine *legein*, or spoken word in all concreteness. One of the most serious errors of which one could be guilty would be to make this *logos tou theou* a concept or abstraction."[18] As a rule, the Pauline reference to *logos* or *logos tou theou* is to the living, preached word of the gospel.

The gospel, when voiced and sounded forth, operates productively, taking effect in the believer (1 Thess. 2:13: *energeitai en hymin tois pisteuousin*). The word is an active force—for better and for worse— creating life for some and destruction for others (1 Cor. 1:18). In Pauline

144

terminology, the gospel is "the power of God" (Rom. 1:16: *dynamis gar tou theou estin*; cf. 1 Thess. 1:5; 1 Cor. 2:4–5; 2 Cor. 6:7). The copula *einai* in Rom. 1:16 (1 Cor. 1:18) serves to connect the subject gospel (or *logos*) with the predicate power, expressing a logical relation and indeed an identity between the two entities. The gospel is inseparable from power. Its "efficacy is supremely concrete,"[19] and to dismiss it as magic or obsolete speculation is to turn a deaf ear on one of the most elementary aspects of Paul's perception of language. Julius Schniewind, in an excellent study on Pauline hermeneutics, noted some seventy years ago that the modern reader tends to associate *logos* and *euaggelion* with doctrine and specific content, whereas Paul's interest does not primarily focus on these aspects.[20] So impressed was Schniewind by the evidence pointing to the efficaciousness of the Pauline *logos* and *euaggelion* that he regarded this aspect as the most important result of his investigation.[21] Paul links the word primarily not with content, but with the effect it has on hearers. Frequently a genitive attached to *logos* is best defined as a genitive *efficaciae*,[22] which may or may not encompass the force of an objective genitive. The "word of life," for example, received by the Philippians (Phil. 2:16: *logon zōēs epechontes*) is less a message about life than the power of life transmitted by the word, and "the word of reconciliation" entrusted to the Corinthians (2 Cor. 5:19: *ton logon tēs katallagēs*) involves not merely the enunciation of a specific message, but the reconciliation effected by its proclamation. By endowing gospel with power, the apostle has assigned it the very quality which is consistent with its oral operation.[23] "Paul connects the word as power with oral word because the real nature of words, their power, is disclosed when they are spoken, pronounced."[24] Spoken words exist only in active production, at the moment of speaking. Being fully caught up in the utterance, they surrender their very being into the act of verbalization. As speech, the gospel actualizes the reality of what is being spoken. On this view, the concept of the gospel as the power of God states nothing less than a fundamental creed of the apostle's oral hermeneutics.[25]

If we are to understand gospel in terms of the efficacy of the sounded word, the agency of the Spirit cannot be neglected. "The interrelation of true word, power, and Spirit are patent for Paul."[26] Words are taught by the Spirit (1 Cor. 2:4, 13), and the confession is spoken in the Holy Spirit (1 Cor. 12:2). The gospel occurs not only in word, but in power and Spirit (1 Thess. 1:5), and the Spirit is received by faith that comes from hearing (Gal. 3:2, 5, 14). In the background lurks the phenomenological connection between sound and spirit or breath, although Paul has not consciously reflected upon it. Because sound comes into existence through the manipulation of air, spoken words owe their very existence to spirit, the breath of life. Operated by the breath of air and endowed with spiritual quality, speech is fluid, hence living, and not subject to the written regimentation of textualization. Moreover, spoken words are invisible and in this regard of the order of God and the Spirit. Energized by spiritual force, the spoken gospel can thus function as carrier of life and give birth to life.

Mouth and heart cooperate in the oral delivery of redemption. "Faith comes from hearing" (Rom. 10:17; au. trans.), and what is heard must first be preached. The heart is the central organ of reception that facilitates communication with Spirit and gospel. Spoken words enter the human heart and enjoy privileged participation in human actuality. They elicit faith and faithful heeding and in turn generate confession (Rom. 10:8–10; 6:17). When one receives the Spirit, one likewise receives it into the heart (Gal. 4:6; 2 Cor. 1:22; Rom. 5:5). The heart, moreover, is the seat of will, intentionality, emotions, and affections (1 Thess. 2:4, 17; Phil. 1:7; Rom. 2:15).[27] For this reason, what enters the human heart affects a person's whole being. In broader hermeneutical perspectives, spoken words are experienced personally and more directly than written words. Sound has a pervasive quality; it permeates one's whole physical existence. "Phenomenologically I do not merely hear with my ears, I hear with my whole body."[28] Whether the heart in Pauline anthropology and hermeneutics functions as central receptive organ or as the locus of personal identity, it signifies the sphere of inwardness, the interiority of a person (Rom. 2:29: *en tō kryptō*), to which the outward appearance can be compared unfavorably (2 Cor. 5:12: *en prosōpō kauchōmenos kai mē en kardia*). The heart as metaphor of human interiority is placed into a curious antithesis to *gramma*. Ideally, Paul asserts, circumcision is to become an inward reality (*en tō kryptō*), in heart and Spirit (*kardias en pneumati*), but not in the *gramma* (Rom. 2:29; cf. 7:6). Similarly, the Corinthians are solicited as a "letter written in our hearts . . . written not with ink, but with the Spirit of the living God; . . . for the *gramma* kills, but the Spirit gives life" (2 Cor. 3:2, 3, 6; au. trans.). We shall return to this notable opposition of spoken words, Spirit, and heart to *gramma,* apparently a symbol of undesirable externalization.

While there is no such thing as a face-to-face encounter with a text, the mouth-to-heart engagement in oral communication fosters personal and intimate relations. The spoken word, emanating from interiority and entering another interiority, creates a deep-set bonding of speaker with auditor. "Sound unites groups of living beings as nothing else does."[29] Without this personalizing engagement oral communication cannot exist.

Oral speech is incapable of transacting its business apart from persons. A message delivered implicates speaker and hearers alike. This personalizing aspect of oral speech registers in Pauline language that identifies the proclamation not only as "the gospel of God" (1 Thess. 2:8; Rom. 1:1; 15:16), or the "gospel of Christ" (1 Cor. 9:12; 2 Cor. 2:12; 9:13), or the "gospel of our Lord Jesus" (1 Thess. 1:8), or the "gospel of his Son" (Rom. 1:9), but notably also as "my gospel" (Rom. 2:16; 16:25), or "my word" (1 Cor. 2:4), or "my message" (1 Cor. 2:4), or "our gospel" (1 Thess. 1:5; 2 Cor. 4:3). This personalization of word and gospel is due to the fact that the speaking of the message breeds familial relations (1 Thess. 2:8). He, Paul, is the father who through the medium of the spoken gospel "begot" children, his hearers (1 Cor. 4:15: *dia tou euaggeliou egō hymas eggenēsa*). What to the modern consciousness may seem to border on paternalism could be more correctly regarded as a manifestation of oral conventions. Spoken words in a sense "create" their audience, joining speaker and hearers together into the intimacy of family life.[30] United by the power of the sounded message, all glorify God and Christ "with a single voice" (Rom. 15:6: *en heni stomati*; cf. 14:11; Phil. 2:11). Because preached words enter into personal engagements, creating a sphere of verbal mutuality, Paul can refer to the gospel as "*logos* of giving and receiving" (Phil. 4:15; au. trans. of *logon doseōs kai lēmpseōs*). Recipient and donor of the word are perforce united in fellowship, and vice versa, wherever the word is, there must also be *koinōnia* (Gal. 6:6; Phil. 1:5). At its optimum, apostolic preaching may thus promote the solidarity of the speaker with the audience, and an equation of the knower with the known. Speaker, message, and audience form the kind of unity that we have earlier referred to as *oral synthesis*.[31]

Oral synthesis creates a tense world of personal loyalties and betrayals. Not only is the message inseparable from the speaker, but the speaker is as important to the recipients as his message. If each speaker promotes "his gospel," binding his hearers' allegiance to "our gospel," a community visited by different apostolic speakers could become fragmented into clusters of shared loyalties. Precisely because "oral cultures have great difficulty in separating the knower from the known,"[32] the appearance of more than one apostle may have divisive effects on the communal whole. From this angle, the well-known phenomenon of Corinthian factionalism may be considered a consequence of the bonding powers of oral speech. Given the fact of a plurality of speakers, the oral gospel, due to its deeply personalizing effects, could well become a cause for divided loyalties in the community: *Egō men eimi Paulou, Egō de Apollō, Egō de Kēpha, Egō de Christou* (1 Cor. 1:12).

The Oral and the Written Gospel

If one asks the question regarding the content of the gospel, no direct answer is forthcoming. Gospel in Pauline hermeneutics is not subject to formal definition. It is, we saw, largely an operational term. There is no indication whatsoever that the gospel equals the transformation of plural, oral traditions into narrative linearity, stretching from birth through a powerful life on to death and resurrection. To the extent that pre-Pauline material is recoverable from Pauline literature, it appears in the form of confessions, formulae, hymns, catechesis, prayer, acclamation, and prophetic words.[33] By and large we encounter pre-Pauline tradition in forms fashioned and favored by oral needs and designed for oral use in worship. The one tradition that expresses the heart of the Pauline gospel is the pairing formula of Jesus' death and resurrection.[34] As for its oral employment, it would be wrong to expect unanimity in tradition or uniformity in Paul. The apostle has received a threefold formula of death, burial, and resurrection (1 Cor. 15:3b–5), but apart from the Corinthian controversy pertaining to the resurrection he attaches little importance to burial. He is manifestly partial to death and resurrection, phrasing, qualifying, and restating the formula in multiple ways, at times stressing death (1 Cor. 1:18), and then again resurrection (1 Cor. 6:14), sometimes attributing soteriological significance to death (Rom. 8:32), or again associating resurrection with exaltation (Rom. 1:4). The formula makes its initial appearance in crystallized form in 1 Thess. 4:14, recurs in variant modes throughout the Pauline Corpus (Gal. 1:1; 2:20; Phil. 3:10–11; 1 Cor. 6:14; 2 Cor. 4:13–14), and articulates its own orally transacted, redemptive functioning in Rom. 10:9: "If you confess with your mouth that Jesus is Lord and believe in your heart that God raised him from the dead, you will be saved" (au. trans.).

If the formula of Jesus' death and resurrection, in all its variants, is constitutive of the Pauline gospel, then this articulation of the fundamentally bifocal message can be said to meet the requirements of oral speech and to respond to the deepest instincts of oral wisdom. Contrasts and antitheses, contending principles and parties aid in the memorization of knowledge.[35] To retrieve and transmit information, the oral performer must organize it in strikingly patterned forms. The very core of Paul's gospel, the rhythmic thematization of death and resurrection, can thus be considered a product of mnemonic, oral dynamics: it is eminently memorable, repeatable, and orally usable.

Faith and hearing, not seeing, constitute the appropriate response to the spoken gospel. The hearing dimension of faith is enunciated as early as 1 Thessalonians in a classic statement on oral hermeneutics: "When you received the Word of God which you heard from us (logon akoēs *par' hēmōn*), you accepted it not as word of men, but for what it truly is, the Word of God, which also performs its [energizing] work in you who believe" (1 Thess. 2:13; au. trans.). At its reception the spoken word functions as "word of hearing" (*logos akoēs*) and in this capacity takes full oral effect (*energeitai*) as Word of God in the hearing believers. In Galatians Paul pits the works of the Law against the Spirit, deeds of power, and a faith that comes from hearing (Gal. 3:2, 5: *ex akoēs pisteōs*). The works of the Law operate in a sphere antithetical to the auditory field of sensory perception. Abraham's exemplary faith, in this context, as well as the righteousness attributed to him, are grounded in obedient hearing. He gave heed to a God who, while inaccessible to sight, came to him in the Word. *Logos akoēs* in 1 Thessalonians and *akoē pisteōs* in Galatians are echoed in the cognate idiom of *hypakoē pisteōs* in Romans. The latter phrase is positioned in the salutation and doxology of Romans (1:5; 16:26), providing a verbal and thematic frame for the letter. Given the auditory dimension of faith (*akoē pisteōs*), obedience (*hypakoē pisteōs*) must likewise be perceived in its authentic, etymological sense, denoting less compliance with instruction and more a faithful heeding of what is being said (2 Thess. 1:8; Rom. 10:16).[36] As obedience, so also is disobedience rooted in the auditory field (2 Cor. 10:6; Rom. 5:19: *parakoē*). It denotes a defective sense of hearing which "will not proceed to the action by which hearing becomes genuine hearing."[37] To sum up, the oral gospel and its proclamation, faith and hearing, heedful listening and failure to heed comprise an auditory field in the midst of which God's righteousness is being delivered.

It is in accord with Paul's developed sense of oral hermeneutics that the gospel displays a decidedly activist character. It enunciates less a principle than a procedure; it is behavioristic more than academic. Apart from its association with terms of speech, the gospel is linked with verbs of action and movement. It operates in the context of sending (1 Thess. 3:2), coming (2 Cor. 2:12), and happening (1 Thess. 1:5). In Rom. 10:14–17, the *locus classicus* of the oral hermeneutics of sound, voice, speaking, and hearing, the apostle almost comically alludes to the gospel's social engagement by citing a quote in praise of the apostolic feet: "How beautiful are the feet of those who preach the good news" (Rom. 10:15; cf. Isa. 52:7). Indeed, the gospel itself has feet, as it were, for it "runs" its course across the globe (2 Thess. 3:1: *ho logos tou kyriou trechē*). Far from being chained to papyrus and scroll, the oral gospel partakes in the itinerant mode of apostolic action.

Thriving in the *vita activa*, the gospel constitutes a form of verbal action that invites reciprocal action. The sounded gospel effects a presentness of what is being said and calls hearers into the center of the message. The ethos inspired by the spoken gospel of Jesus' death and resurrection is that of *participation*. The gospel creates something of an orbit, a sphere of influence, in which one can situate oneself, or to use Pauline terminology, in which to "stand" (1 Cor. 15:1: *to euaggelion . . . en hō hestēkate*). Both grace (Rom. 5:2) and faith (2 Cor. 1:24) exhibit a similar orbital influence. In view of the oral base of faith and gospel, one may call their sphere of influence an *auditory field*. "Standing" in this verbal space of the sounded gospel, one shares in the actuality of the dying and rising Christ. This participatory quality of the gospel is uniquely developed in Pauline theology (1 Thess. 5:10; Gal. 6:14–15; Phil. 3:10–11; 2 Cor. 4:7–14; Rom. 6:3–6), and it furnishes an elementary aspect of the apostle's soteriology, christology, sacramentalism, anthropology, and ethics.[38] It is less susceptible of explanation in terms of Christ mysticism[39] and more readily consonant with the dynamistic aspect of language. The participatory élan distinguishes the Pauline gospel as a genuine oral proclamation, for behind every successful oral performer lies the ability to make hearers live the message. In short, what is implemented in the Pauline language of participation is the epistemological principle of orality that to know actuality is to participate in it.

As missionary of the gospel Paul not merely traveled, but spent much time in the workshop.[40] His trade of making tents and other products of leather "in large measure determined his daily experience and his social status."[41] Like most artisans who lived from the work of their hands, he worked long hours (1 Thess. 2:9: *nyktos kai hēmeras ergazomenos*). The apostle's itinerant life may thus aptly be compared to that of an artisan-missionary.[42] His personal commitment to manual labor is most evident from his spirited defense of his choice to work for a living. According to his own interpretation, the practice of self-support gave him economic independence, freed him from burdening others and, most importantly, allowed him to boast of his weakness as a laborer whose trade was associated with wearisome toil and the stigma of slavishness (1 Cor. 4:11–12; 9:1–19; 2 Cor. 11:7–15; 12:13–16). If it is granted that Paul's trade contributed to his apostolic identity, we may picture him "plying his trade wherever he was preaching the gospel,"[43] and speaking the Word wherever he worked. From this perspective it is reasonable to assume that the artisan-missionary carried on missionary activity in the workshop by discussing the gospel with fellow workers and customers.[44] Significantly, Paul wished to elicit not merely participation in his gospel but imitation of his work as well. He called upon the Thessalonians to work with their hands (1 Thess. 4:11) and held up his own labor as an example to be imitated (2 Thess. 3:8–9). The social background for this equivalence of word and deed may well be the Pauline workshop. But the injunction to imitate the artisan-missionary is rooted in the oral principle of *imitatio magistri*.[45] Accordingly, there are no strict boundaries separating the lessons to be learned from the teacher and his style of life. The student learns by imitating both the teacher's conduct and his message, and vice versa, the teacher lives a life that is paradigmatic in terms of his message. Because in oral hermeneutics words have no existence apart from persons, participation in the message is inseparable from imitation of the speaker: "We decided to share with you not only the gospel of God but also our selves . . . For you recall, brethren, our labor and hardship, how working night and day so as not to be a burden to any of you, we proclaimed to you the gospel of God" (1 Thess. 2:8–9; au. trans.).

THE WRITTEN LAW

Paul's abiding commitment to the oral gospel may cast fresh light on one of the more controversial aspects of his thought, his polemical stance toward the Law. First, we will focus on the apostle's treatment of the Law in Galatians 3. Next we will discuss the famous *pneuma-gramma* antithesis in 2 Cor. 3:1–6. The investigation will conclude with a reflection on Romans 7, Paul's deeply philosophical discourse on the Law.

The Curse of the Law

Recently new insight was provided on the issue of the Law in Galatians by E. P. Sanders in his monumental study on *Paul and Palestinian Judaism*: "We must first note that in Galatians, the reason for not keeping the Law which Bultmann adduces (that keeping it is itself sinning, because it leads to sin: boasting before God) is notably not in evidence."[46] One can go a long way toward agreeing with this statement. It is indeed correct that in Galatians Paul's objection to the Law is not predicated on the formula: observing it is sinning. Bultmann's view, that man's use of the Law *eo ipso* leads to sin because it encourages procurement of salvation by one's own strength,[47] fails to take seriously Paul's fundamentally Jewish conviction that observance of the Law is desirable (Gal. 3:10; Rom. 2:13, 25–26). According to Romans 7, transgression of the Law is a tragedy leading to despair and death. Arrogant boasting before God is once again not the issue. Sanders's own thesis is couched in the formula: "the solution precedes the predicament."[48] By this he meant to say that the apostle's experience of redemption in Christ preceded reflection on sin, and *eo ipso* precluded salvation by the Law. While it may well be true that prior to his call Paul had few, if any, qualms about fulfilling the Law (Phil. 3:6), his letters in fact give us an apostle reflecting on the Law, the dilemma it causes for man, and its relation to faith and gospel. Granted that Paul did not develop a systematic argument on the matter of the Law, full exegetical advantage has yet to be taken of his subtle, linguistic clues pertaining to a deep-seated anxiety over the Law.

We have already touched on the polarization of faith that comes from hearing versus works of the Law in Galatians (3:2, 5: *akoē pisteōs . . . erga nomou*). Paul's meditation on faith and Law (Gal. 3:1–14) brings into convergence hearing (*akoē*), faith (*pistis*), the proclamation of righteousness (*dikaioi . . . proeuēggelisato*), blessing (*eulogia*), and promise of the Spirit (*tēn epaggelian tou pneumatos*)—all features that suggest the transaction of the spoken word and its personalizing effects. The faith of Abraham (3:6) may thus be understood as arising out of hearing, and his righteousness must likewise be tied not only to faith, as is commonly agreed, but to hearing and the oral lifeworld altogether. Undoubtedly, the works of the Law in Galatians refer to circumcision recommended and imposed by rival apostles. But if Abraham's faith results from hearing and obtains the interiorly efficacious righteousness, could not the work of circumcision have resulted from an externalization of the Word of God, which fails to rule in the heart so as to produce true, inward circumcision? This could explain the Pauline antithesis of the works of the Law versus faith which comes from hearing.

The curse of living under the Law, and the implied problem of the Law, are stated in 3:10. The *RSV* translation of the verse is manifestly erroneous: "For all who rely on works of the law are under a curse." The verb "rely" invokes the notion of an unconscionable use of the Law and biases the reader toward a Bultmannian rationale: relying on the Law, one uses it to one's advantage, producing a state of sinfulness. This reading does not, however, conform with the literal wording. The verb "rely" is notably absent from the Greek text which reads as follows: "For as many as are under the works of the Law, are under a curse." As far as it goes, this sentence simply states that life based on works of the Law is subject to a curse. It does not say that use of the Law in terms of "relying" on it constitutes the nature of the curse. The reason for the sinful condition is subsequently provided by the Deuteronomy citation: "Cursed be every one who does not abide by all that is written in the book of the Law to do them" (Gal. 3:10 = Deut. 27:26; au. trans.). Clearly, the curse of the Law is brought about not by "relying" on the Law, but by not doing it! The Law, according to Paul, demands to be acted upon, hence one ought to *do* it (Rom. 2:25: *prassein*; 2:26; 6:13:

phylassein; Gal. 3:10: *poiein*). Indeed, hearers of the Law are not justified, but doers (Rom. 2:13). It is the failure to live up to the Law in all its requirements (Gal. 5:3: *holon ton nomon poiēsai*) that produces the condition of cursedness.

The one feature Paul emphasizes in describing the human condition under the Law is the written nature of the Law. The Law is called "the Scripture" (Gal. 3:8: *he graphē*) or "the book" (3:10: *en tō bibliō*). It exists in written form (3:10: *tois gegrammenois*), and the obedience it claims is to its written totality (3:10: *pasin tois gegrammenois en tō bibliō tou nomou tou poiēsai auta*). Implied in this language is not aversion to the legalistic character of the Law nor skepticism about self-righteous use of it, but a sense of its written totality and complexity. From the standpoint of *akoē pisteōs*, the technology of writing facilitates an unparalleled expansion of mental storage possibilities, effecting a vast augmentation of the Word of God. Insofar as it is recorded by the written medium, the Law renders the obligation to live up to "*all* that is written down in the book" ever more difficult. This written complexification of the Word appears to be contrary to the personalized communication fostered by the oral gospel and faith that comes from hearing. There is, therefore, a linguistic dimension to the Pauline polemic against the Law, which connects the curse of the Law (Gal. 3:13: *tēs kataras tou nomou*), its tragic inability to give life (3:21), with its objectification into a written record.

In reflecting on the purpose of the Law in relation to the Abrahamic covenant, Paul uses obscure and almost mystifying language. The Law "was ordained by angels through the hand [sic] of a mediator; but the mediator is not of one [contradicts the notion of oneness], whereas God is one" (Gal. 3:19–20; au. trans.). These words are designed to stress the mediated, hence derivative, quality of the Law. The concept of mediation is here, contrary to its conventional meaning in religion, used negatively. Both the agency of the angels and the mediatorship of Moses depreciate rather than enhance the status of the Law. Mediation is considered a liability.[49] The Law, when mediated by angels and Moses, perhaps even dictated by angels to Moses,[50] lacks the quality of immediacy. Because the process of mediation filters the Law through the agency of angels and Moses, it communicates by indirection, and for this reason compromises the Word of God. It may not be accidental that the concept of Christ the mediator (*mesitēs*), while developed in the Pastorals (1 Tim. 2:5) and crucial for Hebrews (8:6; 9:15; 12:24), is absent in Pauline theology. The peculiarly negative assessment of the mediation of the Law reflects the hermeneutical conviction of one dedicated to the unmediated, direct, hence oral delivery of the Word of God. In Gal. 3:19–20 the two mediating agents of angels and Moses produce a double distancing effect. The voice of God, when communicated by mediation, no longer speaks directly. In its mediated form, it operates as a fractured, secondary version. Whereas the promises were spoken to Abraham (3:16: *tō de Abraam errethēsan hai epaggeliai*) and renewed in the gospel of Christ, the Law (which came between Abraham and Christ) was equivalent to the interrupted voice of God. The ideal of oneness, invoked by Paul in antithesis to mediatorship, signifies the unmediated, total presence attainable through the personalizing powers of the gospel of Christ. This is how the status of the Law, the written Word of God, must appear to one who is committed to the oral gospel and its participatory effects.

Apart from creating complexification and distanciation, the Law is beset with yet another problem: it produces alienation. The statement that "the Scripture has locked up (*synekleisen*) everything under sin" (Gal. 3:22; au. trans.) conjures up the imagery of the Law as a prison house. The term *sygkleiō* connotes "to lock up," "to shut up," with little hope of freedom or escape. The precise logical connection between sin and Law is left unspecified, but nothing in the immediate context suggests boastful, righteous use of the Law. The following line depicts the Law as a force constraining people within its narrowly contained space, holding all in the clutch of sin: "But before the coming of faith we were kept in custody of the Law, locked up until faith was later to be revealed" (Gal. 3:23; au. trans.). *Phroureisthai*, to be held in custody, is reinforced here by the formerly used *sygkleisthai*, to be locked up, and together the two verbs project the Law as an inescapably closed system. Now the imagery of prison, confining space, controlling and alienating people, leaps to the eye.

As noted before, circumcision constitutes the works of the Law that submit people to the yoke of slavery. But the concrete issue of circumcision leads Paul to deeper reflection on the nature of the Law and its role in history. There is something about the Law itself and its ordained role in history that tends to enslave people in a closed system, prohibiting entrance into the perfection of Abraham's seed. Language that records the curious metaphor of the Law as closure and prison invites exploration into the linguistic, sensory base of Pauline thought. The antithesis of the Law as *graphē* versus the *epaggelia tēs pisteōs* (3:22) indicates affiliations with underlying linguistic realities. The Law that commits man to bondage is the Law in its inscribed existence, *hē graphē*, whereas it is in the form of a spoken message, *hē epaggelia*, that the Word is delivered into the hearts of believers. In depth, the prison house of the Law is constructed in chirographic form. In the words of Ong: "Writing and print effect closure. The written word means constriction."[51] The Law as written Law circumscribes a medium world that is tighter and more sealed off from life than spoken words whose acoustic field is both fluid and open. For Paul the Law as written authority locks Abraham's heirs behind its verbal walls, and, instead of opening up to God, alienates and creates a sphere of sin.

The pertinence of these observations can be strengthened by attending to Paul's insight into the ideal observance of the Law. "For the whole Law is fulfilled in a single word: 'You shall love your neighbor as yourself'" (Gal. 5:14; au. trans.). Far from relinquishing his commitment to the *whole* Law, the apostle chose to sum up the totality of the written Law in a single *logos* (*en heni* [sic] *logō*). The primary unit of oral speech, the *logos*, has been entrusted with carrying the Law in its entirety (cf. Rom. 13:9). The whole Law equals a single *logos*. This *logos* assumes a position of new authority: it becomes "the Law of Christ" (Gal. 6:2). It would be difficult to argue that content makes the crucial difference between the Law of Moses and the Law of Christ, since love of neighbor is a verbatim restatement of Lev. 19:18. What then, according to Paul, accounts for the new authority of the Law of Christ? One is referred back to underlying medium realities. In depth it is not content, but the modality and transformational power of language that discriminates between all that is written down in the book of the Law and the single *logos* of Christ. The latter operates in memorable fashion and bespeaks an ethic of orality: the simple, direct, and personal quality of neighborly love counteracts the complexification, indirection, and alienation brought about by the written Law.

It should be noted that propositions of this kind do not state absolute truths about the matter of the spoken and the written word. Much could be said of the liabilities of orality and the assets of the written word. Paul himself, we shall see, will in 1 Corinthians be driven to a position of questioning the power of the *logos*. By and large, however, his language betrays a singular interest in emphasizing the strictures imposed by the written Law, which is but another way of underscoring his commitment to oral speech.

Spirit versus "Letter"

In 2 Cor. 3:1–6 the apostle's antinomianism takes on a novel aspect. Now the Law is associated with death. The external circumstances that have triggered Paul's language and argument are readily discernible. Divine Man apostles, Paul's principal target in 2 Corinthians,[52] were in the habit of employing letters of recommendation, written either by former hosts to assure them a favorable reception at Corinth, or by Corinthians to recommend them elsewhere (3:1: *systatikōn epistolōn pros hymas ē ex hymōn*). These letters were highly complimentary records of the apostles' virtues and accomplishments, documents, as it were, of their apostolic credentials (12:12: *ta sēmeia tou apostolou*). Paul objects to the practice of using letters of recommendation as a means of assuring apostolic authority. What is surprising, however, is the intricacy of his argument and the depth of his opposition. Why is he not content with stating that the letters induce self-promotion, whereas he, true apostle of Christ, wishes to promote the Lord? Instead, he makes a seemingly excessive statement concerning the *pneuma* that gives life and the *gramma* that takes life away (3:6). To oppose letters of recommendation is one thing, but to equate *gramma* with death is quite another.

One observes two stages in Paul's argument. First, he internalizes and personalizes the concept of letter. Ideally, the letter is written into human hearts. What is more, the people themselves constitute a letter of Christ, universally knowable and readable (3:2–3). One immediately recognizes oral hermeneutics at work in Paul's internalization and personalization of the letter. Second, the apostle contrasts this internalized, personalized letter with the tablets of stone (3:3). Undoubtedly, the latter refer to the Decalogue, the principal authority of the Law. At this point, the argument that began with the issue of letters of recommendation has culminated in an antithesis of Christ's letter "written not with ink but with the Spirit of the living God" (3:3) versus the tablets of the Mosaic Decalogue. This raises a number of questions. What makes Paul depart from the concrete issue of apostolic letters of recommendation and introduce the notion of an internalized, personalized letter? What, if anything, has the Decalogue to do with letters of recommendation? Is there any logic behind the apostle's polemical shift from the apostolic credentials to the Mosaic Law?

In search for an explanation of the curious correlation of letters of recommendation and the Decalogue, it is advisable to probe the theological and hermeneutical predilections of the Divine Man apostles, Paul's principal opponents. When Paul designates the people themselves as a letter of Christ, written neither in ink nor on tablets, he extends by implication the concept of letter to the Decalogue. The people do not constitute a letter written with ink, nor a letter carved on stone. In this one may hear an echo of the apostles' practice of placing confidence both in written credentials and in the Mosaic Law, perceiving both to be letters of recommendation. This opens the way for the concept of the heavenly letter (*Himmelsbrief*), as suggested by Dieter Georgi.[53] Just as the apostles used personal letters of recommendation to advance their reception into the community, so will they also have employed the heavenly letter of the Mosaic Law as a source of inspiration and identification. An active pursuit of self-promotion, pride in Jewish culture, and a high appreciation of written tradition places them into the general context of Hellenistic-Jewish apologetics, according to Georgi's brilliant reconstruction. The Pauline association of letters of recommendation with the Decalogue will therefore find its natural explanation in the Divine Man apostles' identification of the Decalogue as the heavenly letter received by Moses on Sinai and their practice of drawing support from both types of letters.

Against this background Paul's argument appears to engage in a full-blown discussion on hermeneutics.[54] While the shift from the letters of recommendation to the Decalogue is now intelligible, it is of some consequence what he singles out as common denominator of the two types of letters. The personal letters are written in ink (2 Cor. 3:3: *eggegrammenē . . . melani*), the heavenly letter is written on stone (3:3: *eggegrammenē en plaxin lithinais*). Therefore, what both have in common is their written nature. But ideally, Paul asserts, the letter ought to be written in human hearts (3:2; *eggegrammenē en tais kardiais hēmōn*) and embodied in people (3:3: *phaneroumenoi hoti este epistolē Christou*)—hence not written at all in any ordinary sense! The new covenant can thus not be *grammatos,* but must be *pneumatos* (3:6). Paul's objection to all that is *eggegrammenē* with ink or on stone prepares etymologically and conceptually for a reading of the Law in its *written* form. "The letters of the tables of the Law bear eloquent witness to the fact that the *nomos* is only what is written. To translate 'letter' is to miss the deep seriousness of what is said."[55] *To gramma* constitutes what is manifestly *gegrammenon,* and what is written lacks the quality of the Spirit due to its "grammatological" nature. The ideal letter, on the other hand, which is internalized and personalized, has overcome the externalization of the *gramma.*

In view of the identifiably polemical context, one may safely assume that Paul will have formulated his thesis of the incompatibility of *gramma* with *pneuma* in repudiation of the Divine Man hermeneutics. The latter put a high premium on the written word because they will have been convinced of the intrinsic affinity of *pneuma* with *gramma.* Hermeneutically, their inclination to attribute commanding authority to both personal and heavenly letters rested on the conviction that the written word served as carrier of the Spirit. Paul, on his part, operated in the fashion of an *oral traditionalist,* disconnecting the *pneuma* from *gramma* and reconnecting the "Spirit of the living God" with word in its internal, personalizing efficaciousness (3:2–3).

Translations and interpretations of *pneuma* and *gramma* in 2 Cor. 3:1–6 have been informed by theological orientations that have not always paid full attention to underlying hermeneutical tensions. The *RSV* translation, for example, renders *to gramma* with "the written code." The term "code," arbitrarily injected by the translator, may run the gamut of meaning from a set of prearranged symbols or ciphers, to a group of principles and regulations, to a systematized body of law. Frequently interpreters have seized upon the latter, the legal meaning, slanting Paul's hermeneutical concept of *gramma* in the direction of legalism and legalistic self-righteousness. Ernst Käsemann, for example, in discussing the nature of *gramma,* writes of "the Torah in its misunderstood character as a demand for good works."[56] Yet *gramma,* while entirely neutral with respect to the judicial authority of the Law, does carry with it the connotation of *graphein,* to write, a meaning strongly supported by the context. Moreover, Georgi's splendid study on 2 Corinthians has made it abundantly clear that the Divine Man apostles are not representatives of "Jewish legalism," but rather the proponents of a tradition of Hellenistic-Jewish apologetics and hermeneutics. The Pauline response is thus not designed to address the work-character of the Law. It is hardly accidental that in all of 2 Corinthians 3 the term *nomos* is absent. Paul's concern, we observed, is the grammatological nature of the Law. The principal antithesis is not between Spirit versus works, but between Spirit versus the Written. Paul's objection is not to the *nomos* as a legal authority, but rather to the objectification of the Law as *gramma.* It is a tribute to the apostle's theological acumen that he probes in depth the Divine Man apostles' self-promoting posture, discerning its underlying hermeneutical problem.

The recovery of the medium dimension underlying 2 Cor. 3:1–6 casts fresh light on Paul's postulated linkage between *gramma* and death. Startling as this alliance may seem, it is nevertheless plausible if death is perceived in relation to the grammatological identity of the Law. Connections between the written medium and death are manifold, complex, and subtle: "Thousands of references could be cited, open or veiled, to writing and print as death."[57] The freezing of living words into a mute and immutable medium resembles the rite of burial. Laid out stiff and cold, once Spirit-filled words have become "the cadavers of thought."[58] Robbed of oral, spiritual life, they appear despiritualized, hence dead. Thus, the "killing is a consequence of the fact that this Law is only what is written or prescribed."[59] That is, again, not to be taken as an axiomatic statement on the nature of the written Law, but it is the kind of judgment that suggests itself to a mind committed to the oral operation of words.

In a superb survey of the history of interpretation of the *gramma-pneuma* discussion, Bernardin Schneider, O. F. M., detected two principal readings in Christian tradition.[60] The *formalistic* approach understands *gramma* and *pneuma* as two diverse senses inherent in Scripture. *Gramma* denotes the literal sense and *pneuma* the spiritual sense. The *realistic* approach relates *gramma* to the Mosaic Law itself, often in its written form, and designates *pneuma* as the internally active power of the Spirit. In Christian theological history the formalistic approach was widely championed by the Alexandrian tradition (Origen, Athanasius, Gregory of Nyssa, Cyril of Alexandria), and the realistic approach by the Antiochene school of exegesis (Tertullian, Ephraem, Apollinaris of Laodicea, Ambrosiaster, John Chrysostom, Augustin, Pelagius), with a number of early church Fathers supporting both a formalistic and realistic interpretation (Didymus of Alexandria, Theodore of Mopsuestia, Thomas Aquinas).[61] Our own interpretation is squarely based in the realistic, Antiochene tradition. But Schneider's analysis also revealed a persistent, moralistic streak in Antiochene exegesis. There is much talk about the Law punishing transgression, putting an end to a depraved life, or arousing illicit concupiscence. None of the many passages quoted by Schneider manages to demonstrate the *inner logic* linking together the holiness of the Law, its alienating effect, its soteriological defect, its ability to arouse and bring awareness of sin, and its association with death. The written medium, the one quality of the Law that is a principal key to Paul's antinomianism, has not been taken with full seriousness, either theologically or hermeneutically.

Man's Fall Under the Law

Chapter 7 of Romans has long been considered the apostle's philosophically most serious but curiously opaque discourse on the Law. From the hermeneutical perspectives we have developed Romans 7 bears reexamination. It is worth exploring whether Paul's deliberations may be informed, deeply and perhaps subconsciously, by aversion to the Law in its externalized, objectified form.

That the apostle is not entirely unaware of a linguistic dimension is apparent from Rom. 7:6 that defines the distinction between service under the Law and freedom from it in terms of the old status of the grammatological Law (*palaiotēti grammatos*) versus the newness of the Spirit (*kainotēti pneumatos*). This very formulation contrasts the tragically grammatological experience under the Law with the spiritual, nongrammatical power of the gospel. If, moreover, one approaches Romans 7 from a reading of Galatians 3 and especially 2 Cor. 3:1–6, it comes as little surprise to find the Law linked with sin, flesh, and even death. Nor is the well-known apologetic running through the discourse— which affirms the essential holiness (7:12), goodness (7:13), and even spirituality (7:14) of the Law—incompatible with the noted medium realities. To connect the Law with its grammatological confinement is not to deny its inviolability both in Spirit and intentionality.[62]

Its essential goodness notwithstanding, the Law effects knowledge of sin: "But sin I would not have known, if it were not through the Law" (7:7; au. trans.). Instead of delivering salvation, it generates awareness of the human condition. While the existence of sin dates from the genesis of man (Rom. 5:12), it is with the appearance of the Law that human consciousness of sin has been awakened. It is not clear at this point in what sense the Law is empowered to raise awareness of sin.

The Law not only brings knowledge of sin, it also discloses the nature of sin (7:13; *hē hamartia, hina phanē hamartia*). The precise conduct of sin revealed under the Law, however, has remained a controversial issue. According to Bultmann's reading, the Law discloses man's fundamental disposition toward "boasting in works." What constitutes the human predicament under the Law is the very desire to make it the soteriological mainstay. Thus for Bultmann the Law reveals the sinfulness of man's religious reliance upon the Law.[63] A simple check on the vocabulary of Romans 7 raises doubt about Bultmann's proposal. There is no mention in the text of boasting in that upon which one ultimately depends. Absent are the terms *erga tou nomou, dikaiosynē,* and *kauchasthai,* which together could generate a field of meaning congenial to the perception of sin as "boasting in works."

There is little ambiguity in Romans 7 as to what kind of sin Paul has in mind. The Law, over and above raising consciousness of sin, provokes sin to action. That is the meaning of the statement that "sin finding opportunity in the commandment, wrought in me all covetousness" (7:8; au. trans.). Yet the covetousness aroused by the Law is clearly action in violation of the Law that rules: "You shall not covet" (7:7; Exod. 20:17; Deut. 5:21). The sinful conduct brought about through the instrumentality of the Law is therefore transgression of the Law, and not the religiously well-meaning but deeply self-serving use of the Law. Elsewhere in Romans Paul speaks of the introduction of the Law for the purpose of increasing transgression of the Law (5:20: *hina pleonasē to paraptōma*). Its tragically appointed function is therefore to instigate disobedience toward the commandments, rather than compliance with them. Essentially, the Law is holy and good, making a just claim on man's attention (Rom. 8:4), and transgression of the Law, not reliance on it, constitutes the human dilemma.

Transgression of the Law, while undesirable and sinful, does as yet not constitute the depth of sin. When face to face with the Law, a person experiences the inner mechanism of disobedience. Confronted with commandments, one is torn apart between what in accordance with the Law one wishes to do and what concretely one is unable to deliver (7:15–20). The inner self (7:22: *ho esō anthrōpos*) concurs with the mind in observing the Law but is disabled and held in bondage by another law within oneself that contradicts the Law of God. It is this division of the self that constitutes the hell of sin, and death. A person's split identity—and awareness of it—cancels any possible chance of observing the will of God as revealed in the Law. Precisely how the Law brings about consciousness of human self-contradiction is as yet not clear at this point.

More light can be thrown on the subject if one probes the mythological roots that nurtured Paul's thought. Interpreters have at times commented on, but as yet not fully explicated, the myth in the background of Romans 7. There exist ideological and even verbal correspondences between Paul's reflection on the Law and the story of humanity's fall in Genesis 3. An explication of the underlying mythology will clarify the logic upon which the Pauline discourse is built.

The central symbol in the Pauline treatise is the Law. In Genesis it is the tree of the knowledge of good and evil. It is due to the tree that man comes to fall, just as it is under the Law that man experiences the fallen condition. In each case, however, the central symbol is good and holy. A separate agent is introduced: sin in the Pauline discourse, and the serpent in Genesis. The serpent "beguiles" the woman to eat from the tree and thus violates the sanctity of the tree. According to Paul, sin "deceives" man (7:11: *hē gar hamartia . . . exēpatēsen me*) to find an opportunity for sinning in the Law and thus violates the commandments of the Law. In Genesis it is at the instigation of the serpent that the woman desires to eat from the tree. In the Pauline discourse, it is at the instigation of sin that one desires to disobey the Law. In each case the fall brings knowledge of sin. In the Genesis myth, man and woman know that they are naked, that is to say, their consciousness is raised in regard to their character as creatures and their mortality. By learning to discern the difference between good and evil, they have become conscious of their nature. This knowledge, acquired by transgression, leads to expulsion, which ironically marks the beginning of civilized efforts outside the Garden. In Romans 7 man discovers sin. That is to say, one experiences an inability to fulfill the will of God as mandated in the Law. By discovering the nature of sin, one learns to comprehend one's inner self as self-contradiction. This inner conflict, acquired by transgression, leads into utter despair, although it is ironically connected with profound insight into the self.

In paraphrasing a well-known dictum by Paul Ricoeur, it may be said that the Genesis myth has given rise to thought in the apostle.[64] By reenacting the Yahwist story in terms of the fall under the Law, Paul has freed the myth from its first naiveté and promoted it to a mode of intellectual reflectiveness. As revealed by the Law, man's fallen condition is opposite to and in violation of the Law. Interiorly, the Law discloses a division of the self in two contradictory laws. One wills the Law of God; the other operates as counter-will. Theologically, this inner conflict is one between obedience and disobedience. But more is involved here than compliance with or violation of the Law. Hannah Arendt suggested that Paul's exposition in Romans 7 of the two-in-one division, characteristic of mental processes and first explored in Western tradition by Socrates and Plato, amounted to a discovery of what in modern terminology would be called *consciousness*.[65] Indeed, in the struggle between *velle* and *nolle* the self finds itself addressing its self, and in that very process coming to an awareness of its own selfhood. It may thus justly be said that the Law insofar as it makes conscious the struggle between I-will and I-nill serves as midwife in the birth of consciousness itself. But one must hasten to add that the apostle does not, in Socratic fashion, glory in the rise of consciousness. For him, the consciousness obtained under the Law produces a profoundly unhappy state of mind. It is in the experience of self-contradiction that the self comes to awareness of its self-identity. Self-consciousness and the experience of the fall are thus deeply connected phenomena in Paul's discourse on the fall. The Law fails to carry out its assigned role of procuring redemption precisely by exposing the self in the bright light of self-consciousness. While functioning cognitively in raising self-consciousness, it fails to perform soteriologically in bringing about peace and reconciliation. The connection, buried in the myth and boldly reclaimed by Paul, is between the rise in consciousness and expulsion from Eden, self-awareness and the loss of redemption.

It is suggested here that the logic by which the Law performs cognitively but fails soteriologically is most plausibly linked with its existence in objectified, externalized form. Paul himself, we noted, was not unaware of the medium identity of the Law from which Christ effects release

(Rom. 7:7). It is under the grammatological authority of the Law that one suffers the fall, experiencing a heightened sense of the self in conjunction with profound alienation, and even death.

The cognitive faculty Paul attributes to the Law is entirely compatible with the Law as written authority. That writing plays a crucial role, perhaps the crucial role, in the evolution of human consciousness is now an accepted datum of linguistic studies concerned with oral and written modalities. Major aspects of the work by Eric A. Havelock,[66] Walter J. Ong, S. J.,[67] Herbert N. Schneidau,[68] and Jack Goody[69] are devoted to making precisely this point: the transformation of spoken into written words makes vision an analogue of knowing, thereby facilitating a clarity of perception unknown to oral communication. The psycholinguistic realities entailed in the process of pinning down living words on paper are profoundly intricate, but they are conveniently summed up in the fashionable aphorism: spoken words personify, written words objectify. In the performance of the oral gospel the power of words is actualized, and speaker and hearer tend to converge in the message. Spoken words encourage participation *in* the message, not reflection *on* it. The written word of the Law, on the other hand, has become unhinged from the oral, participatory lifeworld. It has assumed an existence as verbal artifact, an object apart from speaker and audience. It is in this posture of detachment that the Law benefits the quality of perception. Laid out before one's eyes, the Law as *gramma* invites scrutiny and fosters critical mental activity. Deliberation of its meaning has replaced participation in its message. The individual self, standing apart from the *gramma*, reflects upon it and comes to awareness of its own inner selfhood. The distance guaranteed by the written Law heightens a sense of self-surveillance and self-criticism. This is the hermeneutical truth behind Paul's statement that I would not have known myself, were it not for the old status of the written Law.

It follows that the soteriological defect Paul imputes to the Law is likewise bound up with its chirographic exteriorization. From a position of commitment to oral synthesis, the written Law spells a loss of being-in-time and a separation from the dynamistic base of language. With writing, salvation has become depersonalized and has ceased to be delivered in the act of speaking. Instead of pledging hearers to a binding contract, the written Law, cut off from oral, participatory life, creates distance between itself and receivers. What results is a posture of reflection upon the Law more than engagement in it. The reader discovers personal identity vis-à-vis the Law. This, from the oral viewpoint, self-alienating process of the objectification of both the Law and the self carries with it the temptation to perceive oneself in a position not merely opposite the Law but also in opposition to it. This is the hermeneutical truth of Paul's statement that the Law releases the sinful desire to transgress the Law.

The deep connection between the cognitive faculty of the Law and its delivery of sin and death is now also clear. Whereas words, when sounded out, display a pervasive and encompassing quality, vision fostered by writing takes reality apart.[70] To say that with writing a disjunctive element has entered the process of knowing is to understate the case. More to the point, writing sanctions cognition as the act of knowing by disjunction. It is significant that the Law, in the apostle's view, raises the self's consciousness by splitting it apart. In describing the depth of the human dilemma under the Law, Paul's language of cognition enlists the verbs of knowing (7:18: *oida*, root FI, *video*, to see), finding (7:21: *heuriskein*), and seeing (7:23: *blepein*), all visually based terms. Under the authority of the written Law, vision has become the dominant metaphor of cognition. But it is not the vision (or reflection) of the glory of the Lord in the Spirit of freedom (2 Cor. 3:12–18), but rather a self-reflection. Knowing by sight opens up the space of interiority, making it available to the inquiring mind. The privacy of the human self is both invaded and fragmented. What one knows, finds, and sees is another law, located in the interior self and locked in combat with the Law of God. Analytic powers have been aroused to the point where the self acquires awareness of its selfhood by reflection on its own interior distances and contradictions. Experience of sin, the conscious realization of one's split identity and consequent inability to do the will of God, is thus built into the structure of knowledge administered by the written Law. But knowledge of this kind, Paul suggests, breeds alienation comparable to expulsion from Eden and makes a parody out of the Law's intent to procure salvation. Once man has fallen under the textuality of the Law, death cannot be far away.

If to the modern typographical consciousness the epistemological flavor of Paul's discourse on the fall inclines toward the pessimistic, one must remember that the apostle approaches the Law in the fashion of an oral traditionalist. In depth his repudiation of the Law arises out of aversion to the objectifying world of visualism and preference for the oral world of dynamism and synthesis. From the standpoint of this conviction, the Law as grammatological authority appears antithetical to the powers of the oral gospel. This is the way the matter of the written Law must present itself to the apostle whose fundamental disposition is not to teach objectification, but to preach participation.

THE ORAL MATRIX OF
THE RIGHTEOUSNESS OF GOD

Modern critical scholarship of the Pauline letters has received a major theological impetus from issues raised in the sixteenth century. The Reformers' application of Pauline theologoumena and the impact of the Reformation on Western history have brought with them unceasing reflection on the apostle's thought. The reasons Paul carried great weight with the Reformers are historically and theologically complex. Among the numerous bonds of kinship the Reformers detected between their own religious experience and that of Paul, the apostle's principled objection to righteousness based on the Law and his companion affirmation of righteousness grounded in faith struck a particularly sensitive chord. Paul's antinomianism proved susceptible of exploitation in terms of a critique of the ecclesiastic indulgences. Justification by faith became the theological principle of redemption from what was perceived to be the Law's righteousness imposed by the church. When in the nineteenth and twentieth centuries historical-critical scholarship began to retroject "the Protestant-Catholic debate into ancient history, with Judaism taking the role of Catholicism and Christianity the role of Lutheranism,"[71] a virtually ineradicable seed of anti-Judaism was planted into Christian theology in general and Pauline scholarship in particular. As documented by E. P. Sanders, New Testament scholars were in the habit of equating ancient Judaism with the legalistic urge to secure redemption in the sight of God by daily weighing individual merits and demerits.[72] Whether it was put subtly or not so subtly, Protestant scholarship especially interpreted the Jewish Law as a tyrant forcing people into earning salvation by compiling good works. It was this legalistic authority of the Law from which Paul was perceived to have liberated mankind. There is in Christian scholarship a growing awareness of the inherent anti-Jewish bias, but moral qualms are no substitute for theological, hermeneutical reflection. Not even Sanders has succeeded in rigorously rethinking the roots of Pauline antinomianism. We noted the unsatisfactory nature of his suggested formula: "the solution precedes the predicament." If we are to overcome the notion of Paul the liberator from Jewish legalism, his theology of the Law must be probed deeply both for its conscious and unconscious motivations. In tracing the linguistic roots of Paul's thinking on gospel and Law, our study attempted to disconnect the apostle's antinomianism from legal, legalistic implication.

Apart from the odious Christian charge of Jewish legalism there is a second less obvious reason that has prevented us from recognizing the

165

linguistic connectedness of the oral gospel with objections to the written Law: the role of the media in the first century as over against the medium situation that obtained during and after the Reformation.[73] The Reformation and its theological ramifications are unthinkable apart from medium realities, that is, the extension and intensification of writing by movable type.[74] This novel technique of producing and managing words directly contributed to the dawning of a new consciousness. Printing multiplied the sheer number of available Bibles, produced vernacular translations, facilitated Bible reading for nonclerical and clerical readers, created a rapidly expanding readership, cultivated the concept of the priesthood of common believers, fostered a literate, scholarly treatment of biblical texts, undercut the thoroughly oral notion of the *verbum efficax* in the sacraments, and so forth. Understandably, the novel technological management of the written medium resulted in the attribution of unprecedented authority to the written Word of the Bible, which in turn launched a challenge to the traditional authority. To be sure, the Reformers, above all the early Luther, retained and in part rediscovered the *viva vox* of the gospel. And yet, the shift in traditional medium priorities inevitably made its impact on Christian theology that both in its Catholic and Protestant affirmation had to come to grips with the rising new consciousness. The written word, magnified and monumentalized by the printing technique, entered Christian consciousness in a manner unmatched in previous theological history. Slowly but surely this elevation of the newly managed medium led interpreters away from awareness of Paul's linguistic frame of reference. As typographical medium consciousness gained the ascendancy, finding its theological formulation in the Protestant principle of *sola scriptura,* the apostle's full disposition to language was increasingly subject to misapprehension. The temptation was irresistible to link the Law with legal authority rather than with the increasingly cherished written medium.

The modern interpreter, experiencing the electronic revolution and its accompanying resurgence of self-consciously managed sound and voice, may at this point in communications' history be able to appreciate afresh the linguistic undercurrents in Pauline theology. The apostle's medium situation, it is now apparent from the distance of the electronic medium stage, is very different from that which existed from the time of the Reformation until very recently. In medium terminology, the Reformers transacted theologically the communications shift from chirographic to typographic consciousness, whereas Pauline theology participates in the dialectic of the oral, auditory versus the written, chirographic implementation of the Word of God. In this situation the apostle refrained from consciously exploiting the religious and linguistic potential of the written medium, but embraced oral hermeneutics as a matter of theological principle.

As was noted above, gospel, faith, and obedience operate for Paul in a verifiable linguistic and specifically auditory sphere of influence. The righteousness of God (*dikaiosynē tou theou*), this infinitely belabored theologoumenon, is likewise rooted in the oral matrix. One must wonder why Paul is strangely noncommittal to a conceptual clarification of one of his key terms. None of the classic *loci* yield anything approximating definitional precision (Phil. 3:9; 2 Cor. 5:21; Rom. 1:16–17; 3:4–5, 21–26; 10:3). The same situation, we remember, applied to the term gospel, and it holds likewise true of the term faith. The answer, one suspects, lies in the oral functioning of gospel, faith, and righteousness of God. Peter Stuhlmacher was probably correct in tracing the concept of righteousness of God to Jewish apocalypticism.[75] It must be added, however, that Paul's use of righteousness of God, irrespective of its derivation from the history of religion, is a perfect expression of the apostle's theology of language. Strictly speaking, righteousness is neither a principle nor a concept, but an event or an act. It is this activist character of righteousness that reveals its oral roots, making it unfit for propositional explication, let alone metaphysical abstraction. The time-honored questions whether righteousness is *iustitia dei activa* or *iustitia dei passiva,* the power or the gift of God, and whether the genitive *tou theou* is of subjective or of objective quality, set up false alternatives.[76] In Rom. 1:16–17 righteousness is not defined in terms of content, but articulated in *statu actionis.* Righteousness of God manifests itself as divine power in the proclamation of the gospel, effecting redemption for all who actively entertain faith,[77] Jews first and also Greeks. Without intending definitional clarity, the *dikaiosynē tou theou* may thus be said to be "a manifestation of the efficaciousness of God,"[78] or the "epiphany of God in the Word of the Gospel,"[79] or "expressing divine activity, treating not of the self-subsistent, but of the self-revealing God."[80] All the features that constitute the orbit of the righteousness of God—its verbal, vocal base, its powerful efficaciousness, its present, revelatory force (*apokalyptetai*), its life-giving character, its universally bonding, unifying potential, and its active engagement of faith—are primary aspects of oral ontology. Gift and power, object and subject are inseparable in this authentically oral synthesis of the proclamation of God's righteousness. Furthermore, Paul's oral ontology brings conceptual unity to what has sometimes been regarded as a peculiar dichotomy in his theology: a forensic, juridical, ethical bent versus a participatory, sacramental, mystical one. Both theological concerns, that of justification and of participation, merge in the *vita activa* of the oral gospel, as was well recognized by Sanders: ". . . righteousness by faith and participation in Christ ultimately amount to the same thing."[81] *Righteousness is God's power insofar as the gospel (of Jesus' death and resurrection) is sounded efficaciously, and a gift for man when hearers partake in the message out of faith.*

The linguistic dimension of Pauline theology was comprehended with remarkable precision by a representative of the Deuteropauline tradition. The author of Colossians singled out the written authority of the Law when he stated that God extinguished "what was written by hand" in the decrees by nailing it to the cross (2:14: *exaleipsas to . . . cheirographon* [sic] *tois dogmasin . . . kai . . . proselōsas auto tō staurō*). In full accord with Paul's linguistic sensibilities, the cross is here perceived as the power that obliterates the Law in its chirographic givenness.

Erhardt Güttgemanns has rightly observed that the distinct opposition of *dikaiosynē ek nomou* versus *dikaiosynē ek pisteōs* is inconceivable in Judaism, whether it be of biblical, intertestamental, apocalyptic, Rabbinic, or modern persuasion.[82] Faith and Law, righteousness and Torah obedience are indivisible in the whole Jewish tradition. Obedience to the Law constitutes *the* appropriate act of faith in response to Israel's election by God. And yet, the hermeneutical impulse of Pauline theology is not entirely foreign to Jewish consciousness.

We have arrived at an understanding of Paul as an oral traditionalist who objects to the Law not on legal, but ultimately on linguistic grounds. The conflict of righteousness derived from the Law versus righteousness by faith is in depth one between the visible, mediated, externalized, and objectified Word of God versus the invisible, unmediated, internalized, and nonobjectified Word of God, and not between the legalistic versus the nonmeritorious function of the Word. This sensibility to the participatory realm of hearing and the repudiation of the externalization and objectification of God, we must now say, places the apostle into the prestigious Jewish tradition of the un-image-able-ness of God. The Law, when taking on a visible form, assumes the posture of a verbal icon. If one lives in a tradition that prohibits the making of a *visual image* of God, then it is entirely in the spirit of this tradition to conclude that there must not be a *verbal image* either, in which case the only acceptable form of expressing divine presence is the invisibility of the spoken word.

THE RUPTURE OF ORAL SYNTHESIS

If Paul senses the disturbing effects of the written objectification of the Word of God, it is not without irony that he has to resort to the written medium himself. To be sure, the letter form allows him to stay in near-oral touch with his addressees. His letters may in fact accommodate the requirements of oral speech more successfully than is commonly acknowledged. Granted also that the letters, dictated by a speaker and intended for hearers as they are, will at least in part have been shaped by oral, prophetic speech patterns.[83] Still, the apostle found himself in a situation where words could not be sounded in oral immediacy, but had to be filtered through the written medium. This raises the question of the impact of the medium on the message with regard to Paul's letters. Notwithstanding the apostle's abiding commitment to the oral gospel, does his own employment of the written medium register effects of alienation? Has the disjunctive force of writing entered into the fiber of his theology, producing strains with the oral gospel?

The oldest extant Pauline texts—1 and 2 Thessalonians[84]—and 1 Corinthians, a particularly striking case in point, will serve as samples of Paul's reflective posture toward his own oral gospel and interpretations of it. The two examples are merely meant to be illustrative. An exhaustive treatment of the apostle's distanciation from the act of primary speech cannot be offered within the scope of this study.

From a historical perspective, Paul is in the Thessalonian letters addressing a situation of radical enthusiasm, sexual libertinism, and social deviation.[85] The religious experience of the believers has found its crystallized expression in the formula: "The day of the Lord has come" (2 Thess. 2:2: *enestēken hē hēmera tou kyriou*). The present arrival of the day of the Lord was equivalent to the experience of personal resurrection. This state of eschatological enthusiasm provides the rationale for other observable phenomena at Thessalonica: shock over the death of members (1 Thess. 4:13), surprise at suffering and affliction (1 Thess. 3:3–4), aberration from the monogamous norm of marriage (1 Thess. 4:1–8), lack of respect for local leadership (1 Thess. 5:12–13), as well as apathy toward work and antagonism toward the Pauline principle of self-sufficient labor (1 Thess. 4:11–12; 5:14; 2 Thess. 3:6–13). Death, suffering, marriage, authority, and work were all considered part of the old world from which the Thessalonian believers in Christ had been redeemed.

Linguistically, one observes a proliferation of oral terms and images in Paul's reflection on his relationship with the people of Thessalonica. The apostle records his reception by and performance in the city in glowing and unusually intimate terms. Faith, love, and hope were the manifestations of the new life in Christ experienced by the Thessalonians (1 Thess. 1:3). The gospel had happened among them "not only in word (1 Thess. 1:5: *ouk egenēthē eis hymas en logō monon*), but also in power (*en dynamei*) and in the Holy Spirit (*en pneumati hagiō*) and with full conviction (*plērophoria pollē*)." They had received the Word with a joy inspired by the Holy Spirit, amid afflictions (1 Thess. 1:6), and they had contributed to the sounding of the gospel in Macedonia and Achaia (1 Thess. 1:8: *exēchētai ho logos tou kyriou*). They had abandoned their idols and turned to the living, true God. He, Paul, had provided for them "like a nurse taking care of her children" (1 Thess. 2:7), and counseled them as a father does his children (1 Thess. 2:11). In all this one recognizes the language of oral efficaciousness, intimacy, and synthesis.

In both 1 and 2 Thessalonians, moreover, the oral principle of *mimesis* is of great moment to Paul. As noted above, Paul elicited not merely participation in the gospel, but imitation of his life and work as well (1 Thess. 2:8; 4:11; 2 Thess. 3:8–9). The apostolic message is inseparable from the speaker. By the same token, the people's imitation of Paul extends to the Lord, the very authority in whose name the apostle speaks. In describing the effect of his preached gospel, Paul writes, with approbation, that in receiving the Word "you became imitators of us and of the Lord" (1 Thess. 1:6: *kai hymeis mimētai hēmōn egenēthete kai tou kyriou*). In its full wording this phrase is exceptional in Pauline literature. Elsewhere hearers are admonished to become imitators of the apostle (2 Thess. 3:7, 9; 1 Cor. 4:16; 11:1; Phil. 3:17), or of other churches (1 Thess. 2:14), but not of the apostle *and of the Lord.* This profoundly mimetic function of the preached gospel corroborates again the oral genius of Paul. Participation in his message entails both imitation of himself, the speaker, and of the resurrected Lord, authoritative source and content of the gospel. Speaker and hearers join with the Lord through the oral bonding of *mimesis.*

Local conditions may have prevailed at Thessalonica that provided a stimulus for religious enthusiasm. But if such were the case, they are not readily ascertainable from the texts. It may be well to exercise caution in labeling the unorthodox piety as gnosticism, apocalypticism, or Hellenistic enthusiasm, terms that themselves are not entirely unambiguous. Since Paul, together with Silvanus and Timothy, was the founding apostle of the Christian community at Thessalonica, the religious phenomena he addresses cannot be entirely unrelated to the message he preached. There is no indication of competing apostles moving in from the outside. Once we recognize Paul's proud recollection of the gospel's emphatically oral and participatory entry among the Thessalonians, it is not implausible to suspect connections between the believers' *mimesis* of the apostles and of the Lord, and the experience of personal resurrection of some. Our suggestion is to accept language as a key to the Thessalonian enthusiasm and to consider the quality of performance of Paul's oral gospel as relevant to the case in question.

In 2 Thess. 2:2 one observes Paul explicitly disengaging himself from the enthusiasts' central creed of realized parousia and resurrection. What is interesting about his repudiation of radical enthusiasm is that he finds it necessary to disavow any possible personal implication in it. The phrasing in 2 Thess. 2:2 is equivocal, perhaps so by design, but its intention clearly is to sever any linkage that might have been construed between Spirit (*pneuma*), word (*logos*), and "a letter purporting to be from us" (*di' epistolēs hōs di' hēmōn*) on the one hand, and the conviction that "the day of the Lord has come" on the other. Did the people, carried away by Spirit and speech, forge an apostolic letter so as to gain Pauline authorization? Or was it Paul's own *logos,* preached in the power of the Spirit, that caused enthusiasm of such magnitude that in his first letter Paul was incapable of rectifying the situation, and in his second letter "could not comprehend how it might have come from his letter or his teachings?"[86] For Paul it was a case of misunderstanding, but one wonders whether it was entirely a matter of faulty hearing and misquoting. Did not the people hear Paul's gospel of the imitation of the apostles *and* of the Lord in a manner in which it could well be apprehended? Was there not something even in the first letter that could have emboldened hearers to a life in enthusiastic faithfulness?

That 1 Thessalonians was incapable of rectifying the situation can in part at least be inferred from Paul's formulated response. We have already observed the existence of enthusiasm prior to the writing of the letter. It cannot be accidental that the fundamental norms of the human condition—death, suffering, marriage, work—were all subject to eschatological challenge. Assuming a connection between Paul's gospel and enthusiastic piety, it is not entirely surprising that certain statements in the first letter could actually be taken to support enthusiasm.[87] When, for example, the apostle writes that the wrath has come upon those who killed the Lord and the prophets (2:16: *ephthasen de ep' autous hē orgē eis telos*), he may have merely strengthened belief in the presence of the day of the Lord. Or, when he writes that Satan has prevented him from returning to the city (2:18), he could have fueled the fire of enthusiasm, since an aggravation of satanic activity was a sign of the end time (2 Thess. 2:3–12). "Might this not give someone the basis to say, 'Since Paul wrote the letter, the parousia has indeed come, for we now enjoy the resurrection state in the spirit'?"[88] Perhaps more than anything else it was the apostle's unflinching oral language concerning the *mimēsis tou kyriou* (1 Thess. 1:6) which could only have encouraged believers to partake in the resurrection of the Lord.

If the first letter still left room for enthusiastic piety, so that a second, more sharply focused letter was required, what does this tell us about Paul's oral *logos* preached in the power of the Spirit? It is difficult to avoid the impression that Paul's gospel in its very oral functioning was itself a source of the enthusiasm. If the gospel of Jesus' death and resurrection called for *mimesis* and interiorization, we should not be surprised to find believers who participated in the resurrection of the one risen from death. It must be stated that Paul's oral gospel is not without self-critical edges against full-blown enthusiasm. The apostle who forfeited communal support and adopted a trade could stress apostolic imitation as a criterion against religiously inspired idleness. But what if one took the imitation of the Lord with utmost seriousness? There are also indications that Paul preached the future coming of Jesus, the parousia (1 Thess. 1:9–10; 5:1–2). But his formulation of the issue of the death of members and the implied lack of hope for a general, future resurrection among some (4:13) suggest that neither he nor Timothy on his mission from Athens to Thessalonica specified a general resurrection of the dead.[89] By leaving the people without specific information about their personal, future resurrection, however, Paul in effect strengthened their mimetic faculty of participating in Jesus' death and resurrection. Given the nature of Paul's oral gospel, the density of the oral milieu at the occasion of its preaching and reception in Thessalonica, the concern for *mimesis* of the apostles and especially of the Lord, and the absence of a future hope in resurrection, it may be reasonably inferred that the Thessalonian enthusiasm was affected by the oral quality and performance of the Pauline gospel.

If one perceives the Thessalonian enthusiasm as a product at least in part engendered by Paul's oral gospel, it is instructive to observe Pauline language "in the mode of primary reflectivity."[90] Distanced from the community by space and time, the apostle has to seize upon the written medium that, despite the letter's close affinity to speech, locates him vis-à-vis the oral gospel. The first time we observe a Christian in the act of writing, the effects are disjunctive more than unitive with regard to orality. While indulging in the oral mode of intimacy, *mimesis*, and participation, he nevertheless inserts critical limitations to full oral synthesis. When, for example, Paul likens the parousia to the unexpected coming of "a thief in the night," he will hardly have reassured those living in "peace and security" (1 Thess. 5:2–3), nor will his striking portrait of the coming

Lord as terrifying judge (1 Thess. 4:6; 5:3; 2 Thess. 1:7–8; 2:8) have been altogether consoling for people living in blissful imitation of the present, resurrected Lord. In response to the question concerning the dead, Paul informs the congregation of the resurrection of the dead at the parousia of the Lord (1 Thess. 4:14). His confirmation of a general resurrection apart from that of Jesus subtly undermines the present participation of all believers in the resurrection of the Lord. The death of members is treated with a seriousness that evidently was lacking in the oral gospel. We shall have occasion to return to the phenomenon of a writer's emphasis on death over against orality's preoccupation with the fullness of life. Furthermore, by also synchronizing the unification of the living with the future parousia of the Lord (4:15–18), he has deflated a present sense of the *mimesis* of the Lord. A new ethical seriousness and commitment to moral authority distinguishes the present as a time in transition toward full time. The principle of the *imitatio Pauli* accentuates the working apostle who could not possibly have encouraged religiously inspired idleness. A differentiated sense of time at the expense of an ontological decrement of present time, an erosion of the full unity of the Lord, hearers, and preached message, a disintegration of the *mimesis* of the Lord, an appeal to strong, ethical norms, and a reawakening of the consciousness of death—these are all the markings of a subtle but "coherent deformation"[91] of the oral gospel and its effects on some hearers.

It is in 1 Corinthians that the critical effects of literary distanciation from the oral lifeworld are most conspicuously in evidence. Of the numerous characteristics of Corinthian culture that scholars have assiduously collected, perhaps none is more spectacular than the possible use of a tradition of sayings of the Lord. To James M. Robinson goes the honor of having first developed the argument on behalf of a sayings tradition at Corinth.[92] After the thesis was confirmed by Helmut Koester,[93] it received its most detailed corroboration from Heinz-Wolfgang Kuhn.[94] Robinson carried further and clarified an observation, first recorded by Bultmann,[95] that there existed an affinity between sayings and wisdom theology. He traced a vast trajectory of sayings traditions from Jewish wisdom to Hellenistic Gnosticism, documenting the persistent influence of wisdom on the genre. In the early Christian tradition the sayings genre Q serves as an example for wisdom providing a focus of crystallization for Jesus sayings, while the *Gospel of Thomas* represents the genre at the stage of gnosticizing transformation. The christological logic that brings together wisdom and sayings is that of Jesus the messenger of wisdom and the speaker of words of wisdom. Once the connection between wisdom and the sayings genre was firmly established, Robinson brought the weight of his insight to bear upon the wisdom section in 1 Cor. 1:18–4:21. Since Paul never mentions wisdom prior to the writing of 1 Corinthians, and only sparingly thereafter, while he engages in a rather specific debate about wisdom in 1 Cor. 1:18–2:16, it must be assumed that wisdom is a concept indigenous to Corinthian theology. If, furthermore, one observes Paul's explicit objection to wisdom sayings (1 Cor. 2:13: *sophias logoi*), one can no longer dismiss the possibility of a sayings tradition at Corinth—given the established connection between wisdom and sayings. Paul's polemic leaves little doubt that the sayings were sounded in their full, life-giving power. When voiced in the Spirit, they became an event. The wisdom made manifest in the proclamation was the present arrival of the kingdom and the realization of personal resurrection. Robinson's suggestion of the operation of wisdom sayings at Corinth conforms with previously observed Corinthian phenomena. Such features as speaking in tongues, realized eschatology, baptismal resurrection, absence of a passion christology, lack of future resurrection hope, ethical libertinism, communal factions centered around individual apostolic leaders, and the management of wisdom sayings in full oral efficaciousness can all be understood as cooperating in the making of a full-fledged oral culture.

Paul's first letter to the Corinthians engages in stressful relations with a distinctly oral, rhetorical nature of wisdom. The first time the term wisdom (*sophia*) appears, it is linked with *logos,* and in this combination criticized by Paul: he came to preach the gospel "not in wisdom of word" (1:17; au. trans. of *ouk en sophia logou*). This line of criticism becomes a recurrent feature in the wisdom controversy. Repeatedly the apostle insists that his proclamation was "not in superior authority of word or wisdom" (2:1; au. trans. of *ou kat' hyperochēn logou ē sophias*), "not in persuasive [seductive?] words of wisdom" (2:4; au. trans. of *ouk en peithoi[s] sophias [logois]*) and "not in words taught by human wisdom" (2:13; au. trans. of *ouk en didaktois anthrōpinēs sophias logois*). Paul's use of the plural *logoi* is atypical, for he "normally speaks in the singular of *logos* in the sense of the 'gospel', and uses the plural only in connection with the wisdom teaching of the Corinthian heretics."[96] His polemic is distinctly directed against the oral powers of wisdom.

Paul counters the power of life-giving wisdom with the power and wisdom of the cross (1:23–24). Precisely why would the *logoi* of wisdom stand condemned by the wisdom of the cross? There is a subtle but inescapable linguistic logic that casts the cross in a position of judging the oral powers of Corinthian wisdom. Insofar as the Christ crucified has ceased to speak, he exercises criticism over the Christ, the messenger of wisdom and speaker of words of power. One must immediately add that Paul has not consciously drawn this far-reaching conclusion. For him the *logos tou staurou* (1:18) is part of the oral gospel through which Christ continues to address hearers. The emphasis on death, therefore, involves a shift in accent in the oral gospel. But it is a shift that poses a threat to the oral lifeworld. If this anti-oral emphasis on death were carried to its natural conclusion, one would arrive at the position of Mark who silenced the post-resurrectional, living Christ by narrating the story of the pre-resurrectional Jesus, making it peak in his death and narrating it in opposition to the oral authorities. But Paul, again, merely gives us a subtle preview of what was to come with Mark. Despite his emphasis on the cross in 1 Corinthians and the implied critique of wisdom's *logoi*, his is still a medium world removed from the literary reflectiveness of Mark.

Paul's discomfort with *logoi* has left traces in his own citation of sayings of the Lord.[97] With one exception (1 Thess. 4:15), it is only in 1 Corinthians that he summons the authority of the Lord when citing a saying or mentioning the unavailability of a saying. In 1 Cor. 7:10–11 he cites the Lord's saying on divorce, versions of which exist both in Q (Matt. 5:32//Luke 16:18) and in Mark (10:11–12). After stating the unconditional prohibition of divorce as the Lord's will, he offers his own amendment that grants divorce if the nonbelieving partner so desires (7:15; cf. 7:12). His own opinion, although not in full agreement with the Lord's, appears fully as authoritative. In 1 Cor. 9:14 Paul cites the Lord's saying concerning remuneration of apostles. A version of it exists in Q (Matt. 10:10//Luke 10:7). No sooner does he expound the Lord's principle of remuneration than he disassociates himself from it. The purpose of his writing, he argues, is not that the saying be applied to him—quite the opposite (9:15). Moreover, Paul points *expressis verbis* to the absence of a dominical saying on the matter of the unmarried (7:25). But that, he adds, can be overcome by his own authority, which is empowered by the Spirit (7:40). The unusual increase in sayings attributed to the Lord in 1 Corinthians, Paul's relative freedom toward them, and the singular reference to the lack of a saying of the Lord will all be features mirroring the apostle's engagement with authorities who are themselves in the habit of invoking sayings of the Lord. On his part Paul does not repudiate the sayings tradition itself, but he takes a critical attitude toward a certain use of sayings. Once again, we observe a preview in miniature of what will happen when Mark undertakes an uncompromising disengagement from synoptic orality. Both in its massive emphasis on death and in its reserved stand toward sayings, Mark's gospel signifies a textuality that has reached the stage of full reflexiveness on oral tradition.

Further evidence of Paul's tense relations with oral tradition in 1 Corinthians is provided by frequent echoes of sayings that have emerged in the *Gospel of Thomas*. The saying 1 Cor. 2:9: "What eye has not seen, nor ear heard, and what has not arisen in the heart of man" (au. trans.), is reiterated in *Gospel of Thomas* 17. Introduced by Paul in reference to its written base in Isa. 64:4, the saying speaks of the incomparable mystery of salvation. The saying 1 Cor. 4:8: "Already you are filled! Already you have become rich! Without us you have become kings!" appears to be an ironic play on *Gospel of Thomas* 81: "Jesus said: 'Let him who has become rich become king.'" The saying 1 Cor. 7:31: "For the form of this world is passing away (*paragein*)" is faintly echoed in the *Gospel of Thomas* 11: "This heaven shall pass away (*paragein*) and the one above shall pass away (*paragein*)." But whereas in Paul the saying underscores a personal commitment to one's appointed status, in *Thomas* it effects transcendence over the world. The saying 1 Cor. 10:27: ". . . eat whatever is set before you," is repeated in *Gospel of Thomas* 14. But in Paul it applies to the specific case of an invitation to the house of an unbeliever, whereas in *Thomas* it sanctions categorical freedom from all dietary laws. The saying 1 Cor. 13:2: ". . . if I have all faith so as to move mountains . . ." appears in Q (Matt. 17:20//Luke 17:6), Mark (11:22–23) and twice in *Gospel of Thomas*, 48 and 106. But whereas the versions in Q, Mark, and *Thomas* extol the omnipotence of faith, Paul subjects mountain-moving faith to the criterion of love. These repeated echoes of sayings, which eventually arrived in the *Gospel of Thomas*, further corroborate the existence of a tradition of sayings at Corinth. Frequently the Pauline text appears to undertake a critical revision of or even parody on an existing saying. It is also noteworthy that, with one exception (1 Cor. 2:9), Paul does not introduce the sayings material with a quotation formula. Were it not for outside evidence provided by Q and *Thomas*, the sayings would be indistinguishable from the Pauline text. In fact, these "sayings" are meant to be integral components of the text of the letter. In observing Paul's engagement of the transformational powers of literacy for the purpose of textualizing the *logoi*, one is again reminded of the Markan text and its power of overriding and transforming oral tradition.

It is precisely in those chapters that urge a break with the oral, life-giving powers of wisdom that Paul strengthens his case by frequent appeal to written authority. When faced with the full consequences of "the superior authority of word or wisdom" (1 Cor. 2:1; au. trans.), he resolutely grasps the formula "for it is written" (*gegraptai gar*), or "as it was written" (*kathōs gegraptai*) for the purpose of substantiating both the foolishness of the wise (1:19; 3:19, 20) and the true wisdom of the crucified Lord (1:31; 2:9). A fivefold appeal to Scripture in the first three chapters of the letter (1:19; 1:31; 2:9; 3:19; 3:20) appears unusually dense when compared with the fivefold use of the formula in the remaining thirteen chapters (9:9; 10:7; 14:21; 15:45; 15:54). By impregnating the wisdom chapters with a formula appealing to scriptural authority, Paul has retextualized the very text that advocates a parting with the oral powers of wisdom.

As if the reweaving of the texture of his letter were not sufficient, Paul has the five references to scriptural authority culminate in a categorical recommitment to Scripture: "Do not go beyond what is written" (1 Cor. 4:6; au. trans. of *mē hyper ha gegraptai*). It would not be too far-fetched to assume with W. Lütgert,[98] Adolf Schlatter,[99] and Otto Michel[100] that Corinthian piety entailed the conviction of having advanced "beyond what is written." If the kingdom had arrived in the power of the *logos*, Scripture would seem to be expendable. When faced with the extreme consequences of oral wisdom, Paul, preacher of the oral gospel, is here compelled to reconsider his hermeneutical priorities and to invoke the norm of Scripture. "Do not go beyond what is written" is a wholly exceptional statement in Pauline theology, and in making it the apostle has at this point sanctioned the written medium as a basis of the new wisdom. The strategy of reinforcing the authority of Scripture combines with a tendency to deflate the power of the *logos*: "for not in a *logos* is the kingdom of God, but in power" (1 Cor. 4:20; au. trans. of *ou gar en logō hē basileia tou theou all' en dynamei*). While in 1 Thess. 1:5 he had in oral fashion emphasized the inseparable unity of *logos*, power (*dynamis*), and Holy Spirit (*pneuma hagion*), he is here forced to dissociate kingdom and power from the *logos*. From the perspective of language, the Paul of the wisdom chapters, who shows himself uneasy about the application of *logoi*, who appeals to scriptural authority and accentuates the Christ crucified, is a subtle but consistent promoter of the values of literacy. In this one case at least we must say that Paul, the oral traditionalist, has activated the powers of the written medium for the purpose of rupturing the oral synthesis.

NOTES

1. Robert W. Funk, "Saying and Seeing: Phenomenology of Language and the New Testament," *JBR* 34 (1966): 197–213; idem, "The Apostolic Parousia: Form and Significance," in *Christian History and Interpretation: Studies Presented to John Knox*, ed. W. R. Farmer, C. F. D. Moule, and R. R. Niebuhr (New York and Cambridge: Cambridge University Press, 1967), pp. 249–68;

idem, *Language, Hermeneutic, and Word of God: The Problem of Language in the New Testament and Contemporary Theology* (New York: Harper & Row, 1966; reprint: Missoula, Mont.: Scholars Press, 1979), pp. 237–74.

2. 1 Thess. 2:17–3:8; Gal. 4:12–20; Phil. 2:19–30; Phlm. 22; 1 Cor. 4:14–21; 2 Cor. 1:8–2:13; 7:5–16; 12:14–13:10; Rom. 1:8–17; 15:14–33.

3. Eph. 6:21–22; Col. 4:7–9; 2 Tim. 4:6–18; Titus 3:12–14; cf. also Heb. 13:18–19, 22–23; 2 John 12; 3 John 13–14.

4. Funk, *Language, Hermeneutic, and Word,* p. 274.

5. Funk, "Apostolic Parousia," p. 259, n. 1.

6. Funk, *Language, Hermeneutic, and Word,* p. 269.

7. In chapter 5 we shall observe that certain pronouncements in Paul's letters are perceived to be empowered with oral efficaciousness. This confirms that the apostle keeps his letters as close as possible to oral speech, but it does not contradict Funk's observation of the travelogue as an indicator of Paul's sensitivity to oral and written verbalization.

8. Dieter Georgi, *Die Gegner des Paulus im 2. Korintherbrief,* WMANT 11 (Neukirchen and Vluyn: Neukirchener Verlag, 1964); Siegfried Schulz, "Die Decke des Moses: Untersuchungen zu einer vorpaulinischen Überlieferung in 2 Kr 3, 7–18," ZNW 49 (1958): 1–30; Gerhard Friedrich, "Die Gegner des Paulus im 2. Korintherbrief," in *Abraham Unser Vater, Juden und Christen im Gespräch über die Bibel: Festschrift für Otto Michel zum 60. Geburtstag,* ed. O. Betz, M. Hengel, P. Schmidt (Leiden: E. J. Brill, 1963), pp. 181–215.

9. For connections between the art of rhetoric, inner vision, and ecstatic, mystical perception, see the extraordinary work by Frances A. Yates, *The Art of Memory* (Chicago: University of Chicago Press, 1966).

10. Willi Marxsen, *The Resurrection of Jesus of Nazareth,* Eng. trans. Margaret Kohl (Philadelphia: Fortress Press, 1970), pp. 98–111.

11. Ibid., p. 105.

12. Johannes Munck, *Paul and the Salvation of Mankind,* Eng. trans. Frank Clark (Richmond: John Knox Press, 1959), pp. 11–35.

13. Krister Stendahl, *Paul Among Jews and Gentiles* (Philadelphia: Fortress Press, 1976), pp. 7–23.

14. Ibid., p. 9.

15. Samuel Terrien, *The Elusive Presence: Toward a New Biblical Theology,* RP 26 (New York: Harper & Row, 1978), pp. 76, 112, passim.

16. Reginald Glanville, "The Predominance of Ear over Eye in the Experience of St. Paul," LonQHR 180 (1955): 297.

17. Walter J. Ong, S. J., *The Presence of the Word: Some Prolegomena for Cultural and Religious History* (New Haven, Conn., and London: Yale University Press, 1967; paperback edition: Minneapolis: University of Minnesota Press, 1981), p. 189.

18. Gerhard Kittel, *"legō,"* TDNT IV: 119.

19. Ibid., p. 118.

20. Julius Schniewind, *Die Begriffe Wort und Evangelium bei Paulus* (Bonn: Carl Georgi, 1910), p. 72: "während wir bei 'Evangelium' fast gar nicht mehr an eine 'Botschaft' denken, sondern nur an einen besondren Komplex von 'Inhalten', gehört es beim paulinischen *euaggelion* zu dessen Wesen, dass es gebotschaftet, ausgerichtet wird."

21. Ibid., p. 24, n. 1: "Dass 'das Wort' unmittelbar als wirksam gedacht wird, ist das Hauptergebnis unsrer Untersuchung . . ."

22. Ibid., pp. 45–46.

23. The noted statement, "His letters are weighty and strong, but his bodily presence is weak, and his speech of no account" (2 Cor. 10:10), cannot be used as an objective basis for Pauline hermeneutics. It is a word spoken by rival apostles. As such it says much about a particular pneumatic oratory cultivated by them. When measured against their hermeneutical standards, Paul's presence and oral speech appears weak. But this cannot possibly be taken to mean that Paul did not subscribe to the primacy of the spoken word.

24. Funk, "Saying and Seeing," p. 212.

25. A monumental and largely forgotten work on early Christian hermeneutics is by the Norwegian scholar Ragnar Asting, *Die Verkündigung des Wortes im Urchristentum: Dargestellt an den Begriffen 'Wort Gottes', 'Evangelium' und 'Zeugnis'* (Stuttgart: W. Kohlhammer, 1939). On the efficacious character of gospel and word of God in Paul, see pp. 135–86, 347–425. Cf. also Adolf von Harnack, *Entstehung und Entwickelung der Kirchenverfassung und des Kirchenrechts in den zwei ersten Jahrhunderten* (Leipzig: J. C. Hinrichs'sche Buchhandlung, 1910), pp. 199–252.

26. Funk, "Saying and Seeing," p. 211.

27. Robert Jewett, *Paul's Anthropological Terms: A Study of Their Use in Conflict Settings*, AGAJU 10 (Leiden: E. J. Brill, 1971), pp. 305–33; Rudolf Bultmann, *Theology of the New Testament*, Eng. trans. Kendrick Grobel (New York: Charles Scribner's Sons, 1951), I, pp. 220–27.

28. Don Ihde, *Listening and Voice: A Phenomenology of Sound* (Athens: Ohio University Press, 1976), p. 45.

29. Ong, *Presence of Word*, p. 122.

30. Pedro Gutierrez, *La Paternité spirituelle selon Saint Paul* (Paris: J. Gabalda et Cⁱᵉ, 1968); Bengt Holmberg, *Paul and Power: The Structure of Authority in the Primitive Church as Reflected in the Pauline Epistles* (Philadelphia: Fortress Press, 1980), pp. 77–79.

31. Chapter 1, p. 19.

32. Walter J. Ong, S. J., "Technology Outside Us and Inside Us," *Communio* 5 (1978): 109.

33. Werner Kramer, *Christ, Lord, Son of God*, SBT 50 (London: SCM Press, 1966). For a summary of studies on the pre-Pauline hymn Phil. 2:5–11, cf. Terrien, *Elusive Presence*, p. 479, n. 20. For a summary of studies on the pre-Pauline confession 1 Cor. 15:3–5, cf. Hans Conzelmann, "Zur Analyse der Bekenntnisformel 1. Kor. 15, 3–5," in *Theologie als Schriftauslegung: Aufsätze zum Neuen Testament* (Munich: Chr. Kaiser, 1974), p. 134, n. 17. Ethelbert Stauffer, *New Testament Theology*, Eng. trans. John Marsh (New York: Macmillan Co.; London: SCM Press, 1955), pp. 233–53; see also Stauffer's compilation of twelve criteria for creedal formulations, pp. 338–39; Archibald M. Hunter, *Paul and His Predecessors* (Philadelphia: Westminster Press, 1961), pp. 9–64.

34. Bultmann, *Theology of New Testament*, I, pp. 292–306; Leander E. Keck, *Paul and His Letters* (Philadelphia: Fortress Press, 1979), pp. 33–42.

35. Walter J. Ong, S. J., *Interfaces of the Word: Studies in the Evolution of Consciousness and Culture* (Ithaca, N.Y., and London: Cornell University Press, 1977), p. 191; Eric A. Havelock, *The Greek Concept of Justice: From Its Shadow in Homer to Its Substance in Plato* (Cambridge, Mass.: Harvard University Press, 1978), pp. 88–91.

36. Ihde, *Listening and Voice*, p. 81.

37. Gerhard Kittel, *"parakouō," TDNT* I: 223.

38. Robert C. Tannehill, *Dying and Rising with Christ: A Study in Pauline Theology*, BZNW 32 (Berlin: Töpelmann, 1966); Eduard Schweizer, "Dying and Rising with Christ," *NTS* 14 (1967): 1–14; E. P. Sanders, *Paul and Palestinian Judaism: A Comparison of Patterns of Religion* (Philadelphia: Fortress Press, 1977), pp. 502–8.

39. Albert Schweitzer, *The Mysticism of Paul the Apostle*, Eng. trans. William Montgomery (London: A. & C. Black, 1931).

40. Ronald F. Hock, *The Social Context of Paul's Ministry: Tentmaking and Apostleship* (Philadelphia: Fortress Press, 1980); idem, "Simon the Shoemaker as an Ideal Cynic," *GRBS* 17 (1976): 41–53; idem, "Paul's Tentmaking and the Problem of His Social Class," *JBL* 97 (1978): 555–64; idem, "The Workshop as a Social Setting for Paul's Missionary Preaching," *CBQ* 41 (1979): 438–50.

41. Hock, *Social Context*, p. 67.

42. Ibid., pp. 17, 27.

43. Ibid., p. 26.

44. Ibid., pp. 31–42.

45. Gabriel Tarde, *Les Lois de l'Imitation*, 2d ed., rev. Eng. trans. Elsie C. Parson (Paris: F. Alcan, 1895); Solomon Gandz, "The Dawn of Literature: Prolegomena to a History of Unwritten Literature," *Osiris* 7 (1939): 271–72; Birger Gerhardsson, *Memory and Manuscript: Oral Tradition and Written Transmission in Rabbinic Judaism and Early Christianity*, ASNU 22 (Lund: C. W. K. Gleerup; Copenhagen: Ejnar Munksgaard, 1961), pp. 181–85.

46. Sanders, *Paul and Palestinian Judaism*, p. 482.

47. Bultmann, *Theology of New Testament*, I, pp. 259–69; see esp. p. 267.

48. Sanders, *Paul and Palestinian Judaism*, p. 484; cf. pp. 474–97.

49. Albrecht Oepke, *"mesitēs," TDNT* IV: 618–20.

50. Joachim Jeremias, "Mōysēs," *TDNT* IV: 866, n. 210.

51. Ong, *Presence of Word*, p. 301.

52. Our reading of 2 Corinthians does not follow Ernst Käsemann ("Die Legitimität des Apostels: Eine Untersuchung zu II Korinther 10–13," *ZNW* 41 [1942]: 33–71), who interpreted the rival apostles in terms of Jewish Christians authorized by the Jerusalem Church. Instead we follow Dieter Georgi (*Die Gegner des Paulus*), who identified them as representatives of a thriving Jewish-Hellenistic missionary movement. The designation Divine Man (*theios anēr*) remains useful, when strictly limited to the apostles of 2 Corinthians. The objection of Carl R. Holladay (*Theios Aner in Hellenistic Judaism: A Critique of the Use of this Category in New Testament Christology*, SBLDS 40 [Missoula, Mont.: Scholars Press, 1977]) to using *theios anēr* as a conceptual umbrella for a variety of christological data in the New Testament is very well taken.

53. Georgi, *Die Gegner des Paulus*, pp. 247–51; L. Röhrich, "Himmelsbrief," *RGG*³ III, cols. 338–39.

54. Georgi, *Die Gegner des Paulus*, pp. 246–51, 272–73.

55. Gottlob Schrenk, *"graphō," TDNT* I: 767. His exposition of the *gramma-pneuma* dichotomy in Paul is a very important contribution to Pauline hermeneutics (pp. 765–68).

56. Ernst Käsemann, "The Spirit and the Letter," in *Perspectives on Paul* (Philadelphia: Fortress Press, 1971), p. 155.

57. Walter J. Ong, S. J., "Maranatha: Death and Life in the Text of the Book," in *Interfaces of Word*, p. 236.

58. The phrase is taken from Miguel de Unamuno, *The Tragic Sense of Life in Men and Nations*, Bollingen Series 85 (Princeton, N.J.: Princeton University Press, 1972), pp. 100–101: "My own thoughts, tumultuous and agitated in the recesses of my mind, once torn up by their roots from my heart, poured out upon this paper and here fixed in unalterable form, are already the cadavers of thought."

59. Schrenk, "*graphō*."

60. Bernardin Schneider, O.F.M., "The Meaning of St. Paul's Antithesis 'The Letter and the Spirit,' " *CBQ* 15 (1953): 163–207.

61. Ibid., p. 187.

62. Lest there be a Marcionite misunderstanding, it is noted that for Paul the Law was written "for our instruction" (1 Cor. 10:11: *pros nouthesian hēmon*; Rom. 15:4: *eis tēn hēmeteran didaskalian*). More than that, insofar as the Abrahamic covenant has entered into written tradition, the Law is the formal carrier of justification by faith (Rom. 4:3). That "the righteous shall live by faith" (Rom. 1:17) is introduced as a quote from Scripture: *kathōs gegraptai*.

63. Rudolf Bultmann, "Römer 7 und die Anthropologie des Paulus," in *Imago Dei: Gustav Krüger zum siebzigsten Geburtstag* (Giessen: Alfred Töpelmann, 1932), pp. 53–62; reprint in *Exegetica: Aufsätze zur Erforschung des Neuen Testaments*, ed. Erich Dinkler (Tübingen: J. C. B. Mohr [Paul Siebeck], 1967), pp. 198–209; in *The Old and New Man in the Letters of Paul*, Eng. trans. Keith R. Crim (Richmond: John Knox Press, 1967).

64. Paul Ricoeur, *The Symbolism of Evil* (Boston: Beacon Press, 1967), p. 19.

65. Hannah Arendt, *The Life of the Mind* (New York and London: Harcourt Brace Jovanovich, 1978), II, pp. 63–73.

66. Eric A. Havelock, *Preface to Plato* (Cambridge, Mass.: Harvard University Press, Belknap Press, 1963); idem, *The Greek Concept of Justice*.

67. Ong, *Presence of Word;* idem, *Interfaces of Word;* idem, "Oral Remembering and Narrative Structures," in *Georgetown University Round Table on Languages and Linguistics 1981*, ed. Deborah Tannen (Washington, D.C.: Georgetown University Press, 1982), pp. 12–24.

68. Herbert N. Schneidau, *Sacred Discontent: The Bible and Western Tradition* (Berkeley—Los Angeles—London: University of California Press, 1976), pp. 1–49, 248–306.

69. Jack Goody, *The Domestication of the Savage Mind* (New York and Cambridge: Cambridge University Press, 1977); Jack Goody and Ian Watt, "The Consequences of Literacy," in *Literacy in Traditional Societies*, ed. Jack Goody (New York and Cambridge: Cambridge University Press, 1968), pp. 27–68.

70. Maurice Merleau-Ponty, "L'Oeil et l'esprit," *Les temps modernes* 18, nos. 184–85 (1961), numéro spécial: Maurice Merleau-Ponty, pp. 193–227; K. A. H. Hidding, "Sehen und Hören," in *Liber Amicorum: Studies in Honour of Professor Dr. C. J. Bleeker*, Numen Supplements XVII (Leiden: E. J. Brill,

1969), pp. 69–79; C. J. Bleeker, "L'Oeil et l'Oreille: Leur Signification Religieuse," in *The Sacred Bridge,* Studies in the History of Religions, Numen Supplements VII (Leiden: E. J. Brill, 1963), pp. 52–71.

71. Sanders, *Paul and Palestinian Judaism,* p. 57.

72. Ibid., pp. 33–59.

73. Eric A. Havelock and Jackson Hershbell, *Communication Arts in the Ancient World* (New York: Hastings House, 1978).

74. Ong, *Presence of Word,* pp. 264–86.

75. Peter Stuhlmacher, *Gerechtigkeit Gottes bei Paulus,* FRLANT 87 (Göttingen: Vandenhoeck & Ruprecht, 1965), pp. 145–75, 238–40.

76. Ernst Käsemann, " 'The Righteousness of God' in Paul," in *New Testament Questions of Today,* Eng. trans. W. J. Montague (Philadelphia: Fortress Press, 1969), pp. 168–82.

77. The formula *ek pisteōs eis pistin* (Rom. 1:17) designates faith *in statu actionis,* just as the formula *apo doxēs eis doxan* (2 Cor. 3:18) indicates the process of inner transformation in the likeness of the Lord.

78. Schniewind, *Die Begriffe Wort und Evangelium bei Paulus,* p. 83.

79. Stuhlmacher, *Gerechtigkeit Gottes bei Paulus,* p. 81.

80. Käsemann, " 'The Righteousness of God' in Paul," p. 174.

81. Sanders, *Paul and Palestinian Judaism,* p. 506.

82. Erhardt Güttgemanns, " 'Gottesgerechtigkeit' und strukturale Semantik: Linguistische Analyse zu *dikaiosyne theou,*" in *Studia Linguistica Neotestamentica* (Munich: Chr. Kaiser, 1971), pp. 59–98.

83. Ulrich B. Müller, *Prophetie und Predigt im Neuen Testament: Formgeschichtliche Untersuchungen zur urchristlichen Prophetie,* SNT 10 (Gütersloh: Gerd Mohn, 1975).

84. We take 2 Thessalonians to be an authentic Pauline letter, following Werner Georg Kümmel, *Introduction to the New Testament,* Eng. trans. A. J. Mattill, Jr., 14th rev. ed. (Nashville: Abingdon Press, 1966), pp. 185–90.

85. W. Lütgert, "Die Vollkommenen im Philipperbrief und die Enthusiasten in Thessalonich," BFCT 13 (1909): 547–654; Robert Jewett, "Enthusiastic Radicalism and the Thessalonian Correspondence," *SBL Seminar Papers* (Missoula, Mont.: Scholars Press, 1972), I, pp. 181–232.

86. Jewett, "Enthusiastic Radicalism," p. 215.

87. Ibid., pp. 216–17.

88. Ibid., p. 217.

89. Willi Marxsen, *Introduction to the New Testament: An Approach to its Problems,* Eng. trans. G. Buswell (Philadelphia: Fortress Press, 1974), pp. 30–36; idem, *Der erste Brief an die Thessalonicher,* Züricher Bibelkommentare 11 (Zurich: Theologischer Verlag, 1979), pp. 64–66.

90. Funk, *Language, Hermeneutic, and Word,* p. 238.

91. Ibid.

92. James M. Robinson, "LOGOI SOPHON: On the Gattung of Q," in *Trajectories through Early Christianity* (Philadelphia: Fortress Press, 1971), p. 97, n. 57; idem, "Kerygma and History in the New Testament," in *Trajectories through Early Christianity,* pp. 37–46.

93. Helmut Koester, "One Jesus and Four Primitive Gospels," in *Trajectories through Early Christianity,* p. 186; cf. also pp. 166–68; idem, "GNOMAI

DIAPHOROI: The Origin and Nature of Diversification in the History of Early Christianity," in *Trajectories through Early Christianity*, pp. 149–51.

94. Heinz-Wolfgang Kuhn, "Der irdische Jesus bei Paulus als traditions-geschichtliches und theologisches Problem," *ZTK* 67 (1970): 295–320.

95. Rudolf Bultmann, *Die Geschichte der synoptischen Tradition*, FRLANT 29, NF 12, 8th ed. (Göttingen: Vandenhoeck & Ruprecht, 1970), p. 73 (69).

96. Robinson, "LOGOI SOPHON," p. 97, n. 57.

97. Kuhn, "Der irdische Jesus bei Paulus," pp. 313–17.

98. W. Lütgert, "Freiheitspredigt und Schwarmgeister in Korinth," BFCT 12 (1908): 129–279.

99. Adolf Schlatter, *Die Theologie der Apostel*, 2d ed. (Stuttgart: Calwer Vereinsbuchhandlung, 1922), p. 508; idem, *Die korinthische Theologie* (Gütersloh: C. Bertelsmann, 1914), pp. 7–8.

100. Otto Michel, *Paulus und seine Bibel* (Gütersloh: C. Bertelsmann, 1929), p. 132.

5. Death and Life in the Word of God

> The association of writing with death is not total, but it is manifold and inescapable.
>
> Walter J. Ong, S. J., "Maranatha: Death
> and Life in the Text of the Book"

> The achievement of Mark, in creating the gospel form and thereby binding the word of the Lord to the pre-Easter Jesus, has not been sufficiently appreciated.
>
> M. Eugene Boring, *Sayings of the Risen Jesus*

> The true tradition is parabolic, because that form moves away from participation (proper to myth) and toward interpretation, proper to that alienated form of communication we call "literature" . . . Interpretation, and alienation, are bound up with writing itself: both imply an absence at the core, not communion with a presence.
>
> Herbert N. Schneidau, "For Interpretation"

We began this book with a study of the oral transmission/composition of the pre-canonical, synoptic tradition. Our first thesis emphasized the diffusive, multidirectional nature of oral speech. Oral traditions do not move through a gradually widening tunnel, showing, as it were, the way toward the light of textuality. The second thesis focused on multiple oral links between the written gospel and primary forms of oral speech. Mark's text is rooted in and surrounded by orality. Synoptic oral traditions preceded the gospel, entered into it, bypassed it, and continued long after its composition. The third thesis defined the gospel as a linguistic form of textual and literary integrity which used but transformed, absorbed but reconstructed the collective memories of oral tradition. The gospel's center of causation was extraneous to, and indeed in tension with, the waxing and waning of oral life. The fourth thesis developed the oral hermeneutics of Paul. If the apostle's thought is perceived as a theology of language, affirmation of the oral power of words and aversion to written objectification lie at its core. The fifth thesis will draw the final conclusion from our reflections on speaking and writing, and designate the written gospel as a counterform to, rather than extension of, oral hermeneutics.

The title of this chapter suggests two different senses. Death and life, in one sense, refers to Jesus himself and to language's ability to handle the one and the other. Our study of Mark's oral legacy focused on Mark 1–13, chapters covering the life of Jesus. Here we must treat the passion narrative and its relative shortage in identifiable oral forms. An examination of the hermeneutics of Q, on the other hand, will demonstrate that genre's concern for continuing the living voice of Jesus. These observations compel us to reflect on connections between orality's attention to Jesus' words and deeds and textuality's power of bringing death to language. In a different sense, both death and life refer to language itself. An oral language deconstructed by textuality undergoes a kind of death. The written language, from this perspective, has risen out of a death in language. The new life it embodies is inseparable from the destruction of a traditional mode of language, and the literary presence it accomplishes is bought at the price of an oral absence.

First, we shall attend to Mark's passion narrative. Linguistically, what differentiates the narration of Jesus' death from that of his life? What were the linguistic, historical, and theological motivations that stimulated the form-critical quest for an older, pre-canonical passion story? What was the oral capacity of absorbing death, and how are we to assess the Markan textualization of it? Next we shall resume discussion of the primary unit of oral speech, the sayings. In terms of the oral ontology of language, an alliance will be observed between Q and Paul's apostolic-prophetic mode of proclamation that sets their oral hermeneutics apart from those of the written gospel. Mark's reservation toward the sayings genre can now be further clarified. Having completed our study of speaking and writing in early Christian traditions, in the third place we will formulate our thesis concerning the relation of the written gospel to oral speech. Finally, we will bring to a conclusion our reflections on the written gospel as parable. Specifically, we shall explore the gospel's parabolic narrative as a key to understanding its place in tradition. Last but not least a statement will be made about the relation between Mark's written parable and Jesus, the speaker in parables.

TEXTUALITY AND THE DEATH OF THE MESSIAH

Mark's passion narrative is laden with death, for it is really a story about three deaths. There is, most obviously, the death of Jesus, which occupies center stage. Divine intervention is not forthcoming during the period of suffering. The heavenly voice is sounded at baptism (1:11) and again at transfiguration (9:7), but it is silent during and after the crucifixion. Nor is there a resurrection story to end the gloomy tale on a victorious note. The resurrection itself is anticipated and reported as having happened, but it is not explicated in narrative discourse. Mark's narrative is truly about passion and death, not passion and resurrection.

There is, secondly, the death of the temple. In fulfillment of Jesus' own temple prophecy (13:2), the rending of the temple curtain at the moment of his expiration (15:38) is symbolic of the destruction of the temple. By placing the fall of the temple into the story of Jesus' death, Mark's narrative has absorbed the two principal traumas suffered in early Christianity. More than that, by connecting and indeed synchronizing the second with the first trauma, a form of theodicy has been accomplished: Jesus' own death proleptically marked the fall of the temple. In reading or hearing the narrative of the first trauma, one finds a rationale for the second trauma.

Thirdly, the passion narrative brings to a logical conclusion the dramatization of the disciples' demise. In chapter 3 we treated the theme both linguistically and literarily. Here we shall interpret it from the perspective of history of religions. Mircea Eliade has discussed the motif of "the message that failed," linking it with a concern for the origin of death. In his *Encyclopedia Britannica* article on myth, he records the following African story:

> God sent the chameleon to the mythical ancestors with the message that they would be immortal, and he sent the lizard with the message that they would die. The chameleon sauntered on the way and the lizard arrived first. After she delivered her message, death entered the world.[1]

The nonarrival of the message of life is a fatally serious matter in the world of religion. Since in Mark the theme of the abortive message of life brings the narration of the disciples' infidelity, and with it the gospel's story, to its conclusion, one cannot possibly infer from it a happy resolution for the disciples. In fact quite to the contrary, it is the very failure of the resurrection message to reach the disciples that provides the rationale for their demise. Whether one looks at the Markan theme of discipleship linguistically as a writer's demotion of the oral authorities, or parabolically as a reversal of the role of insiders, or religiously as a narration of "the message that failed," a rehabilitation of the disciples is positively excluded.[2] In its focus on the death of Jesus, the fall of the temple, and the demise of the disciples, the Markan passion story narrates the genesis of a triple death.

Mark's passion narrative is a tightly plotted story in which oral forms are not as manifestly in evidence as in the preceding story of life. Orally identifiable stories and redundancy of typical stories are less likely to be found in Mark 14–16 than in 1–13. The sayings tradition rapidly diminishes as the story moves toward death. After his arrest Jesus speaks only three more times: the enigmatically brief answer given to Pilate (15:2), the confession before the high priest (14:62), and the cry of dereliction (15:34), the last two sayings being derived from the Hebrew Bible. Directly linked with the relative scarcity of orally discernible materials is an increase in narrative compactness. Local and temporal references give the story of death a topographical coherence and chronological precision that distinguish it from the more thoroughly episodic story of life.

It is this narrative coherence, more than anything else, that lies at the root of the classical, form-critical thesis of an early, written pre-Markan passion narrative. Karl L. Schmidt expressed the opinion of every attentive reader when he stated that in the passion narrative "with compelling necessity and logic one thing follows another."[3] When, moreover, he concluded that the passion narrative was composed "soon after Jesus' death,"[4] he had arrived at a thesis that was to become normative for form criticism. Joachim Jeremias likewise reasoned that, apart from the agreements between John and the synoptics, it was the narrative density of the Markan composition that proved that "the passion narrative constitutes a coherent and very early block of the gospel tradition."[5] Similarly, Martin Dibelius equated narrative coherence with early, written composition, suggesting that "the Passion story is the only piece of Gospel tradition which in early times gave events in their larger connection."[6] Rudolf Bultmann shared the general form-critical presupposition: "Unlike other material of the tradition the passion stories developed early into coherent form; indeed one could almost say that coherence here held primacy."[7] In his view, both confessional creeds and historical remembrance were responsible for bringing the passion materials early under literary control. Implicitly or explicitly the form critics shared the conviction that the assumed early report was in close touch with what actually had happened. Schmidt was most outspoken in this regard: "Before tradition had time to work on events, as was the case with the materials outside of the passion narrative, the report of Jesus' death and resurrection was already fixed."[8] Narrative coherence suggested early written composition, and early documentation implied close proximity to history.

It must be stated categorically that narrative coherence is not necessarily an indication of early composition. To infer from the more tightly plotted story of Jesus' death that it was composed early and in close proximity to the events is to assume direct and unproblematic correspondences between language and extralinguistic actuality. What the coherence, vividness, and realism of a story prove is first and foremost narrative competence. Devices that foster narrative competence—such as the construction of causal connections, logical relations, close followability, and a tight temporal framework—all thrive under textuality. Narrative competence is intimately connected with textuality. What can safely be concluded is that the further a story is removed from oral formalities, the greater its chances to blossom into full textual life. Narrative coherence is thus the direct result of freedom from the restraints of oral formularity and not necessarily of historical closeness to the facts narrated. Is not this uncanny nearness to Jesus' death contingent on the writer's linguistic, temporal, and even geographical distance from it? Is it not perhaps more to the point to claim that the further we are removed from the origin, the more we know about it! It is, in any case, a matter of the utmost importance to understand that the form-critical search for the pre-Markan archetype of the passion narrative was motivated by what could have been an "aesthetic deception."[9] The form critics drew tradition-historical and even historical conclusions before addressing the prior linguistic questions:[10] how does one account for the oral tendency to seize upon the life of Jesus and the greater ability of textuality to appropriate death? Did one not speak about Jesus' death? What is the nexus between death and textuality?

The form-critical thesis of a pre-Markan passion narrative initiated a lively search that yielded a steady flow of increasingly contradictory proposals. A few examples must suffice to delineate the present state of scholarship. Bultmann "assumed" that there was an old report, based on historical recollection, "which narrated very briefly arrest, condemnation by the Sanhedrin and Pilate, the way to the cross, crucifixion and death."[11] It developed by several stages of accretion into the present text. Jeremias likewise believed to have recognized an evolutionary development of the history of the passion tradition. A *short account* that began with the arrest expanded into the *long account* that began with the triumphal entry and ended with the empty tomb, before it was filled out with additional stories and fixed in final form.[12] Vincent Taylor argued for two principal sources prior to Mark: text A, a straightforward, non-Semitic narrative composed for the Roman community, and text B, a Semitically flavored story with details stemming from the reminiscences of Peter.[13] Gottfried Schille suggested an early formulation of the events of the last night (14:18–72, minus the trial before the Sanhedrin), of the crucifixion (15:2–41) and the empty tomb in close connection with a cultic celebration of the anniversary of Jesus' death.[14] Wolfgang Schenk reconstructed two continuous pre-Markan passion sources: a historicizing text characterized by the use of the historical present, and a later report dominated by apocalyptic-gnostic enthusiasm. Mark combined the two, supporting the thrust of the former while setting critical accents against the latter.[15] K. H. Schelkle thought that the pre-Markan passion story approximated our present Markan text rather closely; it was transmitted orally and received its first written form by Mark.[16] Johannes Schreiber again opted for a Markan conflation of two crucifixion texts: a Jerusalem tradition based on Simon of Cyrene and cultivated by the Hellenistic wing of the church, and a gnosticizing text formulated by the Hellenists after their eviction from the city.[17] Detlev Dormeyer offered a detailed analysis of two pre-Markan stages and a final redaction: T, the oldest stratum, belonged to the genre of the Acts of Martyrs; Rs, an intermediary redactor, expanded T into a sequel of thirteen loosely connected scenes; and Rmk, the final redactor, revised Rs without adding essentially new material.[18] More examples could be given, but they would add little to the overall picture. What the search for the pre-Markan passion narrative demonstrates is a substantial lack of agreement as to scope and nature, genre and setting of the passion tradition. Without exaggeration, the stylistic, literary-critical decomposition of the passion text has led to a vast divergence of opinions on almost every single verse. If the scholarship of the past half century teaches us anything, it is that the extraordinarily dense textuality of the Markan passion narrative does not lend itself well to decompositioning.

Recently Helmut Koester has proposed that the apocryphal *"Gospel of Peter* is an independent witness of the formation of the passion narrative."[19] Some sixty years ago Dibelius had offered a very similar suggestion.[20] According to Koester, the *Gospel of Peter* contains a very early, pre-canonical form of the passion (and resurrection) narratives. Interestingly, Koester has dissociated himself from the form-critical assumption that the pre-Markan passion narrative was a historical report. "Form, structure, and life situation of such a historical passion report and its transmission have never been clarified."[21] Instead he believes that the old report was based on scriptural references. But, we must ask, if a major form-critical motivation for the quest after a pre-Markan passion narrative is abandoned, can we continue our search without serious methodological reflection? What are we looking for, and why are we looking for it?

The need for a fresh appraisal of the issue of the passion narrative was fully acknowledged by Rudolf Pesch in his monumental commentary on Mark.[22] He stated forthrightly that the literary, decompositional approach has landed us "in a dead end street,"[23] because the different proposals tend to cancel each other out. The reorientation undertaken by Pesch is based on the hermeneutical principle that characterizes his whole work on Mark: *in dubio pro traditione*. In the case of the passion narrative the author finds Mark 14–16 to be of one cloth, literarily and theologically. The thoroughgoing coherence of the passion narrative suggests to him that it is traditional *in its entirety*. In addition, he adds all preceding references to suffering, such as for example the three passion-resurrection predictions, to this comprehensive pre-Markan passion narrative. The net result is a story that began with 8:27–33, included 9:2–13, 30–35; 10:1, 32–34, 46–52; 11:1–23, 27–33; 12:1–17, 34c–37, 41–44; 13:1–2, and culminated in 14:1–16:8.[24] This traditional narrative is built on a substructure of Old Testament citations and allusions that articulate the motif of the *passio et iustificatio iusti*. It was composed at an early point in the Aramaic-speaking church of Jerusalem and may have served to justify the experience of the church on the model of Jesus' own suffering.

Pesch confronts us with a curious situation. The very evangelist who has such a vested interest in a theology of death as do few early Christian writers is supposed to have refrained from making a single contribution to the narrative dramatization of Jesus' passion. Indeed, according to Pesch, Mark has not added one iota to chapters 14–16. But have we not thereby turned the matter of tradition and composition on its head? By what literary standards is a manifestly heavy narrative engagement a sign not of authorial, but of preauthorial accomplishment? The hermeneutical principle, *in dubio pro traditione*, fails to give Markan composition a fair hearing. If Mark is not merely the author of the gospel's story, but the creator of the form of gospel, as Pesch argues he is,[25] and if the theme of the triple death is carefully anticipated in Mark 1–13, what really allows us not to credit the author with the narrative climax of the death of Jesus, the fall of the temple, and the demise of the disciples?

If there was a pre-canonical passion narrative, how did its formation in the synoptic tradition take place? A standard form-critical answer is that it originated out of brief passion summaries. Jeremias detected such summaries in 1 Cor. 15:3b–5 and in the third passion-resurrection prediction (Mark 10:33–34),[26] Bultmann in all three passion-resurrection predictions (Mark 8:31; 9:31; 10:33–34),[27] and Eduard Lohse again in the longest passion-resurrection prediction (Mark 10:33–34).[28] One could immediately point out that 1 Cor. 15:3b–5 culminates in two christophanies, whereas Mark does not narrate a single one. But the critical, linguistic rejoinder must be that the traditional formula of 1 Cor. 15:3b–5 demonstrates the vitality of the oral gospel, not the existence of a written narrative. What in fact we do observe is a succinct oral formula in the case of Paul, and a densely constructed story in the case of Mark. There is no evidence at hand that would suggest a tradition-historical movement, let alone evolutionary development, from the oral formula to the written passion narrative.

The same judgment applies to the passion-resurrection predictions. If in fact some are pre-Markan, one must ask with Schreiber: "Is it permissible to derive reports and stories from formulae?"[29] and answer with Etienne Trocmé: "we have no evidence at all that the Passion Narrative grew from a small nucleus as a plant develops out of a seed."[30] The investigation, moreover, of the history of tradition of Mark 8:31, 9:31, 10:33–34 is subject to questioning.[31] Georg Strecker, for example, argued that 8:31 was the oldest form, which had been tripled by Mark.[32] Ferdinand Hahn took the shortest form, 9:31, to be the oldest, and 10:33–34, the longest form, to be Markan.[33] Siegfried Schulz likewise thought that 10:33–34 was a Markan composition, whereas 8:31 and 9:31 were largely pre-Markan.[34] Heinz E. Tödt, on the other hand, regarded all three sayings as traditional,[35] while Eta Linnemann again was convinced that Mark had created the longest form on the analogy of the shorter ones.[36] It is precisely this kind of approach to the synoptic tradition that must arouse our deep suspicion. What is the meaning of "oldest form" in oral tradition? Furthermore, does not the scholars' inclination to take the shorter forms (8:31; 9:31) to be traditional suggest that decisions concerning oral tradition are almost instinctively made on the premise of an evolutionary model? Even if scholarship could reach a consensus on the history of tradition of the passion-resurrection predictions, it still remains to be documented how a saying is supposed to have generated an extensive text. What in fact we do observe is that the three sayings are "the latest of all the Son of man sayings to have been developed, and therefore failed to find a place in the logia source,"[37] and that their narrative role is manifestly determined by Mark. But if these sayings are absent from the oral genre of Q, while they are a "key element in what is evidently a very carefully composed section of the Gospel,"[38] one cannot possibly draw inferences as to their tradition-historical role in an alleged evolutionary development of a passion text.

Theological presuppositions played a subtle role in the thesis of a pre-Markan passion narrative. This is most obvious in the case of Dibelius when he declared that "we must presuppose the early existence of a Passion narrative complete in itself since preaching . . . required some such text."[39] Apart from the fact that early Christian preaching required no text at all, one must ask whether the synoptic tradition itself gives evidence of or at least provides a promising climate for a passion narrative. On this, as on many other matters, Tödt sounded the clear voice of the time:

> It has almost become an *opinio communis* to assume that the kerygma of the passion and resurrection is the centre of the synoptic tradition, thus drawing from the function of the passion kerygma in the Gospel of Mark a general conclusion for the synoptic tradition as a whole.[40]

This warning grew out of the author's unsurpassed study of the Son of man tradition and his very keen interest in Q. The one pre-Markan source that can be reconstructed with a degree of certainty, the sayings source Q, does not speak of Jesus' death! This is all the more astounding since Son of man is *the* christological title of the source. The very title that in Mark is linked with Jesus' death, as well as with his earthly power and parousia, is in Q exclusively connected with his present and future power. We shall explore further the deeper implications of the absence of a passion christology in Q, but its specific use of Son of man already suggests that the genre's appropriation of Jesus' present and future power *precluded reflection on his death.* But the moment one acknowledges Q's inherent hermeneutical and theological integrity, one can no longer—in the fashion of leading form critics—relegate the source to a second-class citizenship, assuming that it derived its *raison d'être* from the tradition of passion. Now in fact the tables are turned, and one cannot speak at all of the "omission of passion christology" in Q, as if there had existed a developed text of Jesus' passion prior to Q. The very theology of the sayings source casts doubt on the assumed existence of an early passion narrative. Tödt has drawn this conclusion most vigorously: "The masters of the method of form-criticism, Bultmann and Dibelius, both established, each in his own specific way, the theological priority of the community's kerygma of the passion over the Q material."[41] As a matter of fact, Tödt argued, the history of the Son of man tradition as well as the theology of Q demonstrate the very opposite: ". . . the passion kerygma . . . appears to have been developed within the synoptic tradition later than the material of Q."[42] Dibelius is thus manifestly wrong in assuming that early Christian preaching required the text of a passion narrative. Q, the most prominent oral source of the synoptic tradition, demonstrates that one could very well speak without explicit reference to death.

Apart from Q, does the pre-Markan, synoptic tradition furnish favorable conditions for the composition of a passion narrative? The heroic and polarization stories display an oral christology decidedly antithetical to passion christology. These stories of Jesus' powerful deeds preclude reflection on his death. Nor is there much, if any, room for passion in the didactic stories, for they are pragmatically oriented toward the present needs of the community. Parables could be expected to be the oral form of speech ideally suited for speaking about the unspeakable. Yet Jesus' death, this—for Mark—preeminent aspect of the mystery of the kingdom, is virtually honored with silence in parabolic speech. The parable of the *Wicked Tenants* is a notable exception. One does find scattered sayings which speak in metaphorical indirection of the final stage of Jesus' life: he must drink the cup (Mark 10:38; 14:36), undergo baptism (10:38), serve as ransom for the many (10:45), and be the shepherd who will be struck (14:27). There remain the three passion-resurrection predictions that speak in unambiguous, historicizing fashion of passion. Even if they were part of tradition, they cannot serve as tradition-historical explanations for a passion narrative, as argued above. One must conclude that the bulk of the synoptic tradition—heroic and polarization stories, didactic stories, parables, and most sayings—shows little interest in the suffering and death of Jesus. The oral tradition is preoccupied with aspects of the *vita activa* of Jesus and concerned with the presence of hearers, but silent or reticent with regard to Jesus' death. In other words, the tradition reflects a hermeneutical climate that is anything but favorable to the composition of a passion narrative.

It could, of course, be argued that we have exaggerated the *oral* property of the pre-canonical tradition. The oral appropriation of Jesus' life could presumably have coexisted with a textual assimilation of his passion and death. At this point, literary-aesthetic and psychocultural considerations must be brought to bear on the subject. In a study of the crucifixion in Greco-Roman antiquity, Martin Hengel documented the remarkable paucity of literary references to this *mors turpissima crucis.* "No ancient writer wanted to dwell too long on this cruel procedure."[43] The literary aesthetics of writers, who mostly belonged to the middle class, prevailed to blunt or domesticate the issue, or to prevent the hideous reality from coming to consciousness at all. "Crucifixion was widespread and frequent, above all in Roman times, but the cultured literary world wanted to have nothing to do with it, and as a rule kept quiet about it."[44] In view of widespread reluctance to write about crucifixion, and of synoptic orality's reticence to speak about Jesus' execution, is it plausible that the first recollection early Christians committed to writing would become one of the most realistic of all passion narratives in antiquity? There can be no doubt whatsoever that Jesus' execution was a profoundly traumatic experience for his followers. Early christophanies promoted the living Christ and in part at least will have triggered oral remembering of words and deeds, but not of death. Is not *distance from the trauma* an essential psychocultural prerequisite for most mediations of death? Must we not assume geographical, chronological, and psychological distance before the cross could be assimilated into a developed narrative dramatization?

Jesus' death was not, of course, passed over in complete silence. Orality's hesitation to speak of death and the dubious proposition of an early, written passion narrative bring the focus on the eucharist. It is only when we have become conscious of the difficulty of bringing the death of the Messiah to language that the singular importance of the sacramental meal is appreciated. Although the eucharist is patently oral in cast, there are good reasons for nonsacramental orality to hedge on death. To repeat, voice is alive, and spoken words are consubstantial with life. Synoptic orality is drawn to Jesus' words and deeds, to his activity and exercise of power. Oral speech provides the matrix in which the living Christ flourishes and a sense of God's presence grows. By the same token, synoptic orality shies away from death, which puts an end to active life and to the speaking of words. Death, if it is not to be forgotten altogether, requires a particular mediation. The eucharist provides the special, sacramental medium for assimilating the death of Jesus. In both the activist and participatory character of the words of consecration it discharges the function of primary orality. But added to the spoken, invisible words is the *verbum visibile* of the elements. Bread and wine, transformed by the words of consecration, make death interiorly accessible without reviving realistic aspects of the crucifixion. It is in this sacramentally transfigured space of visible and invisible words that orality's reluctance to speak of death is overcome and participation in death is made possible.

Given the signal importance of the eucharist, could this rite not have furnished the locus for an extended passion narrative? The thesis, developed in fanciful detail by Philip Carrington,[45] and revised with form-critical imagination by Schille,[46] has recently received its most plausible formulation by Trocmé.[47] Passover, Trocmé reminds us, coincided with the anniversary of the death of Jesus. For this reason alone, one may well assume that the Jerusalem Christians celebrated Passover both by commemorating the Exodus and by reenacting the death of Jesus, who had brought liberation from the bondage of sin.[48] If this can be granted, then a liturgical narration of Jesus' passion on the analogy of the Passover Haggadah may have a high degree of probability. It must be readily agreed that of all possible settings for a pre-Markan passion narrative, the eucharist appears to be the most likely candidate. Trocmé's thesis is all the more attractive because he has wisely abstained from a verbatim reconstruction of the assumed text and focused instead on its liturgical aspects. Not all the observed liturgical features are equally convincing, however. It is difficult to see why the threefold division of the Gethsemane prayer should give the impression of "an incantation or a sacred dance,"[49] or why the triple denial of Peter must be located in a cultic drama.[50] Not even the three-hour schematization of Jesus' death (Mark 15:1, 25, 33, 34–37) must necessarily have originated in Jewish-Christian worship. Threefold patterns are noticeable inside the passion narrative and outside of it. They form part of Mark's oral legacy[51] and are used for the purpose of heightening narrative tension. There may be narrative rather than cultic reasons for the tight dramatization of death according to the three-hour rhythm. Death, in contrast to life, comprises a much shorter span of time. The narrative plotting of life does not lend itself to three-hour divisions. But the story of death, especially death by execution, invites a compact, temporally specified frame of time. On a broader scale one must wonder whether Mark's story of the triple death could in this fashion have been narrated by Jerusalem Christians prior to 70 C.E. Even if one were to agree with Günter Klein's thesis of an entrenched anti-Petrinism in the early tradition,[52] it is difficult to imagine Jerusalem Christians reenacting Jesus' death in conjunction with the demise of the pillars and the destruction of the temple. Does not the plot of the triple death point more readily to a composition after 70 C.E.? Most importantly, the thesis of the passion narrative's eucharistic setting must be subjected to stringent linguistic questioning. The eucharistic records of the synoptic tradition show no trace of evidence of an affiliation of a historicizing story of Jesus' death with the sacred meal. The same holds true of Paul's eucharistic tradition. "Paul says almost nothing about the crucifixion except that it occurred. None of the details which appear in any of our gospel accounts are mentioned."[53] May not perhaps the oral, participatory eucharist preclude a historicizing anamnesis? In different words, if we recognize the densely *literary* nature of Mark's passion narrative, why do we continue searching for an *oral* setting? Is this not once again a case of postulating unbroken continuity of oral and written contextuality?

A summary of our findings will compel us to reconsider the history of the tradition of the passion narrative. Mark 14–16 is a tightly plotted text. The search for a text behind the text has brought much confusion, but not the desired result. The linguistic, theological, and tradition-historical motives that gave rise to the quest are not beyond suspicion. The text at hand gives few indications of oral transmission. A prominent exception is provided by the eucharistic tradition (Mark 14:22–24). The relative absence of an oral base is corroborated by the synoptic tradition, which shows a decided preference for the activity of Jesus, both his words and deeds. The form-critical thesis concerning a very early textualization of the tradition of passion is thus undermined on three sides: (1) The assumption that dense textualization, narrative coherence, and realism indicate an early composition, in close touch with history, is untenable. Textual competence is more likely the result of literary distanciation from life, or, in our case, from Jesus' death. (2) The very integrity of the text of the passion narrative has doomed efforts at finding the alleged archetype. Pesch's work, although uncritically beholden to the form-critical thesis, signals a crucial shift toward recognizing the integral nature of the passion text. (3) The synoptic tradition does not provide a favorable climate for the creation of a passion narrative. The thesis of a quasi-organic evolution of the passion tradition, moreover, has no basis in the synoptic tradition, as far as it is subject to examination. At this point a new formulation of the issue is unavoidable. If Mark has a deep investment in Jesus' death, in the demise of the disciples and the fall of the temple, whereas oral tradition by and large does not, and if he writes not to continue but to overcome oral mentality, and if indeed he is the creator of the textualization of Jesus' life and death, what prevents us from crediting him with the composition of the bulk of the passion narrative?

If the passion narrative was for the most part not sewn together out of oral commonplaces, what was its manner of composition? A number of statements about the suffering of the Son of man give us a clue. In Mark 9:11–13 the passion of the Son of man is linked by divine necessity (*dei elthein prōton*) with that of Elijah, and both deaths are in accord with Scripture (9:12: *pōs gegraptai*; 9:13: *kathōs gegraptai*). At the Last Supper Jesus reiterates the mission of the Son of man unto death "as it is written of him" (14:21: *kathōs gegraptai peri autou*). In view of the obvious desire to connect the inevitability of death with a scriptural base, the programmatic "must" (*dei*) of the first passion-resurrection prediction "undoubtedly echoes the motive of the necessity of scriptural fulfilment."[54] This linkage of death with Scripture expounds not merely a theological principle, but a compositional one as well. Dibelius in particular was convinced that Old Testament passages "were read as normative sources for the Passion story,"[55] and Barnabas Lindars demonstrated the substantial scriptural base of early Christian passion theology.[56] For our purpose the most significant contribution has come from Howard C. Kee who studied the scriptural references in Mark 11–16 with unsurpassed care.[57] The author proceeded from the observation that "the number of quotations from and allusions to scripture increases sharply"[58] at the point where the narrative moves toward death. In Mark 11–16 Kee tabulated

57 scriptural quotations, approximately 160 allusions to Scripture and 60 scriptural influences.[59] If in the case of the story of Jesus' life we had reason to observe, "Take the oral units away, and the narrative is gone," we must here say, "Take the scriptural references away, and the story of death has vanished." The existence of allusions and influences, in addition to quotations, suggests that much of Scripture, like much literature in antiquity, was mentally accessible to an oral mode of appropriation. Obviously, orality derived from texts is not the same as primary orality, which operates without the aid of texts. The passion narrative is largely built on texts and texts recycled into the oral medium, that is, secondary orality.

Kee, noting that there was no essential difference in the use of scriptural references between Mark 11–13 and 14–16, wondered whether the pre-Markan passion narrative had begun as early as chapter 11, or, what seemed more likely to him, whether "much or all of the passion narrative should be attributed to Mark."[60] One may add that the multitude of scriptural references are integrated into the text with extraordinary disregard for their original contextual setting. There is, therefore, no compositional difference between Mark's decontextualization and recontextualization of synoptic, oral versus Jewish, scriptural units.

"Passion apologetic" is a favorite scholarly designation for the scriptural rootedness of early Christian passion traditions. The word "apologetic" in this context carries the implication of defensive theological practices out of political or religious embarrassment. But "passion apologetic" may not be the best of terms to comprehend the phenomenon at hand. The tightly woven textual fabric of the passion narrative, which is itself built from other texts, arouses linguistic interests; and considerations of language once again offer new insight. Associations between the written medium and death are not self-evident and do not leap to the eye. And yet, attention to textuality's partiality toward death merely supplements our preceding examination of orality's inclination toward the *vita activa*.

The Jesus who performs deeds of power invites oral remembering, and the heroic and polarization stories appeal to mythopoetic identification. The Jesus who dies in powerlessness is the antihero. If the antihero is to become an attractive figure, distance from and skepticism toward oral clichés is indispensable. Freed from the obligation to shape knowledge in memorable forms and figures, writing can overcome orality's entrenched heroism and cultivate an alternative philosophy. "With writing and print, heroic figures decline."[61] The Jesus who is declared Son of God while dying on the cross is fraught with irony and paradox. Orality is no stranger to the conceptual mode of indirection and inversion. Paradox reaches a height with the parables, and aphoristic sayings can well handle irony. But it is with the written medium that keeps signifier apart from meaning and dissociates knowledge from the self that the mentality of indirection can come to full fruition: the direct sense is not to be trusted, and life, or even death, is not what it seems. Oral speech, moreover, is drawn to presence and present activity. But death, above all else, spells absence. Death also signifies silence. What could be more inimical to the oral medium than an end to speaking? The cross cannot become a focal point for sayings. If *logoi* are collected, they will have to be clustered around the living Christ. Absence and silence are best handled by the medium that has itself withdrawn from sound and personalizing engagement. Furthermore, an oral story must lend itself to repetition. Death, however, does not tolerate repetition. It is intrinsically unrepeatable, because one dies only once. It remains the prerogative of the eucharist to draw death into the oral cycle of repetitiousness. To represent the immobility of death constitutes a strength of written words, which have themselves died to oral life. If one is to face at all the death of the Messiah, the absence it spelled, the silence it entailed, and the grief it brought, distance is an absolute prerequisite. One does not come that close to death unless one stands apart from it. The stunning "realism" of the passion narrative is most likely the result of artistic distanciation by written words that empty events of their immediacy. Close proximity to the event and the oral metaphysics of presence are a persistent obstacle to bringing death to language.

If orality is drawn to the forces of life, and textuality more adept at absorbing death, an emphasis on death may be expected at points where textuality gains the upper hand. In the case of Paul, we remember, death had received a heavy emphasis in 1 Corinthians. The ultimate seriousness with which the apostle treated the Christ crucified in the wisdom chapters was in reaction to Corinthian piety that was characterized by a developed rhetorical consciousness, a probable implementation of sayings of the risen Lord, and an oral enthusiasm for the living Christ and personal resurrection. Paul's emphasis on death together with a defensive posture toward wisdom sayings and his frequent appeal to scriptural authority formed a connected pattern designed to curb the presenting power of oral wisdom. At this point, the often invoked kinship between Paul and Mark appears in a new light. The affirmation of Jesus' death by the two earliest Christian writers available to us must not immediately lead us to assume direct connections. Explanations in terms of causal or genetic relations are not always to be trusted. Mark seized upon the written medium and, not unlike Paul in 1 Corinthians, deemphasized sayings, while making death emphatic with the aid of Scripture. Dramatically, he made the disciples, the oral authorities, come to grief over Jesus' death, the very aspect with which synoptic orality had been ill at ease. Medium and message are once again interconnected. Linguistically, one observes an emergent mode of reflectiveness, rudimentarily in Paul and more fully developed in Mark, that gains distance on the oral regalia of full life and presence. Mark's passion narrative can thus well be understood as a feature intrinsic to an emergent textuality that disengages itself from oral preoccupations.

THE ORAL EQUATION OF THE EARTHLY JESUS WITH THE LIVING LORD

Collecting and speaking words of Jesus or pronouncing words in his name and authority was a standard feature of the early tradition. There is much that seems to favor this process. Sayings of Jesus must have been treasured items, and their oral organization in *loci* formation was ideally suited to preserve his voice and continue his authority. Ironically, sayings were not always accorded the full prestige one might expect them to have enjoyed. It is a curious fact that the genre of sayings came to be a mixed blessing for the emergent orthodox church. We have already observed the paucity of sayings in Mark and Paul's defensive posture in 1 Corinthians. A less than enthusiastic reception of the sayings genre by both evangelists and canonizers suggests tension between those dedicated to the tradition in textual form and the primary unit of oral speech.

In sketching the development of the sayings genre, James M. Robinson noted—*inter alia*—the appropriation of the Q tradition by Matthew and Luke, as well as the genre's appearance in the *Gospel of Thomas*.[62] It is highly significant that the very genre that "continues to be acceptable to the orthodox church only in the context of this other gattung, that of 'gospel',"[63] manifests itself in full force in gnosticism. The discovery of *Thomas*, a sayings collection itself, could well be taken to corroborate the Q hypothesis, but it also brought with it full consciousness of the absence of the genre in the canon. In view of the genre's triumphant rise in gnosticism, its unacceptability to the canonizers except by mediation through the written gospels is all the more significant. When one observes the triumph of the genre in what came to be "heresy," and its subdued existence in developing orthodoxy, a number of data can legitimately be linked together: the canonical rejection of the sayings genre *in its own right*, Paul's defensive attitude in 1 Corinthians, the paucity of sayings in Mark, Matthew's and Luke's absorption of the oral genre into gospel textuality, and its privileged status in gnosticism. What, one must ask, are the traits of the genre that to evangelists and canonizers appeared as defects? How does the process of Matthean and Lukan decontextualization and recontextualization affect the hermeneutical integrity of Q? Eventually we must ask, what all this may tell us about the paucity of sayings in Mark.

In answer to the question of the relation of gospel and sayings genre, Robinson suggested that the gospel replaced the genre as the latter came to be discontinued by the church: "With the final discontinuation of the oral transmission of Jesus' sayings, the *Sitz im Leben* of the gattung was gone; hence orthodoxy contented itself with the canonical gospels."[64] Koester projected a more dynamic view, defining the relation less in terms of replacement than of displacement of the sayings by the gospel. In his words, Q's integration into Matthew and Luke amounted to a "radical critical alteration, not only of the form, but also of the theological intention of this primitive gattung."[65] Our own study would confirm Koester's perception of the trauma Q suffered as it came to take its place in the canonical gospels. Matthew and Luke appropriated Q by revoking its generic, linguistic, and theological integrity. This could well indicate that it was precisely the oral, hermeneutical quality that was unacceptable to evangelists and canonizers alike.

If one asks Robinson about the "heretical" proclivity of the sayings genre, he will point to the early Christian association of wisdom with sayings collections. Jesus' identity as prophetic speaker of words of wisdom could easily modulate into that of a gnostic redeemer, bringer of secret sayings.[66] This observation is indisputably correct. The presence of wisdom in Q,[67] wisdom's function as catalyst for sayings, and the gnosticizing potential of Q are all established features. Wisdom explains how a particular christology could become attached to Jesus and cooperate with the genre of sayings in generating a tradition that was open toward gnosticizing proclivities. But after one has surveyed the historical development of the genre from Jewish wisdom to Hellenistic gnosticism, one is still left wondering precisely why Jesus' sayings, one of the most treasured of early Christian traditions, could become a source of embarrassment and even "heresy."

Koester moved beyond wisdom and gnosticism toward a hermeneutical assessment of the genre of sayings. In his view, the internal principle of the gattung represented by *Thomas* rests on the assumption that "the Jesus who spoke these words was and is the Living One, and thus gives life through his words."[68] It follows that "a direct and almost unbroken continuation of Jesus' own teaching takes place—unparalleled anywhere in the canonical tradition."[69] With this Koester has given us a clear definition of the operating power of the genre of sayings. What must be emphasized is that the principle of the presence of the living Lord is an intrinsic feature of *oral* hermeneutic. Insofar as *logoi* constitute the primary unit of oral tradition, the presence of the living Lord is inseparable from the linguistic ontology of the genre itself. One may also suspect that what was objectionable to the writers of gospels and the compilers of the written canon was this very oral hermeneutic of the sayings genre.

The Oral Hermeneutic of Q

A review of the christological structure and hermeneutical perspective of Q will disclose its fundamentally oral disposition.[70] Q's christology displays a two-pronged emphasis. On the one hand, it prepares for the future, standing as it does "on its tiptoes in anticipation of the parousia."[71] On the other hand, it counsels loyalty to Jesus in the present. Future and present are christologically and soteriologically correlated. The Jesus who verifies his authority as Son of man in the present is expected to return as Son of man in the future. His followers' conduct at present is conditioned by hope for his coming, just as the manner of his coming is contingent on their present attitude toward him. As noted above, Q's christology is an integral entity without reference to suffering and death.[72] Jesus is not a suffering Son of man who died on behalf of the many, but an authoritative prophet, and indeed more than a prophet (Matt. 11:9// Luke 7:26), who demands that he be followed and confessed. In the absence of an encompassing historicizing framework, Q effects a direct address to present hearers. Both in terms of genre and medium the sayings are uniquely qualified to continue the present authority of Jesus. Q ". . . accepted as its central commission the communication of Jesus' teaching."[73] With this understanding of Q's strategy we have arrived at the hermeneutical rationale for its silence with regard to Jesus' death. A tradition that focuses on the continuation of Jesus' words cannot simultaneously bring to consciousness what put an end to his speaking. As long as Jesus is perceived as speaking in the present, there is no need, and hardly a possibility, of recapturing the story of his death. By the same logic, we note again, a heavy narrative emphasis on death, such as one finds in Mark, may imply a critique of the sayings tradition.

Since Q represents an oral genre, the feasibility of its performance is a relevant issue. If the concern is to continue the speech of Jesus, how is his speaking authority actualized? The answer lies in the prophetic self-consciousness of Q. Jesus himself, we noted, is conceived as a prophetic figure who speaks words of judgment and redemption. Israel's prophets serve as a model of discipleship. If Jesus' disciples accept homelessness, they are embracing the life style of the Son of man (Matt. 8:20//Luke

9:58), and if they suffer rejection and persecution, they do so on account of the Son of man (Matt. 5:11//Luke 6:22). But in accepting suffering, both Jesus and the disciples experience what the "fathers did to the prophets" (Luke 6:23; cf. Matt. 5:12). By implication, Jesus is the prophet par excellence, and his followers' suffering is not in imitation of his death, but in tragic repetition of the lot of the prophets. Prophetic speech, moreover, has been shown to permeate the language of Q.[74] Q's present-future orientation is itself a fundamentally prophetic paradigm.[75] The hermeneutical principle of prophetic speech is unequivocally stated in Matt. 10:40// Luke 10:16: "He who hears you hears me, and he who rejects you rejects me, and he who rejects me rejects him who sent me." This formula of legitimation authorizes the prophetic representatives of Q to speak in accordance with the hermeneutical purpose of the genre. Endowed with prophetic authority, they speak the sayings not as mere human words, but as words of Jesus, and not of the Jesus of the past, but in his present authority.

In his massive study of the history of transmission of Q, Siegfried Schulz differentiated a Palestinian stage, characterized by prophetic enthusiasm, from a Jewish-Hellenistic stage, which began to take a retrospective view of the earthly Jesus. One can agree with Schulz that Q is not without reflective and historicizing proclivities. The objective to continue Jesus' teaching does not exclude the work of theological interpretation. The identification of the future Son of man with the earthly Jesus is itself a major exercise in christological reflectiveness. Also, not all Q material is equally well suited for contemporizing words in the prophetic manner. Boring notes a *kai eipen autois* style, which places sayings in past-narrative settings, over against a *legō hymin* style, which represents direct address to hearers.[76] Undoubtedly, Q is already a complex formation of heterogeneous materials. But one must ask Schulz whether it is really possible to determine trends, and even developmental stages, in what constitutes essentially the fluid medium of orality. Whatever its tradition-historical versatility, the hypothetically reconstructed Q comprises a christological and hermeneutical logic of its own. It is structured around a present-future mode of christology and functions in an oral, prophetic manner of speech. Schulz himself concedes that in what for him is the youngest, the Jewish-Hellenistic stage of Q ". . . the exalted-present Son of man continues to speak through his prophets to the community."[77] The encompassing retrospection that casts tradition into a historicizing, pre-resurrectional framework is not within the mental horizon of Q.

Notable hermeneutical distinctions, which are deeply ingrained in modern consciousness, have no validity in Q. The speakers of Q sayings, for example, were not bound to a historical figure of the past, but authorized by a Jesus who continued to speak through their words. A separation between the words of the historical Jesus and those of his followers was thus not only blurred, but often nonexistent. Their words were the words of the Son of man, and his words were their words. Most importantly, the sayings are not christologically divisible into pre-Easter and post-Easter material. This is a point rightly emphasized by Boring more recently[78] and by Tödt in the past.[79] It is unthinkable for Q that Jesus spoke in one mode of existence prior to his death and in another after his resurrection. One must agree with Tödt that "it did not even occur to the members of the community which collected the sayings of Jesus in Q to distinguish between pre-Easter and post-Easter sayings, it being self-evident to them that the earthly Jesus and the risen Jesus are one and the same."[80] The sayings in Q were neither conceived as words of the past, pre-resurrectional Jesus nor strictly speaking as words of the risen Lord. In the oral, prophetic mode of Q the power of speech united the earthly and the future Son of man into the present efficacious one.

The christological and hermeneutical dynamics of Q put the genre's perceived "defect" into perspective. Tödt observed "something like a gulf"[81] separating Q from Mark, comparable only to the other great divide, that between the epistles and the gospels. Obviously the one tradition, the sayings genre of Q, which could conceivably be taken as the missing link in the assumed synoptic evolution toward the gospel, is not that at all. It is now evident what Koester had in mind when he wrote of the "radical critical alteration" Q suffered at the hands of Matthean and Lukan textualization. By pressing the sayings into the service of their written gospels, the authors of Matthew and Luke deprived Q of the very trait constitutive of its oral hermeneutic: the prophetically living voice of Jesus became the unalterable words of Jesus' past authority. A literary mentality, unable to tolerate the oral equation of the earthly Jesus with the living Lord, rigorously tied all sayings to the pre-resurrectional Jesus. Q was preserved at the price of being defeated in its authentic, hermeneutical purpose. One is bound to conclude that it was precisely Q's oral ontology of language that the writers of the written gospels—and one may assume the canonizers—perceived to be its essential "defect."

The Oral Hermeneutic of Paul

We must return to the Pauline gospel and clarify its position vis-à-vis the written gospel. In 1 Corinthians we noted the apostle taking his strongest stand against a full-fledged oral mentality. By emphasizing the crucified Christ and showing reservation toward the words of wisdom, he anticipated developments that would eventually lead to the written gospel. Without the benefit of hindsight, however, the apostle merely shifted the accent from one pole of his gospel to another without releasing the latter from its natural habitat of oral speech. At most, the oral synthesis was ruptured at this point, but not overturned. Fundamentally, Paul's gospel of death and resurrection invites participation. Mark's estrangement from all oral authorities is nowhere to be found in Paul's theology of language. The apostle's disagreements with other apostles arise out of different versions of the oral gospel and competing loyalties to individual speakers, never out of a categorical rejection of the oral conceptualization itself. Neither Paul nor, as far as can be determined, any other apostle contemporaneous with him appears to contemplate an alternative norm by recapturing the pre-resurrectional Jesus in written form. Paul's writings are primarily reflections on his own oral gospel, or that of other apostles, and on its reception in the respective communities. But his reflective posture is effectively restrained by his use of the letter form, which allows maximum oral contact with the recipients. The alienated habit of seeking a lost world by retrieving the past of Jesus' life and death is entirely at odds with his oral hermeneutics. Paul's abiding commitment to the oral gospel, his choice of the letter form, the absence of a developed pre-resurrectional framework, and his firm conviction of the event-character of the word raise the question whether he proclaims his message in the christologically undifferentiated fashion of Q.

That the Pauline mode of address does not conceptually separate a pre-resurrectional from a post-resurrectional christology has recently been intimated by Ulrich B. Müller,[82] and fully developed by Boring.[83] It is instructive to examine Paul's authoritative style of address. One must first note the complete absence of the *egō eimi* style of prophetic proclamation,[84] of the prophetic "truly I say to you" (*amēn legō hymin*) address, of the prophetic messenger formula "thus speaks the one who" (Rev. 2:1, 8, 12, 18; 3:1, 7, 14: *tade legei ho*), and of the *Weckformel* which alerts attention to the speaking authority in the Spirit (Rev. 2:7, 11, 17, 29; 3:6, 13, 22: *ho echōn ous akousatō ti to pneuma legei*). From this absence of the classic, prophetic authorization formulae one may well conclude that Paul was reluctant to identify with the Lord.[85] Paul's professed identity is that of apostle, never prophet.

Despite the absence of established features of prophetic style, aspects of Paul's apostolic self-consciousness are closely related to that of the prophet. Müller discovered a Pauline authorization formula whose affinity to the classic, prophetic formulation is evident.[86] The formula uses the verb *parakalein*, to appeal or exhort, in the first person singular, followed by reference to the Lord Jesus with the preposition *en* or *dia*. The exhortation in or through the Lord articulates the authority that stands behind Paul and in whose name he writes. The full formula is given in 1 Thess. 4:1, 1 Cor. 1:10, and Rom. 15:30, and a modification of it in 2 Cor. 10:1 and Rom. 12:1. Its abbreviated form, without reference to the Lord Jesus, appears in 1 Thess. 4:10, 5:14, Phlm. 9–10, 1 Cor. 4:16, 16:15–16, Phil. 4:2, and Rom. 16:17. Müller's form-critical study identified the formula as an authentically oral one. But whether Paul used it orally or in the first person singular style of letter writing, the exhortation formula attributes the Lord's authority to the apostle's words. As apostle he serves in an ambassadorial role for Christ, speaking on behalf of him as if it were the voice of God (2 Cor. 5:20). "The urgent call of the apostle as he invites men to believe is thus a call which the exalted Christ Himself issues."[87] Although Paul keeps his personal identity apart from Christ's, he perceives his apostolic commission to be less a speaking about Jesus and more a continuation of his authority. There is as yet no sharp line drawn between Jesus the proclaimer and the proclaimed. The proclaimer continues to assert his presence through the mouth of the apostle.

Paul's apostolic-prophetic self-consciousness in proclaiming the gospel in the name and on the authority of the Lord Jesus is echoed in other parts of his letters. In 1 Cor. 5:3–4, for example, he addresses a case of sexual promiscuity by pronouncing judgment. His articulation of excommunication displays a keen sense of the oral, christological efficaciousness of his words. Despite his bodily absence, he writes, he has already pronounced judgment as if he were present, and the community will in his (the apostle's) spiritual presence deliver the offender to his fleshly destruction. The hermeneutics that have informed this statement suggest that Paul's initial enunciation of anathema, presumably his dictation, already carried judgmental powers that became personally effective upon recitation of the letter in the community. But whether dictated or recited, his words take effect "in the name of the Lord Jesus" and "in the power of our Lord Jesus" respectively. Similarly, in 1 Cor. 14:37 the apostle repudiates the Corinthians' practice of identifying prophecy with glossolalia by claiming the authority of the Lord for his own written words: "what I am writing to you: it is a command of the Lord" (au. trans. of *hoti kyriou estin entolē*).

It is in keeping with the apostle's oral interest in extending the living authority of Jesus into the present that he consistently invokes the authority of the Lord (*ho kyrios*) when he refers to or cites a saying of Jesus

(1 Cor. 7:10–11; [7:12, 25;] 9:14; 1 Thess. 4:15–17), legitimizes his own writing (1 Cor. 14:37), or transmits the eucharistic tradition (1 Cor. 11: 23–26).[88] In the mentality of modern scholarship one would tend to subject Paul's claim to critical analysis. One would point out connections between 1 Cor. 7:10–11 and Q (Matt. 5:32//Luke 16:18) as well as Mark (10:11–12), and also between 1 Cor. 9:14 and Q (Matt. 10:10//Luke 10:7). Since Q itself does not differentiate between the earthly Jesus and the post-resurrectional Christ, these sayings could have come from Jesus, but they could just as well have been prophetically functioning sayings of the risen Lord. Interestingly, in Gal. 6:6 Paul paraphrases 1 Cor. 9:14 on his own authority. The eucharistic tradition (1 Cor. 11:23–26) is most likely a liturgical formulation originating in the church of either Jerusalem or Antioch. Paul's apocalyptic saying in 1 Thess. 4:15–17 is widely assumed to stem from prophetic tradition.[89] The analytic approach, it appears obvious, operates on the premise that a saying is either pre-resurrectional, hence coming from the earthly Jesus, or post-resurrectional, hence a word from tradition. The real point to be made is that Paul, unlike modern scholarship, attributes sayings to the Lord irrespective of their historically verifiable genesis. Whether a saying is from the earthly Jesus, prophetically transmitted as a word of the risen Lord, or Paul's own word spoken or written in apostolic-prophetic self-consciousness, it is always legitimized by the authority of the Lord. The overriding concern is to the oral mission of continuing the speaking and living authority of the Lord. This is precisely the purpose of Paul's oral gospel. The oral formula of death and resurrection is functionally designed to continue Jesus' lordship. Pronouncement of death and resurrection is not objective communication about something, but the creation of a reality to participate in.

Orality's Continuing Authority of the Proclaimer

The operating function of the Q sayings and Paul's apostolic-prophetic mode of speech illuminate the oral equation of the earthly Jesus with the living Lord. If traditions as varied in genre and outlook as Q's sayings and Paul's letters subscribe to the same oral functioning of christology, the latter will have been the norm rather than the exception in the early period. Frank W. Beare has stated the case most dramatically: "It is doubtful if any Christian of the first or second century would have been interested in making a clear distinction between words spoken by the historical Jesus in the days of his flesh, and words of the risen Lord— who was, after all, the same person."[90] The sayings of Jesus and speaking in his name did not come down on either side of the great divide separating the earthly Jesus from the post-resurrectional Christ, or the proclaimer from the proclaimed. What Bultmann failed to perceive was that christophanies and the oral functioning of sayings did not bring about the transformation of the proclaimer into the proclaimed, but rather promoted the continuing authority of the proclaimer.[91] But Beare may have over-dramatized the situation insofar as he, like Bultmann, failed to grasp the full impact of Mark's written gospel that cut a christological dividing line in sharp contrast to the oral ontology of the sayings tradition. From the oral perspectives of Q and Paul, the Markan procedure of separating the earthly Jesus from the risen Christ, of relegating all sayings to the former, while silencing the voice of the latter, is a stunning novelty and a deeply alienating experience as well.

Theologians and students of the New Testament appear to be virtually unanimous in viewing the equation of the earthly Jesus with the living Lord as a key to the christology of the canonical gospels. Once again, our study calls for subtle differentiations and a revision of the conventional viewpoint. Strictly speaking, the equation applies to oral christology, especially to the sayings tradition. The written gospel first appeared in the history of the tradition by elevating the earthly Jesus at the price of silencing the living Lord. The oral equation was thereby disrupted, not simply continued.

THE WRITTEN GOSPEL AS COUNTERFORM
TO ORAL SPEECH

Nowhere in early Christianity is it more obvious than in the gospel of Mark that preservation of oral tradition is not a primary function of writing. The gospel's reserved attitude toward sayings, its displacement of all oral authorities, its christological framework, its extensive narrative explication of Jesus' death, and the silence it ascribes to the risen Lord are all features that go against the grain of basic oral impulses. Both in form and content the written gospel constitutes a radical alternative to the oral gospel.[92]

In chapter 3 we attributed the paucity of sayings in Mark to deliberate authorial reservation toward the genre.[93] Undoubtedly the phenomenon is directly related to the virtual absence of Q material in the gospel. Robinson's review of the history of the sayings genre has highlighted the ambiguous role of Q in emergent Christianity. But if Mark composed an alternative to oral speech, and Matthew and Luke accepted Q only through mediation in their written gospels, the virtual absence of Q in Mark may not be as inexplicably odd as it appears in light of the two-source hypothesis.

The issue of Mark's relation to Q is of course a bone of scholarly contention.[94] Unfortunately, the investigation of a possible Markan access to Q material is precluded by virtue of its definition. But if we can free ourselves from the restrictive bonds of the classical definition, tangential connections between Mark and Q-like material are undeniable. A minimal count lists eleven Markan units whose presence in Q is generally assumed: the preaching of John the Baptist: Mark 1:7–8 (Matt. 3:11//Luke 3:16); the saying on measure: Mark 4:24 (Matt. 7:2//Luke 6:38); saying on having and not having: Mark 4:25 (Matt. 25:29//Luke 19:26); mission discourse: Mark 6:7–13 (Matt. 10:1, 9–14//Luke 9:1–6 [cf. 10:2–12]); Beelzebul controversy: Mark 3:22–27 (Matt. 12:22–30//Luke 11:14–30); the sign of Jonah: Mark 8:11–12 (Matt. 12:38–42 [cf. 16:1–4]//Luke 11:16 [cf. 11:29–32]); sin against the Holy Spirit: Mark 3:29 (Matt. 12:32//Luke 12:10); parable of the *Mustard Seed*: Mark 4:30–32 (Matt. 13:31–32//Luke 13:18–19); light under the bushel: Mark 4:21 (Matt. 5:15//Luke 11:33); hiddenness and revelation: Mark 4:22 (Matt. 10:26//Luke 12:2); saying on salt: Mark 9:49–50 (Matt. 5:13//Luke 14:34–35). To these eleven passages one could add diverse materials from the eschatological speech (Mark 13) whose interconnectedness with Q was argued by Jan Lambrecht.[95] If we can bring ourselves to speak of the extreme paucity, rather than the absence, of Q and Q-like material in Mark, we will be a step closer to understanding the gospel's place in tradition.

In the broader context of the history of the sayings genre the relative paucity of sayings in Mark is not an isolated oddity, but part of a syndrome characterized by the absence of the genre in the canon, Matthean and Lukan deconstruction of Q, and the genre's singular preservation in gnosticism. If Matthew and Luke managed to accept and absorb Q, how does one account for Mark's reluctance to do just that? The answer must be that Mark writes primarily not for the sake of continuing the sayings genre, and not at all to duplicate oral christology, but rather to overcome what are perceived to be problems caused by oral speech and its authoritative carriers. Once the form of written gospel existed, Matthew and Luke could "safely" appropriate Q, for deconstructed as the sayings genre then was, it could no longer operate in its oral, prophetic function. But Mark could ill afford to assimilate sayings in full generic integrity because he created the counterform to oral speech.[96]

We have discussed at length Mark's narrative displacement of the principal carriers of oral transmission: the family, the prophets, and the disciples. Distance from the oral authorities marks the strategic point in the synoptic tradition at which a predominantly oral grasp of tradition is restructured by the full force of writing. Once the form of a written gospel existed, Matthew and Luke could relax and even reverse some aspects of Mark's anti-oral bias. But Mark could ill afford the luxury of tolerating the oral authorities because he had to go against them in breaking new ground for a literary consciousness of Jesus' life and death.

The reader or hearer of the Markan gospel is disoriented from the traditional oral authorities and reoriented toward Jesus. But the gospel's christology is an alternative to oral christology. What is most noticeable about Markan christology is its exclusive cast in a pre-resurrectional framework. One cannot fully appreciate this startlingly innovative christological design unless one remembers the lack of pre-resurrectional and post-resurrectional differentiation in Paul and Q. In terms of media, Mark's comprehensive pre-Easter framework typifies the full engagement of the regressive, retrieving powers of textuality.[97] It is the written medium that facilitates this sweeping, retrospective reach for the earthly Jesus, thereby producing a christology that could not differ more sharply from that of the sayings genre. In the oral genre Jesus was essentially a figure of the present with a view toward the future and minimal roots in the past. It is only with writing that a true sense of pastness is possible. The one dimension least developed in orality has become constitutive for written christology. Mark's Jesus takes the *egō eimi* proclamation out of the mouths of the prophets (Mark 13:6) and uses it unprophetically in reference to himself. His own *egō eimi* speech asserts his earthly authority (6:50), which is to be confirmed by death before it will be consummated in the future (14:62). As a historicized figure of the past he has to undergo death, and death in Mark puts an end to his sayings! At this point, the hermeneutical antithesis to the sayings genre could not be more obvious. The very authority of the living Lord, which in the sayings genre continued to address hearers, has been stilled by the gospel's uncompromisingly pre-resurrectional, christological framework. Once the written form of gospel existed, Matthew and Luke, as well as John, could revive the voice of the living Lord. Theirs was, however, the resurrected Lord firmly anchored in an earthly ministry, not the Lord represented by free-floating oral speech. But Mark could ill afford to let the living Lord speak because he created the form that was designed to silence him.

What these observations suggest to us are two fundamental principles that regulate the relation between oral tradition and written gospel. First, the very form of gospel came into existence as a radical alternative to a tradition dominated by an oral ontology of language. Second, and equally important, once the Markan outline was established, it could in the hands of Matthew and Luke serve to deactivate and then absorb the very materials whose oral hermeneutics the form of Mark's gospel had been designed to overcome.

If the oral medium is associated with the presence of Jesus, can the gospel be linked with his absence? The idea of the gospel as a form of absence has been boldly stated by John Dominic Crossan: "One way of adequately summarizing Mark's thought is to call it a message about Jesus' absence, a theology of the Absent Lord."[98] By contrast, Willi Marxsen expressed a traditional opinion of the gospel as embodying a theology of presence in continuity with pre-Markan tradition and the Pauline gospel as well. Mark's gospel "as present address represents the Lord. The presence of the Lord is experienced in the proclamation."[99] The issue of christological absence versus presence can be clarified from the perspective of orality and textuality. Mark's gospel indeed manifests a presence of Jesus, but not in the sense assumed by Marxsen. The presence reconstructed by Mark is a written re-presentation of Jesus' past. Marxsen, postulating continuity from oral to written hermeneutic, mistakes the written re-presentation for oral presence. He therefore fails to recognize that the gospel's presence of Jesus' pre-Easter past is not only not continuous with, but is an alternative to the presence of the living Lord in oral proclamation. Mark's massively reflexive reconstruction of Jesus' past is his form of demythologizing the orally perceived presence of Jesus. It is this gospel's deepest irony that it cannot accomplish the literary re-presentation of Jesus' past without abandoning the oral presence of the speaking Lord. One must agree, therefore, with Crossan that the gospel, insofar as it represents the earthly Jesus at the steep price of silencing the speaking Lord and of withholding his apparition, implies an indelible christological deficit at the core.

Textuality came early to the synoptic tradition. It came, moreover, as a counterform to oral speech and not as an evolutionary progression of it. This gives us reason to reflect on possible causes for the shift. Oral traditions are complex homeostatic systems that can sustain themselves over long periods of time. Their rate of change is unpredictable, but early and radical reconceptualizations via the written medium are likely to occur in response to external circumstances.[100] The early and radical shift that—in the synoptic tradition—constitutes the Markan text is not fully accounted for without the stimulus of environmental factors. The need to disestablish the self-regulating oral process and to implement a new state of consciousness through the vehicle of the written medium suggests the trauma of a major social upheaval. In *The Kingdom in Mark* we proposed that the destruction of Jerusalem in 70 C.E. provided the catalyst for the making of Mark. The narrative decentering from Jerusalem and recentering toward Galilee, the demise of prophetic orality, and the urgency to rebuild a world can all be plausibly linked with the experience of the loss of the center. It is Boring again who has astutely observed the impact of the catastrophe of 70 C.E. upon the history of tradition: "The destruction of the holy city tended to precipitate a fixation of the traditions, which was in fact the beginning of the canon process."[101] This process toward fixation was not limited to Christian traditions. The synoptic shift in media consciousness can well be understood in correlation with a first century C.E. shift in Jewish ontology of Scripture. As the period of the destruction of the temple brought a change in the textual history of the Hebrew Bible from fluidity to protomasoretic stability,[102] so did the synoptic tradition under the impact of the fall of the temple undertake the transit from oral fluidity to textual stability.

The cataclysmic loss of the center called into serious question the orally perceived presence of the Lord, awakening doubts about oral, heroic christology and distrust toward oral authorities. The new medium engineered the textual retrieval of Jesus' past authority, producing a literary re-presentation that still displayed the deep wound of the oral absence of the Lord. The death of Jerusalem, moreover, confronted Christians not only with the absence of the living Lord, but with the irrefutable fact of Jesus' own death. It was the experience of the second trauma that forced full realization of the first trauma.[103] Textuality absorbed the death of Jesus and made it the inescapable culmination of his life, linking it both with the second trauma and with the demise of the disciples. The loss of the center, the textualization of oral commonplaces, a reconstruction of Jesus' past, a strong narrative emphasis on his death, lack of sayings material, a narrative denunciation of oral authorities, and an implied oral, christological absence are all connected phenomena. It may thus not be an exaggeration to claim that it was with Mark's extraordinary narrative that Christian consciousness was jolted out of oral infancy and partial amnesia of Jesus' death toward a fully historicized grasp of the life and death of the Messiah.

PARABOLIC GOSPEL—ORAL TRADITION— JESUS, THE PARABOLIST

Those concerned with understanding early Christian traditions tend to think almost exclusively in terms of progressive development and continuity. Tradition, after all, implies the passing on of information, wisdom, and revelation—a process basic to all human culture. This preference for models of organic progression is most evident in our perception of the synoptic history of traditions and the genesis of the written gospel. We are fond of appealing to the formative stage in tradition, making no serious allowance for the formative elements to undergo deformation themselves in the process of the construction of the written gospel. We like to think of oral tradition as a blueprint for the next generation. Whether the written gospel is explained in organic connection with Petrine recollections, as sequel to the apostolic *logos,* as narrative dramatization of the Pauline gospel, or as the expected culmination of synoptic processes, it is almost uniformly viewed as the guarantor of continuity. What is striking is that the written gospel's relation to tradition has been formulated in such an undialectic fashion.

If one accepts George Kennedy's reading of Papias's statement (*Hist. Eccl.* 3.39.15) in terms of Mark's note-taking of Peter's teachings,[104] one must ask with Wayne Meeks: "What parts of Mark would one identify as summary notes of Peter's preaching?"[105] How could one, for example, demonstrate the Petrine origin of heroic stories, parables, or sayings? Yet even if note-taking could be proven to form a stage in the tradition, one would still have to reckon with linguistic complications far greater than Papias was willing to concede. One must remember that, unless one writes under dictation, not everything that transpires orally can be put into writing. Since, according to Papias, Mark wrote "that which he remembered" (*hosa emnēmoneusen*), hence not under direct dictation, a principle of selectivity would have determined his note-taking from the outset. That Mark "wrote accurately though not in order" (*akribōs egrapsen, ou mentoi taxei*) might be taken in support of note-taking as pure transcription of oral discourse. If there were indeed written notes, their content may therefore have been organized in *loci* formation, lacking biographical sequentiality. In that case, however, the written gospel is left unaccounted for, and one must assume that someone took the crucial step of overcoming the oral arrangement of the material and shaping it into the sequential story, a story, moreover, that denied Peter the very role of apostolic transmitter attributed to him by Papias. One is left with the impression that the Papias account, as reported by Eusebius, has oversimplified the history of the transmission of traditions in the interest of unbroken continuity: a chain of command delegated authoritative information from the Lord to Peter to Mark to the elder to Papias and to Eusebius. It is a model that has hampered more than helped our comprehension of the written gospel and its relation to tradition.

The reason for the writing of the gospel, a matter about which Papias has given us no real clues, is frequently connected with the death of the apostolic generation. The passing of the principal apostles is said to have left a teaching gap. When the living chain of apostolic transmitters of tradition was broken, it became imperative that their message be preserved in as authentic a fashion as possible. Hence the impulse to commit to writing the oral gospel as best one remembered it. This thesis assumes not only the paradigm of linearity for oral tradition, but also the notion of unbroken continuity from the oral to the written gospel. As far as we can delve into pre-Markan tradition, the oral gospels do not even approximate the written gospel, while the written gospel itself shows no evidence of being composed primarily for the purpose of preserving oral tradition. In the words of Alfred Suhl: "The gospel of Mk. offers no basis whatsoever for the assumption that the evangelist put into writing what until then will largely have been oral tradition for the purpose of protecting it from forgetfulness."[106] As long as we regard writing simply as an extension of speaking, we shall find it difficult to come to terms with both the oral functioning of pre-Markan traditions and the dynamics of the written gospel that seeks to overcome, not continue, primary orality.

Few concepts have influenced our thinking on the written gospel as deeply as that of the Paulinism of Mark. We remember Bultmann's proposal that the Pauline kerygma provided the catalyst for shaping the Palestinian Jesus traditions into the written gospel. Both inside and outside the Bultmannian school the Paulinism of Mark is accepted by what appears to be a near majority of scholars. But few in our generation have defended the thesis as outspokenly as Bultmann's student, Helmut Koester. For him, "Mark's basic concept of the 'gospel' is Pauline."[107] The Pauline kerygma set the pattern for the gospel literature, most conspicuously for Mark and John, and for gospels dependent on them. "Indeed, the form of the canonical gospels cannot be explained in any other way. It is, in fact, a creation of the kerygma of the early Christian community. The credal formulation which Paul in 1 Cor. 15:1ff. calls 'gospel', and related creeds of the same kind, have set the pattern for this literature."[108]

One may initially wonder how the Pauline christological pattern of preexistence—life in kenotic humiliation—consummation in death—reversal by the power of resurrection could ever have produced a narrative christology of power received at baptism—life in epiphanic glory—life reversed by death that is paradoxically perceived as elevation *sub contrario*? Hans Conzelmann will have been close on target when he wrote in reference to Phil. 2:6–11: "No gospel could be written in the light of this christology."[109] Second, one must also wonder whether the postulated Pauline genesis of the written gospel is not but one more manifestation of our deep-seated concern for continuity. Why else would form critics display such peculiar insensitivity to form? Is it conceivable that Mark

213

created the form of gospel, which is conspicuously different from that of letter, merely to perpetuate the basic structure of the Pauline gospel? Thirdly, it must be stated that the thesis of the creed setting the pattern for the written gospel has often been presented as a proven fact, whereas it really is a working hypothesis. It has been postulated and emphatically reiterated, but no evidence has been introduced to demonstrate how Paul's oral creeds and oral gospel could have given rise to Mark's written gospel.

If we can rid ourselves of thinking in rectilinear patterns, we may learn to appreciate the hermeneutical distinction between Paul's oral creeds and gospel on the one hand and the written gospel on the other. Paul's gospel is designed to promote the resurrected one and participation in his Lordship. What is readily intelligible is the impact of this gospel on early Christian types of enthusiasm. What is also understandable is the apostle's posthumous popularity with the Gnostics, especially the Valentinians.[110] But the one thing that is next to impossible to grasp is how the oral gospel, programmed to continue the living authority of the resurrected Lord, could have furnished the pattern for the written gospel, which silenced the living Lord by relegating his authority to the pre-Easter framework. Mark's creation of Jesus' pre-Easter career in power and glory at the expense of absenting him in his resurrection glory is precisely what the Pauline gospel does not inspire, let alone provide the pattern for.

There is no need here to recapitulate our central thesis that the written gospel is ill accounted for, and in fact misunderstood, as the sum total of oral rules and drives. Suffice it to say that the history of the sayings tradition may serve as a perennial warning against our habitual thinking along the paradigm of linearity. The one speech form that we had suggested had the greatest chance of preserving the voice of Jesus, because it was a form grasped by Jesus himself and not imposed upon him, proved a mixed blessing for the literary consciousness of the emergent orthodox church. The sayings genre's commitment to the oral equation of the earthly Jesus with the living Lord robbed it of a place in the canon and made it an unwitting contributor to the counterform to oral speech, the written gospel, which immortalized the split between the pre-Easter and the post-Easter Lord.

What the models of expansion of Petrine recollections, extension of the apostolic *logos,* narrative explication of the Pauline creeds and gospel, and summation of synoptic processes illustrate is our deeply entrenched interest in preserving continuity from the oral to the written gospel. In their combined effect these models of continuity suggest that New Testament scholarship conducts its business largely in the Gutenberg galaxy.

While it is widely conceded that the written gospel may be the early Christian movement's most significant contribution to literature, we have tended to operate on the assumption that the written gospel was but a surrogate for oral proclamation. But we cannot flatter ourselves with the path-breaking significance of the written gospel and simultaneously insist on its unbroken connectedness with tradition. If with Mark a creative stage had come when memories were woven into a new form, we must learn to discern and accept the price that was paid for this achievement. Truly creative stages in tradition involve alienation, and genuine innovation is destructive to tradition. That is the reality of the medium transit from the oral to the written gospel, and a religious truth as well.

"Thanks to writing, man and only man has a world and not just a situation."[111] With Mark a world was written into being by distanciation from oral dialogue and remembering. To keep Jesus' own preferred medium at arm's length was indispensable for resurrecting him into the written medium. After he had fully passed into written language, a new world of linguistic reification had come into existence.

If it is the grammar of language and not of history that generates the written gospel, one must postulate a linguistic designation for it. We had determined that parable was the generic key to the gospel of Mark. Our case was based on the leitmotif of kingdom and its metaphorical quality and on the insider-outsider dichotomy, a parabolic hermeneutic itself, that was inverted parabolically. Lest it be assumed that reversal of the disciples' role is unrepresentative of the gospel's narrative mode, we must elaborate the pervasiveness of the dynamics of reversal in Mark.

The written gospel "is powered by paradox."[112] The principal topological valuation of Galilee versus Judea/Jerusalem is turned upside down. Judea/Jerusalem, the traditional seat of power, functions as the locus of abandonment and death, whereas Galilee, habitually suspect in the eyes of southern authorities, becomes the center of unification and redemption. "Thus Judea is linked with the chaos pole of the fundamental opposition, and Galilee with order."[113] New space is created by Jesus' traversing and mastering a hostile sea, while the seat of the establishment is called into question. The roles of temple mount and Mount of Olives are dramatically reversed. The temple, place of God's presence, is declared defunct, while the Mount of Olives operates as seat of Jesus' authoritative teaching and as pointer toward the new place (Mark 14: 28). Announcement of the kingdom of God arouses hopes for an all-powerful Messiah, only to be frustrated by his announcement of his own violent death. His performance of mighty deeds stirs hopes for a kingdom in power, but they are thwarted by the crucifixion. Jesus saves others, but not himself. He solicits followers, but speaks in riddles. He is identified as Nazarene, but rejected in Nazareth. Clean is declared unclean, and unclean becomes clean. The last will be the first, and the first last. The apostolic followers are blind, but a blind beggar receives sight. The Jewish establishment is hostile, but Gentiles believe. Peter the leader denies, and the centurion sees. In Jerusalem Jesus is welcome as the expected inaugurator of "the kingdom of our father David" (11:10), and yet he disconfirms the traditional expectations of the Davidic kingdom on Mount Zion. His anointment at Bethany upsets all conventional messianic hopes. He is anointed outside of Jerusalem, not in the temple. His is not a celebration in royal pomp, but a table fellowship in the house of a leper. He is anointed not by the high priest, but by an anonymous woman. His anointment is not applauded, but criticized. Above all, he is not anointed to power and life, but "beforehand for burying" (14:8). Jesus has his disciples prepare a passover, and yet the meal he celebrates with his disciples is not a passover. Instead of eating a lamb and commemorating the Exodus, Jesus announces the traitor in their midst and enacts participation in his own impending death. Jesus' crucifixion, narrated as a coronation in humiliation, is the gospel's principal paradox. In the end, Jesus is buried in the tomb, but "the boundaries of the tomb are crossed."[114] This is the story in which the inversion of the disciples from insiders to outsiders forms the central parabolic core. Reversal of expectations is the generative force that empowers this narrative to its parabolic ending.

In her structuralist study of the spatial world of Mark, Elizabeth Struthers Malbon posed the question of the gospel's genre in terms of parable versus myth, or parable and myth. She opted for parable-myth, whereby myth has priority over parable because essentially opposing structures are mediated into a new world. In the same study she observed that "Kelber recognizes that the Gospel of Mark functions as myth—it establishes 'a new place and a new time'—but fails to recognize that it functions as parable."[115] While it is true that in *The Kingdom of Mark* we demonstrated the world-creating purpose of the gospel, we did not neglect the parabolic dynamics, a fact recognized by Crossan.[116] The parabolic dimension of the gospel was sharpened in *Mark's Story of Jesus*. Insight into the metaphorical gesturing of the story of Jesus' life and death toward the mystery of the kingdom has further convinced me of the parabolic quality of the gospel. My own work on Mark, therefore, leads me to suggest that parable, rather than myth or parable-myth, is the linguistic designation of the gospel. There can be little question that the narrative momentum is carried both by integrative and disintegrative processes. Yet even a conspicuous mediation such as that of Jews and Gentiles into the kingdom of God is intimately connected with the disciples' reversal from insiders to outsiders. World is created less by mediation and more by inversion. The kingdom is intimated not by balancing structural opposites, but by undercutting structures of expectation. Reorientation toward new place and new time arises out of disorientation from conventional hopes and expectations. That parabolic reorientation by disorientation is the narrative route toward the kingdom is finally confirmed by the gospel's open-endedness. By carrying the insider-outsider dichotomy to its parabolic conclusion, the gospel fails to release its hearers or readers into a perfectly harmonized world, but rather jolts them into the realization of the extravagance of the kingdom of God.

The thesis of Mark as parable sheds light on the gospel's relation to tradition, its own performance quality, its paucity of exclusive parables, its rapport with Matthew and Luke, and last but not least on its relationship to Jesus, the speaker in parables.

No language secure in oral identities sparks the impulse to the writing of Mark's gospel. Models of continuity underrate the integrity and power of living speech and belittle the impact of writing upon it. Transformation of conventional linguistic forms and alienation from a common language fund are the key to the gospel's relation to oral tradition. "Out of alienation, and only out of alienation, certain greater unities can come."[117] It is not without logic that the very writing that breaks the hold on oral tradition is parabolic in the extreme. The written gospel writes itself into parabolic existence as it subverts traditional norms and wrests authority away from the appointed carriers of tradition.

The gospel as parable exemplifies its delicate status in the ancient world of communication. As text, we observed, it absorbed and transformed oral speech into a new linguistic construct. But we also had occasion to suspect that the gospel—like most texts in antiquity—was meant to be read aloud and heard. The text appears to be torn between competing tendencies. How can it be both removed from and committed to orality? The categories of *primary* and *secondary orality* will help clarify the matter. Those oral units that we previously discussed (chap. 2) constitute primary orality. They owe their very existence to oral verbalization. Insofar as they contributed to the building of the gospel, they underwent decontextualization and recontextualization (chap. 3). The resultant text, as all texts, is fixed and in a sense dead, permanently open to visual inspection and the object of unceasing efforts at interpretation. If this text enters the world of hearers by being read aloud, it functions as secondary orality. But now the story narrated is one that was never heard in primary orality, for it comprises textually filtered and contrived language.[118]

From the perspective of the media it is worth noting that parable is a form of communication that embodies the hermeneutics of both speaking and writing. Speaking, we observed, is the natural mode of parabolic discourse. The parable seeks direct engagement with hearers who continue the process initiated by the story. But as it withholds meaning, reveals and conceals simultaneously, the parable feeds on the very distanciation that typifies writing. Hence the extraordinarily astute observation of Schneidau that the parable "contains, in spite of its oral modality, the problematic of writings."[119] Parable is the one form in the synoptic tradition that in its penchant for communication *and* alienation, participation *and* interpretation, can perform the medium transit from orality to textuality and still hold out an invitation to the hearing of an altogether novel story.

The gospel as parable casts light on the paucity and relative tameness of the exclusive parables it carries within itself.[120] On the one hand, Mark learned the hermeneutics of alienation and secrecy from parabolic stories. One may suspect, therefore, that parables were of considerable importance in his tradition. On the other hand, parables, together with sayings, appear to be subject to Markan reservation. This leads us to suggest a preliminary reason for parabolic paucity in the written gospel. *Parables, more than other speech forms, do not well tolerate insertion into texts.* One must differentiate here between parabolic affinity with the hermeneutics of writing, as observed above, and parabolic unfriendliness toward confinement into inclusive textuality. Parables, we repeat, are unfinished stories, and whether they are being heard or read, they are contingent on the work of cocreators. Enclosed in textuality, hemmed in by essentially unrelated words, parables are crippled in their linguistic operation. This violation of the hermeneutical integrity of parables by their insertion into the gospel was noted by Ulrich E. Simon: "These typically Jewish *meshalim* present an enormous difficulty to the present reader, but they must have been even more refractory to Mark at the time of writing."[121]

It appears to be entirely logical to suggest that Mark carries few parables, all of which lack the sting of true extravagance, because he entertains little interest in them. And yet, parable is the one inherited speech form that is subject to hermeneutical reflection. Not only is this gospel not a stranger to parabolic thinking, but it develops its principal parabolic plot out of the parables in chapter 4. This leads us to suggest that the gospel's scarcity of exclusive parables is due not to aversion to parabolic thought, but quite the contrary, to the comprehensive implementation of parabolic hermeneutic across the gospel. To be precise, Mark employs few and relatively tame parables because he has invested parabolic dynamics in the inclusive gospel composition. The gospel of Matthew, a far less parabolic story, contains more and more powerful parables, and Luke, the least parabolic of the synoptic gospels, is the carrier of a large number of decidedly extravagant parables. Mark, by this logic, is not a good carrier of exclusive parables because his is a parabolic story altogether.

The gospel as parable deserves consideration for the bearing it has on the writings of Matthew and Luke. It is not accidental that parable initiates the tradition of written gospels, for parable, and especially a written parable, enacts the condition for interpretation. It seems more likely to suggest with the two-source hypothesis that parable provided the incentive for less parabolic gospels, than to assume with Johann Jakob Griesbach that less parabolic stories produced a shocking parable. With the parable at the outset, the task of interpretation was written into tradition. What triggered additional gospel compositions were not only altered social circumstances, but the disturbing presence of the parabolic story at the outset. Because it is not possible to live in parable alone, accommodations had to be made, whether by closure of Mark's open-ended text or by full-scale reconceptualizations of it.

Now, and only now, may we address the issue of the relation of Mark's parabolic story to Jesus, the speaker in parables. If Jesus was the incarnation of revelation, as Christian tradition identifies him, he could not himself have been a mere transmitter of tradition. A repeater of knowledge scarcely ends on the cross. His parabolic speech placed into tradition from its very inception an alienating element. Parable does not tolerate unbroken continuity. Parabolic speech was the mode of communication that intimated a new voice by dissociation from conventional language. Together with Paul Ricoeur, Crossan, and the late Norman Perrin, Robert Funk has rightly insisted on this aspect of Jesus' parabolic language: "Jesus could not . . . merely hand the tradition on, even after correcting it at this point or that, but had to allow language to collect creatively on his significative intention, by a 'coherent deformation' of the available language fund."[122] Jesus the parabolist is himself not the reassuring foundation of unbroken continuity, and connectedness is not all there is to the tradition he set into motion.

While the gospel does not arise out of the collective drives of oral transmission, it asserts itself in one of the constituent parts of synoptic orality, the parable. Insofar as parable is one of Jesus' primary modes of speech, one can say that it furnishes linguistic and theological connection between the speaker in parables and the written gospel. Both gospel and oral parables transcend their respective narratives by pointing to the kingdom of God. The evangelist enacts the parabolic dynamic of Jesus' language much as the Platonic dialogues represent the Socratic form of philosophical reasoning. The gospel as written parable may thus be understood as Jesus' Word bequeathed to Mark.

In an important sense, however, the written parable is unlike Jesus' parabolic Word. In the oral parables Jesus proclaimed the kingdom of God. Insofar as writing transformed all oral speech, it also affected the very form that was re-presented in the gospel. The interposition of writing facilitated not only a retrieval of the past of Jesus, the confinement of oral speech to a pre-Easter framework, but also the extension of parabolic dynamics across the narrative. The result is a story of Jesus' life and death that functions as a parabolic vehicle of the kingdom. The decisive break in the synoptic tradition did thus not come, as Bultmann thought, with Easter, but when the written medium took full control, transforming Jesus the speaker of kingdom parables into the parable of the kingdom of God.

NOTES

1. Mircea Eliade, "Myth," *Encyclopedia Brittanica*, 1968 ed., XV: 1139.

2. For Norman R. Petersen ("When is the End not the End? Literary Reflections on the Ending of Mark's Narrative," *Int* 34 [1980]: 151–66) the frustration of the readers' expectations in Mark 16:8 is inconsistent with the story whose "principal plot device is one of prediction and fulfillment" (p. 155). This ending, when read literally, effects "the collapse of Jesus' credibility as a predicter" (p. 162). Hence, the "narrator does not mean what he says in Mark 16:8" (p. 162). We refer the reader to chapter 3, pp. 127–28 of this study, and reiterate: (1) In Mark 14:28 Jesus promises to go ahead of the disciples to Galilee. (2) The disciples' disobedience, as well as that of the women, does not damage Jesus' credibility for the readers. Quite the opposite: the readers are to follow, where the disciples failed. (3) I simply submit that Mark means what he says in 16:8. (4) Perhaps Petersen's prediction-fulfillment scheme does not do full justice to Mark's narrative. Hence his uneasiness about the ending. But if we read the narrative parabolically, we can well accept Mark 16:8 for what it says.

3. Karl Ludwig Schmidt, *Der Rahmen der Geschichte Jesu: Literarkritische Untersuchungen zur Ältesten Jesusüberlieferung* (Berlin: Trowitzsch und Sohn, 1919; reprint: Darmstadt: Wissenschaftliche Buchgesellschaft, 1964), pp. 303–4.

4. Ibid., p. 306.

5. Joachim Jeremias, *The Eucharistic Words of Jesus*, Eng. trans. Norman Perrin, 3rd ed., rev. (Philadelphia: Fortress Press, 1977; London: Charles Scribner's Sons, 1965), p. 90.

6. Martin Dibelius, *From Tradition to Gospel*, Eng. trans. Bertram Lee Woolf (New York: Charles Scribner's Sons, 1934), p. 179.

7. Rudolf Bultmann, *Die Geschichte der synoptischen Tradition*, FRLANT 29, NF 12, 8th ed. (Göttingen: Vandenhoeck & Ruprecht, 1970), p. 297 (275).

8. Schmidt, *Der Rahmen der Geschichte Jesu*, p. 305.

9. The term "aesthetic deception" is taken from Erhardt Güttgemanns, *Candid Questions Concerning Gospel Form Criticism: A Methodological Sketch of the Fundamental Problematics of Form and Redaction Criticism*, Eng. trans. William G. Doty, PTMS 26 (Pittsburgh: Pickwick Press, 1979), pp. 380–84. Cf. also chapter 3 of this book, p. 116.

10. A résumé of the present status of the thesis of a pre-Markan passion narrative is given by Gerhard Schneider, "Das Problem einer vorkanonischen Passionserzählung," *BZ* 16 (1972): 222–44. The most scathing criticism of the form-critical thesis is offered by Johannes Schreiber, *Die Markuspassion: Wege zur Erforschung der Leidensgeschichte Jesu* (Hamburg: Furche, 1969). Neither Schneider nor Schreiber has advanced the critique of the form-critical thesis to the level of linguistics. Despite many excellent critical observations, they have not recognized the core of the problem, that is, the assumption that narrative coherence points to a pre-canonical text.

11. Bultmann, *Synoptische Tradition*, pp. 301–2; 298 (279, 275).

12. Jeremias, *Eucharistic Words of Jesus*, pp. 89–96.

13. Vincent Taylor, *The Gospel According to St. Mark*, 2d ed. (London: Macmillan & Co., 1966), pp. 653–64; see also A. Vanhoye, "Structure et théologie des récits de la Passion dans les évangiles synoptiques," *NRT* 99 (1967): 135–63.

14. Gottfried Schille, "Das Leiden des Herrn: Die evangelische Passionstradition und ihr 'Sitz im Leben,'" *ZTK* 52 (1955): 161–205.

15. Wolfgang Schenk, *Der Passionsbericht nach Markus: Untersuchungen zur Überlieferungsgeschichte der Passionstraditionen* (Gütersloh: Gerd Mohn, 1974).

16. K. H. Schelkle, *Die Passion Jesu in der Verkündigung des Neuen Testaments* (Heidelberg: F. H. Kerle, 1949).

17. Johannes Schreiber, *Theologie des Vertrauens: Eine redaktionsgeschichtliche Untersuchung des Markusevangeliums* (Hamburg: Furche, 1967).

18. Detlev Dormeyer, *Die Passion Jesu als Verhaltensmodell: Literarische und theologische Analyse der Traditions- und Redaktionsgeschichte der Markuspassion*, NTAbh 11 (Münster: Aschendorff, 1974).

19. Helmut Koester, "Apocryphal and Canonical Gospels," *HTR* 73 (1980): 105–30.

20. Martin Dibelius, "Die alttestamentlichen Motive in der Leidensgeschichte des Petrus- und des Johannes-Evangeliums," *BZAW* 33 (1918): 125ff.; reprint in *Botschaft und Geschichte*, ed. Günther Bornkamm with Heinz Kraft (Tübingen: J. C. B. Mohr [Paul Siebeck], 1953), I, pp. 221–47.

21. Koester, "Apocryphal and Canonical Gospels," p. 127.

22. Rudolf Pesch, *Das Markusevangelium* (Freiburg—Basel—Vienna: Herder, 1977), II, pp. 1–27.

23. Ibid., p. 10.

24. Ibid., p. 12.

25. Rudolf Pesch, *Das Markusevangelium* (Freiburg—Basel—Vienna: Herder, 1976), I, pp. 1–3.

26. Jeremias, *Eucharistic Words of Jesus*, pp. 93–96.

27. Bultmann, *Synoptische Tradition*, pp. 297–98 (275).

28. Eduard Lohse, *History of the Suffering and Death of Jesus Christ*, Eng. trans. Martin O. Dietrich (Philadelphia: Fortress Press, 1967), pp. 11–14.

29. Schreiber, *Die Markuspassion*, p. 19, n. 39.

30. Etienne Trocmé, *The Passion as Liturgy: A Study in the Origin of the Passion Narratives in the Four Gospels* (unpublished manuscript, Strasbourg, 1981).

31. Güttgemanns, *Candid Questions*, pp. 321–33.

32. Georg Strecker, "Die Leidens- und Auferstehungsvoraussagen im Markusevangelium (Mk. 8,31; 9,31; 10,32–34)," *ZTK* 64 (1967): 16–39.

33. Ferdinand Hahn, *The Titles of Jesus in Christology: Their History in Early Christianity*, Eng. trans. Harold Knight and George Ogg (London: Lutterworth Press, 1969), pp. 37–53.

34. Siegfried Schulz, *Die Stunde der Botschaft: Einführung in die Theologie der vier Evangelisten* (Hamburg: Furche, 1967), pp. 114–17.

35. Heinz Eduard Tödt, *The Son of Man in the Synoptic Tradition*, Eng. trans. Dorothea M. Barton (Philadelphia: Westminster Press; London: SCM Press, 1965), pp. 200–202.

36. Eta Linnemann, *Studien zur Passionsgeschichte*, FRLANT 102 (Göttingen: Vandenhoeck & Ruprecht, 1970), p. 64.

37. Hahn, *Titles of Jesus*, p. 37.

38. Norman Perrin, "The Creative Use of the Son of Man Traditions by Mark," *USQR* 23 (1968): 363–64.

39. Dibelius, *From Tradition to Gospel*, p. 23; for a similar statement, see pp. 178–79: "For what we know of the Christian message makes us expect a description of the whole Passion in the course of a sermon, at least in outline."

40. Tödt, *Son of Man*, p. 233.

41. Ibid., p. 238.

42. Ibid., pp. 244–45.

43. Martin Hengel, *Crucifixion in the Ancient World and the Folly of the Message of the Cross*, Eng. trans. John Bowden (Philadelphia: Fortress Press, 1977), p. 25.

44. Ibid., p. 38.

45. Philip Carrington, *The Primitive Christian Calendar: A Study in the Making of the Marcan Gospel* (Cambridge: At the University Press, 1952).

46. Schille, "Das Leiden des Herrn."

47. Trocmé, *The Passion as Liturgy*.

48. Ibid., p. 68.

49. Ibid., p. 65.

50. Ibid., p. 66.

51. Chapter 2, p. 66.

52. Günter Klein, "Die Verleugnung des Petrus: Eine traditionsgeschichtliche Untersuchung," *ZTK* 58 (1961): 285–328; reprint in *Rekonstruktion und Interpretation: Gesammelte Aufsätze zum Neuen Testament,* BEvT 50 (Munich: Chr. Kaiser, 1969), pp. 49–98.

53. Leander E. Keck, *Paul and His Letters* (Philadelphia: Fortress Press, 1979), p. 38. A possible exception is 1 Cor. 11:23: *ho kyrios Iēsous en tē nykti hē paredideto.* If one translates: "the Lord Jesus, on the night when he was betrayed," the verb *paradidonai* may be taken to refer to the historical betrayal of Judas. But an alternative translation is equally plausible: "the Lord Jesus, on the night when he was delivered," in which case *paradidonai* is a technical, soteriological reference to passion.

54. Hahn, *The Titles of Jesus,* p. 40; Tödt, *The Son of Man,* pp. 188–93.

55. Dibelius, *From Tradition to Gospel,* p. 188; see also "Die alttestamentlichen Motive"; idem, "Das Historische Problem der Leidensgeschichte," in *Botschaft und Geschichte,* pp. 248–57; idem, "Gethsemane," in *Botschaft und Geschichte,* pp. 258–71.

56. Barnabas Lindars, *New Testament Apologetic: The Doctrinal Significance of the Old Testament Quotations* (Philadelphia: Westminster Press; London: SCM Press, 1961), pp. 75–137.

57. Howard C. Kee, "The Function of Scriptural Quotations and Allusions in Mark 11–16," in *Jesus und Paulus: Festschrift für Werner Georg Kümmel zum 70. Geburtstag,* ed. E. Earle Ellis and Erich Grässer (Göttingen: Vandenhoeck & Ruprecht, 1975), pp. 165–88.

58. Ibid., p. 166.

59. Ibid., pp. 167–71.

60. Ibid., p. 175.

61. Walter J. Ong, S. J., *The Presence of the Word: Some Prolegomena for Cultural and Religious History* (New Haven, Conn., and London: Yale University Press, 1967; paperback edition: Minneapolis: University of Minnesota Press, 1981), p. 205.

62. James M. Robinson, "LOGOI SOPHON: On the Gattung of Q," in *Trajectories through Early Christianity* (Philadelphia: Fortress Press, 1971), pp. 71–113.

63. Ibid., p. 113.

64. Ibid., pp. 102–3.

65. Helmut Koester, "GNOMAI DIAPHOROI: The Origin and Nature of Diversification in the History of Early Christianity," in *Trajectories through Early Christianity,* p. 135.

66. Robinson, "LOGOI SOPHON," pp. 103–5.

67. M. Jack Suggs, *Wisdom, Christology, and Law in Matthew's Gospel* (Cambridge, Mass.: Harvard University Press, 1970).

68. Koester, "GNOMAI DIAPHOROI," p. 139.

69. Ibid.

70. Siegfried Schulz, *Q: Die Spruchquelle der Evangelisten* (Zurich: Theologischer Verlag, 1972); Paul Hoffmann, *Studien zur Theologie der Logienquelle,* NTAbh NF 8, 2d ed. (Münster: Aschendorff, 1972); Dieter Lührmann, *Die Redaktion der Logienquelle,* WMANT 33 (Neukirchen and Vluyn: Neu-

kirchener Verlag, 1969); Richard A. Edwards, *A Theology of Q: Eschatology, Prophecy, and Wisdom* (Philadelphia: Fortress Press, 1976).

71. Edwards, *Theology of Q*, p. 154.

72. Lührmann, *Die Redaktion der Logienquelle*, p. 103: "Die Christologie von Q ist ebensowenig vom Passionskerygma geprägt, wie man das bei der synoptischen Tradition im allgemeinen voraussetzen darf . . ."

73. Tödt, *Son of Man*, p. 247.

74. M. Eugene Boring, *Sayings of the Risen Jesus: Christian Prophecy in the Synoptic Tradition* (New York and Cambridge: Cambridge University Press, 1982), pp. 137–82; Edwards, *Theology of Q*, pp. 44–57; Hoffmann, *Theologie der Logienquelle*, pp. 158–90.

75. Werner H. Schmidt, "Die prophetische 'Grundgewissheit'," *EvTh* 31 (1971): 630–50.

76. Boring, *Sayings of Risen Jesus*, pp. 180–81.

77. Schulz, *Spruchquelle der Evangelisten*, p. 482.

78. Boring, *Sayings of Risen Jesus*, pp. 180–81.

79. Tödt, *Son of Man*, pp. 253–65.

80. Ibid., p. 265.

81. Ibid., p. 232.

82. Ulrich B. Müller, *Prophetie und Predigt im Neuen Testament: Formgeschichtliche Untersuchungen zur urchristlichen Prophetie*, SNT 10 (Gütersloh: Gerd Mohn, 1975).

83. Boring, *Sayings of Risen Jesus*, pp. 30–36.

84. Cf. however the related formulae: *ide egō Paulos legō hymin* (Gal. 5:2), *legō gar* (Rom. 12:3), and *legō egō* (1 Cor. 7:12).

85. Müller, *Prophetie und Predigt*, p. 206.

86. Ibid., pp. 116–40.

87. Harald Riesenfeld, *"hyper,"* *TDNT* VIII: 513.

88. Oscar Cullmann, " 'KYRIOS' as Designation for the Oral Tradition Concerning Jesus," *SJT* 3 (1950): 180–97; Boring, *Sayings of Risen Jesus*, pp. 73–75.

89. Müller, *Prophetie und Predigt*, pp. 223–24; Boring, *Sayings of Risen Jesus*, p. 34; Ulrich Luz, *Das Geschichtsverständnis des Paulus*, BEvT 49 (Munich: Chr. Kaiser, 1968), pp. 326–31.

90. Frank W. Beare, "Sayings of the Risen Jesus in the Synoptic Tradition: An Inquiry into Their Origin and Significance," in *Christian History and Interpretation: Studies Presented to John Knox*, ed. W. R. Farmer, C. F. D. Moule, and R. R. Niebuhr (New York and Cambridge: Cambridge University Press, 1967), p. 170.

91. Cf. chapter 1, p. 20.

92. M. Eugene Boring deserves full credit for having first developed the idea of Mark's gospel being an alternative form to oral, prophetic speech. The thesis was initially presented in "The Paucity of Sayings in Mark: A Hypothesis," *SBL Seminar Papers* (Missoula, Mont.: Scholars Press, 1977), pp. 371–77, cf. esp. 374; for a more fully developed version, cf. his *Sayings of Risen Jesus*, pp. 195–203.

93. Cf. chapter 3, pp. 100–102.

94. Burnett Hillman Streeter, "St. Mark's Knowledge and Use of Q," in

Oxford Studies in the Synoptic Problem, ed. W. Sanday (Oxford: At the Clarendon Press, 1911), pp. 165–84; idem, *The Four Gospels* (London: Macmillan & Co., 1924), pp. 186–91; George Dewitt Castor, "The Relation of Mark to the Source Q," *JBL* 31 (1912): 82–91; Carl S. Patton, "Did Mark Use Q? Or Did Q Use Mark?" *AJT* 16 (1912): 634–42; J. M. C. Crum, "Mark and 'Q'," *Theology* 12 (1926): 275–82; T. E. Floyd Honey, "Did Mark Use Q?" *JBL* 62 (1943): 319–31; Burton H. Throckmorton, Jr., "Did Mark Know Q?" *JBL* 67 (1948): 319–39; John Pairman Brown, "Mark as Witness to an Edited Form of Q," *JBL* 80 (1961): 29–44; Werner Georg Kümmel, *Introduction to the New Testament,* Eng. trans. A. J. Mattill, Jr., 14th rev. ed. (Nashville: Abingdon, 1966), p. 55; E. P. Sanders, "The Overlaps of Mark and Q and the Synoptic Problem," *NTS* 19 (1972–73): 453–65; Ernest Best, "An Early Sayings Collection," *NovT* 18 (1976): 1–16.

95. Jan Lambrecht, S. J., *Die Redaktion der Markus-Apokalypse. Literarische Analyse und Strukturuntersuchung,* AnBib 28 (Rome: Pontifical Biblical Institute, 1967), pp. 100–105, 115–20, 257–59. The author's argument is not necessarily convincing. But possible connections between Mark 13 and Q-like materials cannot entirely be ruled out. In the Markan composition, however, the speech takes a position against the presenting power of prophetic proclamation, cf. chapter 3, pp. 99–100.

96. Mark's gospel, it is well known, emphasizes the teaching function of Jesus. This does not contradict the thesis of the gospel's reservation toward sayings. For Mark, the problem is not Jesus, who is the oral performer par excellence, but the sayings genre and its oral, prophetic implementation.

97. Ernst Käsemann ("Blind Alleys in the 'Jesus of History' Controversy," in *New Testament Questions of Today,* Eng. trans. W. J. Montague [Philadelphia: Fortress Press, 1969], p. 62), recognizing the regressive, retrieving function of the written gospel, referred to "the kerygmatic reversion to the narrative form" ("Sackgassen im Streit um den historischen Jesus," in *Exegetische Versuche und Besinnungen,* II, 2d ed. [Göttingen: Vandenhoeck & Ruprecht, 1965], p. 66: ". . . der kerygmatische Rückgriff auf die Form des Berichts"). He thought, however, that the narrative regression became necessary in response to early Christian "enthusiasm." Our thesis states that it was the oral, prophetic ontology of spoken words that necessitated the written gospel.

98. John Dominic Crossan, "A Form for Absence: The Markan Creation of Gospel," *Semeia* 12 (1978): 50.

99. Willi Marxsen, *Mark the Evangelist,* Eng. trans. Roy A. Harrisville et al. (Nashville: Abingdon Press, 1969), p. 135.

100. Berkley Peabody, *The Winged Word: A Study in the Technique of Ancient Greek Oral Composition as Seen Principally Through Hesiod's Works and Days* (Albany: State University of New York Press, 1975), p. 152.

101. Boring, *Sayings of Risen Jesus,* p. 26.

102. James A. Sanders, "Text and Canon: Concepts and Method," *JBL* 98 (1979): 5–29, esp. 12–15.

103. According to Sigmund Freud (*Moses and Monotheism,* Eng. trans. Katherine Jones [New York: Vintage Books, 1939]), both the individual and the human species pass through early traumatic conflicts which are for the most part treated by amnesia in a period of latency. But whenever "events produce

impressions or experiences which are so much like the repressed material . . . they have the power to awaken it" (p. 121). If indeed early Christian prophets pronounced Jesus' parousia in connection with the Roman-Jewish War, the destruction of the holy city was in the experience of Jewish Christians tantamount to Jesus' second death. It could well have been under the impact of the second trauma that the first trauma was brought into full literary consciousness.

104. George Kennedy, "Classical and Christian Source Criticism," in *The Relationships Among the Gospels: An Interdisciplinary Dialogue*, ed. William O. Walker, Jr. (San Antonio: Trinity University Press, 1978), pp. 125–55. Cf. chapter 1, pp. 22–23.

105. Wayne A. Meeks, "Hypomnēmata from an Untamed Sceptic: A Response to George Kennedy," in *Relationships Among Gospels*, p. 171.

106. Alfred Suhl, *Die Funktion der alttestamentlichen Zitate und Anspielungen im Markusevangelium* (Gütersloh: Gerd Mohn, 1965), p. 15.

107. Koester, "GNOMAI DIAPHOROI," p. 152.

108. Helmut Koester, "One Jesus and Four Primitive Gospels," in *Trajectories through Early Christianity*, p. 161.

109. Hans Conzelmann, *An Outline of the Theology of the New Testament*, Eng. trans. John Bowden (New York: Harper & Row; London: SCM Press, 1969), p. 80.

110. Elaine H. Pagels, *The Gnostic Paul: Gnostic Exegesis of the Pauline Letters* (Philadelphia: Fortress Press, 1975).

111. Paul Ricoeur, *Interpretation Theory: Discourse and the Surplus of Meaning* (Fort Worth: Texas Christian University Press, 1976), p. 36.

112. Elizabeth Struthers Malbon, "Narrative Space and Mythic Meaning: A Structural Exegesis of the Gospel of Mark," (Ph.D. diss., Florida State University, 1980), p. 439.

113. Ibid., p. 380.

114. Ibid., p. 368.

115. Ibid., p. 433.

116. John Dominic Crossan, *The Dark Interval: Towards a Theology of Story* (Niles, Ill.: Argus Communications, 1975), p. 126.

117. Walter J. Ong, S. J., *Interfaces of the Word: Studies in the Evolution of Consciousness and Culture* (Ithaca, N.Y., and London: Cornell University Press, 1977), p. 47.

118. In communications theory secondary orality usually refers to electronically mediated sound. We would suggest a differentiation of three types of orality: primary orality, textually mediated or secondary orality, and electronically mediated or tertiary orality.

119. Herbert N. Schneidau, *Sacred Discontent: The Bible and Western Tradition* (Berkeley—Los Angeles—London: University of California Press, 1976), p. 254.

120. Cf. chapter 2, p. 61.

121. Ulrich E. Simon, *Story and Faith in the Biblical Narrative* (London: SPCK, 1975), p. 64.

122. Robert W. Funk, *Language, Hermeneutic, and the Word of God: The Problem of Language in the New Testament and Contemporary Theology* (New York: Harper & Row, 1966; reprint: Missoula, Mont.: Scholars Press, 1979), p. 237.

Bibliography

I
ORALITY AND TEXTUALITY, LITERARY CRITICISM, PHILOSOPHY, AND MYTHOLOGY

Abel, Ernest L. "The Psychology of Memory and Rumor Transmission and their Bearing on Theories of Oral Transmission in Early Christianity." *JR* 51 (1971): 270–81.

Albertz, Martin. *Die Synoptischen Streitgespräche: Ein Beitrag zur Formgeschichte des Urchristentums.* Berlin: Trowitzsch, 1921.

Allport, Gordon, and Postman, Leo. *The Psychology of Rumor.* New York: Henry Holt, 1947.

Alter, Robert. *The Art of Biblical Narrative.* New York: Basic Books, 1981.

Altizer, Thomas J. J. *Total Presence: The Language of Jesus and the Language of Today.* New York: Seabury Press, 1980.

Anderson, Janice Capel. "Grimm's Bible: The Influence of *Deutsche Volkskunde* on the Development of Narrative *Formgeschichte*," unpublished paper, 1977.

Arendt, Hannah. *The Life of the Mind.* New York and London: Harcourt Brace Jovanovich, 1978.

Asting, Ragnar. *Die Verkündigung des Wortes im Urchristentum: Dargestellt an den Begriffen 'Wort Gottes,' 'Evangelium' und 'Zeugnis'.* Stuttgart: W. Kohlhammer Verlag, 1939.

Auerbach, Erich. *Mimesis: The Representation of Reality in Western Literature.* Eng. trans. Willard R. Trask. Princeton, N. J.: Princeton University Press, 1953.

Aune, David E. "Christian Prophecy and the Sayings of Jesus: An Index to Synoptic Pericopae Ostensibly Influenced by Early Christian Prophets." *SBL Seminar Papers* II. Missoula, Mont.: Scholars Press, 1975.

Balogh, Josef. "Voces Paginarum." *Philologus* 82 (1926): 84–109, 202–40.

Baron, Gabrielle. *Marcel Jousse: Introduction à sa Vie et son Oeuvre.* Paris: Casterman, 1965.

Barthes, Roland. *Image—Music—Text.* Selected and translated by Stephen Heath. New York: Hill & Wang, 1977.

Bausinger, Hermann. *Formen der "Volkspoesie."* Grundlagen der Germanistik 6. Berlin: E. Schmidt Verlag, 1968.

Beardslee, William A. *Literary Criticism of the New Testament.* GBS. Philadelphia: Fortress Press, 1970.

———. "Parable, Proverb, and Koan." *Semeia* 12 (1978): 151–77.

———. "Uses of the Proverb in the Synoptic Gospels." *Int* 24 (1970): 61–73.

———. "The Wisdom Tradition and the Synoptic Gospels." *JAAR* 35 (1967): 231–40.

Bibliography

Beare, Frank W. "Sayings of the Risen Jesus in the Synoptic Tradition: An Inquiry into Their Origin and Significance." In *Christian History and Interpretation: Studies Presented to John Knox*, ed. W. R. Farmer, C. F. D. Moule, and R. R. Niebuhr. New York and Cambridge: Cambridge University Press, 1967.

Ben-Amos, Dan. *Folklore Genres*. Publications of the American Folklore Society. Bibliographical and Special Series 26. Austin: University of Texas Press, 1976.

Bertholet, Alfred. *Die Macht der Schrift in Glauben und Aberglauben*. AAWB.PH 1. Berlin: Akademie-Verlag, 1949.

Best, Ernest. "An Early Sayings Collection." *NovT* 18 (1976): 1–16.

Birkeland, Harris. *The Language of Jesus*. Oslo: I kommisjon hos J. Dybwad, 1954.

Black, Matthew. *An Aramaic Approach to the Gospels and Acts*. Oxford: At the Clarendon Press, 1946.

Black, Max. *Models and Metaphors*. Ithaca, N. Y.: Cornell University Press, 1962.

Bleeker, C. J. "L'Oeil et l'Oreille: Leur Signification Religieuse." *The Sacred Bridge*, Studies in the History of Religions, Supplements to *Numen* VII. Leiden: E. J. Brill, 1963.

Bloom, Harold et al., *Deconstruction and Criticism*. New York: Seabury Press, 1979.

Bogatyrev, Petr Grigo'evich, and Jakobson, Roman. "Die Folklore als eine besondere Form des Schaffens." *Donum Natalicium Schrijnen*. Nijmegen and Utrecht: N. V. Dekker & Van de Vegt, 1929.

Boman, Thorleif. *Die Jesus-Überlieferung im Lichte der neueren Volkskunde*. Göttingen: Vandenhoeck & Ruprecht, 1967.

Boomershine, Thomas Eugene. "Mark, the Storyteller: A Rhetorical-Critical Investigation of Mark's Passion and Resurrection Narrative." Ph.D. dissertation, Union Theological Seminary, New York, 1974.

———. "Oral Tradition and Mark." Unpublished manuscript, 1979.

Boring, M. Eugene. "Christian Prophecy and Matthew 10:23: A Test Exegesis." *SBL Seminar Papers*. Missoula, Mont.: Scholars Press, 1976.

———. "Christian Prophecy and Matthew 23:34–36: A Test Exegesis." *SBL Seminar Papers*. Missoula, Mont.: Scholars Press, 1977.

———. "How May We Identify Oracles of Christian Prophets in the Synoptic Tradition? Mark 3:28–29 as a Test Case." *JBL* 91 (1972): 501–21.

———. "The Paucity of Sayings in Mark: A Hypothesis." *SBL Seminar Papers*. Missoula, Mont.: Scholars Press, 1977.

———. *Sayings of the Risen Jesus: Christian Prophecy in the Synoptic Tradition*. New York and Cambridge: Cambridge University Press, 1982.

———. "'What Are We Looking For?' Toward a Definition of the Term 'Christian Prophet'." *SBL Seminar Papers* I. Missoula, Mont.: Scholars Press, 1973.

Boucher, Madeleine. *The Mysterious Parable: A Literary Study*. CBQMS 6. Washington, D.C.: Catholic Biblical Association of America, 1977.

Brown, Raymond E., S. S. "Parable and Allegory Reconsidered." *New Testament Essays*. Garden City, N.Y.: Doubleday & Co., 1968.

Bulkeley, William N. "Chatty Computers." *Wall Street Journal* (December 31, 1980): 1, 12.

Bultmann, Rudolf. "Der Begriff des Wortes Gottes im Neuen Testament." *Glauben und Verstehen*. Vol. I. 3d ed. Tübingen: J. C. B. Mohr [Paul Siebeck], 1958.

————. *Die Geschichte der synoptischen Tradition*. FRLANT 29, NF 12. 8th ed. Göttingen: Vandenhoeck & Ruprecht, 1970 (2d ed., 1931); (*The History of the Synoptic Tradition*. Eng. trans. John Marsh. New York: Harper & Row, 1963).

————. *Der Stil der paulinischen Predigt und die kynisch-stoische Diatribe*. FRLANT 13. Göttingen: Vandenhoeck & Ruprecht, 1910.

Burney, Charles Fox. *The Poetry of Our Lord: An Examination of the Formal Elements of Hebrew Poetry in the Discourses of Jesus Christ*. Oxford: At the Clarendon Press, 1925.

Carlston, Charles E. "Parable and Allegory Revisited: An Interpretive Review." *CBQ* 43 (1981): 235.

————. *The Parables of the Triple Tradition*. Philadelphia: Fortress Press, 1975.

Carothers, John Colin. "Culture, Psychiatry, and the Written Word." *Psychiatry* 22 (1959): 307–20.

Chadwick, H. Munro. *The Heroic Age*. Cambridge: At the University Press, 1912.

Chadwick, H. Munro, and Kershaw, N. *The Growth of Literature*. 3 vols. Cambridge: At the University Press, 1932–40.

Chaytor, Henry John. "The Medieval Reader and Textual Criticism." *BJRL* 26 (1941–42): 49–56.

Clanchy, M. T. *From Memory to Written Record: England, 1066–1307*. Cambridge, Mass.: Harvard University Press, 1979.

Crossan, John Dominic. *Cliffs of Fall: Paradox and Polyvalence in the Parables of Jesus*. New York: Seabury Press, 1980.

————. *The Dark Interval: Towards a Theology of Story*. Niles, Ill.: Argus Communications, 1975.

————. *Finding is the First Act: Trove Folktales and Jesus' Treasure Parable*. Semeia Studies 9. Philadelphia: Fortress Press; Missoula, Mont.: Scholars Press, 1979.

————. "A Form for Absence: The Markan Creation of Gospel." *Semeia* 12 (1978): 41–55.

————. *In Parables: The Challenge of the Historical Jesus*. New York: Harper & Row, 1973.

————. "Parable and Example in the Teaching of Jesus." *NTS* 18 (1971–72): 285–307.

————. *Raid on the Articulate: Comic Eschatology in Jesus and Borges*. New York: Harper & Row, 1976.

Culley, Robert C., ed. "Oral Tradition and Old Testament Studies." *Semeia* 5 (1976).

Cullmann, Oscar. " 'KYRIOS' as Designation for the Oral Tradition Concerning Jesus." *SJT* 3 (1950): 180–97.

Dain, A. *Les Manuscrits*. Paris: Société D'Édition "Les Belles-Lettres," 1964.

Bibliography

Dautzenberg, Gerhard. *Urchristliche Prophetie: Ihre Erforschung, ihre Voraussetzungen im Judentum und ihre Struktur im ersten Korintherbrief.* BWANT 104. Stuttgart—Berlin—Cologne—Mainz: W. Kohlhammer, 1975.

Davids, Peter H. "The Gospels and Jewish Tradition: Twenty Years After Gerhardsson." In *Gospel Perspectives: Studies of History and Tradition in the Four Gospels,* ed. R. T. France and David Wenham. Sheffield: JSOT Press, 1980.

Derrida, Jacques. *Of Grammatology.* Eng. trans. Gayatri Chakravorty Spivak. Baltimore and London: Johns Hopkins University Press, 1976.

―――. *Writing and Difference.* Eng. trans. Alan Bass. Chicago: University of Chicago Press, 1978.

Dibelius, Martin. *From Tradition to Gospel.* Eng. trans. Bertram Lee Woolf. New York: Charles Scribner's Sons, 1934.

Donahue, John R., S. J. "Jesus as Parable of God in the Gospel of Mark." *Int* 32 (1978): 369–86.

Donoghue, Denis. "Deconstructing Deconstruction," review of *Deconstruction and Criticism,* by Harold Bloom, Paul de Man, Jacques Derrida, Geoffrey H. Hartman, and J. Hillis Miller and of *Allegories of Reading: Figural Language in Rousseau, Nietzsche, Rilke, and Proust,* by Paul de Man, in *The New York Review* (June 12, 1980): 37–41.

Doty, William G. "The Concept of Genre in Literary Analysis." *SBL Seminar Papers.* Missoula, Mont.: Scholars Press, 1972.

―――. "The Discipline and Literature of New Testament Form Criticism," *ATR* 51 (1969): 257–321.

―――. *Letters in Primitive Christianity.* Philadelphia: Fortress Press, 1973.

Dundes, Alan. *Folklore Theses and Dissertations in the United States.* Publications of the American Folklore Society. Bibliographical & Special Series 27. Austin: University of Texas Press, 1976.

Ebeling, Gerhard. *Introduction to a Theological Theory of Language.* Eng. trans. R. A. Wilson. Philadelphia: Fortress Press, 1973.

Edwards, Richard A. *A Theology of Q: Eschatology, Prophecy, and Wisdom.* Philadelphia: Fortress Press, 1976.

Eliade, Mircea. *Cosmos and History: The Myth of the Eternal Return.* Eng. trans. Willard R. Trask. New York: Harper & Brothers, 1959.

―――. "Myth." *Encyclopedia Brittanica.* 1968 ed., XV: 1132–42.

Ellis, E. Earle. "New Directions in Form Criticism." In *Jesus Christus in Historie und Geschichte: Neutestamentliche Festschrift für Hans Conzelmann zum 60. Geburtstag,* ed. Georg Strecker. Tübingen: J. C. B. Mohr [Paul Siebeck], 1975.

Entralgo, Pedro La'in. *The Therapy of the Word in Classical Antiquity.* Ed. and Eng. trans. L. J. Rather and John M. Sharp. New Haven, Conn., and London: Yale University Press, 1970.

Fairweather, I. C. M. "Two Different Pedagogical Methods in the Period of Oral Transmission," *SE* VI, TU 112. Berlin: Akademie-Verlag, 1973.

Fascher, Erich. *Die formgeschichtliche Methode: Eine Darstellung und Kritik.* BZNW 2. Giessen: Alfred Töpelmann, 1924.

Finnegan, Ruth. "How Oral is Oral Literature?" *BSOAS* 37 (1974): 52–64.

————. *Oral Literature in Africa.* Oxford: At the Clarendon Press, 1970.

————. *Oral Poetry: Its Nature, Significance and Social Context.* New York and Cambridge: Cambridge University Press, 1977.

Fitzmyer, Joseph A., S. J. "Memory and Manuscript: The Origins and Transmission of the Gospel Tradition." *TS* 23 (1962): 442–57.

Fletcher, Angus. *Allegory: The Theory of a Symbolic Mode.* Ithaca, N.Y.: Cornell University Press, 1964.

Funk, Robert W. "The Apostolic Parousia: Form and Significance." In *Christian History and Interpretation: Studies Presented to John Knox,* ed. W. R. Farmer, C. F. D. Moule, and R. R. Niebuhr. New York and Cambridge: Cambridge University Press, 1967.

————. "The Form of the New Testament Healing Miracle Story." *Semeia* 12 (1978): 57–96.

————. *Jesus as Precursor.* Semeia Studies 2. Philadelphia: Fortress Press; Missoula, Mont.: Scholars Press, 1975.

————. *Language, Hermeneutic, and the Word of God: The Problem of Language in the New Testament and Contemporary Theology.* New York: Harper & Row, 1966; reprint: Missoula, Mont.: Scholars Press, 1979.

————. "The Looking-Glass Tree is for the Birds: Ezekiel 17:22–24; Mark 4:30–32." *Int* 27 (1973): 3–9.

————. "Saying and Seeing: Phenomenology of Language and the New Testament." *JBR* 34 (1966): 197–213.

Gadamer, Hans-Georg. "Plato and the Poets." *Dialogue and Dialectic: Eight Hermeneutical Studies on Plato.* Eng. trans. P. Christopher Smith. New Haven, Conn., and London: Yale University Press, 1980.

Gandz, Solomon. "The Dawn of Literature: Prolegomena to a History of Unwritten Literature." *Osiris* 7 (1939): 261–522.

————. "The Knot in Hebrew Literature, or from the Knot to the Alphabet." *Isis* 14 (1930): 189–214.

Gemoll, Wilhelm. *Das Apophthegma.* Vienna: Hölder-Pichler-Tempsky, 1924.

Gerhardsson, Birger. *Memory and Manuscript: Oral Tradition and Written Transmission in Rabbinic Judaism and Early Christianity.* ASNU 22. Lund: C. W. K. Gleerup; Copenhagen: Ejnar Munksgaard, 1961.

————. *The Origins of the Gospel Traditions.* Philadelphia: Fortress Press, 1979.

————. *Tradition and Transmission in Early Christianity.* ConNT 20. Lund: C. W. K. Gleerup, 1964.

Glanville, Reginald. "The Predominance of Ear Over Eye in the Experience of St Paul." *LonQHR* 180 (1955): 293–97.

Gombrich, Ernst Hans. *Art and Illusion: A Study in the Psychology of Pictorial Representation.* Bollingen Series, vol. 35, no. 5. New York: Pantheon Books, 1960.

————. "Meditations on a Hobby Horse or the Roots of Artistic Form." In *Classic Essays in English,* ed. Josephine Miles. 2d ed. Boston and Toronto: Little, Brown & Company, 1965.

————. *The Story of Art.* 12th rev. and enl. ed. New York and London: Phaidon Press, 1972.

Goody, Jack. *The Domestication of the Savage Mind.* New York and Cambridge: Cambridge University Press, 1977.

————, ed. *Literacy in Traditional Societies.* New York and Cambridge: Cambridge University Press, 1968.

Goody, Jack, and Watt, Ian. "The Consequences of Literacy." In *Literacy in Traditional Societies,* ed. Goody. New York and Cambridge: Cambridge University Press, 1968.

Gray, Bennison. "Repetition in Oral Literature." *JAF* 84 (1971): 289–303.

Greenfield, Patricia M. "Oral or Written Language: The Consequences for Cognitive Development in Africa, the United States and England." *Language and Speech* 15 (1972): 169–78.

Gunkel, Hermann. *The Legends of Genesis: The Biblical Saga and History.* Eng. trans. W. H. Carruth. New York: Schocken Books, 1964.

Güttgemanns, Erhardt. " 'Gottesgerechtigkeit' und strukturale Semantik: Linguistische Analyse zu *dikaiosynē theou.*" *Studia Linguistica Neotestamentica. Gesammelte Aufsätze zur linguistischen Grundlage einer Neutestamentlichen Theologie.* BEvT 60. Munich: Chr. Kaiser, 1971.

————. "Die Linguistisch-Didaktische Methodik der Gleichnisse Jesu." *Studia Linguistica Neotestamentica.* Munich: Chr. Kaiser, 1971.

————. *Offene Fragen zur Formgeschichte des Evangeliums.* BEvT 54. Munich: Chr. Kaiser, 1970; (*Candid Questions Concerning Gospel Form Criticism: A Methodological Sketch of the Fundamental Problematics of Form and Redaction Criticism.* Eng. trans. William G. Doty. PTMS 26. Pittsburgh: Pickwick Press, 1979).

Halbwachs, Maurice. *Les Cadres Sociaux de la Mémoire.* Paris: Félix Alcan, 1925.

Havelock, Eric A. *The Greek Concept of Justice: From Its Shadow in Homer to Its Substance in Plato.* Cambridge, Mass.: Harvard University Press, 1978.

————. *Preface to Plato.* Cambridge, Mass.: Harvard University Press, Belknap Press, 1963.

Havelock, Eric A., and Hershbell, Jackson. *Communication Arts in the Ancient World.* New York: Hastings House, 1978.

Heinrici, Carl Friedrich Georg. *Der litterarische Charakter der neutestamentlichen Schriften.* Leipzig: Dürr'sche Buchhandlung, 1908.

Hendrickson, G. L. "Ancient Reading." *CJ* 25 (1929): 182–96.

Herder, Johann Gottfried. "Von Gottes Sohn, der Welt Heiland." *Herders Sämmtliche Werke,* ed. Bernhard Suphan, Vol. XIX. Berlin: Weidmannsche Buchhandlung, 1880.

————. "Vom Erlöser der Menschen: Nach unsern drei ersten Evangelien." *Herders Sämmtliche Werke,* ed. Bernhard Suphan, Vol. XIX. Berlin: Weidmannsche Buchhandlung, 1880.

Hidding, K. A. H. "Sehen und Hören." *Liber Amicorum: Studies in Honour of Professor Dr. C. J. Bleeker.* Supplements to *Numen* XVII. Leiden: E. J. Brill, 1969.

Hockett, Charles F. "The Origin of Speech." *Scientific American* 203 (1960): 89–96.

Hoffmann, Paul. *Studien zur Theologie der Logienquelle.* NTAbh NF 8. 2d ed. Münster: Aschendorff, 1972.

Ihde, Don. *Listening and Voice: A Phenomenology of Sound.* Athens: Ohio University Press, 1976.

Jones, James H. "Commonplace and Memorization in the Oral Tradition of the English and Scottish Popular Ballads." *JAF* 74 (1961): 97–112.

Jousse, Marcel, S. J. *L'Anthropologie du Geste.* Paris: Gallimard, 1974.

———. *La Manducation de la Parole.* Paris: Gallimard, 1975.

———. *Le Parlant, la Parole et le Souffle.* Paris: Gallimard, 1978.

———. *Études de Psychologie Linguistique: Le Style Oral, Rythmique et Mnémotechnique chez les Verbo-Moteurs.* Paris: Gabriel Beauchesne, 1925.

Kelber, Werner H. "Mark and Oral Tradition." *Semeia* 16 (1979): 7–55.

———. "Markus und die Mündliche Tradition." *LingBib* 45 (1979): 5–58.

———. "Walter Ong's Three Incarnations of the Word: Orality—Literacy—Technology." *PhT* 23 (1979): 70–74.

Kellog, Robert. "Literature, Nonliterature, and Oral Tradition." *NLH* 8 (1977): 531–34.

Kennedy, George A. "Classical and Christian Source Criticism." In *The Relationships Among the Gospels,* ed. William O. Walker, Jr. San Antonio: Trinity University Press, 1978.

———. *Classical Rhetoric and its Christian and Secular Tradition from Ancient to Modern Times.* Chapel Hill: University of North Carolina Press, 1980.

Kermode, Frank. *The Genesis of Secrecy: On the Interpretation of Narrative.* Cambridge, Mass., and London: Harvard University Press, 1979.

———. *The Sense of an Ending: Studies in the Theory of Fiction.* New York and London: Oxford University Press, 1966.

Kirk, Geoffrey Stephen. *Homer and the Oral Tradition.* New York and Cambridge: Cambridge University Press, 1976.

———. *The Songs of Homer.* New York and Cambridge: Cambridge University Press, 1962.

Koester, Helmut. "Die ausserkanonischen Herrenworte als Produkte der christlichen Gemeinde." *ZNW* 48 (1957): 220–37.

———. *Synoptische Überlieferung bei den Apostolischen Vätern.* TU 65. Berlin: Akademie-Verlag, 1957.

Kuhn, Heinz-Wolfgang. *Ältere Sammlungen im Markusevangelium,* SUNT 8. Göttingen: Vandenhoeck & Ruprecht, 1971.

———. "Der irdische Jesus bei Paulus als traditionsgeschichtliches und theologisches Problem." *ZTK* 67 (1970): 295–320.

Lessing, Gotthold Ephraim. *Laokoon.* Ed. Dorothy Reich. New York and London: Oxford University Press, 1965.

Lord, Albert Bates. "Avdo Mededović, Guslar." In *Slavic Folklore: A Symposium,* ed. Albert Bates Lord. Philadelphia: American Folklore Society, 1956.

———. "The Gospels as Oral Traditional Literature." *In The Relationships Among the Gospels,* ed. William O. Walker. San Antonio: Trinity University Press, 1978.

———. *The Singer of Tales.* HSCL 24. Cambridge, Mass.: Harvard University Press, 1960.

———, ed. *Slavic Folklore: A Symposium.* Philadelphia: American Folklore Society, 1956.

Bibliography

Lührmann, Dieter. *Die Redaktion der Logienquelle.* WMANT 33. Neukirchen and Vluyn: Neukirchener Verlag, 1969.

Lumpp, Randolph Franklin. "Culture, Religion, and the Presence of the Word: A Study of the Thought of Walter Jackson Ong." Ph.D. dissertation, University of Ottawa, 1976.

Lüthi, Max. *Volksliteratur und Hochliteratur: Menschenbild—Thematik—Formstreben.* Munich: Francke Verlag, 1970.

Luz, Ulrich. "Das Jesusbild der vormarkinischen Tradition." In *Jesus Christus in Historie und Geschichte: Neutestamentliche Festschrift für Hans Conzelmann zum 60. Geburtstag,* ed. Georg Strecker. Tübingen: J. C. B. Mohr [Paul Siebeck], 1975.

McCartney, Eugene S. "Notes on Reading and Praying Audibly." *CP* 43 (1948): 184–87

McFague, Sallie. *Speaking in Parables: A Study in Metaphor and Theology.* Philadelphia: Fortress Press; London: SCM Press, 1975.

McGinley, Lawrence J., S. J. "Form-Criticism of the Synoptic Healing Narratives." *TS* 3 (1947): 216–30.

McTaggart, Fred. *Wolf That I Am: In Search of the Red Earth People.* Boston: Houghton Mifflin Co., 1976.

Marrou, H. I. *A History of Education in Antiquity.* Eng. trans. George Lamb. New York: Sheed & Ward, 1956.

Merleau-Ponty, Maurice. "L'Oeil et l'esprit." *Les temps modernes* 18, nos. 184–85 (1961): 193–227.

Müller, Ulrich B. *Prophetie und Predigt im Neuen Testament: Formgeschichtliche Untersuchungen zur urchristlichen Prophetie.* SNT 10. Gütersloh: Gerd Mohn, 1975.

Myres, J. L. "Folkmemory." *Folklore* 37 (1926): 12–34.

Neusner, Jacob. "The Rabbinic Traditions about the Pharisees Before 70 A.D. The Problem of Oral Tradition," *Kairos* 14 (1972): 57–70.

Nielsen, Eduard. *Oral Tradition: A Modern Problem in Old Testament Introduction.* SBT 11. London: SCM Press, 1954.

Nohrnberg, James. "On Literature and the Bible." *Centrum* 2 (1974): 5–43.

Norden, Eduard. *Die Antike Kunstprosa: Vom Vl. Jahrhundert v. Chr. bis in die Zeit der Renaissance.* 5th ed. 2 vols. Stuttgart: B. G. Teubner, 1958.

Notopoulos, James A. "Parataxis in Homer: A New Approach to Homeric Literary Criticism." *TAPA* 80 (1949): 1–23.

Olrik, Axel. "Epische Gesetze der Volksdichtung." *ZDA* 51 (1909): 1–12; Eng. trans. "Epic Laws of Folk Narrative." In *The Study of Folklore,* ed. Alan Dundes, pp. 129–41. Englewood Cliffs, N.J.: Prentice-Hall, 1965.

Ong, Walter J., S. J., "Agonistic Structures in Academia: Past to Present." *Interchange* 5 (1974): 1–12.

———. *Fighting for Life: Contest, Sexuality, and Consciousness.* Ithaca, N.Y., and London: Cornell University Press. 1981.

———. "From Mimesis to Irony: The Distancing of Voice." *BMMLA* 9 (1976): 1–24.

———. *Interfaces of the Word: Studies in the Evolution of Consciousness and Culture.* Ithaca, N.Y., and London: Cornell University Press, 1977.

———. "Maranatha: Death and Life in the Text of the Book." In *Interfaces of the Word: Studies in the Evolution of Consciousness and Culture.* Ithaca, N.Y., and London: Cornell University Press, 1977.

————. "Mass in Ewondo." *America* 131 (1974): 148–51.

————. "Milton's Logical Epic and Evolving Consciousness." *PAPS* 120 (1976): 295–305.

————. "Oral Remembering and Narrative Structures." In *Georgetown University Round Table on Languages and Linguistics 1981,* ed. Deborah Tannen. Washington, D.C.: Georgetown University Press, 1982.

————. *Orality and Literacy.* New York and London: Methuen & Co., 1982.

————. *The Presence of the Word: Some Prolegomena for Cultural and Religious History.* New Haven, Conn., and London: Yale University Press, 1967; paperback edition: Minneapolis: University of Minnesota Press, 1981.

————. *Ramus and Talon Inventory.* Cambridge, Mass.: Harvard University Press, 1958.

————. *Ramus, Method, and the Decay of Dialogue.* Cambridge, Mass.: Harvard University Press, 1958.

————. "Technology Outside Us and Inside Us." *Communio* 5 (1978): 100–121.

————. *Why Talk?* Corte Madera, Calif.: Chandler & Sharp, 1973.

————. "The Writer's Audience is Always a Fiction." In *Interfaces of the Word: Studies in the Evolution of Consciousness and Culture.* Ithaca, N.Y., and London: Cornell University Press, 1977.

Overbeck, Franz. "Über die Anfänge der patristischen Literatur." *HZ* 48 (1882): 417–72; reprinted: Basel: Benno Schwabe & Co.

————. *Zur Geschichte des Kanons.* Chemnitz, 1880; reprint: Darmstadt: Wissenschaftliche Buchgesellschaft, 1965.

Parry, Milman. "Studies in the Epic Technique of Oral Verse-Making, I: Homer and Homeric Style." *HSCP* 41 (1930): 73–147.

————. "Studies in the Epic Technique of Oral Verse-Making, II: The Homeric Language as the Language of Oral Poetry." *HSCP* 43 (1932): 1–50.

————. "Whole Formulaic Verses in Greek and Southslavic Heroic Songs." *TAPA* 64 (1933): 179–97.

Patte, Daniel. *Early Jewish Hermeneutic in Palestine.* SBLDS 22. Missoula, Mont.: Scholars Press, 1975.

Peabody, Berkley. *The Winged Word: A Study in the Technique of Ancient Greek Oral Composition as Seen Principally through Hesiod's Works and Days.* Albany: State University of New York Press, 1975.

Perrin, Norman. *Jesus and the Language of the Kingdom: Symbol and Metaphor in New Testament Interpretation.* Philadelphia: Fortress Press; London: SCM Press, 1976.

Petersen, Norman R. *Literary Criticism for New Testament Critics.* GBS. Philadelphia: Fortress Press, 1978.

————. "So-called Gnostic Type Gospels and the Question of the Genre 'Gospel'." Unpublished paper for SBL Task Force on the Gospel Genre, 1970.

————. "When is the End not the End? Literary Reflections on the Ending of Mark's Narrative." *Int* 34 (1980): 151–66.

————, ed. "Perspectives on Mark's Gospel." *Semeia* 16 (1979).

Bibliography

Price, Martin. "The Fictional Contract." In *Literary Theory and Structure: Essays in Honor of William K. Wimsatt,* ed. Frank Brady, John Palmer, and Martin Price. New Haven, Conn., and London: Yale University Press, 1973.

Propp, Vladimir. *Morphology of the Folktale.* Eng. trans. Laurence Scott. Philadelphia: American Folklore Society, 1958; 2d rev. ed. Austin: University of Texas Press, 1968.

———. "Structure and History in the Study of the Fairy Tale." Eng. trans. Hugh T. McElwain. *Semeia* 10 (1978): 57–83.

Räisänen, Heikki. *Die Parabeltheorie im Markusevangelium.* Schriften der Finnischen Exegetischen Gesellschaft 26. Helsinki: Länsi-Suomi, 1973.

Ricoeur, Paul. "Biblical Hermeneutics." *Semeia* 4 (1975): 27–148.

———. *Essays on Biblical Interpretation.* Philadelphia: Fortress Press, 1980.

———. "The Hermeneutical Function of Distanciation." *PhT* 17 (1973): 129–41.

———. *Interpretation Theory: Discourse and the Surplus of Meaning.* Fort Worth: Texas Christian University Press, 1976.

———. *The Rule of Metaphor.* Eng. trans. R. Czerny with K. McLaughlin and J. Costello. University of Toronto Romance Series 37. Toronto and Buffalo: University of Toronto Press, 1977.

———. *The Symbolism of Evil.* Boston: Beacon Press, 1967.

———. "What is a Text? Explanation and Interpretation." In *Mythic-Symbolic Language and Philosophical Anthropology,* by David M. Rasmussen. The Hague: Martinus Nijhoff, 1971.

Riesenfeld, Harald. *The Gospel Tradition.* Philadelphia: Fortress Press, 1970.

Roberts, C. H. "Books in the Graeco-Roman World and in the New Testament." In *The Cambridge History of the Bible.* Vol. I: *From the Beginnings to Jerome,* ed. P. R. Ackroyd and S. F. Evans. New York and Cambridge: Cambridge University Press, 1970.

———. "The Christian Book and the Greek Papyri." *JTS* 50 (1949): 155–68.

Sacks, Sheldon, ed. *On Metaphor.* Chicago and London: University of Chicago Press, 1979.

Scheub, Harold. "Oral Narrative Process and the Use of Models." *NLH* 6 (1975): 353–77.

———. "Translation of African Oral Narrative-Performances to the Written Word." *Yearbook of Comparative and General Literature* 20 (1971): 28–36.

Schmidt, Karl Ludwig. "Die Stellung der Evangelien in der allgemeinen Literaturgeschichte." In *EUCHARISTERION: Studien zur Religion und Literatur des Alten und Neuen Testaments, Hermann Gunkel zum 60. Geburtstag . . . dargebracht,* ed. Hans Schmidt, FRLANT NF 19, 2:50–134. Göttingen: Vandenhoeck & Ruprecht, 1923.

Schmidt, Werner H. "Die prophetische 'Grundgewissheit'." *EvTh* 31 (1971): 630–50.

Schmithals, Walter. "Kritik der Formkritik." *ZTK* 77 (1980): 149–85.

Schneidau, Herbert N. "For Interpretation." *MoRev* 1 (1978): 70–88.

———. *Sacred Discontent: The Bible and Western Tradition.* Berkeley—Los Angeles—London: University of California Press, 1976.

Schniewind, Julius. *Die Begriffe Wort und Evangelium bei Paulus.* Bonn: Carl Georgi, 1910.

Schulz, Siegfried. *Q: Die Spruchquelle der Evangelisten.* Zurich: Theologischer Verlag, 1972.

Schürmann, Heinz. "Die vorösterlichen Anfänge der Logientradition: Versuch eines formgeschichtlichen Zugangs zum Leben Jesu." In *Der historische Jesus und der kerygmatische Christus,* eds. Helmut Ristow and Karl Matthiae. Berlin: Evangelische Verlagsanstalt, 1962; reprinted in *Traditionsgeschichtliche Untersuchungen zu den synoptischen Evangelien.* Düsseldorf: Patmos-Verlag, 1968.

Sedgwick, W. B. "Reading and Writing in Classical Antiquity." *ContRev* 135 (1929): 90–94.

Simon, Ulrich E. *Story and Faith in the Biblical Narrative.* London: SPCK, 1975.

Smith, Morton. "A Comparison of Early Christian and Early Rabbinic Tradition." *JBL* 82 (1963): 169–76.

Sontag, Susan. *On Photography.* New York: Farrar, Straus & Giroux, 1978.

Spencer, Richard A., ed. *Orientation by Disorientation: Studies in Literary Criticism and Biblical Literary Criticism.* Presented in honor of William A. Beardslee. PTMS 35. Pittsburgh: Pickwick Press, 1980.

Strauss, Leo. *Persecution and the Art of Writing.* Glencoe, Ill.: The Free Press, 1952.

Sudhaus, S. "Lautes und leises Beten." *ARW* 9 (1906): 185–200.

Tambiah, S. J. "The Magical Power of Words." *Man* 3 (1968): 175–208.

Tannehill, Robert C. "Attitudinal Shift in Synoptic Pronouncement Stories." In *Orientation by Disorientation: Studies in Literary Criticism and Biblical Literary Criticism.* Presented in Honor of William A. Beardslee, ed. Richard A. Spencer. PTMS 35. Pittsburgh: Pickwick Press, 1980.

———. "The 'Focal Instance' as a Form of New Testament Speech: A Study of Matthew 5:39b–42." *JR* 50 (1970): 372–85.

———. "The Gospel of Mark as Narrative Christology." *Semeia* 16 (1979): 57–95.

———. "Introduction: The Pronouncement Story and Its Types." *Semeia* 20 (1981): 1–13.

———. *The Sword of His Mouth.* Semeia Studies 1. Philadelphia: Fortress Press; Missoula, Mont.: Scholars Press, 1975.

———. "Synoptic Pronouncement Stories: Form and Function." *SBL Seminar Papers.* Chico, Calif.: Scholars Press, 1980.

———. "Varieties of Synoptic Pronouncement Stories." *Semeia* 20 (1981).

Tarde, Gabriel. *Les Lois de l'Imitation.* 2d ed., rev. Paris: F. Alcan, 1895. Eng. trans. Elsie C. Parson. New York: Henry Holt, 1903.

Tedlock, Dennis. "Toward an Oral Poetics." *NLH* 8 (1977): 507–19.

Thompson, Stith. *Motif-Index of Folk-Literature.* 6 vols. Bloomington: Indiana University Press, 1966.

Thomson, James Alexander Kerr. *The Art of the Logos.* London: George Allen & Unwin, 1935.

Tolbert, Mary Ann. *Perspectives on the Parables: An Approach to Multiple Interpretations.* Philadelphia: Fortress Press, 1979.

Tracy, David. *Blessed Rage for Order: The New Pluralism in Theology.* New York: Seabury Press, 1975.

Bibliography

Tyler, Stephen A. *The Said and the Unsaid: Mind, Meaning, and Culture.* New York—San Francisco—London: Academic Press, 1978.

Vachek, Josef. "Zum Problem der geschriebenen Sprache." *TCLP* 8 (1939): 94–104.

Vansina, Jan. *Oral Tradition: A Study in Historical Methodology.* Chicago: Aldine Publishing, 1965.

Via, Dan O. *The Parables: Their Literary and Existential Dimension.* Philadelphia: Fortress Press, 1967.

Vincent, J. J. "The Parables of Jesus as Self-Revelation." *SE* I, TU 73. Berlin: Akademie-Verlag, 1959.

Vischer, Lukas. "Die Rechtfertigung der Schriftstellerei in der alten Kirche." *TZ* 12 (1956): 320–36.

Walker, William O., Jr., ed. *The Relationships Among the Gospels: An Interdisciplinary Dialogue.* TUMSR 5. San Antonio: Trinity University Press, 1978.

Weder, Hans. *Die Gleichnisse Jesu als Metaphern: Traditions- und redaktionsgeschichtliche Analysen und Interpretationen.* 2d ed. Göttingen: Vandenhoeck & Ruprecht, 1980.

Weeden, Theodore J. "Metaphysical Implications of Kelber's Approach to Orality and Textuality." *SBL Seminar Papers.* Missoula, Mont.: Scholars Press, 1979.

———. "Recovering the Parabolic Intent in the Parable of the Sower." *JAAR* 47 (1979): 97–120.

Weiss, Johannes. "Beiträge zur Paulinischen Rhetorik." *Theologische Studien, B. Weiss dargebracht.* Göttingen: Vandenhoeck & Ruprecht, 1897.

Wendland, Paul. "Philo und die kynisch-stoische Diatribe." In *Beiträge zur Geschichte der Griechischen Philosophie und Religion,* ed. Paul Wendland and Otto Kern. Berlin: Georg Reimer, 1895.

———. *Die Urchristlichen Literaturformen.* Tübingen: J. C. B. Mohr [Paul Siebeck], 1912.

Werner, Eric. *A Voice Still Heard: The Songs of the Ashkenazic Synagogue.* University Park: Pennsylvania State University Press, 1976.

Wheelwright, Philip. *Metaphor and Reality.* Bloomington: Indiana University Press, 1962.

Widengren, Geo. "Tradition and Literature in Early Judaism and in the Early Church." *Numen* 10 (1963): 42–83.

Wilder, Amos. "Form-History and the Oldest Tradition." In *Neotestamentica et Patristica: Festschrift for O. Cullmann,* ed. W. C. Unnik. NovTSup 6. Leiden: E. J. Brill, 1962.

———. *The Language of the Gospel: Early Christian Rhetoric.* New York: Harper & Row, 1964.

Wire, Antoinette Clark. "The Structure of the Gospel Miracle Stories and their Tellers." *Semeia* 11 (1978): 83–113.

Wiseman, D. J. "Books in the Ancient Near East and in the Old Testament." In *The Cambridge History of the Bible.* Vol. I: *From the Beginnings to Jerome,* ed. P. R. Ackroyd and S. F. Evans. New York and Cambridge: Cambridge University Press, 1970.

Yates, Frances A. *The Art of Memory.* Chicago: University of Chicago Press, 1966.

II
BIBLICAL SCHOLARSHIP

Achtemeier, Paul J. "An Imperfect Union: Reflections on Gerd Theissen, *Urchristliche Wundergeschichten.*" *Semeia* 11 (1978): 49–68.

———. "The Origin and Function of the Pre-Marcan Miracle Catenae." *JBL* 91 (1972): 198–221.

———. "Toward the Isolation of Pre-Markan Miracle Catenae." *JBL* 89 (1970): 265–91.

Barrett, C. K. *Jesus and the Gospel Tradition.* Philadelphia: Fortress Press, 1968; London: SPCK, 1967.

Bartels, Robert A. *Kerygma or Gospel Tradition . . . Which Came First?* Minneapolis: Augsburg Publishing House, 1961.

Bauernfeind, Otto. *Die Worte der Dämonen im Markusevangelium.* BWANT 8. Stuttgart: Kohlhammer, 1927.

Beach, Curtis. *The Gospel of Mark: Its Making and Meaning.* New York: Harper & Brothers, 1959.

Best, Ernest. *Following Jesus: Discipleship in the Gospel of Mark.* JSNTSup 4. Sheffield: JSOT Press, 1981.

Betz, Hans Dieter. "The Early Christian Miracle Story: Some Observations on the Form Critical Problem." *Semeia* 11 (1978): 69–81.

———. "Jesus as Divine Man." In *Jesus and the Historian: Festschrift for E. C. Colwell,* ed. F. Thomas Trotter. Philadelphia: Westminster Press, 1968.

Bieler, Ludwig. ΘΕΙΟΣ ANHP: *Das Bild des "Göttlichen Menschen" in Spätantike und Frühchristentum.* 2 vols. Vienna: Oskar Höfels, 1935–36.

Bilezikian, Gilbert G. *The Liberated Gospel: A Comparison of the Gospel of Mark and Greek Tragedy.* Grand Rapids: Baker Book House, 1977.

Blenkinsopp, Joseph. *Prophecy and Canon: A Contribution to the Study of Jewish Origins.* UNDCSJCA 3. Notre Dame, Ind., and London: University of Notre Dame Press, 1977.

Boers, Hendrikus. "Sisyphus and His Rock: Concerning Gerd Theissen, *Urchristliche Wundergeschichten.*" *Semeia* 11 (1978): 1–48.

———. *Theology out of the Ghetto: A New Testament Exegetical Study Concerning Religious Exclusiveness.* Leiden: E. J. Brill, 1971.

Bonner, Campbell. "The Technique of Exorcism." *HTR* 36 (1943): 39–49.

———. "Traces of Thaumaturgic Technique in the Miracles." *HTR* 20 (1927): 178–81.

———. "The Violence of Departing Demons." *HTR* 37 (1944): 334–36.

Boobyer, G. H. "The Redaction of Mk 4, 1–34." *NTS* 8 (1961–62): 59–70.

Borsch, Frederick Houk. *God's Parable.* Philadelphia: Westminster Press, 1975.

Bracht, W. "Jüngerschaft und Nachfolge." In *Kirche im Werden,* ed. J. Hainz. Munich—Paderborn—Vienna: Schönigh, 1976.

Breech, Earl. "Kingdom of God and the Parables of Jesus." *Semeia* 12 (1978): 15–40.

Bibliography

Brown, John Pairman. "Mark as Witness to an Edited Form of Q." *JBL* 80 (1961): 29–44.

Budesheim, Thomas L. "Jesus and the Disciples in Conflict with Judaism." *ZNW* 62 (1971): 190–209.

Bultmann, Rudolf. "Römer 7 und die Anthropologie des Paulus." In *Imago Dei: Gustav Krüger zum siebzigsten Geburtstag*. Giessen: Alfred Töpelmann, 1932; reprint: In *Exegetica: Aufsätze zur Erforschung des Neuen Testaments*, ed. Erich Dinkler. Tübingen: J. C. B. Mohr [Paul Siebeck], 1967; *The Old and New Man in the Letters of Paul*. Eng. trans. Keith R. Crim. Richmond: John Knox Press, 1967.

―――. *Theology of the New Testament*. Eng. trans. Kendrick Grobel. New York: Charles Scribner's Sons, 1951.

―――. "Das Verhältnis der urchristlichen Christusbotschaft zum historischen Jesus." In *Exegetica*, ed. Erich Dinkler. Tübingen: J. C. B. Mohr [Paul Siebeck], 1967.

Burch, Ernest W. "Tragic Action in the Second Gospel: A Study of the Narrative of Mark." *JR* 11 (1931): 346–58.

Burkill, T. A. "The Cryptology of Parables in St. Mark's Gospel." *NovT* 1 (1956): 246–62.

Carlston, Charles E., and Norlin, Dennis. "Once More—Statistics and Q." *HTR* 64 (1971): 59–78.

Carrington, Philip. *The Primitive Christian Calendar: A Study in the Making of the Marcan Gospel*. Cambridge: At the University Press, 1952.

Castor, George Dewitt. "The Relation of Mark to the Source Q." *JBL* 31 (1912): 82–91.

Cohen, Boaz. "Note on Letter and Spirit in the New Testament." *HTR* 47 (1954): 197–203.

Coutts, J. " 'Those Outside' (Mark 4, 10–12)." *SE* II, TU 87. Berlin: Akademie-Verlag, 1964.

Crum, J. M. C. "Mark and 'Q'." *Theology* 12 (1926): 275–82.

Dewey, Joanna. *Markan Public Debate: Literary Technique, Concentric Structure and Theology in Mark 2:1–3:6*. SBLDS 48. Chico, Calif.: Scholars Press, 1980.

Dodd, C. H. *According to the Scriptures: The Sub-Structure of New Testament Theology*. London: James Nisbet & Co., 1952.

―――. *The Parables of the Kingdom*. 3d ed. New York: Charles Scribner's Sons, 1961.

Dormeyer, Detlev. *Die Passion Jesu als Verhaltensmodell: Literarische und theologische Analyse der Traditions- und Redaktionsgeschichte der Markuspassion*. NTAbh 11. Münster: Aschendorff, 1974.

Doudna, John Charles. *The Greek of the Gospel of Mark*. JBLMS 12. Philadelphia: Society of Biblical Literature and Exegesis, 1961.

Eitrem, S. "La Magie comme motif littéraire." *SO* 21 (1941): 39–83.

Fitzmyer, Joseph A., S. J. "The Matthean Divorce Texts and Some New Palestinian Evidence." *TS* 37 (1976): 197–226.

Fowler, Robert M. *Loaves and Fishes: The Function of the Feeding Stories in the Gospel of Mark*. SBLDS 54. Chico, Calif.: Scholars Press, 1981.

Friedrich, Gerhard. "Die Gegner des Paulus im 2. Korintherbrief." In *Abraham Unser Vater, Juden und Christen im Gespräch über die Bibel: Festschrift für Otto Michel zum 60. Geburtstag,* ed. O. Betz, M. Hengel, and P. Schmidt. Leiden: E. J. Brill, 1963.

Gealy, Fred D. "The Composition of Mark IV." *ExpT* 48 (1936): 40–43.

Georgi, Dieter. *Die Gegner des Paulus im 2. Korintherbrief.* WMANT 11. Neukirchen and Vluyn: Neukirchener Verlag, 1964.

Gnilka, Joáchim. *Das Evangelium nach Markus.* Zurich—Einsiedeln—Cologne: Benzinger; Neukirchen and Vluyn: Neukirchener Verlag, 1978.

————. *Die Verstockung Israels: Isaias 6, 9–10 in der Theologie der Synoptiker.* SANT 3. Munich: Kösel, 1961.

Gutierrez, Pedro. *La Paternité spirituelle selon Saint Paul.* Paris: J. Gabalda et Cie, 1968.

Hadas, Moses, and Smith, Morton. *Heroes and Gods: Spiritual Biographies in Antiquity.* New York: Harper & Row, 1965.

Hahn, Ferdinand. *The Titles of Jesus in Christology: Their History in Early Christianity.* Eng. trans. Harold Knight and George Ogg. London: Lutterworth Press, 1969.

Harnack, Adolf von. *Entstehung und Entwickelung der Kirchenverfassung und des Kirchenrechts in den zwei ersten Jahrhunderten.* Leipzig: J. C. Hinrichs'sche Buchhandlung, 1910.

Hawkin, David J. "The Incomprehension of the Disciples in the Marcan Redaction." *JBL* 91 (1972): 491–500.

Heard, Richard. "The ΑΠΟΜΝΗΜΟΝΕΥΜΑΤΑ in Papias, Justin, and Irenaeus," *NTS* 1 (1954): 122–34.

Heitmüller, Wilhelm. "Im Namen Jesu." *Eine sprach-u. religionsgeschichtliche Untersuchung zum Neuen Testament, speziell zur altchristlichen Taufe.* FRLANT I, 2. Göttingen: Vandenhoeck & Ruprecht, 1903.

Hengel, Martin. *Acts and the History of Earliest Christianity.* Eng. trans. John Bowden. Philadelphia: Fortress Press; London: SCM Press, 1971.

————. *Crucifixion in the Ancient World and the Folly of the Message of the Cross.* Eng. trans. John Bowden. Philadelphia: Fortress Press, 1977.

Hock, Ronald F. "Paul's Tentmaking and the Problem of His Social Class." *JBL* 97 (1978): 555–64.

————. "Simon the Shoemaker as an Ideal Cynic." *GRBS* 17 (1976): 41–53.

————. *The Social Context of Paul's Ministry: Tentmaking and Apostleship.* Philadelphia: Fortress Press, 1980.

————. "The Workshop as a Social Setting for Paul's Missionary Preaching." *CBQ* 41 (1979): 438–50.

Holladay, Carl R. *Theios Aner in Hellenistic Judaism: A Critique of the Use of this Category in New Testament Christology.* SBLDS 40. Missoula, Mont.: Scholars Press, 1977.

Holmberg, Bengt. *Paul and Power: The Structure of Authority in the Primitive Church as Reflected in the Pauline Epistles.* Philadelphia: Fortress Press, 1980.

Honey, T. E. Floyd. "Did Mark Use Q?" *JBL* 62 (1943): 319–31.

Bibliography

Hunter, Archibald M. *Paul and His Predecessors*. Philadelphia: Westminster Press, 1961.

Jeremias, Joachim. *The Eucharistic Words of Jesus*. 3rd ed., rev. Eng. trans. Norman Perrin. London: Charles Scribner's Sons, 1965; reprint: Philadelphia: Fortress Press, 1977.

Jewett, Robert. "Enthusiastic Radicalism and the Thessalonian Correspondence." *SBL Seminar Papers* I. Missoula, Mont.: Scholars Press, 1972.

─────. *Paul's Anthropological Terms: A Study of Their Use in Conflict Settings*. AGAJU 10. Leiden: E. J. Brill, 1971.

Jülicher, Adolf. *Die Gleichnisreden Jesu*. 2 vols. Tübingen: J. C. B. Mohr [Paul Siebeck] I, 1888, 2d ed. 1899; II, 1899, 2d ed. 1910.

Jüngel, Eberhard. *Paulus und Jesus: Eine Untersuchung zur Präzisierung der Frage nach dem Ursprung der Christologie*. 3d ed. Tübingen: J. C. B. Mohr [Paul Siebeck], 1967.

Käsemann, Ernst. "Gottesgerechtigkeit bei Paulus." *ZTK* 58 (1961): 367–78; " 'The Righteousness of God' in Paul." In *New Testament Questions of Today*, Eng. trans. W. J. Montague. Philadelphia: Fortress Press; London: SCM Press, 1969.

─────. "Die Legitimität des Apostels: Eine Untersuchung zu II Korinther 10–13." *ZNW* 41 (1942): 33–71.

─────. "The Spirit and the Letter." In *Perspectives on Paul*, Eng. trans. Margaret Kohl. Philadelphia: Fortress Press; London: SCM Press, 1971.

Keck, Leander E. "The Introduction to Mark's Gospel." *NTS* 12 (1966): 352–70.

─────. "Mark 3, 7–12 and Mark's Christology." *JBL* 84 (1965): 341–58.

─────. *Paul and His Letters*. Philadelphia: Fortress Press, 1979.

Kee, Howard Clark. *Aretalogies, Hellenistic 'Lives,' and the Sources of Mark*. Protocol of the Colloquy 12. Berkeley, Calif.: Center for Hermeneutical Studies, 1975.

─────. "Aretalogy and Gospel." *JBL* 92 (1973): 402–22.

─────. *Community of the New Age: Studies in Mark's Gospel*. Philadelphia: Westminster Press, 1977.

─────. "The Function of Scriptural Quotations and Allusions in Mark 11–16." In *Jesus und Paulus: Festschrift für Werner Georg Kümmel*, ed. E. Earle Ellis and Erich Grässer. Göttingen: Vandenhoeck & Ruprecht, 1975.

─────. "The Terminology of Mark's Exorcism Stories." *NTS* 14 (1968): 232–46.

Kelber, Werner H. *The Kingdom in Mark: A New Place and a New Time*. Philadelphia: Fortress Press, 1974.

─────. *Mark's Story of Jesus*. Philadelphia: Fortress Press, 1979.

─────, ed. *The Passion in Mark*. Philadelphia: Fortress Press, 1976.

Kertelge, Karl. *Die Wunder Jesu im Markusevangelium: Eine redaktionsgeschichtliche Untersuchung*. SANT 23. Munich: Kösel-Verlag, 1970.

Klein, Günter. "Die Verleugnung des Petrus: Eine traditionsgeschichtliche Untersuchung." *ZTK* 58 (1961): 285–328; reprint: *Rekonstruktion und Interpretation: Gesammelte Aufsätze zum Neuen Testament*. BEvT 50. Munich: Chr. Kaiser, 1969.

Koester, Helmut. "Apocryphal and Canonical Gospels." *HTR* 73 (1980): 105–30.

Kramer, Werner. *Christ, Lord, Son of God.* SBT 50. London: SCM Press, 1966.

Kürzinger, Josef. "Irenäus und sein Zeugnis zur Sprache des Matthäusevangeliums." *NTS* 10 (1963): 108–15.

———. "Das Papiaszeugnis und die Erstgestalt des Matthäusevangeliums." *BZ*, NF 4 (1960): 19–38.

Lake, Kirsopp. "ΕΜΒΡΙΜΗΣΑΜΕΝΟΣ and ΟΡΓΙΣΘΕΙΣ, Mark 1, 40–43." *HTR* 16 (1923): 197–98.

Lambrecht, Jan, S. J., "Die fünf Parabeln in Mk 4." *Bijdr* 29 (1968): 25–53.

———. *Die Redaktion der Markus-Apokalypse: Literarische Analyse und Strukturuntersuchung.* AnBib 28. Rome: Pontifical Biblical Institute, 1967.

Lindars, Barnabas. *New Testament Apologetic: The Doctrinal Significance of the Old Testament Quotations.* Philadelphia: Westminster Press; London: SCM Press, 1961.

Linnemann, Eta. *Jesus of the Parables.* Eng. trans. John Sturdy. New York: Harper & Row; London: SPCK, 1966.

———. *Studien zur Passionsgeschichte.* FRLANT 102. Göttingen: Vandenhoeck & Ruprecht, 1970.

Lohmeyer, Ernst. "Das Gleichnis von den bösen Weingärtnern (Mark. 12, 1–12)." In *Urchristliche Mystik: Neutestamentliche Studien.* 2d ed. Darmstadt: Wissenschaftliche Buchgesellschaft, 1958.

Lohse, Eduard. *History of the Suffering and Death of Jesus Christ.* Eng. trans. Martin O. Dietrich. Philadelphia: Fortress Press, 1967.

Lütgert, W. "Freiheitspredigt und Schwarmgeister in Korinth." BFCT 12 (1908): 129–279.

———. "Die Vollkommenen im Philipperbrief und die Enthusiasten in Thessalonich." BFCT 13 (1909): 547–654.

Malbon, Elizabeth Struthers. "Elements of an Exegesis of the Gospel of Mark according to Lévi-Strauss' Methodology." *SBL Seminar Papers* II. Missoula, Mont.: Scholars Press, 1977.

———. "Narrative Space and Mythic Meaning: A Structural Exegesis of the Gospel of Mark." Ph.D. dissertation, Florida State University, 1980.

Marxsen, Willi. *The Beginnings of Christology.* Eng. trans. Paul J. Achtemeier and Lorenz Nieting. Philadelphia: Fortress Press, 1979.

———. *Mark the Evangelist: Studies on the Redaction History of the Gospel.* Eng. trans. Roy A. Harrisville et al. Nashville: Abingdon Press, 1969.

———. "Redaktionsgeschichtliche Erklärung der sogenannten Parabeltheorie des Markus." *ZTK* 52 (1955): 255–71.

Meagher, John C. *Clumsy Construction in Mark's Gospel: A Critique of Form- and Redaktionsgeschichte.* TorSTh 3. New York and Toronto: Edwin Mellen Press, 1979.

Meeks, Wayne. "Hypomnēmata from an Untamed Sceptic: A Response to George Kennedy." In *The Relationships among the Gospels,* ed. William O. Walker, Jr. San Antonio, Tex.: Trinity University Press, 1978.

Metzger, Bruce M. *The Text of the New Testament: Its Transmission, Corrup-*

tion, and Restoration. New York and London: Oxford University Press, 1964.

Meye, Robert P. "Mark 4, 10: 'Those about Him with the Twelve'." *SE* II, TU 87. Berlin: Akademie-Verlag, 1964.

Michel, Otto. *Paulus und seine Bibel.* Gütersloh: C. Bertelsmann, 1929.

Moule, C. F. D. "Mark 4:1–20 Yet Once More." In *Neotestamentica et Semitica: Studies in Honour of Matthew Black,* ed. E. Earle Ellis and Max Wilcox. Edinburgh: T. & T. Clark, 1969.

Moulton, Warren J. "The Relation of the Gospel of Mark to Primitive Christian Tradition." *HTR* 3 (1910): 403–36.

Murrin, Michael. *The Veil of Allegory.* Chicago: University of Chicago Press, 1969.

Neirynck, Frans. *Duality in Mark: Contributions to the Study of the Markan Redaction.* BETL 31. Louvain: Louvain University Press, 1972.

Patton, Carl S. "Did Mark Use Q? Or Did Q Use Mark?" *AJT* 16 (1912): 634–42.

Perrin, Norman. "The Creative Use of the Son of Man Traditions by Mark." *USQR* 23 (1968): 357–65.

———. *The New Testament: An Introduction.* New York: Harcourt Brace Jovanovich, 1974.

Pesch, Rudolf. *Das Markusevangelium.* Vols. I–II. Freiburg—Basel—Vienna: Herder, 1976–77.

———. *Naherwartungen: Tradition und Redaktion in Mk 13.* Düsseldorf: Patmos-Verlag, 1968.

Petzke, Gerd. *Die Traditionen über Apollonius von Tyana und das Neue Testament.* SCHNT 1. Leiden: E. J. Brill, 1970.

Pryke, E. J. *Redactional Style in the Marcan Gospel: A Study of Syntax and Vocabulary as Guides to Redaction in Mark.* SNTSMS 33. New York and Cambridge: Cambridge University Press, 1978.

Pryor, J. W. "Markan Parable Theology." *ExpT* 83 (1972): 242–45.

Puukko, A. F. "Paulus und das Judentum." *StudOr* 2 (1928): 1–87.

Reploh, Karl-Georg. *Markus—Lehrer der Gemeinde: Eine redaktionsgeschichtliche Studie zu den Jüngerperikopen des Markus-Evangeliums.* SBM 9. Stuttgart: Katholisches Bibelwerk, 1969.

Riddle, Donald W. "Mark 4:1–34: The Evolution of a Gospel Source." *JBL* 56 (1937): 77–90.

———. "The Martyr Motif in the Gospel According to Mark." *JR* 4 (1924): 397–410.

Robinson, James M. "Basic Shifts in German Theology." *Int* 16 (1962): 76–97.

———. *The Problem of History in Mark: And Other Marcan Studies.* Philadelphia: Fortress Press, 1982.

———. *The Problem of History in Mark.* SBT 21. London: SCM Press, 1957. In idem, *Problem of History in Mark: And Other Marcan Studies.*

———. "The Problem of History in Mark, Reconsidered." *USQR* 20 (1965): 131–47. In idem, *Problem of History in Mark: And Other Marcan Studies.*

———. "On the Gattung of Mark (and John)." *Jesus and Man's Hope,* I. Pittsburgh: Pittsburgh Theological Seminary, 1970. In idem, *Problem of History in Mark: And Other Marcan Studies.*

Robinson, James M., and Koester, Helmut. *Trajectories through Early Christianity.* Philadelphia: Fortress Press, 1971.

Roloff, Jürgen. "Das Markusevangelium als Geschichtsdarstellung." *EvTh* 29 (1969): 73–93.

Rudberg, Gunnar. "ΕΥΘΥΣ." *ConNT* 9 (1944): 42–46.

Sanday, W., ed. *Studies in the Synoptic Problem.* (See especially B. H. Streeter, pp. 141–208). Oxford: At the Clarendon Press, 1911.

Sanders, E. P. *Paul and Palestinian Judaism: A Comparison of Patterns of Religion.* Philadelphia: Fortress Press; London: SCM Press, 1977.

———. "The Overlaps of Mark and Q and the Synoptic Problem." *NTS* 19 (1972–73): 453–65.

———. *The Tendencies of the Synoptic Tradition.* SNTSMS 9. New York and Cambridge: Cambridge University Press, 1969.

Sanders, James A. "Text and Canon: Concepts and Method." *JBL* 98 (1979): 5–29.

———. "Torah and Paul." In *God's Christ and His People: Essays Honoring Nils Alstrup Dahl,* ed. W. Meeks and J. Jerrell. Oslo: Universitetsforlaget, 1977.

Schelkle, K. H. *Die Passion Jesu in der Verkündigung des Neuen Testaments.* Heidelberg: F. H. Kerle, 1949.

Schenk, Wolfgang. *Der Passionsbericht nach Markus: Untersuchungen zur Überlieferungsgeschichte der Passionstraditionen.* Gütersloh: Gerd Mohn, 1974.

Schille, Gottfried. "Das Leiden des Herrn: Die evangelische Passionstradition und ihr 'Sitz im Leben'." *ZTK* 52 (1955): 161–205.

Schillebeeckx, Edward. *Jesus: An Experiment in Christology.* Eng. trans. Hubert Hoskins. New York: Seabury Press, 1979.

Schlatter, Adolf. *Die korinthische Theologie.* Gütersloh: C. Bertelsmann, 1914.

———. *Die Theologie der Apostel.* 2d ed. Stuttgart: Calwer Vereinsbuchhandlung, 1922.

Schmidt, Karl Ludwig. *Der Rahmen der Geschichte Jesu: Literarkritische Untersuchungen zur Ältesten Jesusüberlieferung.* 1919; reprint: Darmstadt: Wissenschaftliche Buchgesellschaft, 1964.

Schmithals, Walter. *Das Evangelium nach Markus: Kapitel 1–9,1.* ÖkTNT 2/1. Gütersloh: Gerd Mohn; Würzburg: Echter Verlag, 1979.

Schneider, Bernardin, O. F. M. "The Meaning of St. Paul's Antithesis 'The Letter and the Spirit.'" *CBQ* 15 (1953): 163–207.

Schneider, Gerhard. "Das Problem einer vorkanonischen Passionserzählung." *BZ* 16 (1972): 222–44.

Schreiber, Johannes. *Die Markuspassion: Wege zur Erforschung der Leidensgeschichte Jesu.* Hamburg: Furche, 1969.

———. *Theologie des Vertrauens: Eine redaktionsgeschichtliche Untersuchung des Markusevangeliums.* Hamburg: Furche, 1967.

Schrenk, Gottlob. "gramma." *TDNT* I: 761–69.

Schulz, Siegfried. "Die Decke des Moses: Untersuchungen zu einer vorpaulinischen Überlieferung in 2 Kr 3, 7–18." *ZNW* 49 (1958): 1–30.

———. *Die Stunde der Botschaft: Einführung in die Theologie der vier Evangelisten.* Hamburg: Furche, 1967.

Schweitzer, Albert. *The Mysticism of Paul the Apostle.* Eng. trans. William Montgomery. London: A. & C. Black, 1931.

Schweizer, Eduard. "Dying and Rising with Christ." *NTS* 14 (1967): 1–14.

Bibliography

————. "Zur Frage des Messiasgeheimnisses bei Markus." *ZNW* 56 (1965): 1–8.

Shuler, Philip L. *The Synoptic Gospels and the Problem of Genre.* Ph.D. dissertation, McMaster University, 1975.

————. *A Genre for the Gospels: The Biographical Character of Matthew.* Philadelphia: Fortress Press, 1982.

Smith, Morton. *The Aretalogy Used by Mark.* Protocol of the Colloquy 6. Berkeley, Calif.: Center for Hermeneutical Studies, 1975.

————. *Clement of Alexandria and the Secret Gospel of Mark.* Cambridge, Mass.: Harvard University Press, 1973.

Stauffer, Ethelbert. *New Testament Theology.* Eng. trans. John Marsh. New York: Macmillan Co.; London: SCM Press, 1955.

Stock, Klemens. *Boten aus dem Mit-Ihm-Sein: Das Verhältnis zwischen Jesus und den Zwölf nach Markus.* AnBib 70. Rome: Pontifical Biblical Institute, 1975.

Strecker, Georg. "Die Leidens- und Auferstehungsvoraussagen im Markus-evangelium (Mk 8,31; 9,31; 10,32–34)." *ZTK* 64 (1967): 16–39.

Stuhlmacher, Peter. *Gerechtigkeit Gottes bei Paulus.* FRLANT 87. Göttingen: Vandenhoeck & Ruprecht, 1965.

Suggs, M. Jack. *Wisdom, Christology, and Law in Matthew's Gospel.* Cambridge, Mass.: Harvard University Press, 1970.

Suhl, Alfred. *Die Funktion der alttestamentlichen Zitate und Anspielungen im Markusevangelium.* Gütersloh: Gerd Mohn, 1965.

Tagawa, Kenzo. *Miracles et Evangile.* Paris: Presses Universitaires de France, 1966.

Talbert, Charles H. *What is a Gospel? The Genre of the Canonical Gospels.* Philadelphia: Fortress Press; London: SCM Press, 1977.

Tannehill, Robert C. "The Disciples in Mark: The Function of a Narrative Role." *JR* 57 (1977): 386–405.

————. *Dying and Rising with Christ: A Study in Pauline Theology.* BZNW 32. Berlin: Töpelmann, 1966.

Taylor, Vincent. *The Formation of the Gospel Tradition.* London: Macmillan & Co., 1933.

————. *The Gospel According to St. Mark.* 2d ed. London: Macmillan & Co., 1966.

Terrien, Samuel. *The Elusive Presence: Toward A New Biblical Theology.* RP 26. New York: Harper & Row, 1978.

Theissen, Gerd. *Sociology of Early Palestinian Christianity.* Eng. trans. John Bowden. Philadelphia: Fortress Press, 1977.

————. *Urchristliche Wundergeschichten: Ein Beitrag zur formgeschichtlichen Erforschung der synoptischen Evangelien.* Gütersloh: Gerd Mohn, 1974.

————. "Wanderradikalismus: Literatursoziologische Aspekte der Überlieferung von Worten Jesu im Urchristentum," *ZTK* 70 (1973): 245–71; "Itinerant Radicalism: The Tradition of Jesus Sayings from the Perspective of the Sociology of Literature." Eng. trans. Antoinette C. Wire. *RR* 2 (1975): 84–93.

Throckmorton, Burton H., Jr. "Did Mark Know Q?" *JBL* 67 (1948): 319–39.

Tödt, Heinz Eduard. *The Son of Man in the Synoptic Tradition.* Eng. trans.

Dorothea M. Barton. Philadelphia: Westminster Press, 1965.

Trocmé, Etienne. *The Formation of the Gospel According to Mark*. Eng. trans. Pamela Gaughan. Philadelphia: Westminster Press, 1975.

————. *The Passion as Liturgy: A Study in the Origin of the Passion Narratives in the Four Gospels*. Unpublished manuscript, 1981.

Tyson, Joseph B. "The Blindness of the Disciples in Mark." *JBL* 80 (1961): 261–68.

————. "Sequential Parallelism in the Synoptic Gospels." *NTS* 22 (1976): 276–308.

Vanhoye, A. "Structure et théologie des récits de la Passion dans les évangiles synoptiques." *NRT* 99 (1967): 135–63.

Via, Dan O. *Kerygma and Comedy in the New Testament: A Structuralist Approach to Hermeneutics*. Philadelphia: Fortress Press, 1975.

Votaw, Clyde Weber. *The Gospels and Contemporary Biographies in the Greco-Roman World*. Philadelphia: Fortress Press, 1970.

Walter, Nikolaus. "Tempelzerstörung und Synoptische Apokalypse." *ZNW* 57 (1966): 38–49.

Weeden, Theodore J. "The Heresy That Necessitated Mark's Gospel." *ZNW* 59 (1968): 145–58.

————. *Mark—Traditions in Conflict*. Philadelphia: Fortress Press, 1971.

Wellhausen, Julius. *Einleitung in die Drei Ersten Evangelien*. 2d ed. Berlin: Georg Reimer Verlag, 1911.

Wilckens, Ulrich. *Weisheit und Torheit: Eine exegetisch-religionsgeschichtliche Untersuchung zu 1. Kor. 1 und 2*. BHT 26. Tübingen: J. C. B. Mohr [Paul Siebeck], 1959.

Wrede, William. *The Messianic Secret*. Eng. trans. J. C. G. Greig. London: James Clarke & Co., 1971.

Index of Passages

BIBLE

248

OTHER ANCIENT LITERATURE

Index of Authors